Capacity Mechanisms in EU Energy Law

Energy and Environmental Law and Policy Series

VOLUME 36

Editor

General Editor: Professor Kurt Deketelaere, Professor of Law, University of Leuven, Belgium; Honorary Professor of Law, University of Dundee, UK; Honorary Chief of Staff, Flemish Government; Secretary-General, League of European Research Universities (LERU), Belgium. Kurt's CV – see www.kurtdeketelaere/en/kurt.

Introduction

Environmental protection and energy efficiency/security are important societal challenges. In order to tackle them, policy and legal frameworks are developed at national, regional and global level. Through study and best practices development, the challenges will prove to be solvable.

Contents/Subjects

Environment/Nature/Energy/Climate.

Objective

The aim of this series is to publish works of excellent quality that focus on the study of energy and environmental policy. Through this series the editors:

– contribute to the improvement of the quality of energy/environmental law and policy in general and environmental quality and energy efficiency in particular; increase the access to environmental and energy information for academics, non-governmental organizations, government institutions, and business; and
– facilitate cooperation between academic and non-academic communities in the field of energy and environmental law and policy throughout the world.

Readership

Academics and practitioners in environmental and energy matters.

The titles published in this series are listed at the end of this volume.

Capacity Mechanisms in EU Energy Law

Ensuring Security of Supply in the Energy Transition

Kaisa Huhta

 Wolters Kluwer

Published by:
Kluwer Law International B.V.
PO Box 316
2400 AH Alphen aan den Rijn
The Netherlands
E-mail: international-sales@wolterskluwer.com
Website: lrus.wolterskluwer.com

Sold and distributed in North, Central and South America by:
Wolters Kluwer Legal & Regulatory U.S.
7201 McKinney Circle
Frederick, MD 21704
United States of America
Email: customer.service@wolterskluwer.com

Sold and distributed in all other countries by:
Air Business Subscriptions
Rockwood House
Haywards Heath
West Sussex
RH16 3DH
United Kingdom
Email: international-customerservice@wolterskluwer.com

Printed on acid-free paper.

ISBN 978-94-035-1451-2

e-Book: ISBN 978-94-035-1453-6
web-PDF: ISBN 978-94-035-1455-0

Printed in the United Kingdom.

Table of Contents

Foreword

Capacity mechanisms are a highly topical issue in the European electricity markets. This is not only because of the increasing reliance on electricity and the importance of security of supply but also because of the ongoing European Union (EU) legislative reform regarding capacity mechanisms.

While the analysis in this book follows changes until 5 March 2019, the legislative process has continued. In late March 2019, the European Parliament voted to approve the new legal instruments regarding capacity mechanisms. On 22 May 2019, the Council formally adopted these legal instruments. Although the numbering of the adopted provisions is different in part and the wording of some of the provisions is altered, the general legal approach to capacity mechanisms is the same as in the original proposals by the Commission in 2016. As this book goes into press, it is now certain that Member States' capacity mechanisms will be governed by a new set of EU rules which will require changes in national laws and approaches. I believe this book can offer guidance on understanding that new set of EU rules and its approach to ensuring security of supply in the energy transition.

Kaisa Huhta
Joensuu, Finland 27.5.2019

List of Abbreviations

ACER	Agency for the Cooperation for Energy Regulators
ANODE	French National Association for Retail Energy Providers
CADA	Capacity and Differences Agreement
DG	Directorate-General
ECJ or the Court	European Court of Justice
ECR	European Court Reports
EEAG	Guidelines on State aid for Environmental Protection and Energy 2014-2020
ENTSO-E	European Network of Transmission System Operators for Electricity
EU	European Union
FERC	Federal Energy Regulatory Commission
INPC	Irish National Petroleum Corporation
NYISO	New York Independent System Operator
OGEL	Oil, Gas & Energy Law
OJ	Official Journal
OUP	Oxford University Press
PSO	Public Service Obligation
SGEI	Services of General Economic Interest
TEU	Treaty on the European Union
TFEU or the Treaty	Treaty on the Functioning of the European Union
TSO	Transmission System Operator
UK	United Kingdom

CHAPTER 1
Introduction

§1.01 THE CONCERN FOR GENERATION ADEQUACY IN THE EUROPEAN UNION

European electricity markets are undergoing transition. First and foremost the global concern over the climate has accelerated the process of transition from a fossil fuel-run economy to a decarbonised one where smart technologies and electricity produced from renewable energy sources take the leading role.[1] Furthermore, State-driven and monopolised markets have gradually been merging into a competitive, internal European market.[2] Finally, the supply-oriented market model, where centralised producers and large energy companies are the key players, is morphing into a more polycentric system, where the contribution of demand side actors and distributed generation is given greater emphasis.[3]

---

1. Commission Staff Working Document accompanying the document Report from the Commission Final Report of the Sector Inquiry on Capacity Mechanisms, SWD(2016) 385 final, pp. 5 and 10-13; Proposal for a Regulation of the European Parliament and of the Council on the internal market for electricity, COM(2016) 861 final/2 – (2016)379 (COD) ('Recast Electricity Regulation'), p. 2; Geert Verbong and Frank Geels, 'Future Electricity Systems: Visions, Scenarios and Transition Pathways', in Geert Verbong and Derk Loorbach (eds), *Governing the Energy Transition: Reality, Illusion or Necessity?* (Routledge Studies in Sustainability Transitions, 2012), pp. 203-219.
2. Commission Staff Working Document accompanying the document Report from the Commission Final Report of the Sector Inquiry on Capacity Mechanisms, SWD(2016) 385 final, pp. 10-13; Erik Van Der Vleuten and Per Högselius, 'Resisting Change? The Transnational Dynamics of European Energy Regimes', in Geert Verbong and Derk Loorbach (eds), *Governing the Energy Transition: Reality, Illusion or Necessity?* (Routledge Studies in Sustainability Transitions, 2012), pp. 75-100; Kim Talus, *EU Energy Law and Policy: A Critical Account* (OUP, 2013), pp. 269-286.
3. *See* Commission Staff Working Document, Best practices on Renewable Energy Self-consumption, accompanying the document Communication from the Commission to the European Parliament, the Council, the European Economic and Social Committee and the Committee of the Regions, Delivering a New Deal for Energy Consumers, SWD(2015) 141 final; the Recast Electricity Regulation, p. 3.

Within this transition, there is a growing concern among European Union (hereinafter 'EU') Member States that the market structure that has been designed is unable to ensure generation adequacy in a way that guarantees the overall security of electricity supply, i.e., the uninterrupted availability of affordable electricity. To address this concern, many Member States have adopted national legal instruments that compensate electricity producers for the availability of generation capacity and other resources (measured in kilowatts, kW) to produce electricity in addition to the remuneration these producers receive for the electricity (measured in kilowatt-hours, kWh) they produce and sell in the liberalised energy-only market. This book examines these capacity mechanisms in the context of EU law and the EU energy *acquis*.

The EU approach to capacity mechanisms is cautious due to the potential adverse effects these mechanisms have on fundamental objectives of EU energy law.[4] Such effects include market distortions, increases in consumer prices and detrimental effects on EU sustainability goals.[5] The cautious EU approach is clearly in evidence in recent measures and initiatives undertaken by the European Commission (Commission) concerning generation adequacy, i.e., the ability of installed and expected generation capacity to meet demand at all times.[6] In the context of these initiatives, the Commission acknowledges that EU law allows Member States to address generation adequacy through national laws. However, the Commission is keen to emphasise that EU law also aims to restrict the adoption of capacity mechanisms solely to that necessary to address the issue of generation adequacy. In other words, capacity mechanisms should only be used to fill the gap between the investment that can be achieved through competitive energy-only markets on the one hand and the investment needed to secure

---

4. Article 194 of the Consolidated version of the Treaty on the Functioning of the European Union (OJ C 326, 26.10.2012, pp. 47-390) (hereinafter 'TFEU' or 'the Treaty').
5. *See*, for example, Report from the Commission, Final Report of the Sector Inquiry on Capacity Mechanisms, COM(2016) 752 final; Laurens De Vries and Petra Heijnen, 'The Impact of Electricity Market Design upon Investment under Uncertainty: The Effectiveness of Capacity Mechanisms', 16(3) *Utilities Policy* (2008), pp. 215-227; Carlos Batlle and Pablo Rodilla, 'A Critical Assessment of the Different Approaches Aimed to Secure Electricity Generation Supply', 38(11) *Energy Policy* (2010), pp. 7169-7179; Roland Meyer and Olga Gore, 'Cross-Border Effects of Capacity Mechanisms: Do Uncoordinated Market Design Changes Contradict the Goals of the European Market Integration?', 51 *Energy Economics* (2015), pp. 9-20; Nicolas Hary, Vincent Rious and Marcelo Saguan, 'The Electricity Generation Adequacy Problem: Assessing Dynamic Effects of Capacity Remuneration Mechanisms', 91 *Energy Policy* (2016), pp. 113-127.
6. The EU's concern over the effects of capacity mechanisms is demonstrated through, *inter alia*, the State aid guidelines for energy and environmental protection, the State aid sector inquiry into capacity mechanisms, the Energy Union initiative and various proposals in the Clean Energy for All Europeans legislative package. *See* Commission Decision of 29.4.2015 initiating an inquiry on capacity mechanisms in the electricity sector pursuant to Article 20a of Council Regulation (EC) No 659/1999 of 22 March 1999, C(2015) 2814 final; Report from the Commission, Final Report of the Sector Inquiry on Capacity Mechanisms, COM(2016) 752 final; Commission Staff Working Document accompanying the document Report from the Commission Final Report of the Sector Inquiry on Capacity Mechanisms, SWD(2016) 385 final; Communication from the Commission to the European Parliament, the Council, the European Economic and Social Committee, the Committee of the Regions and the European Investment Bank, A Framework Strategy for a Resilient Energy Union with a Forward-Looking Climate Change Policy, COM(2015) 80 final, pp. 6, 10 and 20; Communication from the Commission, Guidelines on State aid for environmental protection and energy 2014-2020 (OJ C 200, 28.6.2014, pp. 1-55); the Recast Electricity Regulation.

the uninterrupted availability of affordable electricity on the other.[7] Defining the size of this gap and the appropriate measures to address it are, however, strongly debated topics.[8] Within the context of these debates, it is well established that the introduction of capacity mechanisms triggers a number of questions under EU law, the addressing of which has been and continues to be the topic of EU-wide discussion.[9]

On a more general level, the discussion on capacity mechanisms within the EU represents the friction between Member States' needs to prioritise the protection of their national security interests on the one hand and the EU's effort to achieve its objectives through competition and the integration of markets on the other. This friction is rooted in the fact that the EU and its Member States do not have a shared view as to the respective roles of the State, the EU and market forces.[10] This difference in perception is particularly relevant in terms of ensuring sufficient investment in generation adequacy. While EU law emphasises the role of the market in generating investment with the State acting only as the facilitator, Member States consider themselves as the protectors of national security of supply interests, wherein the

---

7. Commission Staff Working Document, Generation Adequacy in the internal electricity market, Guidance on public interventions accompanying the document Communication from the Commission, Delivering the internal electricity market and making the most of public intervention, SWD(2013) 438 final, pp. 5 and 9.
8. There is no definitive consensus on whether energy-only markets can ensure adequate generation capacity or whether forms of capacity mechanism are needed. *See*, for example, Mauricio Cepeda and Dominique Finon, 'Generation Capacity Adequacy in Interdependent Electricity Markets', 39(6) *Energy Policy* (2011), pp. 3128-3143; Peter Cramton, Axel Ockenfels and Steven Stoft, 'Capacity Market Fundamentals', 2(2) *Economics of Energy & Environmental Policy* (2013), pp. 27-46; Michael Hogan, '"Energy-Only Markets" or "a Given form of Capacity Mechanism"? Asking the Wrong Question', conference presentation at *Capacity Mechanisms in Europe: The Fundamental Issues Behind the Ongoing Sector Inquiry*, 29 September 2015, Brussels, available at http://ec.europa.eu/competition/sectors/energy/state_aid_to_secure_electricity_supply_en. html (last accessed 5.3.2019); Jamie Carstairs, 'Market Design: the Energy-Only Market Model', conference presentation at *Capacity Mechanisms in Europe: The Fundamental Issues Behind the Ongoing Sector Inquiry*, 29 September 2015, Brussels, available at http://ec.europa.eu/ competition/sectors/energy/state_aid_to_secure_electricity_supply_en.html (last accessed 5.3.2019).
9. For an overview of these issues, *see* Leigh Hancher, Adrien de Hauteclocque and Malgorzata Sadowska, *Capacity Mechanisms in the EU Energy Market* (OUP, 2015) and the Agency for the Cooperation of Energy Regulators (hereinafter 'ACER'), Capacity Remuneration Mechanisms and the Internal Market for Electricity of 30 July 2013, available at www.acer.europa.eu/official _documents/acts_of_the_agency/publication/crms%20and%20the%20iem%20report%20130 730.pdf (last accessed 5.3.2019); for capacity mechanisms and services in the general economic interest, *see* Christian Held and Jan Ole Voss, 'Legal Limits for Electricity Capacity Markets in the EU and Germany', 245 *Renewable Energy Law & Policy Review* (2013); for cross-border issues *see* Arthur Henriot and Jean-Michel Glachant, 'Capacity Remuneration Mechanisms in the European Market: Now But How?', *Robert Schuman Centre for Advanced Studies Research Paper No 84* (2014); David Newbery, 'Missing Money and Missing Markets: Reliability, Capacity Auctions and Interconnectors', 94 *Energy Policy* (2016), pp. 401-410; and for the security of supply element of capacity mechanisms Marko Sencar, Viljem Pozeb and Tina Krope, 'Development of EU (European Union) Energy Market Agenda and Security of Supply', 77 *Energy* (2014), pp. 117-124; Jan Horst Keppler, 'Rationales for Capacity Remuneration Mechanisms: Security of Supply Externalities and Asymmetric Investment Incentives', 105 *Energy Policy* (2017), pp. 562-570.
10. Heike Schweitzer, 'Services of General Economic Interest: European Law's Impact on the Role of Markets and of Member States', in Marise Cremona (ed.), *Market Integration and Public Services in the European Union* (OUP, 2011), pp. 11-62, at 12.

market-based approach is secondary to the need to guarantee the uninterrupted availability of affordable electricity.

§1.02   RESEARCH OBJECTIVES

Security of electricity supply is a practical necessity to support the functioning of a modern society. The legal framework adopted in the EU to ensure and maintain security of electricity supply stems from a pool of very different needs that must be addressed in order to functionally secure the uninterrupted availability of affordable electricity. In other words, energy law does not and cannot exist in isolation from the physical and economic characteristics of energy. As a consequence, security of electricity supply is an inherently interdisciplinary subject that cannot reasonably be analysed through a legal approach without acknowledging the underlying physical and economic realities.[11]

Capacity mechanisms typically compensate for the provision of generation capacity to ensure generation adequacy. The concepts and functions of generation capacity and generation adequacy within an electricity system are therefore particularly relevant for the purposes of examining the legal framework for capacity mechanisms. Generation capacity is a physical attribute of an electricity generator that describes the maximum output of electricity that the generator can produce under optimal conditions.[12] It is accordingly a physical precondition for the production and supply of electricity. However, the existence of generation capacity is not a value in its own right but only has instrumental value in achieving generation adequacy, which is the ability of the totality of generation capacity to meet demand at all times. This distinction is of fundamental relevance, because generation adequacy can be achieved not only by existing or forthcoming capacity but also by reducing the demand for generation capacity through shifting or reducing electricity demand peaks, for example. Thus, when balancing electricity production against consumption, the objective is not necessarily to increase generation capacity but rather to secure the sufficiency of overall resources to meet demand. Regardless of the approach taken, the security of electricity supply cannot be guaranteed without generation adequacy.

In this context, EU law aims not only to facilitate market-based investment in generation adequacy but also to control the introduction of State intervention, for instance in the form of capacity mechanisms. Nevertheless, State-driven capacity mechanisms that typically compensate for the provision of generation capacity have continued to become more common in the EU.[13]

The objective of this book is to analyse how EU law addresses capacity mechanisms as instruments for ensuring generation adequacy and how the provisions

---

11. Martha Roggenkamp, Catherine Redgwell, Anita Ronne and Inigo del Guayo (eds), *Energy Law in Europe: National, EU and International Regulation* (OUP, 2016), p. 8.
12. This maximum output of a generator can also be referred to as installed capacity, nominal capacity or nameplate capacity.
13. ACER, Annual Report on the Results of Monitoring the Internal Electricity and Gas Markets in 2016: Electricity Wholesale Markets Volume, 6 October 2017, p. 11.

identified should be interpreted within the system of EU law. To achieve this objective, this book addresses the following research questions:

(1) What is the market context in which generation adequacy concerns arise and how do capacity mechanisms address these concerns? (Chapter 2)

(2) What is the EU legal framework that seeks to ensure generation adequacy and how should this framework be interpreted in the context of the adoption of national capacity mechanisms? (Chapter 3)

(3) What are the legal conditions for subsidising generation adequacy and how should this framework be interpreted in the context of the adoption of national capacity mechanisms? (Chapter 4)

(4) What are the free movement rules that address generation adequacy measures and how should these rules be interpreted in the context of the adoption of national capacity mechanisms? (Chapter 5)

(5) What is the broader context of EU energy law in which the objective of generation adequacy operates and how should capacity mechanisms be interpreted in the context of the objectives of EU energy law laid down in Article 194 TFEU? (Chapter 6)

(6) What is the proposed new legal framework for generation adequacy and how do these new proposed rules alter the existing legal framework for national capacity mechanisms? (Chapter 7)

In the context of the questions set out above, the scope of this research is further defined through four overarching features.

First, this book fundamentally examines how EU law addresses legal instruments that its Member States have adopted under national laws. This approach has implications for the scope of the research. Primarily, it means that the focus is on the content and interpretation of EU law itself and not the law of Member States. Because of this, this research does not seek to contribute to the existing literature on the taxonomy or specific designs of national capacity mechanisms.[14] Yet, to determine the compatibility of national legal instruments with EU law, it is necessary to briefly discuss the main characteristics of Member States' capacity mechanisms. However, these are discussed and analysed only to the extent that best serves the purposes of answering the primary research questions.

A focus on the treatment of Member States' legal instruments under EU law also means that certain elements of EU law are excluded from the scope of this book, including, in particular, the application of antitrust rules to capacity mechanisms. This exclusion does not mean that antitrust rules are not relevant to capacity mechanisms. In fact, capacity mechanisms have shown themselves to potentially increase market

---

14. These issues have been extensively discussed in academic literature and on a textbook level. *See*, for example, Leigh Hancher, Adrien de Hauteclocque and Malgorzata Sadowska, *Capacity Mechanisms in the EU Energy Market* (OUP, 2015), pp. 227-382.

concentration and strengthen the dominance of existing incumbents.[15] However, EU antitrust rules are addressed and apply to market players, and therefore, primarily concern the behaviour of private actors and not that of the Member States.[16] In contrast, Member States themselves are the primary addressees of free movement rules, State aid rules and sector-specific rules on electricity.

Second, the scope of this research is further defined by its overall focus on security of electricity supply. It is acknowledged that the existing literature on the general EU law concerning State aid and free movement, for example, is extensive and already goes far beyond the objectives of this research.[17] Therefore, this research does not aim to compete with or contribute to this extensive body of existing literature. Instead, the originality of this research is rooted in its emphasis on how these general and well-established EU rules function and should function when the issue at hand concerns security of electricity supply. Capacity mechanisms are topical and practical examples of instruments that ensure generation adequacy as an element of security of supply. Therefore, they are ideal research subjects for the purposes of demonstrating how EU law not only aims to ensure security of supply but also provides means to govern the instruments designed to bring it about.

Third, the scope of this research is necessarily defined by its focus on both the legal framework currently in force and the proposed rules that will enter into force in the near future.[18] In late 2016, the Commission published a proposal for an extensive legislative package, which addresses the increasing adoption of capacity mechanisms

---

15. Adrien de Hauteclocque, 'Antitrust Law: A Missing Piece in the Regulatory Puzzle?', in Leigh Hancher, Adrien de Hauteclocque and Malgorzata Sadowska, *Capacity Mechanisms in the EU Energy Market* (OUP, 2015), pp. 182-200.
16. *See* Malcolm Jarvis, 'Scope: Persons Bound', in Peter Oliver (ed.), *Oliver on Free Movement of Goods in the European Union* (Hart Publishing, 2010), pp. 55-78 and Adrien de Hauteclocque, 'Antitrust Law: A Missing Piece in the Regulatory Puzzle?', in Leigh Hancher, Adrien de Hauteclocque and Malgorzata Sadowska, *Capacity Mechanisms in the EU Energy Market* (OUP, 2015), pp. 182-200.
17. *See*, among many others, Erika Szyszczak, *The Regulation of the State in Competitive Markets in the EU* (Hart Publishing, 2007); Erika Szyszczak (ed.), *Research Handbook on European State Aid Law* (Edward Elgar, 2011); Juan Jorge Piernas López, *The Concept of State Aid Under EU Law: From Internal Market to Competition and Beyond* (OUP, 2015); Herwig Hofmann and Claire Micheau (eds), *State Aid Law of the European Union* (OUP, 2016); Leigh Hancher, Tom Ottervanger and Piet Jan Slot, *EU State Aids*, 5th edition (Sweet & Maxwell, 2016); Małgorzata Cyndecka, *The Market Economy Investor Test in EU State Aid Law: Applicability and Application* (Kluwer Law International, 2016); Kelyn Bacon, *European Union Law of State Aid*, 3rd edition (OUP, 2017); Philipp Werner and Vinvent Verouden (eds), *EU State Aid Control: Law and Economics* (Wolters Kluwer, 2017); Peter Oliver (ed.), *Oliver on Free Movement of Goods in the European Union* (Hart Publishing, 2010); Laurence Gormley, *EU Law on Free Movement of Goods and Customs Union* (OUP, 2009); Paul Craig and Gráinne de Búrca, *The Evolution of EU Law* (OUP, 2011); Paul Craig and Gráinne de Búrca, *EU Law: Text, Cases, and Materials*, 6th edition (OUP, 2015); Friedl Weiss and Clemens Kaupa, *European Union Internal Market Law* (Cambridge University Press, 2014); Steffen Hindelang, *The Free Movement of Capital and Foreign Direct Investment: The Scope of Protection in EU Law* (OUP, 2009); Vassilis Hatzopoulos, *Regulating Services in the European Union* (OUP, 2012); Panos Koutrakos, Niamh Nic Shuibhne and Phil Syrpis (eds), *Exceptions from EU Free Movement Law: Derogation, Justification and Proportionality* (Hart Publishing, 2016); Morten Broberg and Nina Holst-Christensen, *Free Movement in the European Union*, 3rd edition (DJØF, 2010).
18. This book has followed changes until 5.3.2019.

by Member States.[19] In December 2018, Member States reached a political agreement on the content of these proposals. Some of the provisions of this Clean Energy for All Europeans package directly address and harmonise the adoption criteria for capacity mechanisms.[20] The EU legal setting for capacity mechanisms will change considerably when these proposals enter into force in the future, although their content may still be altered.[21] Finally, the scope of this book is defined by its methodology, which is briefly addressed below.

§1.03 METHODOLOGY AND STRUCTURE

This research comprises a systematic doctrinal analysis of EU law that aims, first, to identify the relevant provisions that govern the introduction and design of capacity mechanisms and, second, to interpret these provisions and their interrelations in the context of EU legal doctrine. This section explains how this analysis is conducted, with specific emphasis on the elements of EU legal doctrine that particularly impact the selected methodological approach.

Capacity mechanisms are not harmonised under EU law. They are governed by a fragmentary body of both primary and secondary provisions that address the broader objectives of security of supply and, occasionally, the provision of adequate generation capacity. In order to identify the relevant EU legal rules that apply to capacity mechanisms within this fragmentary body of legal norms, this book first determines the challenges capacity mechanisms aim to address in the electricity market and the typical shared characteristics of capacity mechanism designs within the EU.

Having identified the applicable legal framework, the book provides a systematic analysis of how capacity mechanisms fall within this framework of rules and which characteristics of capacity mechanisms are likely to raise compatibility issues under EU law. The object of this analysis is the relevant sources of EU law. These include legally binding acts of both primary and secondary law nature, such as treaties, regulations and directives, as well as the case-law of the European Court of Justice (hereinafter the 'ECJ' or 'the Court') and the General Court together with soft-law instruments, such as Commission guidelines. In particular, soft-law instruments expressing the Commission's stand on generation adequacy measures have a significant role in determining the legal compatibility of capacity mechanisms with EU law. As is further discussed in Chapter 4, this is because the legal compatibility of capacity mechanisms is at present primarily evaluated under EU State aid rules, the enforcement of which falls within the exclusive competence of the Commission. Although the Commission guidelines, as soft-law instruments, are not legally binding on the Member States, they bind the

---

19. Communication from the Commission to the European Parliament, the Council, the European Economic and Social Committee, the Committee of the Regions and the European Investment Bank, Clean Energy For All Europeans, COM(2016) 860 final. Capacity mechanisms are directly addressed in the Recast Electricity Regulation.
20. *See*, in particular, Articles 20, 21 and 23 of the Recast Electricity Regulation; and Chapter 7 below.
21. For an analysis of the proposed changes, *see* Chapter 7 below.

Commission itself in its decision-making and are, therefore, valuable in providing legal certainty for Member States in designing their State interventions.[22]

The wording of the specific legal texts under consideration is the starting point for the interpretation of EU legal sources.[23] In accordance with established case-law, however, EU law should not only be interpreted on the basis of its wording but should be evaluated in its context and interpreted in the light of the provisions, objectives and evolution of EU law as a whole.[24] Interpreting EU law in the light of its objectives and its *telos* may be justified by reference to effectiveness, i.e., the *effet utile* of EU law.[25] This interpretational standpoint is particularly relevant in the context of EU energy law, where the objective of security of supply must be balanced against other objectives, which are not always necessarily mutually supportive.[26] In addition to balancing sometimes conflicting interests within the system of EU law, the energy sector is exposed to the friction involved in balancing the objectives pursued by the EU through EU law on the one hand with those of the Member States on the other. The introduction

---

22. 310/85 *Deufil v Commission* [1987] ECR 901, para. 22; C-313/90 *CIRFS v Commission* [1993] ECR I-1125, paras 32-36; and C-311/94 *Ijssel-Vliet* [1996] ECR I-5023, para. 42. This approach is also highlighted from the point of view of the electricity market in the Opinion of the European Economic and Social Committee on the communication from the Commission, Delivering the internal electricity market and making the most of public intervention C(2013) 7243 final, OJ C 226, 16.7.2014, pp. 28-34, para. 2.7.
23. C-53/81 *Levin v Staatssecretaris van Justitie* [1982] ECR 1035, para. 9; C-251/95 *SABEL v Puma, Rudolf Dassler Sport* [1997] ECR I-6191, para. 18; C-404/06 *Quelle* [2008] ECR I-2685, paras 31-33; Rudolf Streinz, 'Interpretation and Development of EU Primary Law', in Karl Riesenhuber (ed.), *European Legal Methodology* (Intersentia, 2017), pp. 151-170, at 160; Karl Riesenhuber, 'Interpretation of EU Secondary Law', in Karl Riesenhuber (ed.), *European Legal Methodology* (Intersentia, 2017), pp. 231-260; Norbert Reich, Annette Nordhausen Scholes and Jeremy Scholes, *Understanding EU Internal Market Law* (Intersentia, 2015), pp. 39-53.
24. C-283/81 *CILFIT v Ministero della Sanità* [1982] ECR 3415, para. 20; 292/82 *Merck* [1983] ECR 3781, para. 12; C-337/82 *St. Nikolaus Brennerei v Hauptzollamt Krefeld* [1984] ECR 1051, para. 10; C-156/98 *Germany v Commission* [2000] ECR I-6882, para. 50; C-223/98 *Adidas AG* [1999] ECR I-7099, para. 23; and more recently C-391/05 *Jan De Nul* [2007] ECR I-1793, para. 20 and C-76/06 P *Britannia Alloys & Chemicals Ltd v Commission of the European Communities* [2007] ECR I-4443, para. 21. In relation to energy, *see* C-17/03 *VEMW and Others* [2005] ECR I-4983, para. 41; Paul Craig and Gráinne de Búrca, *EU Law: Text, Cases, and Materials*, 6th edition (OUP, 2015), pp. 266-315; Matej Avbelj, 'Supremacy or Primacy of EU Law – (Why) Does it Matter?', 17(6) *European Law Journal* (2011), pp. 744-763; Nigel Foster, *Foster on EU Law*, 6th edition (OUP, 2017), pp. 66-68; Norbert Reich, Annette Nordhausen Scholes and Jeremy Scholes, *Understanding EU Internal Market Law* (Intersentia, 2015), pp. 44-45.
25. C-223/98 *Adidas AG* [1999] ECR I-7099, para. 24; C-32/74 *Haaga GmbH* [1974] ECR 1201, para. 6; C-168/00 *Leitner* [2002] ECR I-2631, para. 20; C-315/92 *Verband Sozialer Wettbewerb v Clinique Laboratories and Estée Lauder* [1994] ECR I-317, paras 12-19; 13/72 *Netherlands v Commission* [1973] ECR 27, para. 29; Stefan Mayr, 'Putting a Leash on the Court of Justice? Preconceptions in National Methodology v Effet Utile as a Meta-Rule', 5(2) *European Journal of Legal Studies* (2012), pp. 8-21; Phedon Nicolaides and Maria Geilmann, 'What Is Effective Implementation of EU Law?', 19(3) *Maastricht Journal of European and Comparative Law* (2012), pp. 383-399; Vassilios Skouris, 'Effet Utile Versus Legal Certainty: The Case-Law of the Court of Justice on the Direct Effect of Directives', 17(2) *European Business Law Review* (2006), pp. 241-255; Suvi Sankari, *European Court of Justice Legal Reasoning in Context* (Europa Law Publishing, 2013), pp. 61-71; Norbert Reich, Annette Nordhausen Scholes and Jeremy Scholes, *Understanding EU Internal Market Law* (Intersentia, 2015), pp. 45-46.
26. On the concept of this 'energy trilemma', *see* Raphael Heffron, Darren McCauley and Benjamin Sovacool, 'Resolving Society's Energy Trilemma Through the Energy Justice Metric', 87 *Energy Policy* (2015), pp. 168-176, at 168-169.

of State-driven capacity mechanisms, in particular, demonstrates that Member States are eager to protect domestic security of supply at the expense of the EU's objectives of competitiveness and sustainability.[27]

The methodology utilised in this research is rooted in the EU legal tradition and not in that of individual Member States. It considers EU law an independent order of international law that has unique consequences for the laws of its Member States.[28] This approach invites questions on the relationship and hierarchy between EU and Member State law. The answers to these questions are of fundamental importance when addressing issues of security of supply, the protection of which is traditionally an inherent element of State sovereignty.

The friction between the objectives of Member States' law and the objectives of EU energy law is at the heart of the legal debate on capacity mechanisms. Security of supply is generally considered such a vital interest to the functioning of a modern society that it is always subject to strong national protection. National energy autarky has traditionally been a goal to strive towards because it leaves a State much less exposed to externally unfavourable developments.[29] In contrast, the EU-wide internal market in electricity is built on an entirely different premise in which electricity is produced in the most cost-efficient location and transmitted for consumption to the State where the demand and price are the highest. The EU approach is founded on an idea of interdependence rather than independence.

The established point of departure for determining the relationship between EU and national law is the principle of primacy, which establishes the hierarchical superiority of EU law over national law.[30] As a result, EU law inevitably entails permanent limitation of Member States' sovereign rights.[31] Compliance with the principle of primacy is also a fundamental prerequisite for ensuring the effectiveness of EU law.[32] In practice, the application of this principle means that if an issue of

---

27. For the objectives of EU energy law, *see* Article 194 TFEU.
28. C-26/62 *Van Gend en Loos v Administratie der Belastingen* [1963] ECR 3, p. 12; 6/64 *Costa v ENEL* [1964] ECR 1141, para. 3 and C-106/77 *Amministrazione delle finanze dello Stato v Simmenthal* [1978] ECR 629, pp. 633-634.
29. *See*, for example, Kaisa Huhta, 'Too Important to Be Entrusted to Neighbours? The Dynamics of Security of Electricity Supply and Mutual Trust in EU law', 43(6) *European Law Review* (2018), pp. 920-933; Daniel Yergin, 'Energy Security and Markets', in Jan H. Kalicki and David L. Goldwyn (eds), *Energy & Security*, 2nd edition (John Hopkins University Press, 2013), pp. 69-87, at 73-74; Elisabetta Righini and Juan Carlos González Fernández, 'Capacity Mechanisms and State Aid: Between PSOs, Market Liberalisation, and Security of Supply', 7(10) *Journal of European Competition Law & Practice* (2016), pp. 661-675, at 664.
30. 6/64 *Costa v ENEL* [1964] ECR 1141; 17. Declaration of the TFEU concerning primacy; Rudolf Streinz, 'Interpretation and Development of EU Primary Law', in Karl Riesenhuber (ed.), *European Legal Methodology* (Intersentia, 2017), pp. 151-170, at 162; Gerard Conway, *The Limits of Legal Reasoning and the European Court of Justice* (Cambridge University Press, 2012), pp. 258-265; Matej Avbelj, 'Supremacy or Primacy of EU Law – (Why) Does it Matter?', 17(6) *European Law Journal* (2011), pp. 744-763. Also *see* Allan Rosas and Lorna Armati, *EU Constitutional Law: An Introduction* (Hart Publishing, 2010), p. 55, where it is distinguished that EU law 'prevails over national law but it is not supreme in a strict hierarchical sense'.
31. 6/64 *Costa v ENEL* [1964] ECR 1141, p. 592.
32. 6/64 *Costa v ENEL* [1964] ECR 1141; C-106/77 *Amministrazione delle finanze dello Stato v Simmenthal* [1978] ECR 629, particularly paras 21-23; C-106/89 *Marleasing* [1991] ECR I-7321; Alec Stone Sweet, 'The European Court of Justice', in Paul Craig and Gráinne De Búrca, *The*

incompatibility arises between EU law and a national capacity mechanism or an element of such a mechanism, the provisions of EU law must take precedence over national law. National authorities are automatically prohibited from applying a national provision found to be incompatible with EU law.[33]

The overall research question of how Member States ought to pursue generation adequacy within the EU legal framework has emerged from current, real-life concerns over security of electricity supply. Because of the problem-based nature of the subject and the scope of this research, it is neither reasonable nor justifiable to approach it purely on the basis of legal reasoning. Instead, the physical and economic realities must be included in the analysis, if not always explicitly, then as underlying presumptions by which the electricity markets operate.

This interdisciplinary approach is inherent to the discipline of energy law.[34] It reveals itself in various ways in this research. First, the interdisciplinary character of the research subject is clear from the utilisation of references, which include not only legal sources and legal literature but also literature on, *inter alia*, energy policy, energy engineering and energy economics. Second, it is reflected in the target audience of this book. It is not aimed solely at courts and lawyers but also for the wider group of academics and professionals who deal with EU energy markets.

The problem-based and interdisciplinary character of the research subject invites attempts to comprehensively resolve current concerns over generation adequacy in Europe. However, this is neither a reasonable objective nor one that can be achieved by means of the approach adopted in this research. It is acknowledged that the research questions and methodology selected in this research limit the outcomes that can be reasonably expected. First, the selected research questions and methodology cannot be used to draw conclusions on the effectiveness of the use of capacity mechanisms as a solution for ensuring security of supply or to give recommendations on whether a capacity mechanism should be introduced within a given Member State. Second, the research neither aims to nor is capable of evaluating the impacts of capacity mechanisms or the lack of them. The selected approach is only suitable for analysing how capacity mechanisms are caught by the system of EU law.

Finally, some technical remarks on terminology and referencing are necessary. First, this book inevitably discusses legal sources and case-law dating back to the period prior to the entry into force of the Treaty of Lisbon.[35] However, in the interests of clarity, the Treaty numbering currently in force is used for such purposes in

---

Evolution of EU Law (OUP, 2011), pp. 121-154; Karen Alter, *Establishing the Supremacy of European Law: The Making of an International Rule of Law in Europe* (OUP, 2003).

33. C-106/77 *Amministrazione delle finanze dello Stato v Simmenthal* [1978] ECR 629, pp. 633-634.

34. Raphael Heffron and Kim Talus, 'The Development of Energy Law in the 21st Century: A Paradigm Shift?', 9(1) *The Journal of World Energy Law & Business* (2016), pp. 189-202; Leigh Hancher and Pierre Larouche, 'The Coming of Age of EU Regulation of Network Industries and Services of General Economic Interest', in Paul Craig and Gráinne De Búrca, *The Evolution of EU Law* (OUP, 2011), pp. 743-781, at 744; Martha Roggenkamp, Catherine Redgwell, Anita Ronne and Inigo del Guayo (eds), *Energy Law in Europe: National, EU and International Regulation* (OUP, 2016), p. 8.

35. Treaty of Lisbon amending the Treaty on European Union and the Treaty establishing the European Community, signed at Lisbon, 13 December 2007 (OJ C 306, 17.12.2007, pp. 1-271).

preference to the Treaty numbering used at the time of the judgment at hand.[36] Furthermore, references to the EU in this book should be understood as references to the EU's predecessor organisations (the European Community and the European Economic Community) where relevant. Lastly, the recurring concept of security of supply will be used only to refer to the security of *electricity* supply albeit, in the overall energy security literature, the term is often used to include security of supply of primary energy sources as well.[37]

This book is structured in the following way. Chapter 2 provides an overview of the physical and economic market context from which the wider introduction of capacity mechanisms emerges. It covers the security of supply challenges that Member States have faced and identifies the most typical shared characteristics of capacity mechanisms. Chapter 3 utilises these shared characteristics to determine the applicable provisions of sector-specific energy legislation and their connections with primary law. Chapter 4 analyses capacity remuneration under the EU State aid regime. Chapter 5 evaluates measures to ensure generation adequacy under the EU rules on free movement. Chapter 6 analyses capacity mechanisms in the context of the objectives of EU energy law as a whole. While Chapters 2 to 6 are primarily focused on the existing legal framework and only occasionally reference the forthcoming legal reform, Chapter 7 is entirely dedicated to the proposed provisions of the Clean Energy for All Europeans package. Finally, Chapter 8 concludes by summarising the main findings of the preceding chapters.

---

36. This book has followed changes until 5.3.2019.
37. There have been countless attempts to define the concept of energy security alone. For a collection of these definitions, *see* Benjamin K. Sovacool, 'Introduction', in Benjamin K. Sovacool (eds), *The Routledge Handbook of Energy Security* (Routledge, 2013), pp. 1-42, at 3-6.

CHAPTER 2
Contextualising Capacity Mechanisms

---

§2.01 CAPACITY MECHANISMS AS INSTRUMENTS OF SECURITY OF SUPPLY

[A] The Market Context

The EU project is based on the idea of economic market integration, the effects of which have spread to most areas of law over the years.[1] Electricity is no exception.

The objective of establishing an internal market is specifically laid down in Article 3(3) of the TEU.[2] According to this provision, the internal market will work in favour of objectives such as the sustainable development of Europe based on balanced economic growth and price stability, a highly competitive social market economy, full employment and social progress, and a high level of protection and improvement of the quality of the environment.[3] This particular provision is a manifestation of the underlying assumption that the internal market is an appropriate instrument by which to achieve diverse and complex objectives such as full employment or high environmental quality standards.[4]

The very same logic has been applied to the EU electricity markets. The internal market in electricity, which has been progressively implemented in the EU since the

---

1. Catherine Barnard and Steve Peers (eds), *European Union Law* (OUP, 2014), pp. 1-2; Friedl Weiss and Clemens Kaupa, *European Union Internal Market Law* (Cambridge University Press, 2014), pp. 1-3.
2. Consolidated version of the Treaty on European Union (OJ C 326, 26.10.2012, pp. 13-390) (hereinafter 'TEU' and together with TFEU 'the Treaties').
3. 3(3) TEU; Stephen Weatherill, *The Internal Market as a Legal Concept* (OUP, 2017), pp. 33-48; Wolf Sauter, 'Public Services and the Internal Market: Building Blocks or Persistent Irritant?', 21(6) *European Law Journal* (2015), pp. 738-757, at 743.
4. Friedl Weiss and Clemens Kaupa, *European Union Internal Market Law* (Cambridge University Press, 2014), p. 2; Bruno de Witte, 'A Competence to Protect: The Pursuit of Non-market Aims Through Internal Market Legislation', in Phil Syrpis (ed.), *The Judiciary, the Legislature and the EU Internal Market* (Cambridge University Press, 2012), pp. 49-62.

1990s, aims to deliver real choice for all consumers in the EU, open up new business opportunities and stimulate more cross-border trade in order to achieve efficiency gains, competitive prices and higher standards of service as well as contribute to security of supply as well as sustainability.[5] Again, the underlying idea is that a competitive single market, where electricity flows freely across borders and consumers are able to choose their supplier, will provide the most cost-efficient prices and the highest standards of service, and ensure the achievement of the objectives of sustainability and security of supply.

Ideally, and without the impacts caused by market or regulatory failures and distortions, a system like this would allow power generators to recover their costs and gain their profits through the electricity they produce and sell on the market based on prices determined by demand and supply.[6] This arrangement, also referred to as the energy-only market, is expected to generate the incentives needed to attract investment in generation capacity and thus ensure generation adequacy.[7]

In the energy-only model, sufficient investment in generation capacity is achieved through price signals. Electricity prices are most commonly set by the highest accepted bid in the day-ahead markets, where the bids should, in theory, represent the marginal costs of a generation facility to supply energy.[8] The higher the demand, the

---

5. Recital 1 of Directive 2009/72/EC of the European Parliament and of the Council of 13 July 2009 concerning common rules for the internal market in electricity and repealing Directive 2003/54/EC (OJ L 211, 14.8.2009, pp. 55-93) (hereinafter the 'Electricity Directive').

6. Pablo Rodilla and Carlos Batlle, 'Security of Electricity Supply at the Generation Level: Problem Analysis', 40 *Energy Policy* (2012), pp. 177-185, at 178-181; Laurens de Vries and Petra Heijnen, 'The Impact of Electricity Market Design upon Investment under Uncertainty: The Effectiveness of Capacity Mechanisms', 16(3) *Utilities Policy* (2008), pp. 215-227; Janusz Bielecki and Melaku Geboye Desta (eds), *Electricity Trade in Europe: Review of the Economic and Regulatory Challenges* (Kluwer Law International, 2004), p. 77; ACER, Capacity Remuneration Mechanisms and the Internal Market for Electricity of 30 July 2013, available at www.acer.europa.eu/official _documents/acts_of_the_agency/publication/crms%20and%20the%20iem%20report%20130 730.pdf (last accessed 5.3.2019), p. 3; Philipp Ringler, Dogan Keles and Wolf Fichtner, 'How to Benefit from a Common European Electricity Market Design', 101 *Energy Policy* (2017), pp. 629-643, at 630.

7. Recitals 6 and 56 of the Electricity Directive; William W. Hogan, 'On an "Energy Only" Electricity Market Design for Resource Adequacy', *Harvard University Papers* (2005), available at www. hks.harvard.edu/fs/whogan/Hogan_Energy_Only_092305.pdf (last accessed 5.3.2019), p. 7. For the economics of a functioning energy-only market, *see* Paul Joskow and Jean Tirole, 'Reliability and Competitive Electricity Markets', 38(1) *RAND Journal of Economics* (2007), pp. 60-84; Paul Joskow, 'Capacity Payments in Imperfect Electricity Markets: Need and Design', 16(3) *Utilities Policy* (2008), pp. 15-170, at 160-161; Philipp Ringler, Dogan Keles and Wolf Fichtner, 'How to Benefit from a Common European Electricity Market Design', 101 *Energy Policy* (2017), pp. 629-643, at 631; Commission Staff Working Document accompanying the document Report from the Commission Interim Report of the Sector Inquiry on Capacity Mechanisms, SWD(2016) 119 final, p. 52; Nicolas Hary, Vincent Rious and Marcelo Saguan, 'The Electricity Generation Adequacy Problem: Assessing Dynamic Effects of Capacity Remuneration Mechanisms', 91 *Energy Policy* (2016), pp. 113-127, at 116-117.

8. *Ibid. See also* Peter Cramton, 'Electricity Market Design', 33(4) *Oxford Review of Economic Policy* (2017), pp. 589-612; Peter Cramton, Axel Ockenfels and Steven Stoft, 'Capacity Market Fundamentals', 2(2) *Economics of Energy & Environmental Policy* (2013), pp. 27-46; Paul Joskow, 'Competitive Electricity Markets and Investment in New Generating Capacity', in Dieter Helm (ed.), *The New Energy Paradigm* (OUP, 2007); Goknur Umutlu, André Dorsman and Erdinc Telatar, 'The Electricity Market, Day-Ahead Market and Futures Market', in André Dorsman, Wim Westerman, Mehmet Baha Karan and Özgür Arslan (eds), *Financial Aspects in Energy: A*

higher prices rise. High prices signal scarcity and allow power generators to increase their profitability, which leads to new investment being made in the most effective way.[9]

During these scarcity situations, when electricity prices increase (often drastically and with great volatility), excess demand decreases and the market clears.[10] However, if demand remains greater than supply and the market does not clear, customers are faced with energy rationing, i.e., blackouts, which are considered politically unacceptable in most Member States.[11]

As a physical precondition for generation adequacy, supply has to be balanced with market demand in real time, which means that when demand is low, not all generation units can operate and thus create revenue. Against this background, generation units are typically divided into base, medium and peak-load plants, the latter of which only operate (and thus, recover their costs) during hours of high demand and high prices. Investment and new market entry generally require scarcity rents but investment in this peak-load capacity is particularly dependent on prices occasionally rising to a level that signals scarcity.[12]

It has been rightly pointed out that over the past decade the amount of public EU involvement in, and control over, energy markets has significantly increased due to increasing distrust in the ability of market forces to achieve the objectives of EU energy policy.[13] Nevertheless, the foundations of EU law on energy remain based on the notion that a competitive internal market is the primary driver for investment. This market-driven approach is maintained as the primary means of ensuring security of supply in the EU's plans to further develop the legal framework for electricity.[14] In fact, the extensive legal proposals published by the Commission in late 2016 aim to further

---

European Perspective (Springer, 2011), pp. 109-128; Ronald Huisman, Christian Huurman and Ronald Mahieu, 'Hourly Electricity Prices in Day-Ahead Markets', 29(2) *Energy Economics* (2007), pp. 240-248.

9. For further assessment of European developments, *see* Report from the Commission, Final Report of the Sector Inquiry on Capacity Mechanisms, COM(2016) 752 final, p. 4; European Commission, Investment perspectives in electricity markets, July 2015, available at http://ec.europa.eu/economy_finance/publications/eeip/pdf/ip003_en.pdf (last accessed 5.3.2019).

10. Peter Cramton, Axel Ockenfels and Steven Stoft, 'Capacity Market Fundamentals', 2(2) *Economics of Energy & Environmental Policy* (2013); Peter Cramton and Steven Stoft, 'Forward Reliability Markets: Less Risk, Less Market Power, more Efficiency', 16(3) *Utilities Policy* (2008), pp. 194-201, at 195; Pradyumna Chaitanya Bhagwat, *Security of Supply During the Energy Transition: The Role of Capacity Mechanisms* (Technische Universiteit Delft, PhD thesis 2016), p. 13; and for similar arguments in case-law, *see* SA.46100 *Planned Polish capacity mechanism*, C(2018) 601 final, para. 8.

11. *See* SA.46100 *Planned Polish capacity mechanism*, C(2018) 601 final, para. 6.

12. Paul Joskow, 'Capacity Payments in Imperfect Electricity Markets: Need and Design', 16(3) *Utilities Policy* (2008), pp. 159-170, at 160.

13. Kim Talus, 'Decades of EU Energy Policy: Towards Politically Driven Markets', 10(5) *Journal of World Energy Law and Business* (2017), pp. 1-9, at 1-2.

14. Communication from the Commission to the European Parliament, the Council, the European Economic and Social Committee, the Committee of the Regions and the European Investment Bank, A Framework Strategy for a Resilient Energy Union with a Forward-Looking Climate Change Policy, COM(2015) 80, p. 4; and the Recast Electricity Regulation.

improve the functioning of the market and thereby strengthen the role of the market-driven approach instead of allowing uncontrolled increase in national public intervention.[15]

This idea of ensuring generation adequacy through market-based investment is articulated throughout the sector-specific electricity market legislation. The Electricity Directive states that for the construction of new generation capacity, Member States are to adopt an authorisation procedure based on objective, transparent and non-discriminatory criteria.[16] This authorisation procedure is the primary rule under which investments in generation capacity are expected to be made.

The market context discussed in this section is particularly relevant when examining the steps taken towards achieving security of electricity supply in Europe. The EU internal market in electricity is based on the idea that an integrated market in electricity will be able to contribute to the EU energy policy objectives of sustainability, competitiveness and security set forth in Article 194 TFEU and, therefore, also provide the necessary incentives to invest in electricity generation capacity and ensure security of supply at least cost to the industry and consumers. This is the primary rule and the common thread that informs both the general spirit of the legal framework and its individual provisions.

The internal market has, however, faced challenges in achieving these objectives. There has been criticism as to the suitability of the energy-only approach in relation to the task of ensuring investment in generation capacity while balancing the wider interests of sustainability, security of supply and competitiveness.[17] These challenges are further emphasised in the context of the energy transition, a process which demonstrates that the challenges faced by the EU electricity market and the efforts to resolve them make the reality different from the market-based ideology on which EU electricity legislation is built.

[B]   Challenges Within the Energy Transition

During this millennium, the EU electricity market has been characterised by a number of structural changes that are often referred to as the energy transition.[18] Three

---

15. The Recast Electricity Regulation; and for an analysis of the changes proposed by the Commission, *see* Chapter 7 below.
16. Article 7 of the Electricity Directive. This provision is discussed further in Chapter 3.
17. *See*, for example, Henrik Bjørnebye, *Investing in EU Energy Security: Exploring the Regulatory Approach to Tomorrow's Electricity Production* (University of Oslo, PhD thesis 2009), which analyses the extent to which EU law on generation capacity investment appropriately addresses security of supply issues within a modern electricity market. *See also* Alberto Heimler and Frédéric Jenny, 'The Limitations of European Union Control of State Aid', 28(2) *Oxford Review of Economic Policy* (2012), pp. 347-367; Bram Delvaux, *EU Law and the Development of a Sustainable, Competitive and Secure Energy Policy: Opportunities and Shortcomings* (Intersentia, 2013), pp. 38-46; Mauricio Cepeda, Marcelo Saguan, Dominique Finon and Virginie Pignon, 'Generation Adequacy and Transmission Interconnection in Regional Electricity Markets', 37(12) *Energy Policy* (2009), pp. 5612-5622, which discusses generation adequacy as a public good.
18. This transition is also referred to in the Commission's Clean Energy for All Europeans legal proposals. *See* Recital 3 of the Recast Electricity Regulation. Walter Boltz, 'The Challenges of

developments are identified here as central elements of the energy transition with particular relevance to capacity mechanisms.[19] First, State-driven and monopolised markets have gradually been merging into an integrated and competitive, single European market through the implementation of sector-specific electricity market rules.[20] Second, the supply-oriented market model, where centralised producers and large energy companies are the key players, is morphing into a more polycentric system, where the contribution of demand side actors, distributed generation and so-called 'prosumers' has become more pronounced.[21] Third, global concern for the climate has driven the transition from a fossil fuel-run economy into a decarbonised one where smart technologies and electricity produced from renewable energy sources take the leading role.[22] The challenges caused by and emphasised within this transition are discussed below.

Electricity Market Regulation in the European Union', in Fereidoon Sioshansi (ed.), *Evolution of Global Electricity Markets: New Paradigms, New Challenges, New Approaches* (Elsevier Science & Technology, 2013), pp. 199-224.

19. For further discussion of the character of the energy transition, *see* Geert Verbong and Derk Loorbach, 'Introduction', in Geert Verbong and Derk Loorbach (eds), *Governing the Energy Transition: Reality, Illusion or Necessity?* (Routledge Studies in Sustainability Transitions, 2012), pp. 1-23.

20. The Electricity Directive and the repealed Directive 2003/54/EC of the European Parliament and of the Council of 26 June 2003 concerning common rules for the internal market in electricity and repealing Directive 96/92/EC (OJ L 176, 15.7.2003, pp. 37-56) and Directive 96/92/EC of the European Parliament and of the Council of 19 December 1996 concerning common rules for the internal market in electricity (OJ L 27, 30.1.1997, pp. 20-29). Commission Staff Working Document accompanying the document Report from the Commission Final Report of the Sector Inquiry on Capacity Mechanisms, SWD(2016) 385 final, pp. 10-13; Erik Van Der Vleuten and Per Högselius, 'Resisting Change? The Transnational Dynamics of European Energy Regimes', in Geert Verbong and Derk Loorbach (eds), *Governing the Energy Transition: Reality, Illusion or Necessity?* (Routledge Studies in Sustainability Transitions, 2012), pp. 75-100; Kim Talus, *EU Energy Law and Policy: A Critical Account* (OUP, 2013), pp. 269-286; Eric Hirst and Stan Hadley, 'Generation Adequacy: Who Decides?', 12(8) *The Electricity Journal* (1999), pp. 11-21.

21. In the electricity sector, 'prosumer' refers to an active producer and consumer of energy. *See* Commission Staff Working Document, Best practices on Renewable Energy Self-consumption, accompanying the document Communication from the Commission to the European Parliament, the Council, the European Economic and Social Committee and the Committee of the Regions, Delivering a New Deal for Energy Consumers, SWD(2015) 141 final; the Recast Electricity Regulation, p. 3. In legal literature, *see* Elisabetta Righini and Juan Carlos González Fernández, 'Capacity Mechanisms and State Aid: Between PSOs, Market Liberalisation, and Security of Supply', 7(10) *Journal of European Competition Law & Practice* (2016), pp. 661-675; Jean-Michel Glachant and Sophia Ruester, 'The EU Internal Electricity Market: Done Forever?', 30 *Utilities Policy* (2014), pp. 1-7, at 4; Martha Roggenkamp, Catherine Redgwell, Anita Rønne and Iñigo del Guayo, 'Conclusion', in Martha Roggenkamp, Cathrine Redgwell, Anita Rønne and Iñigo del Guayo (eds), *Energy Law in Europe: National, EU and International Regulation*, 3rd edition (OUP, 2016), pp. 1221-1234, at 1227.

22. Commission Staff Working Document accompanying the document Report from the Commission Final Report of the Sector Inquiry on Capacity Mechanisms, SWD(2016) 385 final, pp. 5 and 10-13; the Recast Electricity Regulation, p. 2; Geert Verbong and Frank Geels, 'Future Electricity Systems: Visions, Scenarios and Transition Pathways', in Geert Verbong and Derk Loorbach (eds), *Governing the Energy Transition: Reality, Illusion or Necessity?* (Routledge Studies in Sustainability Transitions, 2012), pp. 203-219; Bram Delvaux, *EU Law and the Development of a Sustainable, Competitive and Secure Energy Policy: Opportunities and Shortcomings* (Intersentia, 2013), p. 36.

The transition towards a common EU electricity market is a vast undertaking on a continent where electricity systems were initially established within national borders to serve national interests.[23] It remains more realistic to refer to various European electricity markets than to a single European electricity market.[24] These national or regional markets are fragmented, disconnected due to insufficient interconnecting capacity and still, to a large extent, controlled by incumbent energy companies that have a competitive edge against new entrants.[25]

Conventional European electricity markets were structured to emphasise the role of centralised suppliers rather than decentralised 'prosumers' and the role of flexibility or the demand side in general. As a commodity, electricity is characterised by inflexible demand. This is caused largely by the fact that many consumers are rarely able or willing to reduce demand and, even if they are, they still have little information on how and when to reduce it.[26] This results in inflexible demand and lack of short-term price

---

23. Mehmet Baha Karan and Hasan Kazdagli, 'The Development of Energy Markets in Europe', in André Dorsman et al. (eds), *Financial Aspects in Energy: A European Perspective* (Springer, 2011), pp. 11-32; Lionel Kapff and Jacques Pelkmans, 'Interconnector Investment for a Well-Functioning Internal Market: What EU Regime of Regulatory Incentives?', *Bruges European Economic Research Papers* (2010), available at http://aei.pitt.edu/58594/ (last accessed 5.3.2019), p. 4; Graeme Hawker, Keith Bell and Simon Gill, 'Electricity Security in the European Union – The Conflict Between National Capacity Mechanisms and the Single Market', 24 *Energy Research & Social Science* (2017), pp. 51-58, at 52.
24. Peter Cameron, 'Introduction', in Peter Cameron and Raphael Heffron (eds), *Legal Aspects of EU Energy Regulation: The Consolidation of Energy Law Across Europe* (OUP, 2016), pp. 3-31, at 22.
25. The objective of interconnecting at least 10% of installed generation capacity was originally set at the Barcelona Summit in 2002. However, numerous Member States remain below the 10% interconnection target. *See* European Council, Presidency Conclusions, 15-16 March 2002, available at http://ec.europa.eu/invest-in-research/pdf/download_en/barcelona_european_council.pdf (last accessed 5.3.2019), p. 15; Communication from the Commission to the European Parliament and the Council, Achieving the 10% electricity interconnection target Making Europe's electricity grid fit for 2020, 25.2.2015, COM(2015) 82 final; Communication from the Commission to the European Parliament and the Council, European Energy Security Strategy, 28.5.2014, COM(2014) 330 final, p. 10; Muireann Á. Lynch, Richard S.J. Tol and Mark J. O'Malley, 'Optimal Interconnection and Renewable Targets for North-West Europe', 51 *Energy Policy* (2012), pp. 605-617, at 616; DG Competition, The economic impact of enforcement of competition policies on the functioning of EU energy markets, 2016, available at http://ec. europa.eu/competition/publications/reports/kd0216007enn.pdf (last accessed 5.3.2019), pp. 18-19.
26. Commission Staff Working Document accompanying the document Report from the Commission Final Report of the Sector Inquiry on Capacity Mechanisms, SWD(2016) 385 final, p. 29; Report from the Commission, Final Report of the Sector Inquiry on Capacity Mechanisms, COM(2016) 752 final, p. 4; Peter Cramton, Axel Ockenfels and Steven Stoft, 'Capacity Market Fundamentals', 2(2) *Economics of Energy & Environmental Policy* (2013), pp. 27-46; Dominique Finon and Virginie Pignon, 'Electricity and Long-Term Capacity Adequacy: The Quest for Regulatory Mechanism Compatible with Electricity Market', 16(3) *Utilities Policy* (2008), pp. 143-158, at 143; Lawrence Ausubel and Peter Cramton, 'Using Forward Markets to Improve Electricity Market Design', 18(2) *Utilities Policy* (2010), pp. 195-200, at 196; Bram Delvaux, *EU Law and the Development of a Sustainable, Competitive and Secure Energy Policy: Opportunities and Shortcomings* (Intersentia, 2013), p. 41. Limited interconnection has also been used as an argument to defend a capacity remuneration scheme, *see* SA.38968 *Greece Transitory Electricity flexibility remuneration mechanism (FRM)*, C(2016) 1791 final, para. 38.

elasticity, which would signal abundance or scarcity and lead to appropriate invest-ment or divestment decisions.[27] Advances in technology are expected to resolve some of the issues associated with inflexible demand, for example, by facilitating electricity storage and through developments in smart technologies. However, the increasing share of intermittent and publicly subsidised renewable production in the energy mix will require market adjustments that ensure a balance between supply and demand over the long term.[28]

Finally, climate change is perhaps the most urgent driver of the European energy transition. For electricity markets, this is most clearly reflected in increased capacities for renewable production and the production of electricity from renewable energy sources.[29] Additionally, the objectives for energy efficiency and the reduction of energy use play a vital role in the sustainable development policy for EU electricity markets.[30] To enhance this transition, many Member States have introduced State aid schemes for renewable energy, which have accelerated the change in the EU energy mix and given rise to challenges in balancing and predicting supply and demand at times.[31] Further-more, the increased shares of renewable capacity and electricity produced from renewable energy sources have changed the conventional balance and ratio between peak and base-load units.

The structure of the electricity market as well as the energy transition and the challenges associated with it shape the context from which the widespread concerns as to generation adequacy arise in the EU.[32] When electricity is scarce, prices should increase to reflect the scarcity and eventually demand will moderate enough to balance against available supply in an optimal situation.[33] High enough prices will then signal the need and demand for new investment in generation capacity. However, there are

---

27. Pablo Rodilla and Carlos Batlle, 'Security of Electricity Supply at the Generation Level: Problem Analysis', 40 *Energy Policy* (2012), pp. 177-185, at 180; Dominique Finon and Virginie Pignon, 'Electricity and Long-Term Capacity Adequacy: The Quest for Regulatory Mechanism Compat-ible with Electricity Market', 16(3) *Utilities Policy* (2008), pp. 143-158, at 143. In case-law, *see* SA.48648 *Belgian Strategic Reserve*, C(2018) 589 final, para. 13.
28. Pradyumna Bhagwat, Jörn Richstein, Emile Chappin, Kaveri Iychettira and Laurens de Vries, 'Cross-Border Effects of Capacity Mechanisms in Interconnected Power Systems', 46 *Utilities Policy* (2017), pp. 33-47.
29. Eurostat, Renewable energy statistics, July 2016, available at http://ec.europa.eu/eurostat/statistics-explained/index.php/Renewable_energy_statistics (last accessed 5.3.2019).
30. The 2020 targets include a 20% cut in greenhouse gas emissions (from 1990 levels), 20% of EU energy from renewable and a 20% improvement in energy efficiency. The objective is to achieve further cuts of at least 40% in greenhouse gas emissions (from 1990 levels), at least a 27% share for renewable energy and at least a 27% improvement in energy efficiency by 2030.
31. The quantity of renewable energy produced within the EU increased by 73.1% between 2004 and 2014. Eurostat, Renewable energy statistics, July 2016, available at http://ec.europa.eu/eurostat/statistics-explained/index.php/Renewable_energy_statistics (last accessed 5.3.2019). Generally, *see* Leon Freris and David Infield, *Renewable Energy in Power Systems* (John Wiley & Sons, 2008).
32. Report from the Commission, Final Report of the Sector Inquiry on Capacity Mechanisms, COM(2016) 752 final; Report from the Commission, Interim Report of the Sector Inquiry on Capacity Mechanisms, C(2016) 2107 final and Commission Staff Working Document, Interim Report of the Sector Inquiry on Capacity Mechanisms, SWD(2016) 119 final.
33. Peter Cramton, 'Electricity Market Design', 33(4) *Oxford Review of Economic Policy* (2017), pp. 589-612; Peter Cramton, Axel Ockenfels and Steven Stoft, 'Capacity Market Fundamentals', 2(2)

multiple factors that distort the anticipated functioning of the markets. EU electricity markets are fragmented and insufficiently connected; demand is inflexible and decreasing; subsidised and intermittent renewable electricity production is increasing and wholesale prices continue to remain low.[34] Due to the political sensitivity of security of supply issues, many Member States have also capped electricity prices to keep electricity affordable for consumers, thus further preventing prices from rising to a level that would signal scarcity.[35]

Due to the reasons identified above, there appears to be an overcapacity on the market, which does little to incentivise investment.[36] In fact, as many power generators of conventional power plants and particularly peak-load capacities are only able to recover their costs during a few hours each year, there is an incentive to divest rather than invest.[37] As a result, many unprofitable generation facilities are being shut down despite their value for overall generation adequacy. This phenomenon is also referred to as the 'missing money' problem.[38]

Economics of Energy & Environmental Policy (2013); Paul Joskow, 'Competitive Electricity Markets and Investment in New Generating Capacity', in Dieter Helm (ed.), *The New Energy Paradigm* (OUP, 2007).

34. The decrease in electricity demand has been caused by the global economic crisis but is also due to the EU's energy efficiency efforts. Communication from the Commission to the European Parliament, the Council, the European Economic and Social Committee, the Committee of the Regions and the European Investment Bank, Clean Energy For All Europeans, COM(2016) 860 final, p. 10; Report from the Commission, Interim Report of the Sector Inquiry on Capacity Mechanisms, C(2016) 2107 final, pp. 7-10 and Commission Staff Working Document, Interim Report of the Sector Inquiry on Capacity Mechanisms, SWD(2016) 119 final, pp. 13-14.

35. Commission Staff Working Document accompanying the document Report from the Commission Final Report of the Sector Inquiry on Capacity Mechanisms, SWD(2016) 385 final, pp. 34-35; ACER, ACER Market Monitoring Report 2015, available at www.acer.europa.eu/official _documents/acts_of_the_agency/publication/acer_market_monitoring_report_2015.pdf (last accessed 5.3.2019), pp. 87-90. Greece, for example, has a price cap at EUR 150/MWh. *See* SA.38968 *Greece Transitory Electricity flexibility remuneration mechanism (FRM)* C(2016) 1791 final, para. 17; Mauricio Cepeda, Marcelo Saguan, Dominique Finon and Virginie Pignon, 'Generation Adequacy and Transmission Interconnection in Regional Electricity Markets', 37(12) *Energy Policy* (2009), pp. 5612-5622, at 5613. For argumentation in case-law, *see* SA.48648 *Belgian Strategic Reserve*, C(2018) 589 final, para. 14.

36. Commission Staff Working Document accompanying the document Report from the Commission Final Report of the Sector Inquiry on Capacity Mechanisms, SWD(2016) 385 final, p. 17; Report from the Commission, Final Report of the Sector Inquiry on Capacity Mechanisms, COM(2016) 752 final, p. 3; European Commission, Investment perspectives in electricity market, July 2015, available at http://ec.europa.eu/economy_finance/publications/eeip/pdf/ ip003_en.pdf (last accessed 5.3.2019); Commission Staff Working Document, Interim Report of the Sector Inquiry on Capacity Mechanisms, SWD(2016) 119 final, pp. 7-8, 13-16.

37. Hanspeter Höschle, Cedric De Jonghe, Hélène Le Cadre and Ronnie Belmans, 'Electricity Markets for Energy, Flexibility and Availability – Impact of Capacity Mechanisms on the Remuneration of Generation Technologies', 66 *Energy Economics* (2017), pp. 372-383, at 372; Pradyumna Chaitanya Bhagwat, *Security of Supply During the Energy Transition: The Role of Capacity Mechanisms* (Technische Universiteit Delft, PhD thesis 2016), p. 16.

38. In case-law, *see* SA.42011 *Italian capacity mechanism*, C(2018) 617 final, para. 16. For further discussion of this topic, *see* Leigh Hancher and Christoph Riechmann, 'Capacity Mechanisms and Auctions', in Leigh Hancher, Adrien de Hauteclocque and Francesco Maria Salerno (eds), *State Aid and the Energy Sector* (Hart Publishing, 2018), pp. 145-177, at 150-152; *See also* Marcus Hildmann, Andreas Ulbig and Göran Andersson, 'Empirical Analysis of the Merit-Order Effect and the Missing Money Problem in Power Markets With High RES Shares', 30(3) *IEEE Transactions on Power Systems* (2015), pp. 1560-1570; David Newbery, 'Missing Money and

From a legal point of view, the changes required to advance the energy transition discussed above have been gradually introduced through the first, second and third energy packages, the latest of which is in practice still in the process of being fully implemented.[39] In order to achieve these objectives and to create a single competitive and decarbonised electricity market, significant changes in the functioning and design of the electricity market are required. Within this context, Member States have considerable concerns over whether the market-based approach and the energy-only design are in fact able to ensure security of electricity supply and particularly generation adequacy.[40] Specifically, there is a concern that, in the long term, too few generation units will be left to produce electricity during hours of high demand or when intermittent production fails to deliver. These generation adequacy concerns have also been acknowledged in the initiatives for the Energy Union,[41] the redesign of the electricity market[42] and the Clean Energy for all Europeans package,[43] as well as in the State aid sector inquiry into capacity mechanisms.[44]

Missing Markets: Reliability, Capacity Auctions and Interconnectors', 94 *Energy Policy* (2016), pp. 401-410; Peter Cramton and Axel Ockenfels, 'Economics and Design of Capacity Markets for the Power Sector', 36(2) *Zeitschrift für Energiewirtschaft* (2012), pp. 113-134; Paul Joskow, 'Capacity Payments in Imperfect Electricity Markets: Need and Design', 16(3) *Utilities Policy* (2008), pp. 159-170, at 160-161 and 164-166; Hanspeter Höschle, Cedric De Jonghe, Hélène Le Cadre and Ronnie Belmans, 'Electricity Markets for Energy, Flexibility and Availability – Impact of Capacity Mechanisms on the Remuneration of Generation Technologies', 66 *Energy Economics* (2017), pp. 372-383, at 373; Communication From The Commission To The European Parliament, The Council, The European Economic And Social Committee, The Committee Of The Regions And The European Investment Bank, A Framework Strategy for a Resilient Energy Union with a Forward-Looking Climate Change Policy, COM(2015) 80 final, pp. 8-10; Commission Staff Working Document accompanying the document Report from the Commission Final Report of the Sector Inquiry on Capacity Mechanisms, SWD(2016) 385 final, p. 28.

39. The implementation deadline for the third electricity directive was 3 March 2011. Communication from the Commission to the European Parliament, the Council, the European Economic and Social Committee, the Committee of the Regions and the European Investment Bank, A Framework Strategy for a Resilient Energy Union with a Forward-Looking Climate Change Policy, COM(2015) 80 final, p. 9.

40. *See* analysis on when and how energy-only markets are able to ensure generation adequacy in David Newbery, 'Missing Money and Missing Markets: Reliability, Capacity Auctions and Interconnectors', 94 *Energy Policy* (2016), pp. 401-410, at 404-405; Pablo Rodilla and Carlos Batlle, 'Security of Electricity Supply at the Generation Level: Problem Analysis', 40 *Energy Policy* (2012), pp. 177-185, at 177-178.

41. Communication from the Commission to the European Parliament, the Council, the European Economic and Social Committee, the Committee of the Regions and the European Investment Bank, A Framework Strategy for a Resilient Energy Union with a Forward-Looking Climate Change Policy, COM(2015) 80 final.

42. Communication from the Commission to the European Parliament, the Council, the European Economic and Social Committee and the Committee of the Regions, Launching the public consultation process on a new energy market design, COM(2015) 340 final.

43. Communication from the Commission to the European Parliament, the Council, the European Economic and Social Committee, the Committee of the Regions and the European Investment Bank, Clean Energy For All Europeans, COM(2016) 860 final.

44. Commission Decision of 29.4.2015 initiating an inquiry on capacity mechanisms in the electricity sector pursuant to Article 20a of Council Regulation (EC) No 659/1999 of 22 March 1999, C(2015) 2814 final.

[C]   Filling the Gap in EU Security of Supply

The market-based approach to generation investment and its shortcomings within the energy transition is the context from which the wider introduction of capacity mechanisms has emerged.[45] Although the concept of capacity remuneration itself is not · new, EU Member States have started to adopt and use capacity mechanisms with greater frequency to address generation adequacy concerns. Therefore, capacity mechanisms have gained the status of an EU energy policy issue only within this decade.[46]

The introduction of capacity mechanisms by Member States has been met with a reserved response from the EU. On the one hand, Member States' need and right to adopt State-driven measures in the interests of security of supply is recognised.[47] On the other, the EU seems eager to restrict the adoption of capacity mechanisms to that necessary to fill the gap between the level of investment achieved through competitive energy-only markets and the level of investment needed to secure the availability of affordable energy in the most cost-efficient way.[48] The scope and appropriate design of the capacity mechanisms used to fill this gap remain highly debated.[49]

---

45. *See* similar argumentation in Elisabetta Righini and Juan Carlos González Fernández, 'Capacity Mechanisms and State Aid: Between PSOs, Market Liberalisation, and Security of Supply', 7(10) *Journal of European Competition Law & Practice* (2016), pp. 661-675, at 662; Peter Cameron, 'Introduction', in Peter Cameron and Raphael Heffron (eds), *Legal Aspects of EU Energy Regulation: The Consolidation of Energy Law Across Europe* (OUP, 2016), pp. 3-31, at 20.
46. Karsten Neuhoff, Jochen Diekmann, Friedrich Kunz, Sophia Rüster and Wolf-Peter Schill, Sebastian Schwenen, 'A Coordinated Strategic Reserve to Safeguard the European Energy Transition', 41(C) *Utilities Policy* (2016), pp. 1-12, at 2; Leigh Hancher, 'Capacity Mechanisms and State Aid Control: A European Solution to the "Missing Money" Problem?', in Leigh Hancher, Adrien de Hauteclocque and Malgorzata Sadowska (eds), *Capacity Mechanisms in the EU Energy Market* (OUP, 2015), pp. 157-181, at 159.
47. *See* the landmark case 72/83 *Campus Oil Ltd v Minister for Industry and Energy* [1984] ECR 2727.
48. Commission Staff Working Document, Generation Adequacy in the internal electricity market, Guidance on public interventions accompanying the document Communication from the Commission, Delivering the internal electricity market and making the most of public intervention, SWD(2013) 438 final, pp. 5 and 9. The existence of this gap is implicitly recognised in the Electricity Directive, where Article 7 provides for new, market-based generation capacity as the primary rule and Article 8 provides tenders for new capacity where market-based investment is insufficient to ensure security of supply.
49. There is no consensus on whether energy-only markets are able to ensure adequate generation capacity or whether capacity mechanisms are needed. *See*, for example, Mauricio Cepeda and Dominique Finon, 'Generation Capacity Adequacy in Interdependent Electricity Markets', 39(6) *Energy Policy* (2011), pp. 3128-3143; Peter Cramton, Axel Ockenfels and Steven Stoft, 'Capacity Market Fundamentals', 2(2) *Economics of Energy & Environmental Policy* (2013), pp. 27-46; Michael Hogan, '"Energy-Only Markets" or "a Given Form of Capacity Mechanism"? Asking the Wrong Question', conference presentation at *Capacity Mechanisms in Europe: The Fundamental Issues Behind the Ongoing Sector Inquiry*, 29 September 2015, Brussels, available at http://ec. europa.eu/competition/sectors/energy/state_aid_to_secure_electricity_supply_en.html (last accessed 5.3.2019); Jamie Carstairs, 'Market Design: The Energy-Only Market Model', conference presentation at *Capacity Mechanisms in Europe: The Fundamental Issues Behind the Ongoing Sector Inquiry*, 29 September 2015, Brussels, available at http://ec.europa.eu/ competition/sectors/energy/state_aid_to_secure_electricity_supply_en.html (last accessed 5.3. 2019).

Although national designs for capacity remuneration vary, they have one key element in common. Unlike in an energy-only market in which generators are paid only for the electricity they produce and sell, capacity mechanisms involve payment for available capacity as well.[50] In other words, capacity mechanisms address the recognised investment gap in security of supply by *providing compensation for the availability and readiness of installed or forthcoming capacity or other resources to produce and supply electricity*. Therefore, a capacity mechanism is essentially a regulated forward product financed through public funding and often with an obligation for physical delivery.[51] It hedges the commercial risk associated with investment by offering an *ex ante* guarantee of revenues.

Based on the definition set out above, capacity mechanisms should primarily be viewed as instruments to ensure generation adequacy and, to a greater extent, security of supply. As a means to improve security of supply, capacity mechanisms cannot be examined in isolation from other objectives of EU energy law. Article 194 TFEU provides that the EU's energy policy aims to ensure the functioning of the energy market and security of energy supply in the EU, to promote energy efficiency and energy saving and the development of new and renewable forms of energy and to promote the interconnection of energy networks.[52] Capacity mechanisms interact with these objectives in multiple ways. Their usage is partly a reflection of the response to an increase in intermittent electricity production in the energy mix. They reward reliability and predictability rather than sustainability and, therefore, often allocate public funds to conventional generation capacities, which risks undermining the EU sustainability targets. In respect of promoting the interconnection of energy networks, it is clear that remunerating national capacities only is likely to come at the expense of developing intra-Member State networks. Similarly, capacity mechanisms are a potential barrier to the effective functioning of a competitive energy market. Although these mechanisms improve security of supply by increasing generation capacity, this increase is likely to occur at the expense of cost efficiency, which is the main argument for pursuing a competitive internal market. Achieving an equilibrium in which State intervention carried out in the interests of security of supply would fall within the framework of the EU's energy policy objectives clearly involves the balancing of occasionally conflicting interests across a wider spectrum.

As State interventions, capacity mechanisms are a departure from the market-based ideology identified in s §2.01[A] above and, therefore, constitute an exception to the rule governing the EU electricity markets. EU energy law is formulated to facilitate the market-based approach but due to the importance of various interests such as security of supply, it also allows for exemption from these rules. It is well established that an exemption from a fundamental rule should always be interpreted strictly for the

---

50. Janusz Bielecki and Melaku Geboye Desta (eds), *Electricity Trade in Europe: Review of the Economic and Regulatory Challenges* (Kluwer Law International, 2004), p. 77.
51. Lawrence Ausubel and Peter Cramton, 'Using Forward Markets to Improve Electricity Market Design', 18 *Utilities Policy* (2010), pp. 195-200; Simona Benedettini, 'PJM and ISO-NE Forward Capacity Markets: A Critical Assessment', *IEFE Research Report Series* (2013) ISSN 2036-1785, p. 7.
52. Article 194 TFEU.

simple reason that a broad interpretation of an exemption would de facto undermine the rule governing the situation in question.[53] This principle has been repeatedly applied and enforced in EU case-law concerning energy.[54] However, it is not clear how broad or narrow the security of supply exemptions are in practice or where capacity mechanisms should fall within this legal framework. In order to analyse this, the features and background of capacity remuneration models first need to be assessed.

§2.02   THE EVOLUTION OF CAPACITY MECHANISMS

Remunerating capacity is not a particularly new concept, nor is it unique to the EU.[55] Capacity markets were implemented in many parts of the United States in the late 1990s in order to achieve adequate generation standards.[56] New England, for example, still holds capacity auctions to ensure adequate generation capacity[57] and the state of New York has a type of capacity obligation in place.[58] Western Australia has had a reserve capacity mechanism since 2006,[59] although the costs and overcapacity associated with it led to the initiation of a legislative reform in 2016.[60]

At EU level, the possibility of State-driven tendering for capacity was established as a permissible method for procuring generation capacity in the first electricity directive in 1996.[61] A tender refers to a procedure through which planned additional requirements and replacement capacity are covered by supplies from new or existing

---

53. On the strict interpretation, *see* Clemens Kaupa, *The Pluralist Character of the European Economic Constitution* (Hart Publishing, 2016), pp. 197-203 and cases 36/75 *Rutili v Minister for the Interior* [1975] ECR 1219, para. 27; 30/77 *R v Bouchereau* [1977] ECR 1999, para. 30; C-157/94 *Netherlands* [1997] ECR I-5699, para. 37; C-159/94 *Commission v France* [1997] ECR I-5815, paras 53-55; C-54/99 *Église de scientologie* [2000] ECR I-1335, para. 17; C-326/07 *Commission v Italy* [2009] ECR I-2291, para. 70; C-503/99 *Commission v Belgium* [2002] ECR I-4809, para. 47; C-463/00 *Commission v Spain* [2003] ECR I-4581, para. 34; C-483/99 *Commission v France* [2002] ECR I-4781, para. 48.
54. For a landmark ruling, *see* 72/83 *Campus Oil Ltd v Minister for Industry and Energy* [1984] ECR 2727, para. 37. *See also* argumentation in C-439/06 *Citiworks* [2008] ECR I-3913.
55. Elisabetta Righini and Juan Carlos González Fernández, 'Capacity Mechanisms and State Aid: Between PSOs, Market Liberalisation, and Security of Supply', 7(10) *Journal of European Competition Law & Practice* (2016), pp. 661-675, at 661.
56. Pradyumna Chaitanya Bhagwat, *Security of Supply During the Energy Transition: The Role of Capacity Mechanisms* (Technische Universiteit Delft, PhD thesis 2016), pp. 85-87; Consultancy paper for Federal Energy Regulatory Commission (hereinafter 'FERC'), 'Resource Adequacy Requirements: Reliability and Economic Implications', 2013, available at www.ferc.gov/legal/staff-reports/2014/02-07-14-consultant-report.pdf (last accessed 5.3.2019), p. 86.
57. FERC, 'Electric Power Markets: New England (ISO-NE)', August 2017, available at www.ferc.gov/market-oversight/mkt-electric/new-england.asp (last accessed 5.3.2019).
58. The New York Independent System Operator (hereinafter 'NYISO'), 'Installed Capacity Market (ICAP)', 2018, available at www.nyiso.com/installed-capacity-market (last accessed 5.3.2019).
59. Government of Western Australia, 'Electricity Market Review', Discussion paper 2014, available at www.treasury.wa.gov.au/uploadedFiles/Site-content/Public_Utilities_Office/Industry_reform/electricity-market-review-discussion-paper.pdf (last accessed 5.3.2019).
60. Government of Western Australia, 'Electricity reforms ensure fairer system for all', 7 April 2016, available at www.mediastatements.wa.gov.au/Pages/Barnett/2016/04/Electricity-reforms-ensure-fairer-system-for-all.aspx (last accessed 5.3.2019).
61. Directive 96/92/EC of the European Parliament and of the Council of 19 December 1996 concerning common rules for the internal market in electricity (OJ L 027, 30.01.1997 pp. 20-29).

generation capacity.[62] Ireland, for example, introduced a tender in 2003 to facilitate 531 MW of new capacity in response to a long-term generation inadequacy. Based on this mechanism, Irish power generators received payments based on their available capacity.[63]

The EU first began to publicly discuss the potential challenges to generation adequacy in the early 2000s.[64] The liberalisation process for electricity markets had, however, begun from a situation characterised by national overcapacities and inefficiencies, where insufficient investment in new capacity was hardly a problem.[65] Potential issues in ensuring generation adequacy began to gain wider attention after 2005 in various EU policy documents.[66] These documents acknowledged the need for new investment to replace ageing capacities and to cover peak demand.[67] However, they also typically emphasised the importance of a functioning internal electricity market, which was expected to provide all the necessary signals for investment.[68] The market had shifted from being one that was inefficient and clearly suffering from overcapacity in the 1990s to one in which it seemed that there was an abundance of generation capacity but where the need to replace ageing plants, cover peak demand and accommodate intermittent shares of renewable generation had begun to give rise to concern in terms of security of supply.

Despite the high expectations for the functioning of the energy-only model at EU level, several Member States have adopted one or several capacity mechanisms to ensure generation adequacy. For example, Ireland utilises a capacity payment system similar to that evaluated by the Commission under State aid rules in 2003.[69] Sweden has had a strategic reserve scheme in force since 2003[70] and Finland has had a similar scheme in place since 2009.[71] The United Kingdom (hereinafter 'UK') has introduced a centralised capacity market that is based on auctions[72] and an extensive support

---

62. Article 2(24) of the Electricity Directive.
63. N 475/2003 *Irish CADA* 16 December 2003, paras 6-9.
64. Commission Green Paper, Towards a European strategy for the security of energy supply, COM(2000) 769 final.
65. Dominique Finon and Virginie Pignon, 'Electricity and Long-Term Capacity Adequacy: The Quest for Regulatory Mechanism Compatible with Electricity Market', 3(16) *Utilities Policy* (2008), pp. 143-158, at 144; Peter Cramton and Axel Ockenfelds, 'Economics and Design of Capacity Markets for the Power Sector', 36(2) *Zeitschrift für Energiewirtschaft* (2011), pp. 113-134; Henrik Bjørnebye, *Investing in EU Energy Security: Exploring the Regulatory Approach to Tomorrow's Electricity Production* (University of Oslo, PhD thesis 2009), p. 2.
66. Commission Green Paper, A European Strategy for Sustainable, Competitive and Secure Energy, COM(2006) 105 final and Communication from the Commission to the European Council and the European Parliament, An Energy Policy for Europe, COM(2007) 1 final.
67. Commission Green Paper, A European Strategy for Sustainable, Competitive and Secure Energy, COM(2006) 105 final, p. 7.
68. Commission Green Paper, A European Strategy for Sustainable, Competitive and Secure Energy, COM(2006) 105 final, p. 7; and Communication from the Commission to the European Council and the European Parliament, An Energy Policy for Europe, COM(2007) 1 final, p. 4, 7 and 10.
69. N 475/2003 *Irish CADA* 16 December 2003.
70. Lag (2003:436) om effektreserv (Power Reserve Act).
71. Laki sähköntuotannon ja -kulutuksen välistä tasapainoa varmistavasta tehoreservistä (117/2011) (Capacity Reserve Act).
72. SA.34947 *Support to Hinkley Point C Nuclear Power Station* and SA.35980 *GB capacity mechanism*. The Commission's decision to approve the UK capacity market was annulled by the

scheme for a new nuclear unit.[73] Spain has both a targeted capacity payment and a strategic reserve with an interruptibility component.[74] France has adopted a decentralised capacity obligation and a tender for new capacity.[75] Poland has planned a capacity auction scheme to guarantee generation adequacy.[76] EU involvement in most of these cases has comprised an *ex ante* State aid assessment to evaluate whether the national scheme constitutes State aid and whether this aid is compatible with the internal market.[77]

EU institutions began addressing capacity mechanisms and identifying the potential problems involved in their usage around 2010. ACER published a report on capacity mechanisms in 2013 in which it identified that the rationale for many Member States for introducing capacity mechanisms was to mitigate investment uncertainty by providing investment incentives additional to those provided by the market.[78] Generation adequacy was addressed in the 2014 EU energy security strategy[79] and further discussed in the 2014 State aid guidelines for environmental protection and energy.[80] Furthermore, capacity mechanisms and the wider issues of security of electricity supply were among the central elements of the Energy Union agenda established in 2015.[81] That year, the Commission also initiated a State aid sector inquiry into capacity mechanisms, which identified a number of problematic effects that these mechanisms

---

General Court in T-793/14 *Tempus Energy and Tempus Energy Technology v Commission* [2018], judgment of the General Court of 15 November 2018, published in the electronic Reports of Cases. On 21 February 2019, the Commission opened an in-depth investigation into the UK capacity market. *See* European Commission, State aid: Commission opens in-depth investigation into British Capacity Market scheme, 21 February 2019, available at http://europa.eu/rapid/press-release_IP-19-1348_en.htm (last accessed 5.3.2019).

73. SA.34947 *Support to Hinkley Point C Nuclear Power Station*.
74. Commission Staff Working Document, Interim Report of the Sector Inquiry on Capacity Mechanisms, SWD(2016) 119 final, p. 41.
75. SA.39621 *French country-wide capacity mechanism* and SA.40454 *Tender for additional capacity in Brittany*. Both sets of proceedings were initiated in 2015.
76. SA.46100 *Planned Polish capacity mechanism*, C(2018) 601 final.
77. State aid cases on this matter include, for instance T-57/11 *Castelnou Energía v Commission* [2014], judgment of the General Court of 3 December 2014, published in the electronic Reports of Cases; SA.*35980 GB capacity mechanism*; SA.39621 *French country-wide capacity mechanism*; SA.40454 *Tender for additional capacity in Brittany*; N675/2009 *Tender for Aid for New Electricity Generation Capacity* (LV); SA.30531 *Aid for Capacity Payments for Oil-Shale Fuelled Electricity Production (ET)*; N475/2003 *Irish CADA* 16 December 2003; SA.44464 *Irish Capacity Mechanism: reliability option scheme*, C(2017)7789 final; SA.42011 *Italian capacity mechanism*, C(2018) 617 final; SA.45852 *German capacity reserve*, C(2018) 612 final; SA.48490 *Specific demand response tender in France*, C(2018) 588 final; SA.48648 *Belgian Strategic Reserve*, C(2018) 589 final; SA.48780 *Prolongation of the Greek interruptibility scheme*, C(2018) 604 final.
78. ACER, Capacity Remuneration Mechanisms and the Internal Market for Electricity of 30 July 2013, available at www.acer.europa.eu/official_documents/acts_of_the_agency/publication/crms%20and%20the%20iem%20report%20130730.pdf (last accessed 5.3.2019).
79. Communication from the Commission to the European Parliament and the Council, European Energy Security Strategy, COM(2014) 330 final.
80. Communication from the Commission, Guidelines on State aid for environmental protection and energy 2014-2020 (OJ C 200, 28.6.2014, pp. 1-55).
81. Communication from the Commission to the European Parliament, the Council, the European Economic and Social Committee, the Committee of the Regions and the European Investment Bank, a Framework Strategy for a Resilient Energy Union with a Forward-Looking Climate Change Policy, COM(2015) 80 final.

have in relation to EU energy policy objectives.[82] In late 2016, the Commission also published a proposal for an extensive legislative package, which addresses capacity mechanisms in Member States.[83] The prevailing Commission approach to capacity mechanisms in this proposal is cautious: they are tolerated, but treated as a last resort where other means to achieve generation adequacy have failed.

The role of capacity mechanisms in ensuring national security of electricity supply is an illustrative example of the way in which the prevailing market ideology adopted through EU law is balanced against the often protectionist interests of Member States. The idea of sovereign States retreating in favour of market forces, however, does not seem to be fully enforceable in practice.[84] Irrespective of whether capacity mechanisms are considered necessary for the completion of the internal market in electricity, it is clear that their legal status under the EU energy *acquis* and their compatibility with EU law raises unanswered questions. The design and variations of different capacity mechanism models are discussed below.

§2.03 DESIGN OPTIONS FOR CAPACITY MECHANISMS

[A] The Roles of Demand and Supply in a Capacity Mechanism

Capacity mechanisms aim to ensure adequate generation capacity, typically by remunerating electricity producers for new or existing generation capacity. Because of this, capacity mechanisms are generally considered to fall within the category of supply-side measures. Steps taken to improve energy efficiency or demand response, on the other hand, are characteristically demand-side measures, which aim to reduce or shift the amount of electricity consumed. Although these measures are physically different, they are both used to address generation adequacy and can thus be seen as two sides of the same coin when discussing capacity mechanisms.[85] The Commission regards their

---

82. Commission Decision of 29.4.2015 initiating an inquiry on capacity mechanisms in the electricity sector pursuant to Article 20a of Council Regulation (EC) No 659/1999 of 22 March 1999, C(2015) 2814 final; Report from the Commission, Final Report of the Sector Inquiry on Capacity Mechanisms, COM(2016) 752 final.
83. Communication from the Commission to the European Parliament, the Council, the European Economic and Social Committee, the Committee of the Regions and the European Investment Bank, Clean Energy For All Europeans, COM(2016) 860 final. Capacity mechanisms are directly addressed in the Recast Electricity Regulation. *See*, in particular, Articles 20, 21 and 23 of the Recast Electricity Regulation and further analysis in Chapter 7 below.
84. Wolf Sauter and Harm Schepel, *State and Market in European Union Law: The Public and Private Spheres of the Internal Market Before the EU Courts* (Cambridge University Press, 2009), p. 19; Susan Strange, *The Retreat of the State: The Diffusion of Power in the World Economy* (Cambridge University Press, 1996).
85. *See* Xian He, Nico Keyaerts, Isabel Azevedo, Leonardo Meeus, Leigh Hancher and Jean-Michel Glachant, 'How to Engage Consumers in Demand Response: A Contract Perspective', 27 *Utilities Policy* (2013), pp. 108-122; and Commission Consultation paper on generation adequacy, capacity mechanisms and the internal market in electricity, November 2012, available at https://ec.europa.eu/energy/sites/ener/files/documents/20130207_generation_adequacy_con sultation_document.pdf (last accessed 5.3.2019), p. 1.

relationship with one another as a key component in determining the necessity and acceptability of introducing a capacity mechanism under EU law.[86]

Energy efficiency is explicitly mentioned as one of the EU's energy policy objectives under Article 194 TFEU. Article 2(4) of Directive 2012/27/EU of the European Parliament and of the Council (hereinafter the 'Energy Efficiency Directive'), defines energy efficiency as the ratio of output of performance, services, goods or energy, to input of energy.[87] In this context, an improvement in energy efficiency refers to the increase in energy efficiency as a result of technological, behavioural and/or economic changes.[88]

The Electricity Directive offers a more elaborate definition of the concepts of energy efficiency and demand-side management than the Energy Efficiency Directive. Under Article 2(29) of the Electricity Directive, energy efficiency and demand-side management refer to a global or integrated approach aimed at influencing the amount and timing of electricity consumption in order to reduce primary energy consumption and peak loads. Under the EU legal framework for energy efficiency, demand response is seen as an important instrument for improving energy efficiency. This is because it significantly increases the opportunities to reduce or shift consumption, resulting in energy savings not only in final consumption but also in energy generation, transmission and distribution.[89] This definition of demand-side management and energy efficiency is referred to in this book as 'demand side measures'.

Defining energy efficiency and demand-side management as means to address energy demand on the one hand and defining capacity mechanisms as purely supply-side measures on the other amounts, however, to an overly simplistic approach.[90] It appears that the role and status of demand-side measures in achieving the EU's energy policy objectives of security of supply, sustainability and competitiveness have increased within the latest policy initiatives.[91] In its Energy Union Communication, for example, the Commission emphasised that it is necessary to fundamentally rethink the

---

86. Communication from the Commission to the European Parliament and the Council, Energy Efficiency and its contribution to energy security and the 2030 Framework for climate and energy policy, COM(2014) 520; Capacity Mechanisms Working Group, the Participation of Non-Generation Activities, Demand-Side, and Storage in Generation Adequacy Measures, 22 January 2015, available at http://ec.europa.eu/competition/sectors/energy/capacity_mechanisms_working_group_4.pdf (last accessed 5.3.2019).
87. Article 2(4) of Directive 2012/27/EU of the European Parliament and of the Council of 25 October 2012 on energy efficiency, amending Directives 2009/125/EC and 2010/30/EU and repealing Directives 2004/8/EC and 2006/32/EC (OJ L 315, 14.11.2012, pp. 1-57).
88. Article 2(6) of the Energy Efficiency Directive.
89. Recital 44 of the Energy Efficiency Directive.
90. Take the example of interruptibility schemes, which are often caught by the definition of capacity mechanisms but are predominantly demand-side measures. See Commission Staff Working Document accompanying the document Report from the Commission Interim Report of the Sector Inquiry on Capacity Mechanisms, SWD(2016) 119 final, pp. 46-47. Furthermore, the concept of demand-side measures alone is open to definitional challenge. For discussion, see Lorna Greening, 'Demand Response Resources: Who Is Responsible for Implementation in a Deregulated Market?', 35 Energy (2010), pp. 1518-1525, at 1518-1520.
91. The importance of energy efficiency in ensuring energy security has been acknowledged in the EU. See, for example, Communication from the Commission to the European Parliament and the Council, Energy Efficiency and its contribution to energy security and the 2,030 Framework for climate and energy policy, COM(2014) 520.

role of energy efficiency and 'treat it as an energy source in its own right, representing the value of energy saved'.[92] In this approach, the demand side is seen as an independent energy resource, the potential of which is not yet fully exploited.[93] The Commission has also emphasised the need to ensure that energy efficiency and demand-side response can compete on equal terms with generation capacity.[94]

The role of demand-side measures within a capacity design varies according to the capacity mechanism model chosen. Many Member States have included an interruptibility scheme within a supply side oriented capacity mechanism or maintained one alongside such a capacity mechanism.[95] Nevertheless, it is suggested that flexibility and the demand side in general could and should have a larger role in addressing the challenges faced within the energy transition. The Commission estimates the potential of demand side as being 60 GW in the EU.[96] Research indicates that the potential of the demand side as an energy source has not been fully exploited.[97]

[B]   The Taxonomy of Capacity Mechanisms

[1]   *Preliminary Remarks*

Capacity mechanisms can be categorised in different ways, none of which are exhaustive given that real-life designs include variables that depend on the selected national market context as well as institutional and legal setup. However, there are certain key features that distinguish different types of capacity mechanism from each another. The identification of these features is vital in order to understand the applicable legal framework.

---

92. Communication from the Commission to the European Parliament, the Council, the European Economic and Social Committee, the Committee of the Regions and the European Investment Bank, a Framework Strategy for a Resilient Energy Union with a Forward-Looking Climate Change Policy, COM(2015) 80 final, p. 12.
93. Communication from the Commission, Delivering the internal electricity market and making the most of public intervention, C(2013) 7243 final, p. 5; Commission Staff Working Document, Incorporing demand-side flexibility, in particular demand response, in electricity markets, SWD(2013) 442 final.
94. Communication from the Commission to the European Parliament, the Council, the European Economic and Social Committee, the Committee of the Regions and the European Investment Bank, a Framework Strategy for a Resilient Energy Union with a Forward-Looking Climate Change Policy, COM(2015) 80 final, p. 12.
95. Commission Staff Working Document, Interim Report of the Sector Inquiry on Capacity Mechanisms, SWD(2016) 119 final, p. 41.
96. Commission Staff Working Document, Best practices on Renewable Energy Self-consumption accompanying the document Communication from the Commission to the European Parliament, the Council, the European Economic and Social Committee and the Committee of the Regions Delivering a New Deal for Energy Consumers, SWD(2015) 141 final, p. 5.
97. Luis Boscán and Rahmat Poudineh, 'Flexibility-Enabling Contracts in Electricity Markets', Oxford Institute for Energy Studies, July 2016 and Expert Group for Regulatory Recommendations for Smart Grids deployment, Regulatory Recommendations for the Deployment of Flexibility, Report, January 2015, available at http://ec.europa.eu/energy/sites/ener/files/documents/EG3%20Final%20-%20January%202015.pdf (last accessed 5.3.2019).

The most common approach to classifying capacity mechanisms is to begin by looking at how these instruments select and remunerate capacities.[98] Based on the differences between them, capacity mechanisms are often divided into (1) market-wide or targeted mechanisms, (2) price-based or volume-based mechanisms, and (3) centralised and decentralised mechanisms.[99]

Market-wide mechanisms or 'capacity markets' provide payment for all eligible capacity whereas targeted capacity mechanisms only pay for the 'top-up' capacity that is needed in addition to the capacity generated by the markets alone. In respect of the latter, compensation is often allocated based on a certain type of technology or on the location of a generation unit, for example.[100] In centralised capacity mechanisms, the contractual arrangements between capacity providers are set by a central body, whereas in decentralised mechanisms this is done through bilateral agreements.[101]

In price-based capacity mechanisms, the price paid for capacity is fixed and the market determines how much capacity it is willing to offer at that price. Volume-based designs are the mirror image of this. In other words, volume-based mechanisms involve a predetermined amount of capacity, typically set by a regulator, and the market sets the price at which it offers the predetermined capacity.

Figure 2.1   Types of Capacity Mechanisms

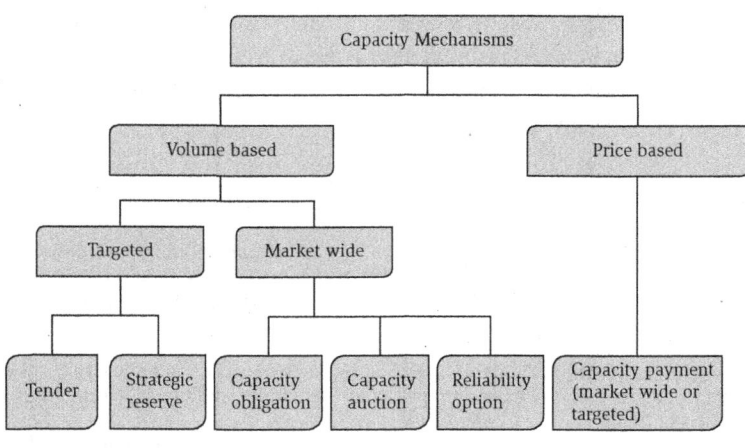

---

98. This approach has been adopted in, for example, ACER, Capacity Remuneration Mechanisms and the Internal Market for Electricity of 30 July 2013, available at www.acer.europa.eu/official_documents/acts_of_the_agency/publication/crms%20and%20the%20iem%20report%2020130730.pdf (last accessed 5.3.2019), pp. 4-5 and in the Report from the Commission, Final Report of the Sector Inquiry on Capacity Mechanisms, COM(2016) 752 final.
99. Commission Staff Working Document, Interim Report of the Sector Inquiry on Capacity Mechanisms, SWD(2016) 119 final, pp. 37-39.
100. Francisco Enrique Gonzáles-Díaz, 'EU Policy on Capacity Mechanisms', in Leigh Hancher, Adrien de Hauteclocque and Malgorzata Sadowska (eds), *Capacity Mechanisms in the EU Energy Market* (OUP, 2015), pp. 3-31, at 10.
101. *Ibid.*

Based on these distinctions, this book identifies six types of capacity mechanisms: tenders for new capacity, strategic reserves, capacity obligations, capacity auctions, reliability options, and capacity payments. However, many Member States have opted to implement several capacity mechanisms or have combined elements of various models into one capacity mechanism design. Member States' design, combination and enforcement of capacity instruments evolve as their national legislation develops.[102]

[2] Tender for New Capacity

A tender for new capacity is a targeted, volume-based mechanism in which a central body grants financing for the construction of a power plant.[103] The requirements for the units that receive financial support vary depending on the objectives of the scheme in question. The requirements can be based on the location, the technology or the minimum size of the generation unit or they can alternate depending on whether the capacity is needed throughout the year or only during peak hours in the winter.[104]

Typically, the entity successful in a tender will receive public financing for the construction of the power plant only, after which they are free to operate and compete on the market without any public guarantees that they will be able to sell the produced electricity.[105] Power purchase agreements concluded with public authorities to finance new generation capacity may also fall within the definition of a tender.[106] Tenders for new capacity have been planned or launched in several Member States, including Belgium, France and Ireland, for example.[107]

A distinction should be made between tenders for new capacity as a type of capacity mechanism on the one hand and the procedure of tendering established in the Electricity Directive on the other.[108] The latter includes tenders as a type of capacity mechanism but is also used more widely to procure capacities in other types of capacity mechanism as well. This is because the wording and interpretation of the Electricity Directive defines tendering broadly to include a wide range of measures to procure resources. For example, the capacity mechanism in Belgium was procured through a tendering procedure within the meaning of the Electricity Directive. However, as a type

---

102. The examples given from Member States' schemes have been updated to include changes up until 5.3.2019.
103. *See*, for example SA.40454 *Tender for additional capacity in Brittany* and SA.34947 *Support to Hinkley Point C Nuclear Power Station*, C(2014) 7142 final.
104. Commission Staff Working Document accompanying the document Report from the Commission, Final Report of the Sector Inquiry on Capacity Mechanisms, SWD(2016) 385 final, p. 56; Graeme Hawker, Keith Bell and Simon Gill, 'Electricity Security in the European Union – The Conflict Between National Capacity Mechanisms and the Single Market', 24 *Energy Research & Social Science* (2017), pp. 51-58, at 53.
105. Commission Staff Working Document accompanying the document Report from the Commission, Final Report of the Sector Inquiry on Capacity Mechanisms, SWD(2016) 385 final, p. 51.
106. *Ibid.*
107. Commission Staff Working Document accompanying the document Report from the Commission, Final Report of the Sector Inquiry on Capacity Mechanisms, SWD(2016) 385 final, p. 55.
108. Article 8 of the Electricity Directive.

of capacity mechanism, it falls within the definition of a strategic reserve.[109] Tendering as a method of procuring capacity in the existing legal framework is extensively analysed in Chapter 3 below.

[3]   Strategic Reserve

A strategic reserve is a volume-based, targeted capacity mechanism in which a centrally predetermined amount of capacity is set aside from the market for use only in exceptional circumstances.[110] For example, a situation in which the market fails to clear could trigger the operation of a strategic reserve.[111] The units that provide the strategic reserve are no longer market participants but back-up units for situations in which the market fails to deliver sufficient generation adequacy.[112]

These capacity units can be existing or, less commonly, new plants. They can also be based on interruptibility schemes in which consumers that are willing to reduce their demand during scarcity hours are contracted. In addition to interruptibility, a strategic reserve may include other instruments that aim to reduce demand or achieve flexibility in respect of it.[113] An independent authority, often the transmission system operator (TSO), is responsible for tendering for the reserve capacity, determining the appropriate volume of reserve capacity and dispatching it when necessary.[114]

Strategic reserve schemes are in use or planned in Belgium, Denmark, Germany, Poland, Finland and Sweden, for example.[115] Not all of these models, however, are referred to as strategic reserves. Instead, the description seems to vary depending on what sort of national challenge the reserve scheme is intended to address. For example, one of the German capacity mechanisms is referred to as the 'network reserve' and has

---

109. SA.48648 *Belgian Strategic Reserve*, C(2018) 589 final, paras 44-61. Similarly, SA.45852 *German capacity reserve*, C(2018) 612 final, para. 9.
110. *See*, for example SA.45852 *German capacity reserve*, C(2018) 612 final, paras 8-20.
111. Pradyumna C. Bhagwat, Jörn C. Richstein, Emile J.L. Chappin, Kaveri K. Iychettira and Laurens J. De Vries, 'Cross-Border Effects of Capacity Mechanisms in Interconnected Power Systems', 46 *Utilities Policy* (2017), pp. 33-47, at 36 and 37-40; Pradyumna Chaitanya Bhagwat, *Security of Supply During the Energy Transition: The Role of Capacity Mechanisms* (Technische Universiteit Delft, PhD thesis 2016), pp. 20-22; Nicolas Hary, Vincent Rious and Marcelo Saguan, 'The Electricity Generation Adequacy Problem: Assessing Dynamic Effects of Capacity Remuneration Mechanisms', 91 *Energy Policy* (2016), pp. 113-127, at 118-119.
112. For example, SA.48648 *Belgian Strategic Reserve*, C(2018) 589 final, para. 8.
113. Commission Staff Working Document accompanying the document Report from the Commission, Final Report of the Sector Inquiry on Capacity Mechanisms, SWD(2016) 385 final, pp. 60-61.
114. In case-law, *see* SA.48648 *Belgian Strategic Reserve*, C(2018) 589 final, para. 50. Note that the capacity for the reserve is often acquired through a tendering procedure similar to that discussed in section §2.03[B][2] above. The underlying difference is that tenders often aim to generate new capacity whereas strategic reserves generally aim to prevent existing plants from shutting down.
115. ACER, Capacity Remuneration Mechanisms and the Internal Market for Electricity of 30 July 2013, available at www.acer.europa.eu/official_documents/acts_of_the_agency/publication/crms%20and%20the%20iem%20report%2020130730.pdf (last accessed 5.3.2019), p. 8; Commission Staff Working Document accompanying the document Report from the Commission, Final Report of the Sector Inquiry on Capacity Mechanisms, SWD(2016) 385 final, p. 57.

the aim of mitigating generation adequacy concerns apparently resulting from insufficient network capacity, and the Polish scheme is referred to as the 'cold contingency reserve' the purpose of which is to address peak-demand hours during the winter.[116]

[4]   Capacity Obligation

A capacity obligation is a volume-based, market-wide capacity mechanism, which imposes obligations on suppliers or large consumers to contract a certain level of capacity linked to their estimated future supply or consumption.[117] Capacity obligations are decentralised mechanisms and there is, accordingly, no central authority that determines the volume required or initiates a bidding process. Instead, suppliers are obliged to contract for their approximated capacity needs plus an additional reserve margin at a price agreed bilaterally between the parties.[118]

The obligations of contracted suppliers can be fulfilled by means of part-ownership of plants or by purchasing tradable capacity certificates, for example.[119] These obligations may also include demand-side capacities. Contracted producers are then obliged to make the contracted capacity available after a certain period of time. Capacity obligations are utilised in France and are in force, albeit not implemented, in Greece.[120]

[5]   Capacity Auction

A capacity auction is a volume-based, market-wide capacity mechanism in which the total required capacity is centrally determined years in advance based on a demand forecast.[121] This capacity is then procured through an auction, where the most competitive bid determines the price of the capacity and demand-side resources.

---

116. However, Poland has committed to terminating the cold contingency reserve. *See* SA.46100 *Planned Polish capacity mechanism*, C(2018) 601 final, para. 16. Also Commission Staff Working Document accompanying the document Report from the Commission, Final Report of the Sector Inquiry on Capacity Mechanisms, SWD(2016) 385 final, p. 58; Graeme Hawker, Keith Bell and Simon Gill, 'Electricity Security in the European Union – The Conflict Between National Capacity Mechanisms and the Single Market', 24 *Energy Research & Social Science* (2017), pp. 51-58, at 52.
117. Pradyumna Chaitanya Bhagwat, *Security of Supply During the Energy Transition: The Role of Capacity Mechanisms* (Technische Universiteit Delft, PhD thesis 2016), pp. 40-42.
118. Regulatory Commission for Electricity and Gas, Study on capacity remuneration mechanisms, 11 October 2012, available at www.creg.info/pdf/Etudes/F1182EN.pdf (last accessed 5.3.2019), p. 11.
119. ACER, Capacity Remuneration Mechanisms and the Internal Market for Electricity of 30 July 2013, available at www.acer.europa.eu/official_documents/acts_of_the_agency/publication/crms%20and%20the%20iem%20report%20130730.pdf (last accessed 5.3.2019), p. 6.
120. SA.38968 *Greece Transitory Electricity flexibility remuneration mechanism (FRM)*, C(2016) 1791 final, paras 6-8; Francisco Enrique Gonzáles-Díaz, 'EU Policy on Capacity Mechanisms', in Leigh Hancher, Adrien de Hauteclocque and Malgorzata Sadowska (eds), *Capacity Mechanisms in the EU Energy Market* (OUP, 2015), pp. 3-31, at 13-14.
121. Pradyumna Chaitanya Bhagwat, *Security of Supply During the Energy Transition: The Role of Capacity Mechanisms* (Technische Universiteit Delft, PhD thesis 2016), pp. 61-72; Nicolas Hary, Vincent Rious and Marcelo Saguan, 'The Electricity Generation Adequacy Problem:

The capacity procured through an auction can participate in the energy-only market similarly to any other unit, regardless of whether it consists of new or existing generation or demand-side units, such as electricity storage units or interruptibility schemes. A capacity auction has been in force in the UK since 2014 and a similar scheme was approved in Poland in 2018.[122] Capacity auctions have also been discussed in other Member States as a long-term solution to ensure generation adequacy.[123]

[6]   Reliability Option

A reliability option is a volume-based, market-wide capacity mechanism where the amount of capacity is centrally determined by an administrative body. In this scheme, capacity providers enter into a contractual arrangement by which they commit to paying the difference between the market price of electricity and an agreed strike price, whenever this difference is positive.[124] In other words, the generator has to make a payment whenever the market price exceeds the reference price. In return, they receive a fixed fee and thus benefit from a more stable and predictable stream of income.[125]

Capacity providers that hold a reliability option contract can also participate in the energy-only market. Depending on the national design, a reliability option may be merely a financial instrument or it may include an obligation to physically deliver electricity. Reliability options also differ from market-based risk hedging agreements because the capacity is set through regulatory means and not negotiated bilaterally on the market.[126] Reliability options are used in Italy and Ireland, for example.[127]

Assessing Dynamic Effects of Capacity Remuneration Mechanisms', 91 *Energy Policy* (2016), pp. 113-127, at 117-118; Graeme Hawker, Keith Bell and Simon Gill, 'Electricity Security in the European Union – The Conflict Between National Capacity Mechanisms and the Single Market', 24 *Energy Research & Social Science* (2017), pp. 51-58, at 52-53.

122. SA.46100 *Planned Polish capacity mechanism*, C(2018) 601 final.
123. Francisco Enrique Gonzáles-Díaz, 'EU Policy on Capacity Mechanisms', in Leigh Hancher, Adrien de Hauteclocque and Malgorzata Sadowska (eds), *Capacity Mechanisms in the EU Energy Market* (OUP, 2015), pp. 3-31, at 13.
124. Paolo Mastropietro, Pablo Rodilla and Carlos Batlle, 'National Capacity Mechanisms in the European Internal Energy Market: Opening the Doors to Neighbours', 82 *Energy Policy* (2015), pp. 38-47, at 42; Regulatory Commission for Electricity and Gas, Study on capacity remuneration mechanisms, 11 October 2012, available at www.creg.info/pdf/Etudes/F1182EN.pdf (last accessed 5.3.2019), p. 11.
125. ACER, Capacity Remuneration Mechanisms and the Internal Market for Electricity of 30 July 2013, available at www.acer.europa.eu/official_documents/acts_of_the_agency/publication/crms%20and%20the%20iem%20report%20130730.pdf (last accessed 5.3.2019), p. 6.
126. Francisco Enrique Gonzáles-Díaz, 'EU Policy on Capacity Mechanisms', in Leigh Hancher, Adrien de Hauteclocque and Malgorzata Sadowska (eds), *Capacity Mechanisms in the EU Energy Market* (OUP, 2015), pp. 3-31, at 14.
127. As examples of reliability option design, *see* SA.42011 *Italian capacity mechanism*, C(2018) 617 final, paras 41-46 and SA.44464 *Irish Capacity Mechanism: reliability option scheme*, C(2017)7789 final. Commission Staff Working Document accompanying the document Report from the Commission, Final Report of the Sector Inquiry on Capacity Mechanisms, SWD(2016) 385 final, p. 126; Graeme Hawker, Keith Bell and Simon Gill, 'Electricity Security in the European Union – The Conflict Between National Capacity Mechanisms and the Single Market', 24 *Energy Research & Social Science* (2017), pp. 51-58, at 52-53.

[7]   Capacity Payment

A capacity payment is a price-based capacity mechanism, whereby generators receive a predetermined premium for some or all of their available capacity in addition to the revenue received through the energy-only market.[128] Capacity payments can either be market-wide, whereby all capacity providers receive remuneration for capacity, or targeted, in which case the recipients of the remuneration are typically selected through a tender or a similar procedure.

The level of compensation for capacity is determined by a public body.[129] The methods that determine the level of remuneration can take into account the likelihood of system failure and the cost of investing in new generation capacity or they can be based on the estimated capacity margin, for instance.[130] Capacity payments are or have been used in Ireland, Portugal, Greece and Spain.[131]

§2.04   THE OVERARCHING FEATURES OF CAPACITY MECHANISMS

The capacity mechanism models described above demonstrate the complexity and diversity in capacity mechanism designs. In addition to variations in the capacity product itself, the eligibility criteria and practical rules of operation and availability vary extensively. Furthermore, it should be borne in mind that these mechanisms are nationally adopted and implemented legal instruments and hence subject to differences in national legal systems, including institutional setup, administrative culture and enforcement rules regarding failure to comply.

In addition to the differences within the designs of the capacity instruments, capacity mechanism designs also vary in terms of what they are intended to do and, therefore, what objectives they can be expected to achieve.[132] A Member State will choose a design that best suits its national needs, whether it is increasing the number

---

128. Regulatory Commission for Electricity and Gas, Study on capacity remuneration mechanisms, 11 October 2012, available at www.creg.info/pdf/Etudes/F1182EN.pdf (last accessed 5.3.2019), p. 12.
129. ACER, Capacity Remuneration Mechanisms and the Internal Market for Electricity of 30 July 2013, available at www.acer.europa.eu/official_documents/acts_of_the_agency/publication/ crms%20and%20the%20iem%20report%20130730.pdf (last accessed 5.3.2019), p. 7.
130. Regulatory Commission for Electricity and Gas, Study on capacity remuneration mechanisms, 11 October 2012, available at www.creg.info/pdf/Etudes/F1182EN.pdf (last accessed 5.3.2019), p. 12.
131. ACER, Capacity Remuneration Mechanisms and the Internal Market for Electricity of 30 July 2013, available at www.acer.europa.eu/official_documents/acts_of_the_agency/publication/ crms%20and%20the%20iem%20report%20130730.pdf (last accessed 5.3.2019), p. 6; Graeme Hawker, Keith Bell and Simon Gill, 'Electricity Security in the European Union – The Conflict Between National Capacity Mechanisms and the Single Market', 24 Energy Research & Social Science (2017), pp. 51-58, at 52-53.
132. These distinctions are based on ACER, Capacity Remuneration Mechanisms and the Internal Market for Electricity of 30 July 2013, available at www.acer.europa.eu/official_documents/ acts_of_the_agency/publication/crms%20and%20the%20iem%20report%20130730.pdf (last accessed 5.3.2019), pp. 7-8 and the findings in the State aid sector inquiry. See Report from the Commission, Final Report of the Sector Inquiry on Capacity Mechanisms, COM(2016) 752 final, pp. 8-12.

of peak-load units, mitigating the missing money problem or preventing the closure of unprofitable conventional units.[133] There is no single design that is capable of addressing all these objectives, but different types of mechanisms respond to different national needs.[134]

The optimal design for a capacity mechanism, therefore, depends on the Member State's circumstances and market structure. First, the challenges addressed through a capacity mechanism can vary geographically from local to national or regional level.[135] For example, the German strategic reserve was first implemented as means of mitigating the insufficient network capacity between northern and southern Germany.[136] Second, capacity mechanisms have a temporal aspect, which determines the timeframe of the obligations within the mechanism. In other words, the Member State's generation adequacy challenges can be medium-term, long-term or only transitional. This affects the instrument of choice.

Despite the inherent differences between national designs, a number of overarching features are common to most capacity mechanisms. It is necessary to identify these features in order to determine the applicable framework under EU law.

First, capacity mechanisms, regardless of their design, are all responses to a generation adequacy concern at the Member State level. This raises the questions of how an adequate level of capacity is determined, which entity sets the threshold for (in)adequacy and how EU law will then treat the national measures adopted to rectify the problems identified.

Generation adequacy is a necessary component in maintaining security of electricity supply but there is no conclusive consensus as to what it entails or how it should be understood.[137] One way of understanding generation adequacy is to examine its role in relation to other elements of security of supply. Carrying out this exercise makes it necessary to define the concept of security of supply. The Electricity Directive offers a loose definition, in which 'security' means both security of supply and the provision of electricity, and technical safety.[138] Directive 2005/89/EC of the European Parliament and of the Council concerning measures to safeguard security of electricity

---

133. In case-law, *see* SA.42011 *Italian capacity mechanism*, C(2018) 617 final, para. 143 and SA.44464 *Irish Capacity Mechanism: reliability option scheme*, C(2017) 7789 final, para. 15, for example. More generally on the drivers for implementing capacity mechanisms, *see* Graeme Hawker, Keith Bell and Simon Gill, 'Electricity Security in the European Union – The Conflict Between National Capacity Mechanisms and the Single Market', 24 *Energy Research & Social Science* (2017), pp. 51-58.

134. This was also the conclusion of the State aid sector inquiry. Report from the Commission, Final Report of the Sector Inquiry on Capacity Mechanisms, COM(2016) 752 final.

135. For a discussion on capacity mechanisms in a local context, *see* Fabien Roques, 'Market Design for Generation Adequacy: Healing Causes Rather than Symptoms', 16(3) *Utilities Policy* (2008), pp. 171-183, at 175-182.

136. Kai Uwe Pritzsche and Katharina Reinhardt, 'Germany', in Leigh Hancher, Adrien de Hauteclocque and Malgorzata Sadowska (eds), *Capacity Mechanisms in the EU Energy Market* (OUP, 2015), pp. 271-287, at 276.

137. For a collection of definitions of energy security, *see* Benjamin K. Sovacool, 'Introduction', in Benjamin K. Sovacool (eds), *The Routledge Handbook of Energy Security* (Routledge, 2013), pp. 1-42, at 3-6; Eric Hirst and Stan Hadley, 'Generation Adequacy: Who Decides?', 12(8) *The Electricity Journal* (1999), pp. 11-21.

138. Article 2(28) of the Electricity Directive.

supply and infrastructure investment (hereinafter the 'Security of Supply Directive') defines security of electricity supply as the ability of an electricity system to supply final customers with electricity, as provided for under the Directive.[139] This definition seems to indicate that achieving the objectives and successfully implementing the tasks set out in the Security of Supply Directive will lead to a de facto state of security of supply. In other words, the Security of Supply Directive is, in its entirety, an attempt to define what security of supply entails and, as such, does not provide a very compact definition of this multifaceted concept.[140]

For the purposes of this book, security of supply is taken to mean *the uninterrupted availability of affordable electricity*. This definition includes a broad variety of elements ranging from safeguarding the availability of primary energy sources for electricity production to the safety of specific components in the electricity grid. It inevitably also includes a short-term element of security and safety that is often referred to as the ability of the electricity system to respond to sudden disturbances of supply and demand in real time.[141] In contrast, generation adequacy as *the ability of installed and expected generation capacity to meet demand at all times* is focused on the equilibrium between supply and demand and, specifically, the sufficiency of resources to meet demand in the long-term.[142] Generation adequacy should, therefore, also be distinguished from the broader concept of system adequacy, which refers to the ability of the entire system, including networks, to meet demand at all times. While balancing demand and supply in real time is often the responsibility of the system operator, generation adequacy and long-term sufficiency of investment in generation resources are legal and political issues and often protected as national security interests.[143]

Another way of understanding the concept of generation adequacy is to identify the different levels on which it operates. There is capacity, the acceptable *level* of which is determined by individual Member States but pursued primarily through market forces.[144] In addition to the level of capacity, however, the *timing* of the capacity

---

139. Article 2(b) of Directive 2005/89/EC of the European Parliament and of the Council of 18 January 2006 concerning measures to safeguard security of electricity supply and infrastructure investment (OJ L 33, 4.2.2006, p. 22-27).
140. Bram Delvaux, *EU Law and the Development of a Sustainable, Competitive and Secure Energy Policy: Opportunities and Shortcomings* (Intersentia, 2013), pp. 336-338.
141. Pablo Rodilla, Álvaro Baíllo, Santiago Cerisola and Carlos Batlle, 'Regulatory Intervention to Ensure an Efficient Medium-Term Generating Resource Planning In Electricity Markets', *Working Paper IIT-10-008A* (2010), pp. 1-2.
142. Pablo Rodilla, Álvaro Baíllo, Santiago Cerisola and Carlos Batlle, Regulatory Intervention to Ensure an Efficient Medium-Term Generating Resource Planning In Electricity Markets, *Working Paper IIT-10-008A* (2010), pp. 1-2; Simona Benedettini, 'PJM and ISO-NE Forward Capacity Markets: A Critical Assessment', *IEFE Research Report Series* (2013) ISSN 2036-1785; Commission Staff Working Document accompanying the document Report from the Commission, Final Report of the Sector Inquiry on Capacity Mechanisms, SWD(2016) 385 final, p. 68.
143. Angus Johnston and Guy Block, *EU Energy Law* (OUP, 2012), p. 10; Sirja-Leena Penttinen, 'The Role of the Court of Justice of the European Union in the Energy Market Liberalisation', in Kim Talus (ed.), *Research Handbook on International Energy Law* (Edward Elgar, 2014), pp. 241-271, at 241. David Newbery, 'Missing Money and Missing Markets: Reliability, Capacity Auctions and Interconnectors', 94 *Energy Policy* (2016), pp. 401-410, at 402.
144. The Member States' right to determine the pursued level of generation adequacy will change if the Clean Energy for All Europeans package enters into force. *See* Communication from the Commission to the European Parliament, the Council, the European Economic and Social

investment has to be suitable to meet demand. Finally, generation adequacy requires the right *mix* of technologies in order to guarantee security of supply.[145] This dimension connects the issue of generation adequacy to EU sustainability targets and the objective of increasing the share of electricity produced from renewable sources. An energy mix with a high share of renewable electricity production contributes to the EU sustainability targets but nevertheless increases the intermittency of electricity production. Hence, the increase in intermittent production has the potential of threatening generation adequacy. Capacity mechanisms, on the other hand, improve generation adequacy, but in doing so may create disincentives for further investment in intermittent renewable capacities.

Under the EU's legal framework for the internal electricity market, an appropriate level of capacity as well as the right timing and mix of generation investment should be achieved by market forces and, more specifically, by the energy-only market. Capacity mechanisms are an exception to this rule. Unlike in the energy-only model, in which generators are rewarded only for the electricity they actually produce and sell on the market, capacity mechanisms involve compensation for available capacity as well.[146] The required level, timing and mix of capacity are, therefore, directly or indirectly determined by the State rather than market forces.[147] This overarching feature of capacity mechanisms requires the identification and interpretation of the relevant sector-specific rules on electricity, which is the topic of Chapter 3.

Second, capacity mechanisms typically receive public funding. The allocation and level of financing vary depending on the design of the mechanism but nonetheless capacity mechanisms shift some of the financial risk associated with investment from the investor to the State. This triggers the applicability of EU State aid rules, which is further assessed from the point of view of capacity remuneration in Chapter 4.

Third, capacity mechanisms as instruments of safeguarding security of supply operate at the heart of Member States' national security. Energy independence and protectionism have traditionally been the main national approaches to security of supply. In contrast, the EU's approach to security of supply is based on the idea that pooling and sharing the natural resources of larger geographical areas ensures security of supply in a more cost-efficient and sustainable way. From a legal point of view, this approach is implemented through free movement rules, which are the topic of Chapter 5.

Committee, the Committee of the Regions and the European Investment Bank, Clean Energy For All Europeans, COM(2016) 860 final; Articles 20, 21 and 23 of the Recast Electricity Regulation.

145. For further discussion of these three elements, *see* Fabien Roques, 'Market Design for Generation Adequacy: Healing Causes Rather than Symptoms', 16(3) *Utilities Policy* (2008), pp. 171-183, at 172.

146. Janusz Bielecki and Melaku Geboye Desta (eds), *Electricity Trade in Europe: Review of the Economic and Regulatory Challenges* (Kluwer Law International, 2004), p. 77.

147. Commission, Consultation paper on generation adequacy, capacity mechanisms and the internal market in electricity, November 2012, available at https://ec.europa.eu/energy/sites/ener/files/documents/20130207_generation_adequacy_consultation_document.pdf (last accessed 5.3.2019), p. 1.

Fourth, capacity mechanisms inevitably interact with the internal market in electricity as interventions to the energy-only model. In addition to the country-specific design challenges involved, capacity mechanisms are a potential obstacle to achieving the other objectives of the EU electricity market set through both Treaty law and sector-specific electricity market legislation. This interaction, and the balancing, on a wider scale, of the sometimes contradictory objectives of EU energy law, is addressed in Chapter 6. Finally, Chapter 7 focuses on how the *status quo* will change when the proposed legal measures of the Clean Energy for All Europeans package enter into force.

CHAPTER 3

The EU Legal Framework for Ensuring Generation Adequacy

§3.01 CAPACITY MECHANISMS IN EU SECONDARY LEGISLATION

EU electricity legislation is based on the principle that prices formed in the energy-only market should produce the appropriate incentives for investing in secure yet cost-efficient amount of electricity generation capacity.[1] Nationally implemented capacity mechanisms constitute an intervention and an exception to this principle.

Security of electricity supply and facilitation of investment in the generation capacity required to ensure it are generally addressed through secondary legal instruments. Although this legal framework is founded on market-based ideology, it generally recognises that the uninterrupted availability of affordable electricity is such a vital component of a functioning modern society that instruments to address security of supply must be in place to fill the gap in the event that the market fails to deliver an adequate level of generation adequacy. This chapter concentrates on identifying and interpreting this legal framework and the ways in which capacity mechanisms are caught by its application.

There is no single legal instrument in force in the EU that directly and exhaustively addresses legal issues related to capacity mechanisms.[2] Instead, there is a fragmentary body of provisions, which apply to State-driven safeguards for generation adequacy for when the market alone does not deliver an adequate level of security of supply.

There are two main secondary legislative instruments that address the objective of security of supply from the point of view of generation adequacy. The first of these

---

1. For more on the dynamics and functioning of the electricity markets, *see* Chapter 2 above.
2. *See* Paolo Mastropietro, Pablo Rodilla and Carlos Batlle, 'National Capacity Mechanisms in the European Internal Energy Market: Opening the Doors to Neighbours', 82 *Energy Policy* (2015), pp. 38-47, at 39-40.

is the Security of Supply Directive.[3] It establishes measures aimed at safeguarding security of electricity supply in order to ensure the proper functioning of the internal market for electricity, an adequate level of generation capacity and an adequate balance between supply and demand.[4]

Under the Security of Supply Directive, Member States are responsible for maintaining a balance between the demand for electricity and the availability of generation capacity.[5] In accordance with the principles on which the internal market in electricity is based, this obligation should be fulfilled through market-based approaches. Member States are to ensure a high level of security in respect of the electricity supply by taking the necessary measures to facilitate a stable investment climate and by defining the roles and responsibilities of competent authorities, including regulatory authorities and all relevant market actors.[6] In implementing measures to achieve these objectives, Member States should consider, *inter alia*, the importance of ensuring continuity of electricity supplies as well as the importance both of maintaining a transparent and stable regulatory framework and of encouraging the establishment of liquid wholesale markets.[7] They should also take into account the internal market and the possibilities for cross-border cooperation in relation to security of electricity supply.[8]

When adopting measures to ensure a high level of security of electricity supply and to facilitate a stable investment climate, Member States may also consider the degree of diversity in electricity generation, the importance of reducing the long-term effects of the growth of electricity demand, the importance of encouraging energy efficiency and the adoption of new technologies and the importance of removing administrative barriers to investment in infrastructure and generation capacity.[9] In particular, Member States are obliged to encourage the establishment of a liquid

---

3. Directive 2005/89/EC of the European Parliament and of the Council of 18 January 2006 concerning measures to safeguard security of electricity supply and infrastructure investment (OJ L 33, 4.2.2006, pp. 22-27).
4. Article 1 of the Security of Supply Directive. There is little literature on the Security of Supply Directive, as was pointed out in the Clean Energy for All Europeans legislative proposals published in November 2016. Commission Staff Working Document, Evaluation Report covering the Evaluation of the EU's regulatory framework for electricity market design and consumer protection in the fields of electricity and gas Evaluation of the EU rules on measures to safeguard security of electricity supply and infrastructure investment (Directive 2005/89) accompanying the document Proposal for a Directive of the European Parliament and of the Council on common rules for the internal market in electricity (recast), Proposal for a Regulation of the European Parliament and of the Council on the electricity market (recast), Proposal for a Regulation of the European Parliament and of the Council establishing a European Union Agency for the Cooperation of Energy Regulators (recast), Proposal for a Regulation of the European Parliament and of the Council on risk-preparedness in the electricity sector, SWD(2016) 412 final, pp. 50-51. By way of exception to this, *see* Peter Cameron, *Competition in Energy Markets* (OUP, 2007), pp. 528-533; Henrik Bjørnebye, *Investing in EU Energy Security: Exploring the Regulatory Approach to Tomorrow's Electricity Production* (University of Oslo, PhD thesis 2009).
5. Article 5 of the Security of Supply Directive.
6. Article 3(1) and Recital 12 of the Security of Supply Directive.
7. Article 3(2) of the Security of Supply Directive.
8. For further discussion on the prioritisation of cross-border solutions to ensure generation adequacy, *see* Chapter 6.
9. Article 3 of the Security of Supply Directive.

wholesale market framework that provides suitable price signals for generation and consumption and to require TSOs to ensure that an appropriate level of reserve generation capacity is available for balancing purposes and/or to adopt equivalent market-based measures.[10]

The Security of Supply Directive establishes a framework within which Member States are to define transparent, stable and non-discriminatory policies on security of electricity supply that are *compatible with the requirements of a competitive internal market for electricity.*[11] Consequently, the Directive is primarily an instrument to guide the facilitation of the market-based approach to security of supply, not an instrument of State intervention. However, the broadly formulated provisions contained in the Directive impose few enforceable obligations on Member States.[12] Because of this, the Directive may be characterised as a mere declaration of what security of supply is thought to entail under EU law.[13] Due to the nature of this Directive, it has little independent value as a source of legal obligations but can rather be used as an instrument for interpreting the intended meaning of and approaches to security of supply under EU law.

The second sector-specific legal instrument for the internal market in electricity is the Electricity Directive, which establishes common rules for the generation, transmission, distribution and supply of electricity, together with consumer protection provisions.[14] Aligned with the market-based approach, these common rules were established with a view to improving and integrating competitive electricity markets within the EU. The Electricity Directive, however, contains provisions on how and when it is acceptable to resort to State interventions such as capacity mechanisms to ensure security of electricity supply. These provisions and their interpretation offer an appropriate point of departure for analysing capacity mechanisms under EU law. This analysis is the focus of this chapter. However, as identified in Chapter 1, capacity mechanisms are characteristically Member State measures designed to address national concerns about generation adequacy in a sector extensively regulated by the EU. Because of this interplay between EU law and Member State law, it is first necessary to assess and analyse the competences based on which security of supply can be

---

10. Article 5(1)(a) to (b) of the Security of Supply Directive.
11. Article 1(2) of the Security of Supply Directive.
12. *See* analysis of the limited impact of the Security of Supply Directive in Commission Staff Working Document, Evaluation Report covering the Evaluation of the EU's regulatory framework for electricity market design and consumer protection in the fields of electricity and gas Evaluation of the EU rules on measures to safeguard security of electricity supply and infrastructure investment (Directive 2005/89) accompanying the document Proposal for a Directive of the European Parliament and of the Council on common rules for the internal market in electricity (recast) Proposal for a Regulation of the European Parliament and of the Council on the electricity market (recast) Proposal for a Regulation of the European Parliament and of the Council establishing a European Union Agency for the Cooperation of Energy Regulators (recast) Proposal for a Regulation of the European Parliament and of the Council on risk-preparedness in the electricity sector, SWD(2016) 412 final, pp. 50-51.
13. *See* argumentation in T-57/11 *Castelnou Energía v Commission* [2014], judgment of the General Court of 3 December 2014, published in the electronic Reports of Cases, paras 205-207; Henrik Bjørnebye, *Investing in EU Energy Security: Exploring the Regulatory Approach to Tomorrow's Electricity Production* (University of Oslo, PhD thesis 2009), pp. 221-222.
14. Article 1 of the Electricity Directive.

addressed in EU law in the first place. After this, the provisions under which capacity mechanisms can be introduced are addressed.

§3.02   THE EU'S COMPETENCE TO ADDRESS SECURITY OF SUPPLY

[A]   Legal Bases

EU competences are governed by the principle of conferral, under which the Union can only act to the extent permitted by the Member States to achieve the objectives set out in the EU Treaties.[15] Member States retain all competences that have not been conferred upon the Union through the Treaties.[16] This principle applies to actions taken in all sectors but has particular relevance to the energy sector, which is traditionally subject to national protectionism and national security concerns.[17] Furthermore, the Treaties clearly recognise the importance of protecting certain interests in Member States and by Member States. The EU is expected to respect Member States' essential functions, including safeguarding national security.[18] National security remains the sole responsibility of each Member State and inevitably includes certain aspects of security of electricity supply.[19]

Generally, however, EU measures in the energy sector fall within the application of shared competence in accordance with Article 4 TFEU.[20] The energy-specific legal basis for applying this competence is established in Article 194 TFEU, which states that EU energy policy aims to:

(a) ensure the functioning of the energy market;
(b) ensure security of energy supply in the Union;
(c) promote energy efficiency and energy saving and the development of new and renewable forms of energy; and

---

15. Article 5(2) TEU; Paul Craig and Gráinne de Búrca, *EU Law: Text, Cases, and Materials*, 6th edition (OUP, 2015), pp. 73-104; Armin von Bogdandy, 'Founding Principles', in Armin von Bogdandy and Jürge Bast (eds), *Principles of European Constitutional Law*, revised 2nd edition (Hart Publishing, 2011), pp. 9-54, at 3-37.
16. Article 5(2) TEU. *See also* Bram Delvaux, *EU Law and the Development of a Sustainable, Competitive and Secure Energy Policy: Opportunities and Shortcomings* (Intersentia, 2013), pp. 107-112; Leigh Hancher and Sally Janssen, 'Shared Competences and Multi-Faceted Concepts – European Legal Framework for Security of Supply', in Barry Barton et al. (eds), *Energy Security: Managing Risk in a Dynamic Legal and Regulatory Environment* (OUP, 2004), pp. 85-119.
17. Armin von Bogdandy, 'Founding Principles', in Armin von Bogdandy and Jürge Bast, *Principles of European Constitutional Law*, revised 2nd edition (Hart Publishing, 2011), pp. 11-54, at 35-37.
18. Article 4(2) TFEU.
19. Article 4(2) TFEU; Bram Delvaux, *EU Law and the Development of a Sustainable, Competitive and Secure Energy Policy: Opportunities and Shortcomings* (Intersentia, 2013), pp. 304-312.
20. Internal market and environmental matters, the legal bases that have previously been used to introduce energy legislation, also fall within the area of shared competence. *See* Armin von Bogdandy and Jürge Bast, 'The Federal Order of Competences', in Armin von Bogdandy and Jürge Bast, *Principles of European Constitutional Law*, revised 2nd edition (Hart Publishing, 2011), pp. 275-307, at 305-307.

(d) promote the interconnection of energy networks.[21]

In addition to Article 194 TFEU, the Treaty also provides that, without prejudice to any other procedures provided for in the Treaties, the Council may also decide on measures appropriate to address certain economic situations particularly if severe difficulties arise in the supply of energy.[22] The wording of this provision indicates that its application should be limited to short-term shocks and emergencies. It is accordingly clear that its application cannot be extended to State intervention to facilitate investment in generation capacity in the long term.

The measures necessary to achieve the policy objectives established in Article 194 TFEU are adopted in accordance with the ordinary legislative procedure.[23] The adopted measures, however, should not affect a Member State's right to determine the conditions for exploiting its energy resources, its choice between different energy sources and the general structure of its energy supply.[24] This provision, laid down in Article 194(2) TFEU, leaves the ambiguous impression that Member States have a wide margin of discretion in independently determining measures that affect the national exploitation of energy resources and the choice between these resources as well as the structure of the energy supply. Furthermore, a broad interpretation of this provision would suggest that Member States could refuse to apply EU law that effectively restricted this margin of discretion. Capacity mechanisms are an illustrative example of how a broad interpretation such as this would play out in practice. Capacity mechanisms, as adopted by Member States, tend to favour conventional generation capacities and interfere with the sustainability objectives of the Union. Because of these potential adverse effects, the EU is keen to restrict the adoption of such mechanisms, particularly where it entails the provision of public funding for capacity with characteristically high greenhouse gas emissions.[25] The arguments raised by Member States in response to such efforts on the part of the EU to restrict the adoption of certain capacity mechanisms are likely to involve invoking Article 194(2) TFEU.

However, the scope of application for Article 194(2) TFEU has been interpreted narrowly in case-law. In T-370/11 *Poland v Commission,* the General Court held that the Commission's decision Poland had contested was not incompatible with Article 194(2) TFEU. Although the subject matter of the contested decision concerned energy, it had been adopted based on the environmental competence under Article 191(1) TFEU and did not therefore fall within the application of Article 194(2).[26] Due to the

---

21. Article 194(1) TFEU; Leigh Hancher and Francesco Maria Salerno, 'Energy Policy after Lisbon', in Andrea Biondi, Piet Eeckhout and Stefanie Ripley (eds), *EU Law after Lisbon* (OUP, 2012), pp. 367-402.
22. Article 122 TFEU; Bram Delvaux, *EU Law and the Development of a Sustainable, Competitive and Secure Energy Policy: Opportunities and Shortcomings* (Intersentia, 2013), p. 283.
23. Articles 194(2), 289 and 294 TFEU; Paul Craig and Gráinne de Búrca, *EU Law: Text, Cases, and Materials,* 6th edition (OUP, 2015), pp. 126-132.
24. T-370/11 *Poland v Commission* [2013], judgment of the General Court of 7 March 2013, published in the electronic Reports of Cases.
25. *See* Article 23 of the Recast Electricity Regulation.
26. T-370/11 *Poland v Commission* [2013], judgment of the General Court of 7 March 2013, published in the electronic Reports of Cases, para. 13.

different legal basis, Article 194(2) TFEU could not be successfully invoked to protect the national choice between energy resources.

Based on this narrow interpretation, Article 194(2) TFEU seems to have limited practical relevance in the current legal setting.[27] This is particularly the case because the relevant secondary legal instruments for capacity mechanisms were introduced before the Treaty of Lisbon, which first introduced explicit objectives for energy policy and a specific competence on energy matters.[28] Hence, the existing secondary provisions that govern the introduction of capacity mechanisms were not adopted with Article 194 TFEU as their legal basis. Nevertheless, the overall objectives set out in Article 194 TFEU, including security of supply, have been the fundamental drivers of EU energy policy since the first sector-specific energy rules in the 1990s. Because of the lack of an energy-specific competence, however, both the Electricity Directive and the Security of Supply Directive were introduced with Article 114 TFEU as the legal basis. Therefore, these directives are subject to potential limitations under Article 114 TFEU but not under Article 194 TFEU.

Article 114 TFEU allows the EU to adopt measures with the aim of establishing or ensuring the functioning of the internal market, an area which also falls within the application of shared competences. The internal market is to comprise an area without internal frontiers in which the free movement of goods, persons, services and capital is ensured.[29] Due to this legal basis, both the Security of Supply Directive and the Electricity Directive should be viewed and interpreted as instruments of market integration. Measures adopted for the approximation of laws under 114 TFEU should follow the ordinary legislative procedure similarly to Article 194 TFEU.[30]

In addition to the principle of conferral, the Treaties lay down the principles of subsidiarity and proportionality, both of which can have particular relevance when measures in the interests of security of supply are introduced.[31] Under the principle of proportionality, the content and form of Union action may not go beyond that

---

27. However, the relevance of Article 194(2) TFEU is likely to change should the proposed legislative changes in the Clean Energy for All Europeans package enter into force. This is because Article 194 TFEU would be used as the legal basis for the first time. *See* Communication from the Commission to the European Parliament, the Council, the European Economic and Social Committee, the Committee of the Regions and the European Investment Bank, Clean Energy For All Europeans, COM(2016) 860 final; and analysis in Chapter 7 below. Also *see* T-356/15 *Austria v Commission* [2018], judgment of the General Court of 12 July 2018, published in the electronic Reports of Cases, para. 507; Leigh Hancher, 'State Aid to the Nuclear Power Sector: The General Court's Ruling on the UK Reactor at Hinkley Point C', *OGEL* (2018).
28. Treaty of Lisbon amending the Treaty on European Union and the Treaty establishing the European Community, signed at Lisbon, 13 December 2007 (OJ C 306, 17.12.2007, pp. 1-271).
29. Articles 26 and 114 TFEU.
30. Rik Ruiter, 'Under the Radar? National Parliaments and the Ordinary Legislative Procedure in the European Union', 20(8) *Journal of European Public Policy* (2013), pp. 1196-1212; Jenny Helstroffer and Marie Obidzinski, 'Codecision Procedure Bias: The European Legislation Game', 38(1) *European Journal of Law and Economics* (2014), pp. 29-46; Charlotte Burns, Anne Rasmussen and Christine Reh, 'Legislative Codecision and Its Impact on the Political System of the European Union', 20(7) *Journal of European Public Policy* (2013), pp. 941-952; Paul Craig and Gráinne de Búrca, *EU Law: Text, Cases, and Materials*, 6th edition (OUP, 2015), pp. 126-132.
31. Andrea Biondi, 'Subsidiarity in the Courtroom', in Andrea Biondi, Piet Eeckhout and Stefanie Ripley (eds), *EU Law after Lisbon* (OUP, 2012), pp. 213-227; Armin von Bogdandy, 'Founding Principles', in Armin von Bogdandy and Jürge Bast (eds), *Principles of European Constitutional*

necessary to achieve the objectives laid down for EU energy policy.[32] In the context of achieving EU energy policy objectives, it has been established that security of electricity supply cannot be sufficiently achieved by the Member States alone but can be better achieved at EU level.[33] Under the principle of subsidiarity, the EU can only act if and in so far as the objectives of the proposed action cannot be sufficiently achieved by the Member States.[34] The assessment of this principle will prove important with regard to capacity remuneration if the EU adopts legal measures to further control the national introduction of capacity mechanisms.[35] On the one hand, national capacity mechanisms have been designed to respond to such different capacity adequacy concerns that an integrated EU capacity mechanism would be unlikely to achieve the objectives of security of supply better than purely national measures. On the other hand, it is also uncontroversial to state that a situation in which individual Member States introduce mechanisms that are incompatible with one another will hinder the development of an effective internal market in electricity.

Despite the apparent applicability of the subsidiarity principle, its practical relevance is likely to remain limited. The subsidiarity principle seems to have acquired more of a procedural and a political status than a legal one and has never been successfully invoked before the EU courts.[36]

[B]   Roles and Responsibilities of the EU and the Member States

As noted above, the Security of Supply Directive requires Member States to ensure a high level of security of electricity supply by taking the necessary measures to facilitate

Law, revised 2nd edition (Hart Publishing, 2011), pp. 9-54, at 35-36; Wolf Sauter, 'Proportionality in EU Law: A Balancing Act?', 15(2) *Cambridge Yearbook of European Legal Studies* (2012), pp. 439-466; Ulrich Everling, 'The European Union as a Federal Association of States and Citizens', in Armin von Bogdandy and Jürge Bast (eds), *Principles of European Constitutional Law*, revised 2nd edition (Hart Publishing, 2011), pp. 701-734; Tor-Inge Harbo, *The Function of Proportionality Analysis in European Law* (Brill Nijhoff, 2015); Nigel Foster, *Foster on EU Law* (OUP, 2015), pp. 78 and 86-91.

32. Article 5(4) TEU. Wolf Sauter, 'Proportionality in EU Law: A Balancing Act?', 15(2) *Cambridge Yearbook of European Legal Studies* (2012), pp. 439-466; Tor-Inge Harbo, *The Function of Proportionality Analysis in European Law* (Brill Nijhoff, 2015); Nigel Foster, *Foster on EU Law* (OUP, 2015), pp. 88-89; Jürgen Kühling, 'Fundamental Rights', in Armin von Bogdandy and Jürge Bast (eds), *Principles of European Constitutional Law*, revised 2nd edition (Hart Publishing, 2011), pp. 479-514, at 505-511.

33. Recital 18 of the Security of Supply Directive.

34. Article 5(3) TEU; Paul Craig and Gráinne de Búrca, *EU Law: Text, Cases, and Materials*, 6th edition (OUP, 2015), pp. 95-101.

35. The Clean Energy for All Europeans proposal includes an extensive assessment of proportionality and subsidiarity. *See*, Communication from the Commission to the European Parliament, the Council, the European Economic and Social Committee, the Committee of the Regions and the European Investment Bank, Clean Energy For All Europeans, COM(2016) 860 final and, in particular, the Recast Electricity Regulation.

36. Andrea Biondi, 'Subsidiarity in the Courtroom', in Andrea Biondi, Piet Eeckhout and Stefanie Ripley (eds), *EU Law after Lisbon* (OUP, 2012), pp. 213-227; Nigel Foster, *Foster on EU Law* (OUP, 2015), pp. 86-89; Armin von Bogdandy, 'Founding Frinciples', in Armin von Bogdandy and Jürge Bast (eds), *Principles of European Constitutional Law*, revised 2nd edition (Hart Publishing, 2011), pp. 9-54, at 35-37.

a stable investment climate and by defining the roles and responsibilities of competent authorities, including regulatory authorities and all relevant market actors.[37] From a legal point of view, the process of defining and dividing responsibilities between the EU and Member States begins with the relevant provisions on competence regarding energy.[38] Shared competences allow both the EU and Member States to adopt legally binding acts in the energy sector. However, Member States' competence to do so is secondary to that of the EU in the sense that they can only exercise their competence in relation to a particular subject to the extent that the EU has not exercised its competence.[39] This limitation can be relevant when determining whether security of supply is so extensively regulated by the EU that it limits Member States' ability to exercise their shared competence.

The ECJ has consistently held that if a matter has been the subject of exhaustive harmonisation at EU level, any related national measure should be assessed in the light of the provisions of that harmonising measure and not in the light of primary law.[40] Because of this, it is necessary to determine whether the existing harmonisation is extensive enough to trigger this effect.

Security of electricity supply and, in particular, State intervention to facilitate investment in generation capacity are not addressed in detail through secondary legislation. Furthermore, the Security of Supply Directive explicitly provides that Member States are, in fact, responsible for the balancing of supply and demand in relation to electricity.[41] As a result, Member States retain a high level of discretion in adopting national capacity mechanisms. However, they need to comply with both Treaty law and relevant secondary rules. The ongoing legal discussion on the distortive effects of national capacity remuneration schemes has led to a higher level of EU involvement, which will effectively limit Member States' competence in respect of the subject matter.[42] However, the legal framework that currently addresses capacity

---

37. Article 3(1) and Recital 12 of the Security of Supply Directive.
38. Article 4 TFEU.
39. Article 2(2) TFEU. *See also* Leigh Hancher and Francesco Maria Salerno, 'Energy Policy after Lisbon', in Andrea Biondi, Piet Eeckhout and Stefanie Ripley (eds), *EU Law after Lisbon* (OUP, 2012), pp. 367-402; Leigh Hancher and Sally Janssen, 'Shared Competences and Multi-Faceted Concepts – European Legal Framework for Security of Supply', in Barry Barton, Catherine Redgwell, Anita Rønne and Donald N. Zillman (eds), *Energy Security: Managing Risk in a Dynamic Legal and Regulatory Environment* (OUP, 2004), pp. 85-119. On EU competences generally, *see* Catherine Barnard and Okeoghene Odudu (eds), *The Outer Limits of European Union Law* (Hart Publishing, 2009); Theodore Konstadinides, *Division of Powers in European Union Law: The Delimitation of Internal Competence between the EU and the Member States* (Kluwer Law International, 2009).
40. *See* cases C573/12 *Ålands Vindkraft AB v Energimyndigheten* [2014] ECR II-2037, para. 57; C-309/02 *Radlberger Getränkegesellschaft and S. Spitz* [2004] ECR I-11763, para. 53; C-324/99 *DaimlerChrysler* [2001] ECR I-9897, para. 32; and C-322/01 *Deutscher Apothekerverband* [2003] ECR I-14887, para. 64.
41. Article 5 of the Security of Supply Directive.
42. *See* the Recast Electricity Regulation. On the ongoing discussion on capacity mechanisms, *see* Eric Hirst and Stan Hadley, 'Generation Adequacy: Who Decides?', 12(8) *The Electricity Journal* (1999), pp. 11-21; Fabien Roques, 'Market Design for Generation Adequacy: Healing Causes Rather than Symptoms', 16(3) *Utilities Policy* (2008), pp. 171-183; Nicolas Hary, Vincent Rious and Marcelo Saguan, 'The Electricity Generation Adequacy Problem: Assessing Dynamic Effects of Capacity Remuneration Mechanisms', 91 *Energy Policy* (2016), pp. 113-127; Pradyumna

mechanisms is not exhaustive and does not harmonise the matter extensively enough to exclude the application of primary law.

EU electricity legislation establishes that defining the roles and responsibilities of Member States and relevant market actors has great significance in safeguarding security of electricity supply and the proper functioning of the internal market, while at the same time avoiding creating obstacles to market entrants.[43] Two Member State responsibilities with particular relevance to capacity mechanisms are identified here. The first is Member States' responsibility to communicate their security of supply levels and approaches to the EU. The second, which is a more substantive responsibility, is that of maintaining a balance between the supply of and demand for electricity.

Under this second category of responsibilities, Member States are to take appropriate measures to ensure and maintain the availability of generation capacity.[44] With particular relevance to capacity mechanisms, they are obliged to encourage the establishment of a wholesale market framework that provides suitable price signals for generation and consumption.[45] This, again, underlines the market-based approach to attracting generation investment and highlights the importance of capacity mechanisms being treated as a last resort to address security of supply. Nevertheless, the Security of Supply Directive also provides that Member States may take additional

---

Bhagwat, Jörn Richstein, Emile Chappin, Kaveri Iychettira and Laurens De Vries, 'Cross-Border Effects of Capacity Mechanisms in Interconnected Power Systems', 46 *Utilities Policy* (2017), pp. 33-47; Pradyumna Chaitanya Bhagwat, *Security of Supply During the Energy Transition: The Role of Capacity Mechanisms* (Technische Universiteit Delft, PhD thesis 2016); Leigh Hancher, Adrien de Hauteclocque and Malgorzata Sadowska (eds), *Capacity Mechanisms in the EU Energy Market* (OUP, 2015); Dominique Finon and Virginie Pignon, 'Electricity and Long-Term Capacity Adequacy: The Quest for Regulatory Mechanism Compatible with Electricity Market', 3(16) *Utilities Policy* (2008), pp. 143-158; Elisabetta Righini and Juan Carlos González Fernández, 'Capacity Mechanisms and State Aid: Between PSOs, Market Liberalisation, and Security of Supply', 7(10) *Journal of European Competition Law & Practice* (2016), pp. 661-675; Kaisa Huhta, 'Prioritising Energy Efficiency and Demand Side Measures over Capacity Mechanisms under EU Energy Law', 35(1) *Journal of Energy & Natural Resources Law* (2017), pp. 7-24; Mauricio Cepeda and Dominique Finon, 'Generation Capacity Adequacy in Interdependent Electricity Markets', 39(6) *Energy Policy* (2011), pp. 3128-3143; Peter Cramton, Axel Ockenfels and Steven Stoft, 'Capacity Market Fundamentals', 2(2) *Economics of Energy & Environmental Policy* (2013), pp. 27-46; Pablo Rodilla and Carlos Batlle, 'Security of Electricity Supply at the Generation Level: Problem Analysis', 40 *Energy Policy* (2012), pp. 177-185, at 177-178; Marcus Hildmann, Andreas Ulbig and Göran Andersson, 'Empirical Analysis of the Merit-Order Effect and the Missing Money Problem in Power Markets With High RES Shares', 30(3) *IEEE Transactions on Power Systems* (2015), pp. 1560-1570; David Newbery, 'Missing Money and Missing Markets: Reliability, Capacity Auctions and Interconnectors', 94 *Energy Policy* (2016), pp. 401-410; Peter Cramton and Axel Ockenfels, 'Economics and Design of Capacity Markets for the Power Sector', 36(2) *Zeitschrift für Energiewirtschaft* (2012), pp. 113-134; Paul Joskow, 'Capacity Payments in Imperfect Electricity Markets: Need and Design', 16(3) *Utilities Policy* (2008), pp. 159-170, at 160-161 and 164-166; Hanspeter Höschle, Cedric De Jonghe, Hélène Le Cadre and Ronnie Belmans, 'Electricity Markets for Energy, Flexibility and Availability – Impact of Capacity Mechanisms on the Remuneration of Generation Technologies', 66 *Energy Economics* (2017), pp. 372-383; Paolo Mastropietro, Pablo Rodilla, Carlos Batlle, 'National Capacity Mechanisms in the European Internal Energy Market: Opening the Doors to Neighbours', 82 *Energy Policy* (2015), pp. 38-47.
43. Recital 3 of the Security of Supply Directive.
44. Article 5 of the Security of Supply Directive.
45. *Ibid.*

measures to ensure the balancing of supply and demand.[46] These measures include provisions on facilitating new generation capacity, on the entry of new generation companies into the market, on the removal of barriers preventing the use of interruptible contracts and on tendering procedures within the meaning of the Electricity Directive.[47] These measures must be compatible with Treaty law, in particular, the State aid provisions of the Treaty.[48] Although these provisions of the Security of Supply Directive do not impose any concrete obligations on Member States, they communicate the intention underlying the legal framework: ensuring conditions under which generation adequacy is ensured is the responsibility of each Member State. In fulfilling this responsibility, capacity mechanisms are to be treated as measures of last resort.

Member States are also obliged to communicate their security of supply levels and approaches to the Commission. Monitoring and reporting obligations are included in both the Electricity Directive and the Security of Supply Directive.[49] In relation to capacity mechanisms, monitoring security of supply should cover the balance of supply and demand on the national market, the level of expected future demand and envisaged additional capacity being planned or under construction.[50] Such monitoring should also include measures to cover peak demand and to deal with shortfalls in the amount of electricity supplied on the part of one or more suppliers.[51] These monitoring obligations can be delegated to the competent regulatory authority and should cover short, medium and long-term factors relevant to security of supply.[52] The reporting conducted in respect of this monitoring should cover the overall ability of the electricity system to meet current and projected demand for electricity.[53] Because of these monitoring and reporting requirements, the content of the reports may prove to be of value in determining the necessity and appropriateness of introducing capacity mechanisms.

---

46. *Ibid.*
47. Article 5 of the Security of Supply Directive; Article 8 of the Electricity Directive; Natalia Fiedziuk, 'Putting Services of General Economic Interest up for Tender: Reflections on Applicable EU Rules', 50(1) *Common Market Law Review* (2013), pp. 87-114; Philipp Kiiver, *The Practice of Public Procurement: Tendering, Selection and Award* (Intersentia, 2014).
48. Article 5 of the Security of Supply Directive.
49. *See,* generally Recital 44 of the Electricity Directive and Recital 11 of the Security of Supply Directive.
50. Article 4 of the Electricity Directive. Monitoring security of supply is typically the responsibility of the national regulatory authority. *See* Raphael Heffron, 'Shared Governance', in Peter Cameron and Raphael Heffron (eds), *Legal Aspects of EU Energy Regulation: The Consolidation of Energy Law Across Europe* (OUP, 2016), pp. 52-58; Hans Vedder, Anita Rønne, Martha Roggenkamp and Iñigo del Guayo, 'EU Energy Law', in Martha Roggenkamp, Catherine Redgwell, Anita Rønne and Iñigo del Guayo (eds), *Energy Law in Europe: National, EU and International Regulation* (OUP, 2016), pp. 187-366, at 290-292.
51. Article 4 of the Electricity Directive. Peter Cameron, *Competition in Energy Markets* (OUP, 2007), p. 523.
52. Article 4 and Article 37(1)(r) of the Electricity Directive and Recital 16 of the Security of Supply Directive.
53. Article 7 of the Security of Supply Directive.

§3.03 PROCURING GENERATION CAPACITY THROUGH TENDERING OR EQUIVALENT PROCEDURES

[A] High Threshold for Public Intervention

The market-based approach to new generation investment is articulated in Article 7 of the Electricity Directive. This provides for the establishment by Member States of an authorisation procedure for the construction of new generation capacity and stipulates that this procedure is to be conducted in accordance with objective, transparent and non-discriminatory criteria.[54] In determining the criteria based on which the authorisation is conducted, Member States are to consider different elements of the construction process. These include, among other issues, the safety and security of the electricity system, installations and associated equipment, the protection of the environment and the nature of the primary energy sources.[55] The authorisation procedures and criteria should be made public, which is a specific condition for the fulfilment of the general requirement of transparency. Applicants have the right to be informed of the reasons for refusal to grant authorisation and to have access to an appeal process to contest such a refusal.[56]

The authorisation procedure is a legal manifestation of the market-based approach under which investment in the European electricity market should occur. However, the Electricity Directive enables Member States to deviate from this rule by ensuring the possibility to contribute to security of supply through a tendering or an equivalent procedure whereby capacity is publicly procured to ensure a sufficient level of generation capacity.[57] In addition to governing the introduction of a tender or an equivalent procedure, Article 8 of the Electricity Directive includes a set of restrictive criteria for the application of such procedures. These restrictions stipulate that such procedures may be launched only if, on the basis of the authorisation procedure, the generating capacity to be built or the energy efficiency/demand side management measures to be taken are insufficient to ensure security of supply. The inclusion of these restrictions indicates that tendering and equivalent procedures are to be treated as derogations from and interventions in the market-based approach.[58]

---

54. Article 7(1) of the Electricity Directive; Peter Cameron, *Competition in Energy Markets* (OUP, 2007), p. 133. On the approaches taken in the 3rd energy package, *see* generally Leigh Hancher and Francesco Maria Salerno, 'Energy Policy after Lisbon', in Andrea Biondi, Piet Eeckhout and Stefanie Ripley (eds), *EU Law after Lisbon* (OUP, 2012), pp. 367-402; Hans Vedder, Anita Rønne, Martha Roggenkamp and Iñigo del Guayo, 'EU Energy Law', in Martha Roggenkamp, Catherine Redgwell, Anita Rønne and Iñigo del Guayo (eds), *Energy Law in Europe: National, EU and International Regulation* (OUP, 2016), pp. 187-366, at 253-298.
55. Article 7(2) of the Electricity Directive.
56. Article 7(4) of the Electricity Directive.
57. Article 8 of the Electricity Directive. *See also* Recital 43 of the Electricity Directive; Hans Vedder, Anita Rønne, Martha Roggenkamp and Iñigo del Guayo, 'EU Energy Law', in Martha Roggenkamp, Catherine Redgwell, Anita Rønne and Iñigo del Guayo (eds), *Energy Law in Europe: National, EU and International Regulation* (OUP, 2016), pp. 187-366, at 266-267; Peter Cameron, *Competition in Energy Markets* (OUP, 2007), pp. 523-525.
58. Peter Cameron, *Competition in Energy Markets* (OUP, 2007), p. 524, refers to tendering as 'a measure that is clearly an intervention in the market with potentially wide distorting effects'.

The existence of this option is supported by the importance of security of electricity supply. However, the economic rationale for the EU's adoption of the market-based approach also explains why the use of such derogations from the primary market-based approach should be subject to stringent criteria that are interpreted narrowly.[59] On the one hand, the risk of inefficient and ineffective public interventions is high and the launching of tenders or equivalent procedures can trigger opportunistic investor behaviour whereby, instead of investing based on market signals, investors wait for the launching of public tenders to gain access to public funding and hedged risks.[60] On the other hand, including the legal option to launch tenders or equivalent procedures indicates the importance attributed to ensuring the security of the electricity supply under EU law.

The concern for generation adequacy that has resulted in the widespread adoption of capacity mechanisms in Member States demonstrates that the investment incentives generated through the energy-only approach do not ensure generation investment in the right place and at the right time, at any rate not in a manner acceptable to Member States. The possibility of the market failing to deliver adequate electricity generation capacity is explicitly identified in Article 8 of the Electricity Directive, which provides as follows:

> Member States shall ensure the possibility, in the interests of security of supply, of providing for new capacity or energy efficiency/demand-side management measures through a tendering procedure or any procedure equivalent in terms of transparency and non-discrimination, on the basis of published criteria. Those procedures may, however, be launched only where, on the basis of the authorisation procedure, the generating capacity to be built or the energy efficiency/demand-side management measures to be taken are insufficient to ensure security of supply.

The definition of tendering is set out in Article 2(24) of the Electricity Directive, according to which a tendering or an equivalent procedure refers to a procedure through which planned additional requirements and replacement capacity are covered by supplies from new or existing generation capacity.[61] Therefore, tendering or equivalent procedures under Article 8 of the Electricity Directive should be clearly distinguished and separated from the tenders referred to above in section §2.03[B][2]

---

59. For more on the rationale behind the market-based approach, *see* Chapter 2 above.
60. Commission Staff Working Document accompanying the document Report from the Commission Final Report of the Sector Inquiry on Capacity Mechanisms, SWD(2016) 385 final, p. 144; Communication from the Commission to the European Parliament and the Council, Energy Infrastructure and Security of Supply, COM(2003) 743 final, pp. 8-9; Dominique Finon and Virginie Pignon, 'Electricity and Long-Term Capacity Adequacy: The Quest for Regulatory Mechanism Compatible with Electricity Market', 16(3) *Utilities Policy* (2008), pp. 143-158, at 150.
61. Article 8 of the Electricity Directive; Natalia Fiedziuk, 'Putting Services of General Economic Interest up for Tender: Reflections on Applicable EU Rules', 50(1) *Common Market Law Review* (2013), pp. 87-114; Philipp Kiiver, *The Practice of Public Procurement: Tendering, Selection and Award* (Intersentia, 2014).

of Chapter 2, but rather viewed as a wider selection of the procedural means by which capacities can be procured.[62]

The reference to planned *additional* requirements in Article 8 of the Electricity Directive implies that the capacity procured through a tender or an equivalent procedure has to fulfil requirements that are needed to ensure security of supply but not achieved through the authorisation procedure under Article 7 of the Electricity Directive. These requirements can relate not only to the amount of capacity available but also to a certain location or type of capacity, for example peak-load capacity. Capacity mechanisms may, depending on the design, fall within this definition of tendering. However, if they do not, they are typically caught by the alternative wording 'any procedure equivalent', which refers to any procedure that fulfils the same requirements of transparency and non-discrimination as tendering itself.[63] Measures such as these have been established to include strategic reserves, capacity payments, long-term contracts, capacity obligations and reliability options, for example.[64] In fact, all the capacity mechanisms discussed in Chapter 2 above may be caught by this definition of tendering and equivalent procedures pursuant to Article 8 of the Electricity Directive if the allocation of public funds in the mechanism is competitive. The distinction between a tender and an equivalent procedure was clarified by the General Court in a recent case concerning a nuclear power plant at Hinkley Point C.[65] The General Court confirmed that Article 8 of the Electricity Directive allows for not just tendering procedures but also other procedures, which fulfil the requirements of transparency and non-discrimination.[66]

The content of Article 8(1) of the Electricity Directive should be understood as twofold. First, it contains a procedural obligation. Under this obligation, Member States are to establish a procedure in which suppliers of electricity can bid to offer new or existing capacity or flexibility when necessary. This procedure is established in the security of supply interest and should be based on published and publicly available

---

62. Peter Cameron, *Competition in Energy Markets* (OUP, 2007), pp. 524-525.
63. Article 8 of the Electricity Directive.
64. *See* Recital 10 of the Security of Supply Directive; Communication from the Commission, Delivering the internal electricity market and making the most of public intervention, C(2013) 7243 final, p. 14; and Note of DG Energy & Transport on Directives 2003/54/EC and 2003/55/EC on the Internal Market in Electricity and Natural Gas: Measures to Secure Electricity Supply, 16.1.2004, available at www.rae.gr/old/europe/sub4/security_of_electricity_supply_DGTREN. pdf (last accessed 5.3.2019), pp. 6-7. This note was published at a time when Directive 2003/54/EC of the European Parliament and of the Council of 26 June 2003 concerning common rules for the internal market in electricity and repealing Directive 96/92/EC (OJ L 176, 15.7.2003, pp. 37-56) was still in force. The provision on tendering for new capacity has, however, remained the same in the Electricity Directive now in force. For further analysis, *see* Peter Cameron, *Competition in Energy Markets* (OUP, 2007), pp. 524-525; and interpretation in case-law in SA.34947 *Support to Hinkley Point C Nuclear Power Station*, C(2014) 7142 final, para. 359.
65. T-356/15 *Austria v Commission* [2018], judgment of the General Court of 12 July 2018, published in the electronic Reports of Cases.
66. T-356/15 *Austria v Commission* [2018], judgment of the General Court of 12 July 2018, published in the electronic Reports of Cases, para. 682.

criteria.[67] Member States must also designate an independent authority or a public or private entity to be responsible for the organisation, monitoring and control of this procedure.[68] In essence, Member States must have a procedural and institutional platform for acquiring additional capacity if it is required in the interests of security of supply.

Second, Article 8 contains substantive rules on the circumstances in which Member States may resort to this procedure. In other words, it is mandatory to establish a legal framework under which procuring additional capacity is possible but the application of that framework is subject to a set of additional criteria. Although the definition of tendering and equivalent procedures alone would allow for a relatively broad spectrum of measures to address generation adequacy, this narrows significantly when the definition is interpreted together with the requirements under which the procedure under Article 8 can be invoked.

The wording of Article 8 of the Electricity Directive leaves much room for interpretation of these requirements, which in practice allows varying implementation between Member States as demonstrated by the broad variety of capacity mechanism designs in Member States. Nevertheless, Article 8 is one of the only legally binding, electricity-specific provisions to directly address the conditions under which capacity mechanisms *may* be introduced and the requirements that such measures must fulfil within the EU. Because of this, it is important to define the scope and content of the conditions under which tendering or equivalent procedures can be utilised in Member States to introduce a capacity mechanism.

To determine the scope and content of the requirements laid down in Article 8 of the Electricity Directive, it is first necessary to determine what qualifies as a security of supply interest as provided for in that article. Second, it is vital to analyse what constitutes insufficiency of the authorisation procedure under Article 7 of the Electricity Directive. After these interpretative challenges have been met, the analysis will move on to examine how Member States can ensure that the procedures they launch fulfil the requirements of transparency and non-discrimination.

[B]   A Justifiable Security of Supply Interest

Article 8(1) of the Electricity Directive establishes that tendering or equivalent procedures can only be launched if the generation capacity to be built or the energy efficiency and demand-side management measures to be taken under the authorisation procedure are insufficient to ensure security of supply. This legal limitation on the

---

67. In accordance with Article 8(3) of the Electricity Directive, details of the tendering procedure for means of generation capacity and energy efficiency/demand-side management measures shall be published in the Official Journal of the European Union at least six months prior to the closing date for tenders.
68. Article 8(5) of the Electricity Directive. This authority or a public or private body must be independent from electricity generation, transmission and distribution as well as supply activities. The transmission system operator may also hold this position but only if the transmission system operator is fully independent from other activities that do not relate to the ownership of the transmission system.

application of a tender or an equivalent procedure raises the questions (1) of how to define security of supply or its insufficiency and, more importantly, (2) of where capacity mechanisms fall within this definition.[69]

Security of electricity supply is not exhaustively defined in EU law. However, within the context of the EU electricity market legislation, security of supply can be understood as the uninterrupted availability of affordable electricity.[70] This definition has two elements. The first is the uninterrupted availability of electricity, which entails not only the de facto capability of a system to deliver electricity but also access to the electricity system. The second element concerns affordability, which refers to the price of electricity and its relevance to security of supply. These elements are discussed below in connection with Article 8 of the Electricity Directive.

Interruptions in and the unavailability of electricity supply are politically sensitive issues. Even short disruptions in electricity supply are considered unacceptable in Member States.[71] To avoid these disruptions, the electricity system needs certain qualities, such as a functioning electricity network. Furthermore, ensuring the uninterrupted availability of electricity requires that the system's installed and planned capacity is able to meet demand, i.e., produce a sufficient amount of electricity in the long term.[72] In addition to a sufficient overall capacity level, there must also be a functional mix of base-load and peak-load capacity.[73] In planning these criteria in a capacity mechanism design, Member States may consider elements such as the safety and security of the electricity system, compliance with public service obligations (PSOs),[74] and protection of public health and safety and the environment.[75] They may also consider energy efficiency, the nature of the primary sources and the contribution

---

69. On defining a legitimate security of supply interest, *see*, for instance, SA.675/2009 *Tender for Aid for New Electricity Generation Capacity (LV)*, C(2010) 4146, paras 23-37.
70. For further discussion of this topic, *see* Chapter 2 above.
71. David Newbery, 'Missing Money and Missing Markets: Reliability, Capacity Auctions and Interconnectors', 94 *Energy Policy* (2016), pp. 401-410, at 402; Angus Johnston and Guy Block, *EU Energy Law* (OUP, 2012), p. 10; Sirja-Leena Penttinen, 'The Role of the Court of Justice of the European Union in the Energy Market Liberalisation', in Kim Talus (ed.), *Research Handbook on International Energy Law* (Edward Elgar, 2014), pp. 241-271, at 241; Mauricio Cepeda, Marcelo Saguan, Dominique Finon and Virginie Pignon, 'Generation Adequacy and Transmission Interconnection in Regional Electricity Markets', 37(12) *Energy Policy* (2009), pp. 5612-5622, at 5612; Mauricio Cepeda and Dominique Finon, 'Generation Capacity Adequacy in Interdependent Electricity Markets', 39 *Energy Policy* (2011), pp. 3128-3143, at 3128.
72. Pablo Rodilla, Álvaro Baíllo, Santiago Cerisola and Carlos Batlle, 'Regulatory Intervention to Ensure an Efficient Medium-Term Generating Resource Planning In Electricity Markets', *Working Paper IIT-10-008A* (2010), pp. 1-2; Simona Benedettini, 'PJM and ISO-NE Forward Capacity Markets: A Critical Assessment', *IEFE Research Report Series* (2013) ISSN 2036-1785; Commission Staff Working Document accompanying the document Report from the Commission Interim Report of the Sector Inquiry on Capacity Mechanisms, SWD(2016) 119 final, p. 52.
73. Nevertheless, Article 8 of the Electricity Directive does not explicitly differentiate between investment in base-load, medium-load or in peak-load capacity. Henrik Bjørnebye, *Investing in EU Energy Security: Exploring the Regulatory Approach to Tomorrow's Electricity Production* (University of Oslo, PhD thesis 2009), p. 231.
74. For further discussion of this topic, *see* section §3.04 below.
75. Article 8(3) of the Electricity Directive.

of the planned generation capacity to meeting the EU's renewable energy targets and the contribution of generation capacity to reducing emissions.[76]

There is also a temporal element in the uninterrupted availability of electricity. Tenders and equivalent procedures are intended to address security of supply concerns in the medium to long term. For shorter term issues, Article 42 of the Electricity Directive provides that a Member State may temporarily take the necessary safeguard measures in the event of a sudden crisis in the electricity market. This requires that there is a threat to the physical safety or security of persons, apparatus or installations or system integrity.[77] However, capacity mechanisms are characteristically not adopted to address an emergency or a sudden shock that has already taken place, and therefore, they are unlikely ever to fall within the scope of application of Article 42 of the Electricity Directive.

As an element of security of supply, the affordability of electricity is strongly connected with the role and rights of energy consumers and the ongoing discussion on access to energy, energy justice and energy poverty.[78] The Electricity Directive requires Member States to ensure that all household customers and, where appropriate, small enterprises enjoy universal service.[79] Universal service is a type of public service, which refers to the right to be supplied with electricity of a specified quality within their territory at *reasonable*, easily and clearly comparable, transparent and non-discriminatory prices.[80] The requirement for electricity prices to be reasonable can sometimes even warrant price regulation, which is otherwise considered detrimental to the functioning of the internal electricity market.[81] In general, the universal service obligation sets requirements designed to ensure that certain services of a specified

---

76. *Ibid.*
77. Article 42 of the Electricity Directive. *See also* Article 122 TFEU. The measures adopted under Article 42 of the Electricity Directive must cause the least possible disturbance in the functioning of the internal market and must not be wider in scope than is strictly necessary to remedy the sudden difficulties which have arisen.
78. *See* Articles 3(7) and 3(8) and Recital 53 of the Electricity Directive; Communication from the Commission to the European Parliament, the Council, the European Economic and Social Committee, the Committee of the Regions and the European Investment Bank, Clean Energy For All Europeans, COM(2016) 860 final, pp. 3 and 11; Benjamin K. Sovacool, Roman V. Sidortsov and Benjamin R. Jones, *Energy Security, Equality and Justice* (Routledge, 2014); Benjamin K. Sovacool, Roman V. Sidortsov and Benjamin R. Jones, 'Energy Justice' in Raphael Heffron and Gavin Little (eds), *Delivering Energy Law and Policy in the EU and the US* (Edinburgh University Press, 2016), pp. 377-390.
79. Article 3(3) of the Electricity Directive. There is a deeper emphasis on the protection of vulnerable customers and universal service in the Clean Energy for All Europeans proposals. *See* Proposal for a Directive of the European Parliament and of the Council on Common Rules for the Internal Market in Electricity (recast), COM(2016) 864 final.
80. Article 3(3) of the Electricity Directive; Heike Schweitzer, 'Services of General Economic Interest: European Law's Impact on the Role of Markets and of Member States', in Marise Cremona (ed.), *Market Integration and Public Services in the European Union* (OUP, 2011), pp. 11-62, at 32-35.
81. C-265/08 *Federutility and Others v Autorità per l'energia elettrica e il gas* [2010] ECR I-3377; Despoina Mantzari, 'The Quest for Reasonable Retail Energy Prices in Europe: Positive and Normative Dimensions', 36(1) *Yearbook of European Law* (2017), pp. 599-627; Henrik Bjørnebye, 'Electricity Generation Capacity Tenders in the Security of Supply Interest: EU Regulation of Internal Electricity Market Facilitation and Intervention', 4 *OGEL* (2007), p. 7. However, price regulation is discouraged to prevent market distortion and will be limited even

quality are made available to all consumers and users in a Member State at an affordable price while taking national circumstances into account.[82] The possibility of price regulation constituting a public service has also been established in case-law.[83]

It seems that uninterrupted availability and affordability have different levels of importance in the context of Article 8 of the Electricity Directive. Invoking a threat to the uninterrupted availability of electricity alone is a sufficient argument for the introduction of tenders or equivalent procedures.[84] However, it seems that, despite the universal service requirements, the argument for affordability is significantly weaker than that concerning the uninterrupted availability of electricity in the context of introducing tenders or equivalent procedures. There are two reasons for this. First, even under the market-based approach under which electricity investment should primarily be made a relatively high level of price fluctuation and even price spikes are required to signal scarcity. It would seem counterintuitive to argue that temporary price increases are acceptable when the market operates based on Article 7 of the Electricity Directive but not when the derogation under Article 8 of the Electricity Directive applies.[85] Second, it is established case-law that derogations from EU law are not allowed either in the interests of explicit or in the interests of implicit economic protectionism. The Court has consistently held that purely economic interests cannot be invoked to justify exemptions from EU law.[86]

Tenders or equivalent procedures under Article 8 of the Electricity Directive are adopted to ensure the reliability of the electricity system in terms of supplying electricity in the medium and long term. Capacity mechanisms apply the same rationale: Member States resort to paying compensation for the availability and readiness of installed or forthcoming capacity to produce and supply electricity. Despite the common rationale, capacity mechanisms do not fall uncontroversially within the definition of security of supply provided. The idea of capacity mechanisms is to ensure an additional contribution to generation adequacy which, in turn, is an

---

further should the proposed changes in the Clean Energy for All Europeans package enter into force. *See* the Recast Electricity Regulation.

82. Commission Communication, A Quality Framework for Services of General Interest in Europe, COM(2011) 900 final, p. 4. Also *see* C-265/08 *Federutility and Others v Autorità per l'energia elettrica e il gas* [2010] ECR I-3377; C-36/14 *Commission v Poland* [2015], judgment of the Court of 10 September 2015, published in the electronic Reports of Cases; and C-121/15 *ANODE* [2016], judgment of the Court of 7 September 2016, published in the electronic Reports of Cases.

83. C-265/08 *Federutility and Others v Autorità per l'energia elettrica e il gas* [2010] ECR I-3377; and C-121/15 *ANODE* [2016], judgment of the Court of 7 September 2016, published in the electronic Reports of Cases.

84. *See*, for example, N475/2003 *Irish CADA*, 16 December 2003; SA.675/2009 *Tender for Aid for New Electricity Generation Capacity (LV)*, C(2010) 4146; and SA.30531 *Aid for Capacity Payments for Oil-Shale Fuelled Electricity Production (ET)*.

85. *See* supportive arguments in Henrik Bjørnebye, 'Electricity Generation Capacity Tenders in the Security of Supply Interest: EU Regulation of Internal Electricity Market Facilitation and Intervention', 4 *OGEL* (2007), pp. 11-12.

86. C-352/85 *Bond van Adverteerders v State of the Netherlands* [1988] ECR 2085, para. 34; C-398/95 *Syndesmos ton en Elladi Touristikon kai Taxidiotikon Grafeion v Ypourgos Ergasias* [1997] ECR I-3091 paras 22-25; C-158/96 *Kohll v Union des Caisses de Maladie* [1998] ECR I-1931, para. 41; C-171/08 *Commission v Portugal* [2010] ECR I-6817, para. 39.

integral element of ensuring the uninterrupted availability of electricity. This connection with capacity mechanisms and security of supply is undisputed.[87] However, explicitly providing remuneration for the existence of capacity also means that someone has to cover the cost of doing so, which means that the expenses caused by a capacity mechanism are recovered from final consumers of electricity in one way or another. Therefore, capacity mechanisms typically increase the price of electricity for final customers and make it less rather than more affordable. It has been demonstrated that the increasing share of intermittent, subsidised renewable production and the subsequent need for back-up capacity supported by capacity remuneration will significantly increase the cost of electricity.[88]

The controversial role of capacity mechanisms in EU electricity legislation has been acknowledged in the European debate on generation adequacy.[89] Using State remuneration to ensure the uninterrupted availability of electricity reduces its affordability. The Commission, in particular, has raised concerns over the inefficiencies and market distortions caused by the premature introduction of capacity mechanisms.[90] It has emphasised that nationally set generation adequacy levels, which fail to take into account cross-border capacities, can result in the over-procurement and thus overcompensation of generation capacity.[91] It seems clear that placing emphasis on uninterrupted availability to the extent that allows unjustified overcapacity is not justifiable in the interests of security of supply. Despite this, the widespread introduction of capacity mechanisms in Member States seems to indicate that Member States strongly prioritise uninterrupted availability of electricity over affordability. This tendency is in line with the interpretation of Article 8 presented above.

To conclude, the above analysis indicates that when identifying a legitimate security of supply interest, the uninterrupted availability of electricity is considered a

---

87. Pradyumna Bhagwat, Jörn Richstein, Emile Chappin, Kaveri Iychettira and Laurens De Vries, 'Cross-Border Effects of Capacity Mechanisms in Interconnected Power Systems', 46 *Utilities Policy* (2017), pp. 33-47, at 43-44.

88. For example, the price of electricity in Germany and Denmark is approximately three times as high as in some of the eastern Member States. *See* European Commission, Electricity and natural gas price statistics, 4.9.2014, available at http://ec.europa.eu/eurostat/statistics-explained/index.php/Electricity_price_statistics (last accessed 5.3.2019). *See* analysis in the Opinion of the European Economic and Social Committee on The economic effects from electricity systems created by increased and intermittent supply from renewable sources (exploratory opinion), OJ C 198, 10.7.2013, p. 5.

89. Communication from the Commission to the European Parliament, the Council, the European Economic and Social Committee and the Committee of the Regions, Progress towards completing the Internal Energy Market, COM(2014) 634 final, p. 6; and European Network of Transmission System Operators for Electricity (hereinafter 'ENTSO-E'), Communication Paper on Capacity Remuneration Mechanisms, available at www.entsoe.eu/fileadmin/user_upload/_library/position_papers/120510_MC_TOP_11_CRM_memorandum_external.pdf (last accessed 5.3.20 19), p. 3.

90. Commission Staff Working Document accompanying the document Report from the Commission Interim Report of the Sector Inquiry on Capacity Mechanisms, SWD(2016) 119 final, particularly at p. 4; Commission Staff Working Document accompanying the document Report from the Commission Final Report of the Sector Inquiry on Capacity Mechanisms, SWD(2016) 385 final.

91. Report from the Commission, Final Report of the Sector Inquiry on Capacity Mechanisms, COM(2016) 752 final, p. 13.

priority in comparison with the affordability of electricity under Article 8 of the Electricity Directive. This allows Member States to resort to tendering or equivalent procedures insofar as they are first able to show that the additional capacity is procured in the interests of security of supply, and second, that the procured capacity does not exceed the level needed to ensure generation adequacy.

In addition to a legitimate security of supply interest, however, resorting to the procedures under Article 8(1) of the Electricity Directive requires that investment under the authorisation procedure is *insufficient* to ensure security of supply as discussed in this section. This prerequisite for a failure in the market-based approach is analysed below.

[C]   Failure in the Market-Based Approach

Being able to identify justifiable interests of security of supply is not in itself a sufficient reason to launch a capacity mechanism. The measures taken under the authorisation procedure also need to be *insufficient* to ensure the level of security of supply established above. Since capacity mechanisms are intended for ensuring security of supply in the medium to long term, Member States will typically introduce such measures to prevent supply disruptions in the future rather than to address an immediate risk of unavailability. Therefore, they need to be able to evaluate and prove where the perceived risk of unavailability lies and why it seems likely that this risk will materialise in the future without State intervention. This raises the question as to whether a mere concern for generation adequacy is enough or whether Member States need to be able to prove that expected capacity will not be able to meet demand in the future.[92] This is a matter of drawing a line between a nationally subjective concern for generation adequacy and an objectively proven threat that is likely to materialise.

In practice, Member States have introduced measures to ensure security of supply based on different arguments and varying concerns for national generation adequacy. These include, *inter alia*, the need to adapt to the needs of the energy transition, high import dependency, delays in grid expansion, nuclear phase-out, growing demand, the risk that existing capacities will be decommissioned, increasing variable generation, low interconnectivity, spiking peak demand, long-term capacity deficits, the missing money problem and decreasing capacity margins.[93] It may be

---

92. The Clean Energy for All Europeans package proposes common assessment criteria by which to evaluate generation adequacy.
93. *See* N475/2003 *Irish CADA*, 16 December 2003; SA.675/2009 *Tender for Aid for New Electricity Generation Capacity (LV)*, C(2010) 4146, paras 4-5 and 22-30; and SA.38968 *Greece Transitory Electricity flexibility remuneration mechanism (FRM)*, C(2016) 1791 final, paras 12-16; SA.34947 *Support to Hinkley Point C Nuclear Power Station*, C(2013) 9073 final, paras 9-10; SA.35980 *GB capacity mechanism*, C(2014) 5083 final, paras 85-86; NN24/2010 *Compensation for the provision of instant interruptibility services in Sardinia and Sicily*, C(2010) 3222 final, para. 7; SA.42955 *German Network Reserve*, C(2016) 8742 final, paras 4-7; SA.43735 *German ABLAV Interruptibility Scheme*, C(2016) 6765 final, paras 4-5; SA.39621 *French country-wide capacity mechanism*, C(2016) 7086 final, paras 43-44; SA.42011 *Italian capacity mechanism*, C(2018) 617 final, para. 144; SA.44464 *Irish Capacity Mechanism: reliability option scheme*, C(2017)7789 final, para. 16; SA.46100 *Planned Polish capacity mechanism*, C(2018) 601 final,

contended that the arguments available to Member States to prove the perceived generation inadequacy seem to have evolved along with the developments in the energy transition. In particular, the growing share of State-funded renewable electricity capacities increases the demand for back-up capacity to mitigate the intermittency of renewable production.[94] State aid to support renewable capacities or generation has also brought about a significant overcapacity in some national markets, which, prima facie, do not appear to raise concerns as to security of supply. However, as demonstrated in *Castelnou Energía*, even circumstances of apparent overcapacity can create a generation adequacy problem that warrants State intervention in the form of, for example, a capacity mechanism.[95] In this case, Spain defended its capacity remuneration scheme using arguments concerning the structural aspects of its domestic electricity market, such as the increasing proportion of electricity produced from renewable energy sources, the isolation of the Spanish electricity market from other European markets and a sharp decline in demand.[96] Spain argued that without public intervention, significant capacities would be mothballed, endangering security of supply.[97] The Commission accepted the Spanish support scheme and the General Court dismissed an appeal against it.

Evaluating the risk to long-term security of supply in a reliable way can prove a difficult task for Member States not only due to the multiple variables in play but also because of the poor market visibility left by the economic crisis as well as legal and policy uncertainty.[98] Nevertheless, there is no harmonised methodology based on which Member States are obliged to evaluate the sufficiency or insufficiency of their national generation capacity.[99] This allows for the adoption of national, mutually incompatible capacity mechanism designs. The level of security of supply that is regarded as sufficient, therefore, entirely depends on the nature of the security of supply risks in the Member State in question and the strength of the arguments that Member State is able to muster to defend its public intervention.[100] It seems that this

---

paras 5-9. For further discussion of the drivers of capacity mechanisms, *see* Graeme Hawker, Keith Bell and Simon Gill, 'Electricity Security in the European Union – The Conflict Between National Capacity Mechanisms and the Single Market', 24 *Energy Research & Social Science* (2017), pp. 51-58, at 52-54.

94. This development was acknowledged as early as 2005. *See* Recital 5 of the Security of Supply Directive, which states that '[w]hen promoting electricity from renewable energy sources, it is necessary to ensure the availability of associated back-up capacity, where technically necessary, in order to maintain the reliability and security of the network'.

95. T-57/11 *Castelnou Energía v Commission* [2014], judgment of the General Court of 3 December 2014, published in the electronic Reports of Cases.

96. Case T-57/11 *Castelnou Energía v Commission* [2014], judgment of the General Court of 3 December 2014, published in the electronic Reports of Cases, paras 138 and 140.

97. Similar argumentation also in SA.46100 *Planned Polish capacity mechanism*, C(2018) 601 final, para. 6.

98. Eurostat, Consumption of energy, June 2017, available at http://ec.europa.eu/eurostat/statistics-explained/index.php/Consumption_of_energy (last accessed 5.3.2019).

99. This matter will change should the Clean Energy for All Europeans proposals enter into force. *See* Chapter 7 below.

100. Angus Johnston and Guy Block, *EU Energy Law* (OUP, 2012), p. 262. For examples of how Member State have defined their pursued level of security of supply, *see* SA.48648 *Belgian Strategic Reserve*, C(2018) 589 final, paras 10-11 and SA.46100 *Planned Polish capacity mechanism*, C(2018) 601 final, paras 29-32.

broad margin of discretion applies irrespective of the reasons as to why the market has failed to deliver adequate generation capacity.[101] Due to the fact that capacity mechanisms commonly involve State funding, the compatibility of these measures with EU law is typically assessed under State aid provisions.[102] This assessment will implicitly also evaluate the adequacy of the arguments used by Member States to demonstrate the market's inability to deliver sufficient generation capacity.

[D]   Requirements for Transparency and Non-discrimination

Article 8 of the Electricity Directive establishes that any tender or an equivalent procedure, such as a capacity mechanism, must fulfil the requirements of transparency and non-discrimination.[103] Article 8(3) of the Electricity Directive sheds light on what transparency and non-discrimination are intended to entail. First, the details of the procedure have to be published in the Official Journal (hereinafter 'OJ') of the EU at least six months prior to the closing date for tenders. The specifications within these procedures should be made available to any undertaking established within the EU in a manner that allows sufficient time in which to submit a tender.[104] This requirement is intended to ensure that capacity located in other Member States or capacity providers willing to invest in capacity located within the territory of another Member State can participate in tendering or similar procedures. This requirement has a strong connection with the prohibition on quantitative restrictions on imports and all measures having equivalent effect.[105] Second, the tender specifications must include a detailed description of the procedure to be followed by all tenderers. The specifications should also include an exhaustive list of criteria that will be used to select the successful participants and the incentives granted to these participants.[106] It seems that the requirements for non-discrimination and transparency cover not only the procedural framework under which tendering or equivalent procedures may be adopted but also the individual tenders or equivalent procedures that are launched in practice.

---

101. It has even been argued that Member States would be allowed to resort to tendering or equivalent procedures even if the reason for the generation inadequacy was a Member State's own failure to implement the internal market rules in electricity. *See* Henrik Bjørnebye, 'Electricity Generation Capacity Tenders in the Security of Supply Interest: EU Regulation of Internal Electricity Market Facilitation and Intervention', 4 *OGEL* (2007), p. 16.
102. For further discussion of this topic, *see* Chapter 4 below.
103. On tendering in respect of public services in general, *see* Natalia Fiedziuk, 'Putting Services of General Economic Interest up for Tender: Reflections on Applicable EU Rules', 50(1) *Common Market Law Review* (2013), pp. 87-114.
104. Article 8(3) of the Electricity Directive.
105. Articles 34 and 35 TFEU. For further discussion of this topic, *see* Chapter 5 below.
106. Articles 8(3) and 7(2) of the Electricity Directive. The tender specifications can also relate to the safety and security of the electricity system, installations and associated equipment, the protection of public health and safety, the protection of the environment, land use and siting, the use of public land, energy efficiency and the nature of the primary sources. They can also relate to characteristics particular to the applicant, such as technical, economic and financial capabilities or compliance with PSOs and universal service under Article 3 of the Electricity Directive, and the contribution of the generation capacity to meeting the EU's renewable energy targets and to reducing emissions.

It is widely acknowledged that Member States have not been successful in ensuring transparency or non-discrimination within capacity mechanisms in their domestic markets.[107] The model followed in terms of inviting electricity providers to participate in a capacity mechanism scheme, establishing and defining the selection criteria and remunerating successful participants can either support or undermine the requirements for transparency and non-discrimination. These issues are discussed below in relation to capacity mechanisms.

Transparency is not explicitly defined in the Electricity Directive. It is, however, addressed through various other legal instruments under EU energy law.[108] These legal instruments establish that the objective of increasing transparency is intended to ensure open and fair competition to the benefit of final consumers.[109] In the context of the electricity market, furthermore, lack of transparency is seen as a hindrance to the efficient allocation of resources, risk hedging and new entry.[110]

Based on the issues discussed above, transparency should be viewed as the availability of and access to information relevant to participation in the electricity market.[111] This is relevant in terms of capacity mechanisms from two points of view. First, the procurement criteria based on which additional capacity or demand-side response is acquired must be made available and accessible ahead of time, thus making it possible for all interested participants to submit a bid.[112] Second, lack of transparency can negatively affect investment signals.[113] This is relevant because capacity mechanisms are typically introduced to mitigate the effects of distorted or weak price signals, so their impact on appropriate investment signals should be positive, not negative.

---

107. Report from the Commission, Final Report of the Sector Inquiry on Capacity Mechanisms, COM(2016) 752 final, pp. 2 and 13-14; Commission Staff Working Document accompanying the document Report from the Commission Interim Report of the Sector Inquiry on Capacity Mechanisms, SWD(2016) 119 final, pp. 66-78.
108. See Regulation (EU) No 1227/2011 of the European Parliament and of the Council of 25 October 2011 on wholesale energy market integrity and transparency (OJ L 326, 8.12.2011, pp. 1-16) (hereinafter 'REMIT'); and Commission Regulation (EU) No 543/2013 of 14 June 2013 on submission and publication of data in electricity markets and amending Annex I to Regulation (EC) No 714/2009 of the European Parliament and of the Council (OJ L 163, 15.6.2013, pp. 1-12). For an overview, see Hans Vedder, Anita Rønne, Martha Roggenkamp and Iñigo del Guayo, 'EU Energy Law', in Martha Roggenkamp, Catherine Redgwell, Anita Rønne and Iñigo del Guayo (eds), Energy Law in Europe: National, EU and International Regulation (OUP, 2016), pp. 187-366, at 284.
109. Recital 2 of REMIT.
110. Recital 39 of the Electricity Directive. Lack of transparency was identified as a challenge to creating a competitive internal market in electricity back in 2007. See Proposal for a Directive of the European Parliament and of the Council amending Directive 2003/54/EC concerning common rules for the internal market in electricity, COM(2007) 528 final, p. 16.
111. See, for example, Recital 25 of REMIT.
112. Article 8(3) of the Electricity Directive.
113. This has been the case in some decentralised capacity mechanisms, where capacity is bilaterally contracted. See Commission Staff Working Document accompanying the document Report from the Commission Interim Report of the Sector Inquiry on Capacity Mechanisms, SWD(2016) 119 final, pp. 98-99; Communication from the Commission to the European Parliament, the Council, the European Economic and Social Committee and the Committee of the Regions, Making the internal energy market work, COM(2012) 663 final, p. 15; Commission Staff Working Document accompanying the document Report from the Commission Final Report of the Sector Inquiry on Capacity Mechanisms, SWD(2016) 385 final, p. 123.

Where State aid for capacity mechanisms is concerned, the requirement of transparency involves publishing decisions to grant such aid together with their implementing provisions and the identities of the beneficiaries of the aid.[114]

The requirement of non-discrimination in a capacity mechanism is largely a question of eligibility. In other words, non-discrimination concerns the entities that are allowed to participate in the capacity mechanism scheme and the criteria on which they are selected or excluded from it. Failing to fulfil the requirement for non-discrimination involves the risk of having to pay more than necessary for capacity and the possibility of distortion or hindrance of competition in the electricity market.[115] The Commission takes the view that non-discriminatory capacity remuneration should be allocated following an open, competitive bidding process[116] and should be open to *any* capacity that can contribute to meeting the required generation adequacy standard and security of supply.[117]

The Commission has raised particular concerns as to the potential of capacity mechanisms to favour certain producers or technologies, creating obstacles to trade in electricity and hindering the completion of the internal market in electricity.[118] For example, capacity mechanisms can provide remuneration for certain types of generation or technologies only.[119] They can fail to take into account both new and existing capacities or completely exclude demand response, cross-border capacity or foreign participation.[120] For example, the 2016 report on the State aid sector inquiry demonstrated that Member States often focused either entirely on attracting new capacity or on avoiding the closure of existing capacity, rather than allowing both to compete

---

114. Communication from the Commission, Guidelines on State aid for environmental protection and energy 2014-2020 (OJ C 200, 28.6.2014, pp. 1-55), paras 104-106.
115. Commission Staff Working Document accompanying the document Report from the Commission Final Report of the Sector Inquiry on Capacity Mechanisms, SWD(2016) 385 final, pp. 104-105; Communication from the Commission, Delivering the internal electricity market and making the most of public intervention, C(2013) 7243 final, p. 3; Communication from the Commission to the European Parliament, the Council, the European Economic and Social Committee and the Committee of the Regions, Making the internal energy market work, COM(2012) 663 final, p. 15; Commission Staff Working Document accompanying the document Report from the Commission Interim Report of the Sector Inquiry on Capacity Mechanisms, SWD(2016) 119 final, pp. 66-78.
116. European Commission, Consultation Paper on generation adequacy, capacity mechanisms and the internal market in electricity, 15.11.2012, p. 13.
117. Commission Staff Working Document, Generation Adequacy in the internal electricity market – guidance on public interventions accompanying the document Communication from the Commission Delivering the internal electricity market and making the most of public intervention, SWD(2013) 438 final, p. 29.
118. European Commission, Interim Report of the Sector Inquiry on Capacity Mechanisms, C(2016) 2107 final, p. 2.
119. Commission Staff Working Document accompanying the document Report from the Commission Final Report of the Sector Inquiry on Capacity Mechanisms, SWD(2016) 385 final, p. 83.
120. European Commission, Interim Report of the Sector Inquiry on Capacity Mechanisms, C(2016) 2107 final, p. 3; Commission Staff Working Document accompanying the document Report from the Commission Interim Report of the Sector Inquiry on Capacity Mechanisms, SWD(2016) 119 final, pp. 42-43 and 48.

on equal terms.[121] This tendency can easily lead to overcompensation, which unnecessarily increases the price of electricity and, again, contributes to making electricity less rather than more affordable.[122]

A capacity mechanism does not have to be explicitly discriminatory in order to fail to comply with the requirement of non-discrimination. Exclusion can also be implicit in the sense that participation is allowed but the predetermined performance criteria de facto limit participation.[123] For example, a large size requirement may exclude demand response participation and a very short lead time between a successful bid and the delivery of the contracted capacity may exclude capacities that take a long time to construct.[124] Interestingly, this may lead to a situation where some requirements, such as environmental standards, are explicitly allowed under Article 8(3) of the Electricity Directive, while being simultaneously discouraged because of their discriminatory effects.

The results of the 2016 State aid sector inquiry into capacity mechanisms found that the capacity mechanisms included in the inquiry largely failed to fulfil the requirement for non-discrimination. They were highly selective and implicitly or explicitly excluded certain technologies, certain locations, certain providers, certain sizes and so on.[125] Furthermore, and in the absence of a common assessment methodology to evaluate appropriate and sufficient levels of security of supply, Member States' capacity mechanisms were considered unlikely to genuinely fulfil the requirement for transparency. This was regarded as being particularly the case because the results of Member States' different generation adequacy evaluations are not mutually comparable. Therefore, they cannot provide objective information to market

---

121. Commission Staff Working Document accompanying the document Report from the Commission Final Report of the Sector Inquiry on Capacity Mechanisms, SWD(2016) 385 final, pp. 84-112; and European Commission, Interim Report of the Sector Inquiry on Capacity Mechanisms, C(2016) 2107 final, p. 13.

122. Communication from the Commission, Delivering the internal electricity market and making the most of public intervention, C(2013) 7243 final, p. 3; SA.34947 *Support to Hinkley Point C Nuclear Power Station*, C(2013) 9073 final, para. 111.

123. Paolo Mastropietro, Pablo Rodilla, Carlos Batlle, 'National Capacity Mechanisms in the European Internal Energy Market: Opening the Doors to Neighbours', 82 *Energy Policy* (2015), pp. 38-47, at 39; Commission Staff Working Document accompanying the document Report from the Commission Interim Report of the Sector Inquiry on Capacity Mechanisms, SWD(2016) 119 final, p. 63; Commission Staff Working Document accompanying the document Report from the Commission Final Report of the Sector Inquiry on Capacity Mechanisms, SWD(2016) 385 final, pp. 92-98.

124. European Commission, Interim Report of the Sector Inquiry on Capacity Mechanisms, C(2016) 2107 final, p. 13. Commission Staff Working Document accompanying the document Report from the Commission Interim Report of the Sector Inquiry on Capacity Mechanisms, SWD(2016) 119 final, pp. 63-64.

125. Commission Staff Working Document accompanying the document Report from the Commission Final Report of the Sector Inquiry on Capacity Mechanisms, SWD(2016) 385 final; Commission Staff Working Document accompanying the document Report from the Commission Interim Report of the Sector Inquiry on Capacity Mechanisms, SWD(2016) 119 final, p. 79; European Commission, Interim Report of the Sector Inquiry on Capacity Mechanisms, C(2016) 2107 final, p. 13.

participants.[126] This is a problem of legal predictability as well as transparency. The compatibility of Member States' measures with EU law should be determined by means of an objectively and consistently conducted legal evaluation. However, due to the different methodologies utilised in national assessments, one Member State's capacity inadequacy may seem more severe than another's, while objectively the results could be vice versa. In other words, the lack of common assessment criteria allows the EU's transparency assessment to be based upon the degree to which the arguments presented in a Member State's assessment appear convincing and not necessarily on objectively proven levels of security of supply.

If the requirements for non-discrimination and transparency under Article 8 of the Electricity Directive were to be followed strictly, most capacity mechanism designs would not be permitted under EU law. It seems, however, that the strong security of supply interest, the broad margin of discretion allowed in implementing Article 8 and the public service nature of certain electricity services outweigh such prima facie incompatibility. With a view to further developing this argument, capacity mechanism as public services are analysed below.

§3.04   GENERATION ADEQUACY AS A PUBLIC SERVICE

[A]   The Concept of a Service of General Economic Interest

Services of general economic interest (hereinafter 'SGEIs') are economic activities that have, first, been identified as particularly important for the functioning of a society and, second, would not be sufficiently ensured without State intervention.[127] The concept, furthermore, refers to services of an economic nature which the Member States subject to specific PSOs on the basis of a general interest criterion.[128] The SGEI concept is an evolving one whose definition depends on the needs of citizens, technological and market developments and social and political preferences in Member States.[129]

---

126. Commission Staff Working Document accompanying the document Report from the Commission Interim Report of the Sector Inquiry on Capacity Mechanisms, SWD(2016) 119 final, pp. 56-57.
127. Philipp Werner and Vincent Verouden, 'Services of General Economic Interest', in Philipp Werner and Vincent Verouden (eds), *EU State Aid Control: Law and Economics* (Wolters Kluwer, 2017), pp. 439-465; Leigh Hancher and Pierre Larouche, 'The Coming of Age of EU Regulation of Network Industries and Services of General Economic Interest', in Paul Craig and Gráinne De Búrca, *The Evolution of EU Law* (OUP, 2011), pp. 743-781; Erika Szyszczak and Johan van de Gronden (eds), *Financing Services of General Economic Interest: Reform and Modernization* (T.M.C. Asser Press, 2013).
128. Commission White Paper on Services of General Interest, COM(2004) 374 final, p. 22; Commission Green Paper on services of general interest, COM(2003) 270 final, p. 7; Wolf Sauter, 'Public Services and the Internal Market: Building Blocks or Persistent Irritant?', 21(6) *European Law Journal* (2015), pp. 738-757.
129. Commission Communication on the application of the European Union State aid rules to compensation granted for the provision of services of general economic interest, OJ C 8, 11.1.2012, p. 11.

The EU's policy on SGEIs aims to serve the interests and needs of EU citizens.[130] These services are different from any others in the sense that Member States consider them necessary even where the market has insufficient incentive to provide them.[131] SGEIs are often subject to extensive State intervention to ensure that the consumers have access to certain services that are considered fundamental to the functioning of a society.

There is no clear and exhaustive definition of an SGEI.[132] Furthermore, there is no exhaustive list of conditions that need to be fulfilled before a Member State can invoke the existence and protection of an SGEI.[133]

The existence of SGEIs and the need to safeguard them are, however, identified in primary EU law. Article 14 TFEU recognises the 'place occupied by services of general economic interest in the shared values of the Union'. Furthermore, it states that the EU and its Member States are to take care that SGEI operate on the basis of principles and conditions, particularly economic and financial conditions, which enable them to fulfil their missions.

SGEI are also acknowledged in Protocol 26 to the Treaties and in Article 36 of the Charter of Fundamental Rights of the EU. The latter recognises SGEIs as important instruments for promoting the social and territorial cohesion of the Union.[134] Article 106(2) TFEU, however, is the Treaty provision that provides the most insight into what can and cannot be done in respect of SGEIs. It provides that undertakings entrusted with the operation of SGEIs are subject to the rules contained in the Treaties, in

---

130. Communication from the Commission, Services of general interest in Europe, OJ C 17, 19.1.2001, pp. 4-23, para. 8.
131. Communication from the Commission, Services of general interest in Europe, OJ C 17, 19.1.2001, pp. 4-23, para. 14.
132. T-57/11 *Castelnou Energía v Commission* [2014], judgment of the General Court of 3 December 2014, published in the electronic Reports of Cases, para. 132; and T-289/03 *BUPA* [2008] ECR II-81, para. 165; Nuno Albuquerque Matos, 'The Role of the BUPA Judgement in the Legal Framework for Services of General Economic Interest', 16(1) *Tilburg Law Review* (2011), pp. 83-104.; Wolf Sauter, *Public Services in EU Law* (Cambridge University Press, 2015), pp. 9-20; Heike Schweitzer, 'Services of General Economic Interest: European Law's Impact on the Role of Markets and of Member States', in Marise Cremona (ed.), *Market Integration and Public Services in the European Union* (OUP, 2011), pp. 11-62; Natalia Fiedziuk, 'Services of General Economic Interest and the Treaty of Lisbon: Opening Doors to a Whole New Approach or Maintaining the "Status Quo"', 36(2) *European Law Review* (2011), pp. 226-242; Natalia Fiedziuk, 'Putting Services of General Economic Interest up for Tender: Reflections on Applicable EU Rules', 50(1) *Common Market Law Review* (2013), pp. 87-114; Natalia Fiedziuk, 'Towards a More Refined Economic Approach to Services of General Economic Interest', 16(2) *European Public Law* (2010), pp. 271-288, at 275-276; Wolf Sauter, 'Public Services and the Internal Market: Building Blocks or Persistent Irritant?', 21(6) *European Law Journal* (2015), pp. 738-757, at 741.
133. T-57/11 *Castelnou Energía v Commission* [2014], judgment of the General Court of 3 December 2014, published in the electronic Reports of Cases, para. 132; and T-289/03 *BUPA* [2008] ECR II-81, para. 165.
134. TEU Protocol (No 26) on services of general interest (O J 115, 09.05.2008, pp. 308-308); Charter of Fundamental Rights of the European Union (OJ C 326, 26.10.2012, pp. 391-407); Wolf Sauter, *Public Services in EU Law* (Cambridge University Press, 2015), pp. 12-17 and 21-22; Natalia Fiedziuk, 'Services of General Economic Interest and the Treaty of Lisbon: Opening Doors to a Whole New Approach or Maintaining the "Status Quo"', 36(2) *European Law Review* (2011), pp. 226-242.

particular those governing competition. However, these undertakings are only subject to the rules contained in the Treaties insofar as the application of such rules does not prevent them from performing the tasks assigned to them. This exemption is qualified by the further statement in Article 106(2) TFEU that the development of trade should not be affected to such an extent as would be contrary to the interests of the Union.[135] It is established case-law that Article 106 TFEU concerns undertakings for whose actions States must take special responsibility because of the influence that they may exert over such actions.[136] Article 106 TFEU should, therefore, be interpreted as being intended to ensure that Member States do not take advantage of their relations with those undertakings in order to circumvent other rules contained in the Treaties, such as those concerning free movement.[137] It has been argued that Article 106 TFEU has direct effect, which means that individuals or undertakings are able to invoke the provision directly in proceedings before national or EU courts,[138] but it has also been argued that it might not have direct effect in its entirety.[139]

The concept of SGEIs is often used interchangeably with that of public services, although the latter seems to be less precise.[140] However, using these concepts synonymously for the purposes of analysing capacity mechanisms within the context of EU electricity legislation can be defended.[141] The supply of electricity is considered such a vital component of a functioning modern society that the Electricity Directive was formulated to include guarantees of certain public services in the electricity sector.

---

135. Article 106(2) TFEU; Wolf Sauter, *Public Services in EU Law* (Cambridge University Press, 2015), pp. 53-64; Alvaro Pliego Selie, 'Article 106', in Weijer Ver Loren van Themaat and Berend Reuder (eds), *European Competition Law: A Case Commentary* (Edward Elgar, 2014), pp. 195-215, at 202-211.
136. Joined cases 188/80, 189/80 and 190/80 *France, Italy and United Kingdom v Commission* [1982] ECR 2545, para. 12 and C-157/94 *Commission v Netherlands* [1997] ECR I-5699, para. 29.
137. C-157/94 *Commission v Netherlands* [1997] ECR I-5699, paras 27-33 and the very same arguments in almost exactly the same formulation in C-158/94 *Commission v Italy* [1997] ECR I-5789, paras 38-44; C-159/94 *Commission v France* [1997] ECR I-5815, paras 44-50. For further discussion of the free movement provisions, *see* Chapter 5 below.
138. C-260/89 *Elliniki Radiophonia Tiléorassi AE and Panellinia Omospondia Syllogon Prossopikou v Dimotiki Etairia Pliroforissis and Sotirios Kouvelas and Nicolaos Avdellas and others* [1991] ECR I-2925; Angus Johnston and Guy Block, *EU Energy Law* (OUP, 2012), p. 245.
139. C-260/89 *ERT v DEP* [1991] ECR I-2925, para. 34; C-320/91 *Corbeau* [1993] ECR I-2533, para. 21; Richard Whish and David Bailey, *Competition Law*, 8th edition (OUP, 2015), p. 253; Natalia Fiedziuk, 'Towards Decentralization of State Aid Control: The Case of Services of General Economic Interest', 36(3) *World Competition Law and Economics Review* (2013), pp. 387-408, at 391-392; Paul Craig and Gráinne de Búrca, *EU Law: Text, Cases, and Materials*, 6th edition (OUP, 2015), pp. 184-224.
140. *See* Commission Green Paper on services of general interest, COM(2003) 270 final, pp. 6-7, in which the Commission states that a PSO 'refers to specific requirements that are imposed by public authorities on the provider of the service in order to ensure that certain public interest objectives are met, for instance, in the matter of air, rail and road transport and energy'. On the definitions in legal literature, *see* Leigh Hancer and Wolf Sauter, 'Public Services and EU Law', in Catherine Barnard and Steve Peers (eds), *European Union Law* (OUP, 2013), pp. 539-566, at 546-552; Wolf Sauter, *Public Services in EU Law* (Cambridge University Press, 2015), pp. 1-3.
141. The concepts are often used interchangeably in EU legal documents. For discussion of definitions, *see* Wolf Sauter, *Public Services in EU Law* (Cambridge University Press, 2015), pp. 9-20; Natalia Fiedziuk, 'Putting Services of General Economic Interest up for Tender: Reflections on Applicable EU Rules', 50(1) *Common Market Law Review* (2013), pp. 87-114, at 87-89.

The Directive refers to these guarantees as PSOs, which can be introduced as SGEIs.[142] The connection and similarity between these concepts is therefore apparent, as further demonstrated in the next section.

In the context of EU energy law, a public service has been referred to as 'the guaranteeing, through regulatory standards, measures or requirements, of levels of consumer or environmental protection that might otherwise not be maintained through the simple operation of the market mechanism'.[143] This definition appears to have gained wider scholarly acceptance,[144] although it does not explicitly include the possibility of imposing PSOs in the interests of security of supply. Security of supply is, nevertheless, specifically considered an acceptable reason for introducing PSOs in the general economic interest under Article 3(2) of the Electricity Directive. This provision is analysed below from the point of view of security of supply and, in particular, capacity mechanisms.

[B]   PSOs in the Interests of Security of Electricity Supply

The issue of using PSOs to pursue the objective of security of supply is specifically addressed in Article 3 of the Electricity Directive. Member States may impose PSOs in the general economic interest on undertakings operating in the electricity sector.[145] These obligations may relate to security of supply, regularity, the quality and price of supplies and environmental protection. Environmental protection in this context specifically includes energy efficiency, energy from renewable sources and climate protection.[146] Security of electricity supply has also been confirmed in EU case-law as an acceptable interest in respect of which to impose PSOs.[147]

Article 3 of the Electricity Directive also imposes general requirements for PSOs imposed in the interests of security of supply. The obligations are to be clearly defined, transparent, non-discriminatory and verifiable and should guarantee equality of access for EU electricity undertakings to national consumers.

---

142. Article 3(2) of the Electricity Directive.
143. Christopher Jones (ed.), *EU Energy Law – Volume I: The Internal Energy Market – The Third Liberalisation Package* (Claeys & Casteels, 2010), p. 395.
144. It is referred to, *inter alia*, in Angus Johnston and Guy Block, *EU Energy Law* (OUP, 2012), p. 163; Kim Talus, *Introduction to EU Energy Law* (OUP, 2016), p. 29.
145. Article 3(2) of the Electricity Directive. Ana Stanic, 'An Overview of EU Energy Law', in Peter Cameron and Raphael Heffron (eds), *Legal Aspects of EU Energy Regulation: The Consolidation of Energy Law Across Europe* (OUP, 2016), pp. 32-65, at 41-43; Hans Vedder, Anita Rønne, Martha Roggenkamp and Iñigo del Guayo, 'EU Energy Law', in Martha Roggenkamp, Catherine Redgwell, Anita Rønne and Iñigo del Guayo (eds), *Energy Law in Europe: National, EU and International Regulation* (OUP, 2016), pp. 187-366; Peter Cameron, *Competition in Energy Markets* (OUP, 2007), pp. 128-132.
146. Article 3(2) of the Electricity Directive.
147. C-393/92 *Amelo* [1994] ECR I-1477; T-57/11 *Castelnou Energía v Commission* [2014], judgment of the General Court of 3 December 2014, published in the electronic Reports of Cases, para. 126.

The wording of Article 3(2) of the Electricity Directive confirms that the provision should be interpreted in the light of Article 106(2) TFEU.[148] As noted in the previous section, Article 106(2) TFEU provides that electricity undertakings entrusted with the operation of services of general economic interest are subject to the rules set out in the Treaties but that exemption from these rules may be granted if applying them would prevent these undertakings from performing the tasks assigned to them and if such exemption would not affect the development of trade to such an extent as would be contrary to the interests of the Union.[149] In other words, PSOs are as a rule subject to Treaty law, but can be used to justify exemption from the relevant provisions of the Treaties. Therefore, defining the scope of PSOs and the acceptable measures that can be taken to pursue the objective of security of supply is relevant because these obligations can, under specific circumstances, be used to justify exemptions from fundamental Treaty rules, including State aid rules.[150]

In general, permitted derogations from Treaty provisions should be interpreted narrowly.[151] Moreover, it should be noted that although the public service provision must be interpreted in the light of the exemption permitted under Article 106(2) TFEU, the sector-specific requirements laid down in the Electricity Directive further narrow the range of situations in which Article 106(2) TFEU can be successfully invoked.[152] Therefore, the apparently broad formulation of Article 106(2) TFEU should not be understood as allowing unlimited leeway for exemptions.

Article 3 of the Electricity Directive contains a non-exhaustive list of issues that can be considered PSOs.[153] It is clear from the wording of Article 3 that PSOs in the interests of security of supply are acceptable. However, as noted in section §3.03[B] above, security of supply has many elements, which have been evaluated individually in case-law. For instance, it is established case-law that securing reasonable prices can be a legitimate SGEI.[154] Furthermore, financial support for a certain fuel has been accepted as an SGEI.[155] Article 3 of the Electricity Directive does not differentiate

---

148. Article 3(2) of the Electricity Directive; C-265/08 *Federutility and Others v Autorità per l'energia elettrica e il gas* [2010] ECR I-3377, para. 26 and C-121/15 *ANODE* [2016], judgment of the Court of 7 September 2016, published in the electronic Reports of Cases, para. 38.
149. In this context, there is no material difference between public services and SGEIs. *See* Henrik Bjørnebye, *Investing in EU Energy Security: Exploring the Regulatory Approach to Tomorrow's Electricity Production* (University of Oslo, PhD thesis 2009), pp. 283-285.
150. *See* Chapters 4 and 5 below.
151. C-157/94 *Commission v Netherlands* [1997] ECR I-5699, para. 37; C-159/94 *Commission v France* [1997] ECR I-5815, paras 53-55; Leigh Hancher and Pierre Larouche, 'The Coming of Age of EU Regulation of Network Industries and Services of General Economic Interest', in Paul Craig and Gráinne De Búrca, *The Evolution of EU Law* (OUP, 2011), pp. 743-781, at 575.
152. C-17/03 *VEMW and Others* [2005] I-4983; Leigh Hancer and Wolf Sauter, 'Public Services and EU Law', in Catherine Barnard and Steve Peers (eds), *European Union Law* (OUP, 2013), pp. 539-566, at 554; Angus Johnston and Guy Block, *EU Energy Law* (OUP, 2012), pp. 246-247.
153. AG opinion in C-121/15 *ANODE* [2016], judgment of the Court of 7 September 2016, published in the electronic Reports of Cases, paras 52-54.
154. C-265/08 *Federutility and Others v Autorità per l'energia elettrica e il gas* [2010] ECR I-3377 and C-121/15 *ANODE* [2016], judgment of the Court of 7 September 2016, published in the electronic Reports of Cases.
155. T-57/11 *Castelnou Energía v Commission* [2014], judgment of the General Court of 3 December 2014, published in the electronic Reports of Cases.

between peak-load or base-load capacity, or indeed refer to capacity at all, but incentivising investment in peak-load generation capacity has, nevertheless, also been accepted as an SGEI in case-law.[156]

Despite the non-exhaustive list of issues that can be addressed through PSOs, it seems clear that market failure is a precondition for imposing PSOs in the interest of security of supply.[157] PSOs constitute a method of structuring State intervention in the event that the market does not function adequately.[158] This was aptly discussed by Advocate General Colomer in *Federutility*, where he stated that '[i]f public service can be defined, [...] as "the extension of the market by other means, where the market has failed, and not the other way around", then, in a situation of diminished competition, the state would have to intervene in order to mitigate the effects of this difficult situation. Yet state involvement in the market must be limited so as not to postpone true liberalisation indefinitely, and should focus on the protection of the rights of the consumer.'[159] The role of market failure has also been confirmed by the Commission to be particularly relevant in terms of capacity mechanisms. Capacity mechanisms can, in theory, constitute PSOs if their goal is to ensure that electricity undertakings assume a responsibility for the provision of generation capacity that they would not assume, or at least not to the same extent, under normal market conditions.[160]

If the requirement for market failure is interpreted together with the requirements for tendering or equivalent procedures, it is clear that the adoption of a capacity mechanism requires that the capacity remunerated through the mechanism is not satisfactorily provided under normal market conditions.[161] Therefore, in order to adopt a capacity mechanism, Member States need to demonstrate that the internal market in electricity is unable to solve the identified problem or at least unlikely to do so.[162] In demonstrating this, and the need for intervention, Member States have a significant margin of discretion, which is next discussed.

---

156. *See* N475/2003 *Irish CADA*, 16 December 2003, para. 22, for the differentiation between 'normal' and 'reserve' capacity.
157. On the requirement of market failure in imposing PSOs, *see* Wolf Sauter, *Public Services in EU Law* (Cambridge University Press, 2015), pp. 29-34; Ramona Ianus and Massimo Francesco Orzan, 'Aid Subject to Discretionary Assessment under Article 107(3) TFEU', in Herwig Hofmann and Claire Micheau (eds), *State Aid Law of the European Union* (OUP, 2016), pp. 240-307, at 292-293; Wolf Sauter, 'Public Services and the Internal Market: Building Blocks or Persistent Irritant?', 21(6) *European Law Journal* (2015), pp. 738-757, at 743-744.
158. AG opinion in C-265/08 *Federutility and Others v Autorità per l'energia elettrica e il gas* [2010] ECR I-3377, para. 43.
159. AG opinion in C-265/08 *Federutility and Others v Autorità per l'energia elettrica e il gas* [2010] ECR I-3377, para. 6.
160. European Commission, Consultation Paper on generation adequacy, capacity mechanisms and the internal market in electricity, 15.11.2012, p. 9.
161. SA. 34947 *Support to Hinkley Point C Nuclear Power Station*, C(2013) 9073 final, para. 103; Wolf Sauter, *Public Services in EU Law* (Cambridge University Press, 2015), pp. 29-34.
162. Communication from the Commission, Delivering the internal electricity market and making the most of public intervention, C(2013) 7243 final, p. 7.

[C] Member States' Discretion in Defining PSOs

Traditionally and in accordance with the principle of subsidiarity, Member States have had a wide margin of discretion in determining what they regard as SGEIs and in defining PSOs.[163] This is explicitly stated in Protocol 26 to the Treaties. The Protocol establishes that the shared values of the Union in respect of SGEIs include, in particular, the essential role and the wide discretion of national, regional and local authorities in providing, commissioning and organising services of general economic interest as closely as possible to the needs of the users.[164] The Protocol also highlights the diversity between various SGEIs and the differences in the needs and preferences of users that may result from different geographical, social or cultural situations.[165]

Member States' leeway in defining the scope and operation of SGEIs is confirmed not only by the fact that the Treaties do not contain a definition of the term but also by the fact that they do not confer competence on Union institutions to provide such a definition.[166] Whether a service is to be regarded as an SGEI and how it should be operated are issues that should be defined and interpreted primarily at national level.[167] As noted in the well-known *BUPA* case from 2008, the broad margin of discretion afforded to Member States should not be interpreted as meaning that they do not have an obligation to prove the necessity of an SGEI.[168] A Member State must ensure that the SGEI satisfies the general criteria laid down for such services and that

---

163. Cases T-106/95 *FFSA and Others v Commission* [1997] ECR II-229, para. 99; T-17/02 *Fred Olsen v Commission* [2005] ECR II-2031, para. 216; T-289/03 *BUPA* [2008] ECR II-81, para. 166; C-265/08, *Federutility* [2010] ECR I-3377, para. 29; C-67/96 *Albany* [1999] ECR I-5751, para. 104; Communication from the Commission, Services of general interest in Europe, OJ C 17, 19.1.2001, pp. 4-23, para. 22; Heike Schweitzer, 'Services of General Economic Interest: European Law's Impact on the Role of Markets and of Member States', in Marise Cremona (ed.), *Market Integration and Public Services in the European Union* (OUP, 2011), pp. 11-62, at 32-35; Natalia Fiedziuk, 'Services of General Economic Interest and the Treaty of Lisbon: Opening Doors to a Whole New Approach or Maintaining the "Status Quo"', 36(2) *European Law Review* (2011), pp. 226-242, at 229-230.
164. Consolidated version of the Treaty on European Union, Protocol (No 26) on services of general interest (OJ 115, 09.05.2008, p. 308); Natalia Fiedziuk, 'Services of General Economic Interest and the Treaty of Lisbon: Opening Doors to a Whole New Approach or Maintaining the "Status Quo"', 36(2) *European Law Review* (2011), pp. 226-242.
165. Consolidated version of the Treaty on European Union, Protocol (No 26) on services of general interest (O J 115, 09.05.2008 p. 308).
166. *See* T-289/03 *BUPA* [2008] ECR II-81, para. 167; Nuno Albuquerque Matos, 'The Role of the BUPA Judgement in the Legal Framework for Services of General Economic Interest', 16(1) *Tilburg Law Review* (2011), pp. 83-104.
167. C-67/96 *Albany* [1999] ECR I-5751, para. 104; Communication from the Commission, Services of general interest in Europe, OJ C 17, 19.1.2001, pp. 4-23, para. 22.
168. T-289/03 *BUPA* [2008] ECR II-81, para. 172; Wolf Sauter, 'Case T–289/03, British United Provident Association Ltd (BUPA), BUPA Insurance Ltd, BUPA Ireland Ltd v. Commission of the European Communities, Judgement of the Court of First Instance of 12 February 2008, nyr', 46(1) *Common Market Law Review* (2009), pp. 269-286, at 273-286 and criticism on the BUPA case at 285-286. *See also* Julian Nowag, *Competition Law, State Aid Law and Free-Movement Law: The Case of the Environmental Integration Obligation* (University of Oxford, PhD thesis 2014), p. 122; Nuno Albuquerque Matos, 'The Role of the BUPA Judgement in the Legal Framework for Services of General Economic Interest', 16(1) *Tilburg Law Review* (2011), pp. 83-104.

these criteria are indeed fulfilled in the particular case at hand.[169] These general criteria include, in particular, that a public authority has entrusted an entity with the mandatory performance of an SGEI and that the SGEI in question is universal in nature.[170] Furthermore, the service should be uninterrupted (continuity), provided at uniform tariff rates and of similar quality (equality).[171] In relation to electricity, these criteria are further defined in the Electricity Directive. The definition of an SGEI given by a Member State can be challenged by the Commission only in the event of manifest error.[172] Failure to prove that there is a legitimate SGEI mission may, for example, constitute such an error.[173]

Member States' margin of discretion is narrower in sectors, such as electricity, where there is harmonised legislation.[174] The absence of a definition of a PSO in the Electricity Directive, however, demonstrates that even the sector-specific legislation allows a broad margin of discretion to the Member States.[175] The Electricity Directive only sets common *minimum* standards for the establishment of PSOs in the electricity sector.[176] These minimum standards emphasise the importance of fair and reasonable prices and the overall protection of consumers,[177] while complying with general EU law and pursuing the objectives of EU energy law.[178] It is established case-law that a Member State introducing a PSO must be able to prove that the requirements set for

---

169. T-289/03 *BUPA* [2008] ECR II-81, para. 172.
170. T-289/03 *BUPA* [2008] ECR II-81, para. 172. Universality, in this context, means that the service is for the benefit of all consumers throughout the relevant territory. Nuno Albuquerque Matos, 'The Role of the BUPA Judgement in the Legal Framework for Services of General Economic Interest', 16(1) *Tilburg Law Review* (2011), pp. 83-104. On the concept of entrustment, *see* Heike Schweitzer, 'Services of General Economic Interest: European Law's Impact on the Role of Markets and of Member States', in Marise Cremona (ed.), *Market Integration and Public Services in the European Union* (OUP, 2011), pp. 11-62, at 35-38.
171. AG opinion in C-265/08 *Federutility and Others v Autorità per l'energia elettrica e il gas* [2010] ECR I-3377, paras 54-55.
172. *See* cases T-106/95 *FFSA and Others v Commission* [1997] ECR II-229, paras 98-100; T-17/02 *Fred Olsen v Commission* [2005] ECR II-2031, paras 209 and 216; T-289/03 *BUPA* [2008] ECR II-81, paras 100-101, 148 and 164-166; Communication from the Commission, Services of general interest in Europe, OJ C 17, 19.1.2001, pp. 4-23, para. 22; Wolf Sauter, 'Case T–289/03, British United Provident Association Ltd (BUPA), BUPA Insurance Ltd, BUPA Ireland Ltd v. Commission of the European Communities, Judgement of the Court of First Instance of 12 February 2008, nyr', 46(1) *Common Market Law Review* (2009), pp. 269-286, at 276-277.
173. T-289/03 *BUPA* [2008] ECR II-81, para. 172.
174. C-206/98 *Commission v Belgium* [2000] ECR I-3509, para. 45. Commission Communication on the application of the European Union State aid rules to compensation granted for the provision of services of general economic interest, OJ C 8, 11.1.2012, p. 9.
175. C-265/08 *Federutility and Others v Autorità per l'energia elettrica e il gas* [2010] ECR I-3377, paras 29-30; and AG opinion in C-265/08 *Federutility and Others v Autorità per l'energia elettrica e il gas* [2010] ECR I-3377, para. 46. *See also* argumentation on the role of harmonisation in T-289/03 *BUPA* [2008] ECR II-81, para. 167; Wolf Sauter, 'Case T–289/03, British United Provident Association Ltd (BUPA), BUPA Insurance Ltd, BUPA Ireland Ltd v. Commission of the European Communities, Judgement of the Court of First Instance of 12 February 2008, nyr', 46(1) *Common Market Law Review* (2009), pp. 269-286, at 277-278.
176. Recitals 46 and 50 of the Electricity Directive.
177. Article 3 and Recital 50 of the Electricity Directive and discussion in AG opinion in C-265/08 *Federutility and Others v Autorità per l'energia elettrica e il gas* [2010] ECR I-3377, para. 6.
178. Recitals 46 and 50 of the Electricity Directive.

imposing such an obligation are fulfilled.[179] Furthermore, all PSOs are subject to Treaty law if they do not fall within the scope of the exemption provided in Article 106(2) TFEU.

Article 3 of the Electricity Directive, nevertheless, limits Member States' freedom in determining what measures they can take to ensure SGEIs.[180] The EU exercises control over Member States' PSOs through the obligation to inform the Commission of any measures adopted to fulfil PSOs under Article 3(15) of the Electricity Directive.[181] The Commission must also be notified every two years of any changes to such measures, irrespective of whether or not they require a derogation from the Directive.

Despite the existence of extensive sector-specific legislation that narrows Member States' margin of discretion, the Court has been reluctant to extend the Commission's competence in determining the scope of PSOs.[182] Nevertheless, the scope and content of a SGEI obligation is subject to control by the EU institutions.[183] The framework for exercising this control was laid down in the well-known *Federutility* case, which clarifies the interpretation of Article 3 of the Electricity Directive.[184]

The interpretation of Article 3 of the Electricity Directive, Article 106(2) TFEU and the assessment in the *Federutility* case together indicate that under the current legal setting, PSOs must:

(1) be developed with full regard for the rules contained in the Treaties;
(2) be adopted in the general economic interest;
(3) be compatible with the principle of proportionality;
(4) be clearly defined, transparent, non-discriminatory, and verifiable;
(5) guarantee equality of access to national consumers for EU electricity companies.

Because of the broad margin of discretion and the existing body of case-law on security of supply and public services, it can be argued that generation adequacy is a legitimate general economic interest.[185] Paying compensation for services in the general economic interest in the form of capacity mechanisms, however, should be

---

179. T-289/03 *BUPA* [2008] ECR II-81, paras 171-172; Nuno Albuquerque Matos, 'The Role of the BUPA Judgement in the Legal Framework for Services of General Economic Interest', 16(1) *Tilburg Law Review* (2011), pp. 83-104.
180. AG opinion in C-265/08 *Federutility and Others v Autorità per l'energia elettrica e il gas* [2010] ECR I-3377, para. 47.
181. C-265/08 *Federutility and Others v Autorità per l'energia elettrica e il gas* [2010] ECR I-3377, para. 23.
182. C-265/08 *Federutility and Others v Autorità per l'energia elettrica e il gas* [2010] ECR I-3377; Leigh Hancher and Pierre Larouche, 'From a Formalistic to an Integrative Model: The Case of EU Economic Regulation' in Pierre Larouche and Péter Cserne (eds), *National Legal Systems and Globalization: New Role, Continuing Relevance* (T.M.C. Asser Press, 2013), p. 137.
183. C-41/83 *Italy v Commission* [1985] ECR 873, para. 30; and T-289/03 *BUPA* [2008] ECR II-81, para. 100.
184. C-265/08 *Federutility and Others v Autorità per l'energia elettrica e il gas* [2010] ECR I-3377; Leigh Hancher and Pierre Larouche, 'The coming of age of EU regulation of network industries and services of general economic interest', in Paul Craig and Gráinne De Búrca, *The Evolution of EU Law* (OUP, 2011), pp. 743-781, at 754-755.
185. Capacity mechanisms and EU State aid rules are further examined in Chapter 4.

assessed separately. Nevertheless, imposing PSOs to ensure security of supply is essentially a matter of national circumstances and national demand for intervention.[186] However, the adoption and operation of such mechanisms are required to fulfil the criteria established in Article 3 and related case-law. These requirements are assessed below in relation to capacity mechanisms.

[D]   Conditions for Imposing Capacity Mechanisms as PSOs

[1]   Justification for SGEIs

As discussed in section §3.04[C] above, Member States have a broad margin of discretion in defining the objective and scope of their PSOs. Article 3(2) of the Electricity Directive and Article 106(2) TFEU, however, establish a set of requirements for the lawful introduction of PSOs.[187] Capacity mechanisms introduced in the interests of security of supply must fulfil these requirements, the first of which is the existence of a general economic interest justification. In other words, the introduction of capacity mechanisms must be defensible in the general economic interest.

Aligned with the broad margin of discretion afforded to Member States, concrete obligations imposed in the general economic interest may take into account Member States' national policy objectives.[188] Pursuing purely economic interests in the guise of PSOs, however, is not compatible with EU law.[189] For example, introducing capacity mechanisms that protect national energy undertakings in the absence of a legitimate security of supply concern would not be justifiable. However, there is case-law that indicates that even a measure that is prima facie protectionist in nature may be compatible with EU law if a Member State can show that the measure is necessary to prevent disruptions in the supply of electricity.[190] Nevertheless, PSOs should not result in the creation of generation capacity that goes beyond that needed to prevent undue interruptions in the supply of electricity to final consumers.[191]

---

186. Member States may take their national policy objectives into account. See C-67/96 *Albany* [1999] ECR I-5751, para. 104; C-265/08 *Federutility and Others v Autorità per l'energia elettrica e il gas* [2010] ECR I-3377, para. 29; and conversely, C-36/14 *Commission v Poland* [2015], judgment of the Court of 10 September 2015, published in the electronic Reports of Cases.

187. For an overview, *see* Luc Gyselen, 'Services of General Economic Interest and Competition under European Law – A Delicate Balance', 1(1) *Journal of European Competition Law & Practice* (2010), pp. 491-499.

188. C-67/96 *Albany* [1999] ECR I-5751, para. 104; and C-265/08 *Federutility and Others v Autorità per l'energia elettrica e il gas* [2010] ECR I-3377, para. 29. *See also* Leigh Hancher and Pierre Larouche, 'The Coming of Age of EU Regulation of Network Industries and Services of General Economic Interest', in Paul Craig and Gráinne De Búrca, *The Evolution of EU Law* (OUP, 2011), pp. 743-781, at 754-755.

189. C-352/85 *Bond van Adverteerders v State of the Netherlands* [1988] ECR 2085, para. 34; C-398/95 *Syndesmos ton en Elladi Touristikon kai Taxidiotikon Grafeion v Ypourgos Ergasias* [1997] ECR I-3091, paras 22-25; C-158/96 *Kohll v Union des Caisses de Maladie* [1998] ECR I-1931, para. 41; C-171/08 *Commission v Portugal* [2010] ECR I-6817, para. 39.

190. T-57/11 *Castelnou Energía v Commission* [2014], judgment of the General Court of 3 December 2014, published in the electronic Reports of Cases and 72/83 *Campus Oil* [1984] ECR 2727.

191. Recital 1 of the Security of Supply Directive.

It is established case-law that the formulation of Article 106(2) TFEU aims to reconcile Member States' interest in using certain undertakings as instruments of economic or social policy with the EU's interest in ensuring compliance with the rules on competition and preservation of the unity of the internal market.[192] It has been rightly argued, furthermore, that the large number of cases that have centred around the issue of reconciling Member States' interests and those of the EU is ultimately a matter of varying conceptions of the role of the market on the one hand and the role of the State on the other.[193] This balancing of sometimes mutually conflicting, multidimensional interests involves evaluating whether the adopted measure is limited to what is necessary to achieve an objective. This requirement of proportionality is analysed below.

[2]   Compliance with the Principle of Proportionality

The requirement of proportionality in PSOs is enshrined in the wording of Article 106(2) TFEU. This states, as noted above, that undertakings entrusted with the operation of SGEIs are, in principle, subject to the rules contained in the Treaties. However, derogation from these Treaty rules is possible in circumstances where applying them would obstruct the performance, in law or in fact, of the particular tasks assigned to the undertakings involved. Based on the wording of this provision, the application of Treaty rules is not intended to prevent Member States' discretion to utilise PSOs. However, in order for this derogation to apply, the development of trade must not be affected to such an extent as would be contrary to the interests of the Union.[194] This requirement lies at the core of the proportionality assessment for PSOs. It implies that the measures adopted to ensure the SGEIs should not create unnecessary distortions of trade.[195]

---

192. C-265/08 *Federutility and Others v Autorità per l'energia elettrica e il gas* [2010] ECR I-3377, para. 27; C-67/96 *Albany* [1999] ECR I-5751, para. 103; C-202/88 *France v Commission* [1991] ECR I-1223, para. 12; C-157/94 *Commission v Netherlands* [1997] ECR I-5699, para. 39; C-159/94 *Commission v France* [1997] ECR I-5815, para. 55; and C-121/15 *ANODE* [2016], judgment of the Court of 7 September 2016, published in the electronic Reports of Cases, para. 43; Heike Schweitzer, 'Services of General Economic Interest: European Law's Impact on the Role of Markets and of Member States', in Marise Cremona (ed.), *Market Integration and Public Services in the European Union* (OUP, 2011), pp. 11-62, at 12. This balancing act between the market, European integration and individual Member States' interests has also been referred to as a 'persistent irritant'. *See* Mario Monti, A New Strategy for the Single Market, at the Service of Europe's Economy and Society, Report to the President of the European Commission, 9 May 2000, p. 73.
193. Heike Schweitzer, 'Services of General Economic Interest: European Law's Impact on the Role of Markets and of Member States', in Marise Cremona (ed.), *Market Integration and Public Services in the European Union* (OUP, 2011), pp. 11-62, at 12; Leigh Hancher and Pierre Larouche, 'The Coming of Age of EU Regulation of Network Industries and Services of General Economic Interest', in Paul Craig and Gráinne De Búrca, *The Evolution of EU Law* (OUP, 2011), pp. 743-781, at 757.
194. Article 106(2) TFEU.
195. *See* Communication from the Commission, Services of general interest in Europe, OJ C 17, 19.1.2001, pp. 4-23, para. 23; and, for capacity mechanisms, T-57/11 *Castelnou Energía v Commission* [2014], judgment of the General Court of 3 December 2014, published in the

It is established case-law that if a Member State's public intervention in the general economic interest fulfils the proportionality requirements under 106(2) TFEU, PSOs in the interests of security of supply are compatible with the requirement of proportionality under EU law.[196] Determining whether a capacity mechanism fulfils the proportionality criteria is, however, complex. This is due to not only their exceptional nature as derogations from the market-based principle fundamental to the sector-specific electricity market legislation but also because of their potentially highly distortive effects on the internal electricity market.

The wording of Article 106(2) TFEU is designed to allow for a flexible and context-sensitive interpretation that allows Member States' different circumstances and national objectives to be taken into account.[197] In the absence of harmonisation, it allows for the introduction of measures for different types and levels of generation adequacy risks. However, the potentially distortive impacts of capacity mechanisms upon, *inter alia*, long-term investment behaviour, price development, free movement of goods and the concentration of market incumbents mean that the necessity for and positive outcomes of a capacity mechanism must outweigh the negative distortive effects of the measure. Alternatively, the negative impacts of not adopting a capacity mechanism have to be greater than the negative impacts of adopting one. In other words, the concern for generation adequacy must be substantial in order for a capacity mechanism to fall within the scope of the derogation permitted under Article 106(2) TFEU. It is a matter of balancing conflicting and fundamentally important interests: national generation adequacy on the one hand and the undistorted functioning of the internal market in electricity on the other.[198]

Evaluation of the principle of proportionality has been extensively discussed in the ECJ's case-law. The Court has established criteria for assessing compliance with the principle of proportionality and has applied these criteria in numerous cases. In situations where the introduction of PSOs has been harmonised, as is the case for electricity, the Court has applied a strict approach to proportionality.[199] The criteria applied in relation to capacity mechanisms are discussed below.

First, in order to fulfil the proportionality requirement the capacity mechanism in question must be appropriate for securing the general economic interest objective that

electronic Reports of Cases, para. 148; Heike Schweitzer, 'Services of General Economic Interest: European Law's Impact on the Role of Markets and of Member States', in Marise Cremona (ed.), *Market Integration and Public Services in the European Union* (OUP, 2011), pp. 11-62, at 38-42.

196. Cases C-393/92 *Almelo* [1994] ECR I-01477 and C-157/94 *Commission v Netherlands* [1997] ECR I-5699.

197. Communication from the Commission, Services of general interest in Europe, OJ C 17, 19.1.2001, pp. 4-23, para. 24.

198. AG opinion in C-265/08 *Federutility and Others v Autorità per l'energia elettrica e il gas* [2010] ECR I-3377, para. 53.

199. C-265/08 *Federutility and Others v Autorità per l'energia elettrica e il gas* [2010] ECR I-3377; and analysis in Koen Lenaerts, 'Defining the Concept of "Services of General Interest" in Light of the "Checks and Balances" Set out in the EU Treaties', 19(4) *Jurisprudence* (2012), pp. 1247-1267, at 1259.

it pursues.[200] Essentially, this criterion requires that the measure adopted is *suitable* to achieve the objective pursued.[201] For capacity mechanisms, this implies that there is an objective understanding of the issues that are causing a generation adequacy problem and that the instruments adopted to rectify these issues are specifically tailored to address these problems.

Second, the intervention in question must be limited in duration to that strictly necessary in order for it to achieve its objective.[202] The rationale for such a requirement can be derived from the free market ideology on which the EU internal market is based: a measure that fundamentally derogates from a fundamental market principle should not be permanent.[203] The Commission has confirmed the importance of this requirement in terms of capacity mechanisms[204] and has directly applied it in its assessment of a national capacity mechanism.[205] In the context of a derogation regime, it is logical for the justification for such an exemption to be lost if the amount of generation capacity increases to an adequate level.[206]

The Court interpreted the requirement for temporality strictly in *Federutility*. It found that national law under which an intervention was characterised as temporary would not in itself constitute a sufficient ground on which to conclude that the intervention is proportionate from the point of view of its duration, but that this would have to be independently assessed by a national court.[207]

Third, the intervention used should be limited to that necessary to achieve the objective that is being pursued in the general economic interest.[208] PSOs should not be attached to activities that may be carried on under normal market conditions.[209] Furthermore, if the market may be expected to deliver an adequate level of capacity using less distortive measures, these should be exhausted before resorting to PSOs. In order to objectively determine whether a less interventionist measure is available, a comparison between alternative measures should be made.[210] In addition to the proportionality of the capacity mechanism design itself, the timing of its usage should

---

200. Cases C-242/10 *Enel Produzione SpA v Autorità per l'energia elettrica e il gas* [2010] ECR I-13665, para. 55; and C-121/15 *ANODE* [2016], judgment of the Court of 7 September 2016, published in the electronic Reports of Cases, para. 55.
201. Leigh Hancer and Wolf Sauter, 'Public Services and EU Law', in Catherine Barnard and Steve Peers (eds), *European Union Law* (OUP, 2013), pp. 539-566, at 544.
202. C-265/08 *Federutility and Others v Autorità per l'energia elettrica e il gas* [2010] ECR I-3377, para. 35.
203. *Ibid.*
204. Communication from the Commission, Delivering the internal electricity market and making the most of public intervention, C(2013) 7243 final, pp. 7 and 18.
205. SA.35980 *GB capacity mechanism*, C(2014) 5083 final, para. 6; N178/2010 *Preferential dispatch of indigenous coal plants*, C(2010) 4499, paras 32-34.
206. AG Opinion C-265/08 *Federutility and Others v Autorità per l'energia elettrica e il gas* [2010] ECR I-3377, para. 70.
207. C-265/08 *Federutility and Others v Autorità per l'energia elettrica e il gas* [2010] ECR I-3377, para. 35.
208. C-265/08 *Federutility and Others v Autorità per l'energia elettrica e il gas* [2010] ECR I-3377, para. 36.
209. European Commission, Consultation Paper on generation adequacy, capacity mechanisms and the internal market in electricity, 15.11.2012, p. 9. In respect of case-law concerning capacity mechanisms, *see* SA.45852 *German capacity reserve*, C(2018) 612 final, para. 94.
210. For more on alternative measures to address generation adequacy, *see* Chapter 6.

also be proportionate.[211] This is because capacity mechanisms have enormous potential to distort competition and trade in the internal market if they are adopted prematurely and in an uncoordinated way without proper assessment of the underlying causes of generation inadequacy.[212] The fulfilment of this criterion is also for the national courts to assess.

Finally, the requirement of proportionality must also be assessed with regard to the scope *ratione personae* of the measure.[213] In particular, this requires an assessment of the beneficiaries of the measure.[214] This criterion was particularly relevant in *Federutility*, where it was established that price regulation could constitute a PSO. It was, however, strongly emphasised that the group of beneficiaries of lower gas prices should not be more extensive than required to achieve the objective pursued.[215] This criterion is less essential in the context of capacity mechanisms, because there is no separable group of final consumers that would not need the provision of uninterrupted electricity.

The proportionality principle is an instrument that can ensure that Article 106(2) TFEU is strictly interpreted to prevent broad derogations from Treaty law.[216] However, the evaluation should not be so strict that it would de facto exclude or limit the discretion granted to Member States in defining the scope of SGEIs. Typically, it is for the national courts to review compliance with the principle of proportionality.[217] This review is subject to EU control only to determine, first, whether the measure is necessary in order for the service to be performed and, second, whether it is manifestly inappropriate in relation to the objective pursued.[218]

The burden of proof with regard to fulfilling the proportionality criteria falls on Member States.[219] A Member State has to be able to demonstrate that the capacity mechanism it has adopted fulfils the requirement of proportionality. However, the burden of proof does not extend so far as to require Member States to demonstrate that

---

211. AG opinion in C-265/08 *Federutility and Others v Autorità per l'energia elettrica e il gas* [2010] ECR I-3377, para. 6.
212. ACER, Capacity Remuneration Mechanisms and the Internal Market for Electricity of 30 July 2013, available at www.acer.europa.eu/official_documents/acts_of_the_agency/publication/crms%20and%20the%20iem%20report%20130730.pdf (last accessed 5.3.2019), para. 51; European Commission, Interim Report of the Sector Inquiry on Capacity Mechanisms, C(2016) 2107 final, p. 3.
213. C-265/08 *Federutility and Others v Autorità per l'energia elettrica e il gas* [2010] ECR I-3377, para. 39.
214. *Ibid.*
215. *Ibid.*
216. C-157/94 *Commission v Netherlands* [1997] ECR I-5699, para. 37.
217. C-265/08 *Federutility and Others v Autorità per l'energia elettrica e il gas* [2010] ECR I-3377, para. 34.
218. T-57/11 *Castelnou Energía v Commission* [2014], judgment of the General Court of 3 December 2014, published in the electronic Reports of Cases, para. 150; T-289/03 *BUPA* [2008] ECR II-81, paras 222, 266 and 287; C-157/94 *Commission v Netherlands* [1997] ECR I-5699, para. 53; C-67/96 *Albany* [1999] ECR I-5751, paras 107 and 111; and joined cases T-125/96 and T-152/96 *Boehringer v Council and Commission* [1999] ECR II-3427, paras 73-74.
219. C-157/94 *Commission v Netherlands* [1997] ECR I-5699, para. 51.

no other conceivable measure, by definition hypothetical, would guarantee the same results as the selected capacity mechanism.[220]

In addition to the proportionality criteria established in case-law, Article 106(2) TFEU specifically requires that imposing a PSO in the general economic interest should not affect trade to such extent as would be contrary to the interests of the EU. Contrary to the proportionality assessment, the burden of proof falls on the Commission to demonstrate that Member States' measures affect trade in a way that would be contrary to the interests of the EU.[221]

[3]   Additional Sector-Specific Requirements for Introducing PSOs

Article 3 of the Electricity Directive establishes both procedural and material criteria for the introduction of PSOs, in addition to balancing conflicting interests in respect of this process. The obligations must be clearly defined, transparent, non-discriminatory and verifiable, and guarantee equal access for EU electricity companies to consumers.[222] Member States must also inform the Commission of all measures adopted to fulfil PSOs, irrespective of whether these measures require derogations from the rules of the Directive, and by extension, from Article 106(2) TFEU.[223]

In terms of capacity mechanisms, the tendency for them to fail to fulfil the requirements of transparency and non-discrimination has been widely discussed.[224] This is largely due to the great difficulties Member States have faced in trying to incorporate these criteria into the design of a capacity mechanism. In order for a capacity mechanism to be non-discriminatory, it should not differentiate between cross-border contracts and national contracts,[225] nor should it reserve capacity for purely national purposes.[226] In practice, however, this is hardly ever achieved.[227]

---

220. C-157/94 *Commission v Netherlands* [1997] ECR I-5699, para. 58; C-158/94 *Commission v Italy* [1997] ECR I-5789, para. 54; and C-159/94 *Commission v France* [1997] ECR I-5815, para. 101.
221. C-157/94 *Commission v Netherlands* [1997] ECR I-5699, paras 67-69; C-158/94 *Commission v Italy* [1997] ECR I-5789, paras 63-65; C-159/94 *Commission v France* [1997] ECR I-5815, paras 111-113; and further analysis in AG opinion in C-265/08 *Federutility and Others v Autorità per l'energia elettrica e il gas* [2010] ECR I-3377, paras 77-79.
222. Article 3(2) of the Electricity Directive; Hans Vedder, Anita Rønne, Martha Roggenkamp and Iñigo del Guayo, 'EU Energy Law', in Martha Roggenkamp, Catherine Redgwell, Anita Rønne and Iñigo del Guayo (eds), *Energy Law in Europe: National, EU and International Regulation* (OUP, 2016), pp. 187-366; Peter Cameron, *Competition in Energy Markets* (OUP, 2007), pp. 128-132.
223. Article 3(15) of the Electricity Directive. The Commission should additionally be informed every two years of any changes to national PSOs.
224. Commission Staff Working Document accompanying the document Report from the Commission Final Report of the Sector Inquiry on Capacity Mechanisms, SWD(2016) 385 final; Report from the Commission, Final Report of the Sector Inquiry on Capacity Mechanisms, COM(2016) 752 final; Commission Staff Working Document accompanying the document Report from the Commission Interim Report of the Sector Inquiry on Capacity Mechanisms, SWD(2016) 119 final. For more on this topic, *see* section §3.03[D] above.
225. Article 4 of the Security of Supply Directive.
226. Commission Staff Working Document, Generation adequacy in the internal electricity market – guidance on public interventions, SWD(2013) 438 final, p. 30.
227. Commission Staff Working Document accompanying the document Report from the Commission Interim Report of the Sector Inquiry on Capacity Mechanisms, SWD(2016) 119 final, p. 79;

§3.05   THE RELATIONSHIP BETWEEN TENDERS AND PSOs UNDER THE ELECTRICITY DIRECTIVE

As noted above, introducing capacity mechanisms under EU electricity legislation requires, first and foremost, that the market is not expected to deliver by itself a sufficient level of generation capacity to ensure security of supply. This requirement is incorporated in both tendering and equivalent procedures under Article 8 of the Electricity Directive and PSOs under Article 3 of the Electricity Directive, both of which establish conditions for the adoption of capacity mechanisms.

Articles 3 and 8 of the Electricity Directive are both exceptions to the market-based approach.[228] They are both autonomous provisions that can be applied independently of one another. From the point of view of capacity mechanisms, however, these provisions are highly intertwined as Article 8 lays down the procedural requirements for imposing PSOs under Article 3.[229] Applying these provisions or successfully invoking the derogations they potentially allow requires fulfilment of the criteria identified above. This, however, raises the question of the legal relationship between these provisions.

Article 3(14) of the Electricity Directive addresses the relationship between PSOs under Article 3 and tendering or equivalent procedures under Article 8 of the Electricity Directive. It states that Member States may decide not to apply the provisions of Article 8 of the Electricity Directive. This derogation is applicable only insofar as the application of Article 8 would obstruct the performance, in law or in fact, of the obligations imposed on electricity undertakings in the general economic interest. In other words, Member States can derogate from the tendering procedure in Article 8 of the Electricity Directive only to the extent that applying this provision would prevent the performance of lawfully introduced PSOs. However, it is established case-law that tendering or equivalent procedures are the preferred method for procuring public services.[230]

Nevertheless, at first glance the wording of Article 3(14) of the Electricity Directive appears to indicate that Member States may circumvent the design criteria laid down for the tendering procedure in Article 8 of the Electricity Directive.

European Commission, Interim Report of the Sector Inquiry on Capacity Mechanisms, C(2016) 2107 final, p. 13; Paolo Mastropietro, Pablo Rodilla and Carlos Batlle, 'National Capacity Mechanisms in the European Internal Energy Market: Opening the Doors to Neighbours', 82 *Energy Policy* (2015), pp. 38-47, at 40.
228. Articles 8(1) and 3(14) of the Electricity Directive.
229. Natalia Fiedziuk, 'Putting Services of General Economic Interest up for Tender: Reflections on Applicable EU Rules', 50(1) *Common Market Law Review* (2013), pp. 87-114.
230. C-280/00 *Altmark* [2003] ECR I-7747. For further discussion of this topic in legal literature, *see* Philipp Kiiver, *The Practice of Public Procurement: Tendering, Selection and Award* (Intersentia, 2014); Christopher Bovis, 'Public Procurement and State Aid', Herwig Hofmann and Claire Micheau (eds), *State Aid Law of the European Union* (OUP, 2016), pp. 161-186; Heike Schweitzer, 'Services of General Economic Interest: European Law's Impact on the Role of Markets and of Member States', in Marise Cremona (ed.), *Market Integration and Public Services in the European Union* (OUP, 2011), pp. 11-62, at 29-30; Natalia Fiedziuk, 'Putting Services of General Economic Interest up for Tender: Reflections on Applicable EU Rules', 50(1) *Common Market Law Review* (2013), pp. 87-114.

Transparency and non-discrimination, however, are requirements set for both PSOs and tendering or equivalent procedures. As a result, Member States cannot be exempted from these requirements even if they are able to invoke the exemption and not apply Article 8 of the Electricity Directive.

Article 3(14) of the Electricity Directive establishes that Member States may decide not to apply Article 8 of the Electricity Directive only insofar as the development of trade would not be affected to such an extent as would be contrary to the interests of the EU. The formulation of Article 3(14) of the Electricity Directive is identical to that of Article 106(2) TFEU and should be interpreted in the same narrow way. The interests of the EU refer, *inter alia*, to competition with regard to eligible customers.[231]

If there is a legitimate general economic interest and the other requirements for imposing PSOs are fulfilled, Member States may decide not to resort to tendering or equivalent procedures and, instead, directly impose PSOs in the interests of security of supply. Overall, Member States have an incentive to formulate their State interventions as PSOs, as compensation for such obligations is evaluated differently from State aid.[232] State-driven remuneration for capacity and the exemptions potentially available under EU law are discussed in the next chapter.

---

231. Article 3(14) of the Electricity Directive.
232. Conor Quigley, *European State Aid Law and Policy* (Hart Publishing, 2015), pp. 231-254; Thomas von Danwitz, 'The Concept of State Aid in Liberalized Sectors', in Marise Cremona (ed.), *Market Integration and Public Services in the European Union* (OUP, 2011), pp. 103-115.

CHAPTER 4

Remunerating Generation Adequacy

§4.01 REMUNERATION AS THE OVERARCHING ELEMENT IN CAPACITY MECHANISMS

The previous chapters outline the context in which the wider introduction of capacity mechanisms arises and show how these mechanisms are treated in EU electricity legislation.[1] This secondary legislative framework addresses capacity mechanisms as Member State interventions that aim to ensure that the market provides a higher level of security of supply than would otherwise be the case.

The reasons for introducing capacity mechanisms vary significantly between Member States. They may relate to the changing structure of the electricity market, such as increasing variable generation, nuclear phase-out, decommissioning of existing capacities and decreasing capacity margins; or to the need to adapt to the energy transition in general. These reasons can also be partly external and include issues such as increasing import dependencies, a Member State's peripheral location and low interconnectivity. Member States have also introduced capacity mechanisms on grounds of growing demand and, in particular, spiking peak demand and long-term investment issues such as capacity deficits and the missing money problem.[2]

---

1. Chapters 2 and 3 above.
2. For the different arguments that have been used to defend the adoption of a capacity mechanism, see N475/2003 *Irish CADA*, 16 December 2003; SA.675/2009 *Tender for Aid for New Electricity Generation Capacity (LV)*, C(2010) 4146, paras 4-5 and 22-30; SA.38968 *Greece Transitory Electricity flexibility remuneration mechanism (FRM)*, C(2016) 1791 final, paras 12-16; SA.34947 *Support to Hinkley Point C Nuclear Power Station*, C(2013) 9073 final, paras 9-10; SA.35980 *GB capacity mechanism*, C(2014) 5083 final, paras 85-86; NN24/2010 *Compensation for the provision of instant interruptibility services in Sardinia and Sicily*, C(2010) 3222 final, para. 7; T-57/11 *Castelnou Energía v Commission* [2014], judgment of the General Court of 3 December 2014, published in the electronic Reports of Cases; SA.42955 *German Network Reserve*, C(2016) 8742 final, paras 4-7; SA.43735 *German ABLAV Interruptibility Scheme*, C(2016) 6765 final, paras 4-5; SA.39621 *French country-wide capacity mechanism*, C(2016) 7086 final, paras 43-44.

From a legal point of view, the obligation to ensure a sufficient level of generation capacity and the balance between supply and demand lies with individual Member States.[3] In an effort to fulfil this obligation, Member States have adopted different capacity mechanisms to address different national issues that affect generation adequacy. Because of these different functions assigned to capacity mechanisms, there is natural variation between the instruments adopted by Member States.

The key unifying element between these mechanisms, however, is the economic incentives they provide to increase the level of security of supply.[4] International experience on capacity mechanisms shows that the existence of capacity mechanisms can cost up to 10% to 20% of wholesale electricity prices.[5] Because of the great administrative costs associated with the adoption and operation of a capacity mechanism and the costs caused by paying for the capacity itself, it is essential to determine how these mechanisms are and can be financed. When additional economic incentives for generation capacity are adopted by a government, they are likely to fall within the application of the EU State aid regime, which is the topic of this chapter.[6] The focus is on the substantive provisions of State aid, whereas the procedural aspects are only be analysed insofar as so doing serves the purposes of analysing the substantive provisions and the relevance of the EU State aid regime to capacity remuneration.

The significance of EU State aid rules in the context of capacity remuneration is well illustrated in the State aid sector inquiry that was initiated by the Commission in April 2015 to investigate capacity mechanisms.[7] Launching such an inquiry requires that there is a reason to suspect that State aid measures in a particular sector or based on a particular aid instrument may materially restrict or distort competition within the internal market in several Member States.[8] This was the first, and so far the last, time

---

3. Article 5 of the Security of Supply Directive.
4. Report from the Commission, Final Report of the Sector Inquiry on Capacity Mechanisms, COM(2016) 752 final, p. 7.
5. Commission Staff Working Document, Generation Adequacy in the internal electricity market – guidance on public interventions accompanying the document Communication from the Commission Delivering the internal electricity market and making the most of public intervention, SWD(2013) 438 final, p. 32.
6. For an analysis of state aid in the energy sector more generally, *see* Leigh Hancher and Francesco Salerno, 'State Aid in the Energy Sector', in Erika Szyszczak (ed.), *Research Handbook on European State Aid Law* (Edward Elgar, 2011), pp. 246-276; Angus Johnston, 'The Impact of the New EU Commission Guidelines on State Aid for Environmental Protection and Energy on the Promotion of Renewable Energies', in Franz Jürgen Säcker, Lydia Scholz and Thea Sveen (eds), *EU Renewable Energy Law: Legal Challenges and New Perspectives* (Oslo Sjørettsfondet, 2014), pp. 13-57; Elisabetta Righini and Juan Carlos González Fernández, 'Capacity Mechanisms and State Aid: Between PSOs, Market Liberalisation, and Security of Supply', 7(10) *Journal of European Competition Law & Practice* (2016), pp. 661-675.
7. Commission Decision of 29.4.2015 initiating an inquiry on capacity mechanisms in the electricity sector pursuant to Article 20a of Council Regulation (EC) No 659/1999 of 22 March 1999, C(2015) 2814 final.
8. Article 20a(1) of Council Regulation (EC) No 659/1999 of 22 March 1999 laying down detailed rules for the application of Article 108 of the treaty on the functioning of the European Union and as amended by Council Regulation (EU) No 734/2013 of 22 July 2013 amending Regulation (EC) No 659/1999 laying down detailed rules for the application of Article 93 of the EC Treaty (OJ L 204, 31.7.2013, pp. 15-22).

that the Commission has initiated a sector inquiry, which demonstrates the significance of capacity remuneration in the electricity market.

The purpose of the sector inquiry into capacity mechanisms was to gain a better
understanding of the existence and functioning of capacity mechanisms across Member States.[9] The findings of the inquiry confirmed that public remuneration for capacity
risks creating competitive distortions in the electricity market and, in principle,
constitutes State aid.[10] However, the inquiry only provided a general analysis of
capacity remuneration schemes in eleven Member States. Consequently, it did not
replace the need to conduct case-by-case State aid analyses on capacity mechanisms.[11]
It did, however, acknowledge a general need to reform the electricity markets.[12] The
inquiry also established some preferences between different capacity mechanism
designs.[13] For example, capacity payments were generally considered unlikely to
constitute an appropriate measure to address generation adequacy.[14] Although the
final report is not legally binding, the Commission has relied on its findings in the
interpretation of EU State aid rules when assessing Member States' aid schemes in the
electricity sector.[15]

The allocation of public funding to generation adequacy is an illustrative example
of the rationales underpinning EU State aid control.[16] On the one hand, well-designed
State aid can be used to target market failures and objectives of common interest, such
as SGEI.[17] On the other hand, the supranational rules on State aid are in place to ensure
the efficiency and effectiveness of public spending and to limit the potential adverse

---

9. Commission Decision of 29.4.2015 initiating an inquiry on capacity mechanisms in the electricity sector pursuant to Article 20a of Council Regulation (EC) No 659/1999 of 22 March 1999,
C(2015) 2814 final, para. 6.
10. Report from the Commission, Final Report of the Sector Inquiry on Capacity Mechanisms,
COM(2016) 752 final, p. 2.
11. Report from the Commission, Final Report of the Sector Inquiry on Capacity Mechanisms,
COM(2016) 752 final, footnote 4.
12. Report from the Commission, Final Report of the Sector Inquiry on Capacity Mechanisms,
COM(2016) 752 final, pp. 5-6. Leigh Hancher and Christoph Riechmann, 'Capacity Mechanisms
and Auctions', in Leigh Hancher, Adrien de Hauteclocque and Francesco Maria Salerno (eds),
State Aid and the Energy Sector (Hart Publishing, 2018), pp. 145-177, at 162-163.
13. Report from the Commission, Final Report of the Sector Inquiry on Capacity Mechanisms,
COM(2016) 752 final, p. 10.
14. Report from the Commission, Final Report of the Sector Inquiry on Capacity Mechanisms,
COM(2016) 752 final, p. 10.
15. SA.43735 German ABLAV Interruptibility Scheme, C(2016) 6765 final; Leigh Hancher and
Christoph Riechmann, 'Capacity Mechanisms and Auctions', in Leigh Hancher, Adrien de
Hauteclocque and Francesco Maria Salerno (eds), State Aid and the Energy Sector (Hart
Publishing, 2018), pp. 145-177, at 172-173.
16. On the origins and objectives of EU State aid control, see Juan Jorge Piernas López, The Concept
of State Aid Under EU Law: From Internal Market to Competition and Beyond (OUP, 2015), pp.
21-64; Herwig Hofmann, 'State aid Review in a Multi-Level System: Motivations for Aid, Why
Control It, and the Evolution of State Aid Law in the EU', in Herwig Hofmann and Claire Micheau
(eds), State Aid Law of the European Union (OUP, 2016), pp. 3-11; Alberto Heimler and Frédéric
Jenny, 'The limitations of European Union Control of State Aid', 28(2) Oxford Review of
Economic Policy (2012), pp. 347-367, at 348-352; Kelyn Bacon, European Union Law of State Aid,
3rd edition (OUP, 2017), pp. 3-16.
17. Philipp Werner and Vincent Verouden, 'Introduction: The Law and Econmics of EU State Aid
Control', in Philipp Werner and Vincent Verouden (eds), EU State Aid Control: Law and
Economics (Wolters Kluwer, 2017), pp. 7-62, at 30-31.

effects of State aid on competition.[18] Overall, compliance with State aid rules requires that an objective of EU law, such as security of supply, is being pursued.[19]

The State aid sector inquiry into capacity mechanisms demonstrates the different adverse effects that unnecessary adoption or unsuitable design of capacity mechanisms may have on the internal market in electricity. Some capacity mechanisms risk overcompensation and, as a result, inefficient use of public funds.[20] Administratively set capacity prices are unlikely to reflect the market value of capacity and may not, therefore, provide the necessary investment incentives.[21] Furthermore, certain capacity mechanisms are likely to create implicit price caps or distort the functioning of the energy-only market in other ways.[22] Many capacity mechanisms target certain capacities over others and fail to take into account cross-border capacities, thus undermining the pursuit of an integrated internal market in electricity.[23] These tendencies are addressed, among other issues, through EU State aid control, the elements of which are discussed below.

§4.02 GENERAL PROHIBITION ON DISTORTIVE STATE AID

[A] The Concept of Aid

Article 107(1) TFEU prohibits aid in any form whatsoever if it fulfils four cumulative criteria. First, the aid must be granted by a Member State or through State resources. Second, it must distort or threaten to distort competition. Third, it must favour certain undertakings or the production of certain goods. Finally, it must affect trade between Member States. If these conditions are met, the aid is considered incompatible with the internal market within the meaning of Article 107(1) TFEU.

The concept of aid under Article 107(1) TFEU has been given a broad interpretation by the Commission and the EU courts. Generally speaking, aid has been understood to refer to an economic advantage and, as such, the concept encompasses a much more extensive variety of economic support schemes than merely a direct

---

18. European Commission, State aid modernization, COM(2012) 209 final, p. 12; Leigh Hancher, Tom Ottervanger and Piet Jan Slot, *EU State Aids*, 5th edition (Sweet & Maxwell, 2016), pp. 32-39.
19. Wolf Sauter, *Public Services in EU Law* (Cambridge University Press, 2015), p. 153.
20. European Commission, Interim Report of the Sector Inquiry on Capacity Mechanisms, C(2016) 2107 final, p. 14.
21. Commission Staff Working Document accompanying the document Report from the Commission Final Report of the Sector Inquiry on Capacity Mechanisms, SWD(2016) 385 final, para. 364.
22. Commission Staff Working Document accompanying the document Report from the Commission Final Report of the Sector Inquiry on Capacity Mechanisms, SWD(2016) 385 final, para. 384.
23. Jean-Michel Glachant and Sophia Ruester, 'The EU Internal Electricity Market: Done Forever?', 31 *Utilities Policy* (2014), pp. 221-228; Commission Staff Working Document accompanying the document Report from the Commission Final Report of the Sector Inquiry on Capacity Mechanisms, SWD(2016) 385 final, para. 4.

transfer of State funds to an undertaking.[24] An undertaking, furthermore, has consistently been defined broadly as an entity engaged in economic activities irrespective of its legal status and the manner in which it is financed.[25]

It is settled case-law that the concept of aid set out in Article 107(1) TFEU does not distinguish between measures of State intervention by reference to their causes or their aims but rather defines aid in relation to its effects.[26] In other words, a State measure can constitute prohibited State aid irrespective of whether it has a legitimate aim such as security of supply.[27] However, the ECJ has rejected the extension of the concept of State aid to measures having equivalent effects to State aid.[28]

The existence of an economic advantage is evaluated against what an undertaking would be able to recover under normal market conditions.[29] Furthermore, an investment in an undertaking by the State constitutes State aid if a market operator would not have made that investment under normal market conditions.[30] This

---

24. C-399/08 P *Commission v Deutsche Post* [2010] ECR I-7831, para. 40; C-237/04 *Enirisorse* [2006] ECR I-2843, para. 30; C-206/06 *Essent Netwerk Noord and Others* [2008] ECR I-5497, para. 79; C-522/13 *Ministerio de Defensa and Navantia* [2014], judgment of the Court 9 October 2014, published in the electronic Reports of Cases, para. 21; Giuseppe Conte and James Kavanagh, 'Advantage', in Philipp Werner and Vincent Verouden (eds), *EU State Aid Control: Law and Economics* (Wolters Kluwer, 2017), pp. 66-86; Conor Quigley, *European State Aid Law and Policy* (Hart Publishing, 2015), pp. 12-26; Kelyn Bacon, *European Union Law of State Aid*, 3rd edition (OUP, 2017), pp. 17-60; Peter Vesterdorf and Stephen Harris, *State Aid Law of the European Union* (Sweet & Maxwell, 2008), pp. 3-15.
25. Joined cases C-180/98 to C-184/98 *Pavlov and Others* [2000] ECR I-6451, para. 74; C-41/90 *Höfner and Elser* [1991] ECR I-1979, para. 21; joined cases C-159/91 and C-160/91 *Poucet and Pistre* [1993] ECR I-637, para. 17; C-244/94 *Fédération Française des Sociétés d'Assurance* [1995] ECR I-4013, para. 14; C-67/96 *Albany* [1999] ECR I-5751, para. 77; C-117/97 *Brentjens'* [1999] ECR I-6025, para. 77; C-219/97 *Drijvende Bokken* [1999] ECR I-6121, para. 67; Communication from the Commission on the application of the European Union State aid rules to compensation granted for the provision of services of general economic interest, OJ C 8, 11.1.2012, pp. 4-14, para. 9; Wolf Sauter, 'The Notion of Undertaking', in Herwig Hofmann and Claire Micheau (eds), *State Aid Law of the European Union* (OUP, 2016), pp. 74-83.
26. 173/73 *Italy v Commission* [1974] ECR 709, para. 13; 310/85 *Deufil v Commission* [1987] ECR 901, para. 8; C-56/93 *Belgium v Commission* [1996] ECR I-723, para. 79; C-75/97 *Belgium v Commission* [1999] ECR I-3671, para. 25; C-241/94 *France v Commission* [1996] ECR I-4551, para. 20; joined cases C-106/09 P and C-107/09 P *Commission and Spain v Government of Gibraltar and United Kingdom* [2011] ECR I-11113, para. 48. In legal literature, *see* Erika Szyszczak, *The Regulation of the State in Competitive Markets in the EU* (Hart Publishing, 2007), pp. 223-224; Małgorzata Cyndecka, *The Market Economy Investor Test in EU State Aid Law: Applicability and Application* (Kluwer Law International, 2016); Carles Esteva Mosso, 'The More Economic Approach Paradigm – An Effects-Based Approach to EU Competition Policy', in Jürgen Basedow and Wolfgang Wurmnest (eds), *Structure and Effects in EU Competition Law: Studies on Exclusionary Conduct and State Aid* (Kluwer Law International, 2011), pp. 11-22.
27. Henrik Bjørnebye, *Investing in EU Energy Security: Exploring the Regulatory Approach to Tomorrow's Electricity Production* (University of Oslo, PhD thesis 2009), p. 326.
28. C-379/98 *PreussenElektra* [2001] ECR I-2099. *See also* Falk Schöning and Clemens Ziegler, 'What Is State Aid?', in Leigh Hancher, Adrien de Hautecloque and Francesco Maria Salerno (eds), *State Aid and the Energy Sector* (Hart Publishing, 2018), pp. 3-29, at 5-6.
29. Cases C-280/00 *Altmark* [2003] ECR I-7747, para. 84; C-39/94 *SFEI and Others* [1996] ECR I-3547, para. 60; C-342/96 *Spain v Commission* [1999] ECR I-2459, para. 41; C-256/97 *DM Transport* [1999] ECR I-3913, para. 22; Juan Jorge Piernas López, *The Concept of State Aid Under EU Law: From Internal Market to Competition and Beyond* (OUP, 2015), pp. 79-84.
30. 234/84 *Kingdom of Belgium v Commission of the European Communities* [1986] ECR 2263; Małgorzata Cyndecka, *The Market Economy Investor Test in EU State Aid Law: Applicability and*

interpretation broadens the concept of aid from that of a positive contribution to any measure that mitigates the normal charges an undertaking would include in its budget.[31] Aid can be direct financing through loans or guarantees or reverse support through tax deductions or other material advantages.[32] Aid can also be indirect.[33] A charge that is applied under non-discriminatory conditions to both domestic and imported products can constitute State aid if the collected charge is used solely for the benefit of domestic products.[34] A State measure that mitigates or hedges the risks associated with the undertaking's economic activities is also likely to constitute State aid.[35] For instance, reliability options are an illustrative example of a government hedging investors' risks by guaranteeing them a stable stream of revenues irrespective of market prices.[36] Furthermore, a waiver of charges can constitute State aid if a State chooses not to charge market prices for an undertaking's services.[37] For example, the French capacity guarantee constituted aid because France had surrendered its funds by allocating capacity certificates to capacity operators free of charge instead of selling them.[38]

A single capacity mechanism can also include more than one measure that constitutes State aid within the meaning of Article 107(1) TFEU. For example, the UK support scheme for the new nuclear power station Hinkley Point C comprised three different support measures. The main form of support was a subsidy by which the beneficiary was to receive a steady stream of revenue, the amount of which was to be determined by reference to the difference between a predetermined strike price and a

---

Application (Kluwer Law International, 2016); Juan Jorge Piernas López, *The Concept of State Aid under EU Law: From Internal Market to Competition and Beyond* (OUP, 2015), pp. 75-79.

31. Cases 30/59 *De Gezamenlijke Steenkolenmijnen in Limburg v High Authority* [1961] ECR 1, para. 9; C-387/92 *Banco Exterior de España* [1994] ECR I-877, para. 13; C-241/94 *France v Commission* [1996] ECR I-4551, para. 34; C-256/97 *DM Transport* [1999] ECR I-3913, para. 19; C-53/00 *Ferring* [2001] ECR I-9067, para. 15; Juan Jorge Piernas López, *The Concept of State Aid Under EU Law: From Internal Market to Competition and Beyond* (OUP, 2015), pp. 67-75.

32. C-379/98 *PreussenElektra* [2001] ECR I-2099, para. 58; Rein Wesseling and Marieke Bredenoord-Spoek, 'State Measure', in Philipp Werner and Vincent Verouden (eds), *EU State Aid Control: Law and Economics* (Wolters Kluwer, 2017), pp. 87-118, at 114-116; Commission Notice on the notion of State aid as referred to in Article 107(1) of the Treaty on the Functioning of the European Union, OJ C 262, 19.7.2016, pp. 1-50, para. 51.

33. Giuseppe Conte and James Kavanagh, 'Advantage', in Philipp Werner and Vincent Verouden (eds), *EU State Aid Control: Law and Economics* (Wolters Kluwer, 2017), pp. 66-86, at 66-67.

34. C-206/06 *Essent Netwerk Noord and Others* [2008] ECR I-5497, para. 58; C-17/91 *Lornoy and Others* [1992] ECR I-6523, para. 32; C-72/92 *Scharbatke* [1993] ECR I-5509, para. 18.

35. C-379/98 *PreussenElektra* [2001] ECR I-2099, para. 54; Aindrias Ó Caoimh and Wolf Sauter, 'Criterion of Advantage', in Herwig Hofmann and Claire Micheau (eds), *State Aid Law of the European Union* (OUP, 2016), pp. 84-128, at 84-86.

36. For more information on the functioning of a reliability option, *see* Chapter 2 above.

37. Communication from the Commission on the application of the European Union State aid rules to compensation granted for the provision of services of general economic interest, OJ C 8, 11.1.2012, pp. 4-14, para. 32; Jacques Derenne, 'Article 107 TFEU', in Weijer Ver Loren van Themaat and Berend Reuder (eds), *European Competition Law: A Case Commentary* (Edward Elgar, 2014), pp. 216-255, at 238-250.

38. SA.39621 *French country-wide capacity mechanism*, C(2016) 7086 final, para. 54; Leigh Hancher and Christoph Riechmann, 'Capacity Mechanisms and Auctions', in Leigh Hancher, Adrien de Hauteclocque and Francesco Maria Salerno (eds), *State Aid and the Energy Sector* (Hart Publishing, 2018), pp. 145-177, at 169-171.

reference price set by wholesale prices.[39] In addition, the scheme involved a credit guarantee by the State, which was also regarded as State aid.[40] Furthermore, the support scheme for Hinkley Point C involved a so-called Secretary of State Agreement by which investors would be entitled to compensation in the event that the UK government shut down the nuclear facility on political grounds.[41]

As noted above, the broad interpretation of aid under Article 107(1) TFEU leaves little room for measures that fall outside the concept of State aid. Nevertheless, it is possible to identify certain State measures that do transfer State resources to an undertaking but do not confer any economic advantage. This is possible when the Member State in question procures services from the market like any other market participant. This was the conclusion of the Commission's State aid assessment in two cases relevant to capacity remuneration. Both concerned the procurement of interruptibility services to balance the electricity system, the first in Italy and the second in Greece.[42]

The Italian scheme comprised a system of compensation for undertakings located in Sardinia and Sicily that provided instant interruptibility services.[43] The Greek mechanism compensated certain undertakings located in the Greek interconnected system for reducing their electricity consumption during peak hours.[44] In both schemes, the undertakings entered into contracts with the TSO for a limited duration. The Commission declared that neither scheme constituted aid as they did not confer an economic advantage on the contracted undertakings but rather constituted compensation for services that were necessary in order to balance the real-time fluctuation between electricity supply and demand. However, it is exceptional for these types of measures to fall outside the scope of aid.[45]

In the case of Italy, the Commission argued that the services, necessary for the functioning of the electricity system, were provided at market price. Therefore, the TSO was acting like a rational market economy operator.[46] Furthermore, the Commission

---

39. SA.34947 *Support to Hinkley Point C Nuclear Power Station*, C(2014) 7142 final, paras 6-14.
40. SA.34947 *Support to Hinkley Point C Nuclear Power Station*, C(2014) 7142 final, paras 48-73.
41. SA.34947 *Support to Hinkley Point C Nuclear Power Station*, C(2014) 7142 final, paras 74-75. In legal literature, *see* Kai Struckmann and Geza Sapi, 'Energy and Environmental Aid', in Philipp Werner and Vincent Verouden (eds), *EU State Aid Control: Law and Economics* (Wolters Kluwer, 2017), pp. 663-713, at 710-712; Filip Černoch and Veronika Zapletalová, 'Hinkley Point C: A New Chance for Nuclear Power Plant Construction in Central Europe?' 83 *Energy Policy* (2015), pp. 165-168.
42. SA.38711 *Interruptibility service for the electric system in Greece*, C(2014) 7374 final; NN24/2010 *Compensation for the provision of instant interruptibility services in Sardinia and Sicily*, C(2010) 3222 final; SA.35119 *Prolongation of the scheme for compensation of instant interruptibility services in Sardinia and Sicily*, C(2012) D 6779 final.
43. NN24/2010 *Compensation for the provision of instant interruptibility services in Sardinia and Sicily*, C(2010) 3222 final, para. 5.
44. SA.38711 *Interruptibility service for the electric system in Greece*, C(2014) 7374 final, para. 2.
45. SA.43735 *German ABLAV Interruptibility Scheme*, C(2016) 6765 final, paras 29-32.
46. C-119/97 *SFEI and Others* [1999] ECR I-1341, paras 60-61; Commission Notice on the notion of State aid as referred to in Article 107(1) of the Treaty on the Functioning of the European Union, OJ C 262, 19.7.2016, pp. 1-50, paras 73-116; and for capacity mechanisms NN24/2010 *Compensation for the provision of instant interruptibility services in Sardinia and Sicily*, C(2010) 3222 final, para. 68; Falk Schöning and Clemens Ziegler, 'What Is State Aid?', in Leigh Hancher,

concluded that the advantages acquired by the contracted undertaking could equally have been acquired, under normal market conditions, from other market participants.[47] The Commission used similar arguments in the Greek case. It argued that because there was a genuine need for the interruptible load and the services were procured at least cost to the system, the Greek measure did not involve an undue economic advantage and did not, consequently, constitute State aid.[48] The distinction between the State purchasing goods and services as a rational market operator on the one hand and the State as the provider of aid on the other has been discussed in case-law. The Court has held as follows:

> a tariff charged to a category of undertakings for a source of energy at a lower level than that which would normally have been applied may be regarded as State aid if that tariff, adopted by a body subject to the control and direction of public authorities, is attributable to the Member State concerned and that State, unlike an ordinary economic operator, uses its powers to confer a pecuniary advantage on energy consumers by foregoing the profit which it could normally realise.[49]

It is clear that the concept of aid under Article 107(1) TFEU is intended to have a broad meaning. This is further demonstrated by the expression 'any form whatsoever'. However, as pointed out by the ECJ, the prohibition of State aid is neither absolute nor unconditional.[50] Article 107(1) TFEU establishes four cumulative criteria, all of which must be fulfilled in order for the EU State aid regime to apply.[51] First, the intervention has to be organised by the State or through State resources. Second, it must confer a selective advantage on the beneficiary. Third, it has to affect trade between Member States. Fourth, it should distort or threaten to distort competition in order to constitute prohibited State aid within the meaning of Article 107(1) TFEU. These criteria are analysed below from the capacity remuneration perspective.

[B]   State Resources and Aid Attributable to the State

As noted above, capacity mechanisms are highly likely to constitute an economic advantage within the meaning of Article 107(1) TFEU. Whether such an advantage is granted by the State or through State resources is less obvious.

Adrien de Hauteclocque and Francesco Maria Salerno (eds), *State Aid and the Energy Sector* (Hart Publishing, 2018), pp. 3-29, at 10-14.

47. NN24/2010 *Compensation for the provision of instant interruptibility services in Sardinia and Sicily,* C(2010) 3222 final, paras 21-25.
48. SA.38711 *Interruptibility service for the electric system in Greece,* C(2014) 7374 final, paras 76 and 86.
49. C-143/99 *Adria-Wien* [2001] ECR I-8365, para. 39; joined cases 67/85, 68/85 and 70/85 *Van der Kooy and Others v Commission* [1988] ECR 219, para. 28.
50. C-143/99 *Adria-Wien* [2001] ECR I-8365, para. 30.
51. C-280/00 *Altmark* [2003] ECR I-7747, para. 74; C-399/08 *P Commission v Deutsche Post* [2010] ECR I-7831, para. 39; C-142/87 *Belgium v Commission* [1990] ECR I-959, para. 25; joined cases C-278/92 to C-280/92 *Spain v Commission* [1994] ECR I-4103, para. 20; and C-482/99 *France v Commission* [2002] ECR I-4397, para. 68.

It is established case-law that only advantages that are directly or indirectly granted through State resources can constitute State aid.[52] This does not necessarily require a direct transfer of State resources, as a waiver of charges that places some undertakings in a more favourable financial position than others can constitute State aid within the meaning of Article 107(1) TFEU.[53] In addition, the aid must be attributable to the State. This means that a public authority must be involved in the adoption of the aid measure in question.[54] Economic advantages financed through private resources can strengthen the position of an undertaking or a group of undertakings but, nevertheless, do not constitute aid within the meaning of Article 107(1) TFEU.[55] However, the distinction is not entirely clear-cut.

The ECJ has consistently held that aid within the meaning of Article 107(1) TFEU covers all financial means that can be used to confer an economic advantage on undertakings.[56] Therefore, even if the financial means in question are not held by a public authority, they can be regarded as State resources if they remain under public control.[57] Public control over resources may be held to exist if national legislation

---

52. Joined cases C-52/97 to C-54/97 *Viscido and Others* [1998] ECR I-2629, para. 13; C-53/00 *Ferring* [2001] ECR I-9067, para. 16; 82/77 *Openbaar* [1978] ECR 25, paras 24-25; C-189/91 *Kirsammer-Hack* [1993] ECR I-6185, para. 16; C-200/97 *Ecotrade* [1998] ECR I-7907, para. 35; C-295/97 *Piaggio* [1999] ECR I-3735, para. 35; C-379/98 *PreussenElektra* [2001] ECR I-2099, para. 58; C-677/11 *Doux Élevage SNC* [2013], judgment of the Court of 30 May 2013, published in the electronic Reports of Cases, para. 27; C-482/99 *France v Commission* [2002] ECR I-4397, para. 24; C-345/02 *Pearle and Others* [2004] ECR I-7139, para. 35; C-303/88 *Italy v Commission* [1991] ECR I-1433, para. 11; C-126/91 *GEMO* [2003] ECR I-2361, para. 23; Communication from the Commission on the application of the European Union State aid rules to compensation granted for the provision of services of general economic interest, OJ C 8, 11.1.2012, pp. 4-14, para. 31; Rein Wesseling and Marieke Bredenoord-Spoek, 'State Measure', in Philipp Werner and Vincent Verouden (eds), *EU State Aid Control: Law and Economics* (Wolters Kluwer, 2017), pp. 87-118; Kelyn Bacon, *European Union Law of State Aid*, 3rd edition (OUP, 2017), pp. 60-69.
53. C-262/12 *Vent De Colère and Others* [2013], judgment of the Court of 19 December 2013, published in the electronic Reports of Cases, para. 19; C-387/92 *Banco Exterior de España* [1994] ECR I-877, para. 14; C-6/97 *Italy v Commission* [1999] ECR I-2981, para. 16; Conor Quigley, *European State Aid Law and Policy* (Hart Publishing, 2015), pp. 27-52.
54. C-262/12 *Vent De Colère and Others* [2013], judgment of the Court of 19 December 2013, published in the electronic Reports of Cases, para. 17; C-482/99 *France v Commission* [2002] ECR I-4397, para. 52; SA.48648 *Belgian Strategic Reserve*, C(2018) 589 final, para. 91; SA.42011 *Italian capacity mechanism*, C(2018) 617 final, para. 112; SA.46100 *Planned Polish capacity mechanism*, C(2018) 601 final, para. 114; SA.44464 *Irish Capacity Mechanism: reliability option scheme*, C(2017)7789 final, para. 71; Jacques Derenne, 'Article 107 TFEU', in Weijer Ver Loren van Themaat and Berend Reuder (eds), *European Competition Law: A Case Commentary* (Edward Elgar, 2014), pp. 216-255, at 217-222; Falk Schöning and Clemens Ziegler, 'What is State aid?', in Leigh Hancher, Adrien de Hauteclocque and Francesco Maria Salerno (eds), *State Aid and the Energy Sector* (Hart Publishing, 2018), pp. 3-29, at 17-23.
55. Communication from the Commission on the application of the European Union State aid rules to compensation granted for the provision of services of general economic interest, OJ C 8, 11.1.2012, pp. 4-14, para. 31.
56. C-262/12 *Vent De Colère and Others* [2013], judgment of the Court of 19 December 2013, published in the electronic Reports of Cases, para. 21.
57. C-482/99 *France v Commission* [2002] ECR I-4397, para. 37; C-206/06 *Essent Netwerk Noord and Others* [2008] ECR I-5497, para. 70; C-677/11 *Doux Élevage SNC* [2013], judgment of the Court of 30 May 2013, published in the electronic Reports of Cases, para. 35; C-262/12 *Vent De Colère and Others* [2013], judgment of the Court of 19 December 2013, published in the electronic Reports of Cases, paras 21-33; Thomas von Danwitz, 'The Concept of State Aid in Liberalized

obliges a private party to collect compulsory charges, which are managed and reallocated in accordance with national law.[58] In other words, aid provided through State resources includes advantages granted through a private body appointed or established by a State to administer the aid.[59]

This distinction is relevant in relation to capacity remuneration, because most capacity mechanisms are not directly financed by a transfer of State funds.[60] Instead, they often involve a levy or a surcharge on suppliers which ultimately recovers these costs from their customers.[61] However, when the funds are collected through a compulsory charge laid down in legislation and then reallocated to achieve an objective set in this legislation, the requirement for State control is fulfilled.[62]

The Commission addressed this issue in its decision on the UK capacity market, which consists of centralised capacity auctions in which contracted bidders receive remuneration in exchange for delivering energy whenever needed during the delivery year.[63] The capacity market is financed through a surcharge on all suppliers, which is collected by a State-owned body. In this case, it was argued that the notified capacity mechanism was imputable to the State and from State resources because the State retained control over the measure. Furthermore, the capacity market was put in place through national legislation under which the State remained responsible for approving the amount of capacity to be auctioned.[64]

TSOs are often of key significance in relation to capacity remuneration due to the operational role they frequently have, alongside the national regulatory authorities, in the functioning of capacity mechanisms. For example, TSOs may be responsible for dispatching capacity in strategic reserves.[65] They can also have a central role in collecting the charges that finance a capacity mechanism. Because of this, it is necessary to determine whether national law that requires a TSO to collect levies or

---

Sectors', in Marise Cremona (ed.), *Market Integration and Public Services in the European Union* (OUP, 2011), pp. 103-115, at 109-110.

58. C-262/12 *Vent De Colère and Others* [2013], judgment of the Court of 19 December 2013, published in the electronic Reports of Cases, paras 25 and 27.

59. C-262/12 *Vent De Colère and Others* [2013], judgment of the Court of 19 December 2013, published in the electronic Reports of Cases, para. 20; 78/76 *Steinike & Weinlig* [1977] ECR 595, para. 21; C-73/91 *Sloman Neptun* [1993] ECR I-887, para. 19; C-677/11 *Doux Élevage SNC* [2013], judgment of the Court of 30 May 2013, published in the electronic Reports of Cases, para. 26; C-379/98 *PreussenElektra* [2001] ECR I-2099, para. 58.

60. Leigh Hancher, 'Capacity Mechanisms and State Aid Control: A European Solution to the "Missing Money" Problem?', in Leigh Hancher, Adrien de Hauteclocque and Malgorzata Sadowska (eds), *Capacity Mechanisms in the EU Energy Market* (OUP, 2015), pp. 157-181, at 167.

61. *See*, for example, SA.43735 *German ABLAV Interruptibility Scheme*, C(2016) 6765 final, para. 18.

62. C C-262/12 *Vent De Colère and Others* [2013], judgment of the Court of 19 December 2013, published in the electronic Reports of Cases, paras 25 and 27; C-482/99 *France v Commission* [2002] ECR I-4397.

63. SA.35980 *GB capacity mechanism*, C(2014) 5083 final.

64. SA.35980 *GB capacity mechanism*, C(2014) 5083 final, paras 109-111.

65. For instance, the role of the TSO in the German network reserve scheme is explained in Commission Staff Working Document accompanying the document Report from the Commission Final Report of the Sector Inquiry on Capacity Mechanisms, SWD(2016) 385 final, paras 165-166. *See also*, SA.45852 *German capacity reserve*, C(2018) 612 final.

charges from suppliers or customers and allocate a portion of the revenues to support a capacity remuneration scheme constitutes State resources.

Irrespective of whether the TSO is privately or publicly owned, the measure cannot escape qualifying as aid if the State retains control over it.[66] This issue was discussed in a State aid case concerning a tender for new generation capacity in Latvia.[67] The Latvian government argued that the measure did not constitute State aid because the funds were collected from consumers by the TSO and passed on to the beneficiary without ever passing through the State budget. This argument was rejected in the final decision because the TSO was a 100% subsidiary of the State. Even if the TSO had been privately owned, the rules governing the collection and allocation of the charges were established by the State and, therefore, the funds would have constituted State resources.[68] Similar argumentation was used in a State aid case concerning the German Network Reserve.[69] The Commission argued that since the TSOs were mandated to collect and redistribute the funds by law, the financial flows were constantly under the control of the State even if the transactions took place between private parties.[70] Therefore, the German measure was considered imputable to the State.

The established expansive interpretation of State resources and imputation to the State was narrowed in the well-known *PreussenElektra* case.[71] The case concerned German legislation under which private electricity supply undertakings were obliged to purchase electricity produced in their area from renewable energy sources at minimum prices, which were higher than the real economic value of that type of electricity. These undertakings were then required to distribute the financial burden resulting from this purchase obligation between those electricity supply undertakings and upstream private electricity network operators. The matter was referred to the ECJ for a preliminary ruling. The questions referred essentially aimed to ascertain whether the German scheme constituted aid within the meaning of Article 107(1) TFEU. The Commission's broad interpretation of the scope of State aid was rejected in both the Advocate General's opinion and in the judgment itself, and the Court ruled that the measure was not State aid.

The ECJ first took the well-established view that only advantages granted directly or indirectly through State resources are to be considered aid.[72] It clarified that the reference to State resources should not be understood to indicate that all advantages granted by a State, whether financed through State resources or not, constitute aid. Instead, the aim of the definition is to include both advantages that are conferred

---

66. C-482/99 *France v Commission* [2002] ECR I-4397, para. 37; C-83/98 P *France v Ladbroke Racing and Commission* [2000] ECR I-3271, para. 50; Rein Wesseling and Marieke Bredenoord-Spoek, 'State Measure', in Philipp Werner and Vincent Verouden (eds), *EU State Aid Control: Law and Economics* (Wolters Kluwer, 2017), pp. 87-118, at 89-98 and 100-114.
67. N675/2009 *Tender for Aid for New Electricity Generation Capacity (LV)*, C(2010) 4146.
68. N675/2009 *Tender for Aid for New Electricity Generation Capacity (LV)*, C(2010) 4146, para. 18.
69. SA.42955 *German Network Reserve*, C(2016) 8742 final.
70. SA.42955 *German Network Reserve*, C(2016) 8742 final, para. 32. *See also* SA.45852 *German capacity reserve*, C(2018) 612 final.
71. C-379/98 *PreussenElektra* [2001] ECR I-2099.
72. C-379/98 *PreussenElektra* [2001] ECR I-2099, para. 58.

directly by the State and those conferred by a public or private body designated or established by the State to perform a State-governed task.[73] The obligation imposed on private electricity supply undertakings to purchase electricity produced from renewable energy sources at fixed minimum prices did not, under this definition of aid, involve a direct or indirect transfer of State resources to undertakings that produced renewable electricity.[74] Due to this distinction, the allocation of the financial burden set for the electricity supply undertakings could not constitute a transfer of State resources.[75] The obvious economic advantage conferred on the producers of renewable electricity was not in itself enough to constitute State aid.

In subsequent case-law, the ECJ has further clarified the interpretation in *PreussenElektra*. It has stated that the private undertakings had not been appointed by the Member State to manage State resources.[76] Instead, they were bound by a purchasing obligation the costs of which they were expected to cover from their own financial resources.[77] This finding emphasises the importance of State control over the collected funds.

The Court's approach in *PreussenElektra* has been criticised on the grounds that it constituted a narrow and formalistic interpretation of State aid that failed to take into account the effects of a measure that was essentially identical to State aid.[78] In subsequent cases on similar State measures, the ECJ has been reluctant to reinforce the strict approach it took to the concept of State control in that case. In *Essent Netwerk Noord,* the Court reached the opposite conclusion to the one it arrived at in *PreussenElektra*.[79] The facts of this case were that under Dutch law domestic purchasers of electricity were required to pay their net operator a surcharge for electricity. This surcharge was then redistributed to undertakings to recover non-market-compatible costs dating back to before the liberalisation of the electricity market. The ECJ ruled that this surcharge constituted State resources because it was imposed through State legislation. Furthermore, the collectors of the surcharge were publicly owned and had been tasked with the responsibility of managing the collected funds.[80] The measure was declared to be State aid and incompatible with the internal market.

---

73. 82/77 *Openbaar* [1978] ECR 25, paras 24 and 25; C-189/91 *Kirsammer-Hack* [1993] ECR I-6185, para. 16; joined cases C-52/97, C-53/97 and C-54/97 *Viscido* [1998] ECR I-2629, para. 13; C-200/97 *Ecotrade* [1998] ECR I-7907, para. 35; C-295/97 *Piaggio* [1999] ECR I-3735, para. 35; C-379/98 *PreussenElektra* [2001] ECR I-2099, para. 58.
74. C-379/98 *PreussenElektra* [2001] ECR I-2099, para. 59.
75. C-379/98 *PreussenElektra* [2001] ECR I-2099, para. 60.
76. C-206/06 *Essent Netwerk Noord and Others* [2008] ECR I-5497, para. 74.
77. C-262/12 *Vent De Colère and Others* [2013], judgment of the Court of 19 December 2013, published in the electronic Reports of Cases, para. 35.
78. Julio Baquero Cruz and Fernando Castillo de la Torre, 'A Note on PreussenElektra', 26 *European Law Review* (2001), p. 494; and more recently, Kim Talus, *EU Energy Law and Policy: A Critical Account* (OUP, 2013), pp. 142-143.
79. C-206/06 *Essent Netwerk Noord and Others* [2008] ECR I-5497; for an analysis in legal literature, *see* Bent Ole Gram Mortensen, 'The European Court of Justice Decision in Case C-206/06, Essent Netwerk Noord BV', 17(6) *European Energy and Environmental Law Review* (2008), pp. 389-393.
80. C-206/06 *Essent Netwerk Noord and Others* [2008] ECR I-5497, paras 61-75; for an analysis in legal literature, *see* Henrik Bjørnebye, *Investing in EU Energy Security: Exploring the Regulatory Approach to Tomorrow's Electricity Production* (University of Oslo, PhD thesis 2009), p. 331. *See*

The different conclusions reached by the Court in relation to seemingly similar circumstances in the cases of *PreussenElektra* and *Essent Netwerk Noord* demonstrate the fine line involved in determining State control over resources.[81] The essential difference between these cases was that in *PreussenElektra* the undertakings responsible for reallocating their resources had not been appointed by the State to manage that role, whereas in *Essent Netwerk Noord* the task of managing the collected resources was specifically entrusted to a company under State law. Furthermore, the objective of the State measure in *PreussenElektra* was environmental protection, whereas in *Essent Netwerk Noord* it aimed to mitigate stranded costs associated with market liberalisation. In general, cases that involve an environmental justification seem to be interpreted less narrowly by the Court compared to justifications in the interests of security of supply, for example.[82]

The analysis in this section indicates that despite the subtle distinction between *PreussenElektra* and *Essent Netwerk Noord*, it is unlikely that Member States would be able to design a capacity remuneration scheme that would be interpreted as not being imputable to the State or not drawing on State resources. The controversial ruling in *PreussenElektra* seems only to apply to a narrow category of schemes where little or no State intervention has taken place in managing the resources that are allocated. This narrow interpretation of 'State control' is unlikely to impact upon the evaluation of capacity mechanisms, which are characteristically measures to fulfil a State-defined objective of generation adequacy and typically include State involvement in the collection and allocation of resources.

[C] The Requirement of Selectivity

In order for a State measure to amount to State aid, it must have the effect of favouring certain undertakings or the production of certain goods.[83] Both these requirements are

---

also cases T-25/07 *Iride and Iride Energia v Commission* [2009] ECR II-245; and T-47/15 *Germany v Commission* [2016], judgment of the General Court of 10 May 2016 published in the electronic Reports of Cases, paras 81-128.

81. For an analysis, *see* Leigh Hancher, Tom Ottervanger and Piet Jan Slot, *EU State Aids*, 5th edition (Sweet & Maxwell, 2016), p. 824.

82. *See*, for example, C-379/98 *PreussenElektra* [2001] ECR I-2099, paras 68-81, where instead of scrutinising the applicability of the established grounds for justification, the Court simply declared that the contested measure was 'not incompatible' with free movement rules. Similar arguments on the broad interpretative approach taken in respect of environmental justifications are discussed in Henrik Bjørnebye, *Investing in EU Energy Security: Exploring the Regulatory Approach to Tomorrow's Electricity Production* (University of Oslo, PhD thesis 2009), pp. 63, 65 and 92-99; Kim Talus, EU *Energy Law and Policy: A Critical Account* (OUP, 2013), pp. 167-174.

83. Andreas Bartosch, 'The Concept of Selectivity?', in Erika Szyszczak (ed.), *Research Handbook on European State Aid Law* (Edward Elgar, 2011), pp. 176-192; Michael Honoré, 'Selectivity', in Philipp Werner and Vincent Verouden (eds), *EU State Aid Control: Law and Economics* (Wolters Kluwer, 2017), pp. 119-168; Conor Quigley, *European State Aid Law and Policy* (Hart Publishing, 2015), pp. 63-75; Roberto Cisotta, 'Criterion of Selectivity', in Herwig Hofmann and Claire Micheau (eds), *State Aid Law of the European Union* (OUP, 2016), pp. 129-150; José Luís Da Cruz Vilaça, *EU Law and Integration: Twenty Years of Judicial Application of EU Law* (Hart Publishing, 2014), pp. 237-250; Jacques Derenne, 'Article 107 TFEU', in Weijer Ver Loren van

often easily fulfilled in the case of capacity remuneration, because electricity generation capacity, as a good, is financially supported over other goods.[84] Furthermore, the
payment of capacity remuneration does not merely amount to support for one sector of
the economy, but is typically also made on a selective basis within the electricity sector
and as between different production technologies. As a result, the making of such
payments tends to favour certain undertakings or groups of undertakings over others.[85]

Determining the selectivity of a State measure can prove challenging because law
generally treats undertakings and sectors differently.[86] The ECJ has addressed this in its
case-law concerning the energy sector. In *Adria-Wien*, the Court determined that a
national measure that provided for a rebate on taxes on natural gas and electricity did
not constitute State aid if it applied to all undertakings in the national territory.[87]
Furthermore, it is settled case-law that a measure that is justified by the nature or
general scheme of the system of which it is part does not fulfil the condition of
selectivity even if it confers an advantage on its recipient.[88]

The requirement for selectivity was further analysed in *Netherlands v Commission*, a case which concerned a Dutch emissions trading scheme.[89] Dutch law established a national emissions target for large industrial facilities, which, the Commission
claimed, benefited from an economic advantage because such facilities received
tradable emissions allowances under the national legislation.[90] The General Court,
however, rejected the Commission's argument and annulled the Commission's decision due to lack of selectivity within the contested measure. The General Court noted
that selectivity between undertakings should entail a comparison between undertakings which are in a legal and factual situation that is comparable in the light of the
objective pursued by the measure in question.[91] The General Court held that the

---

Themaat and Berend Reuder (eds), *European Competition Law: A Case Commentary* (Edward
Elgar, 2014), pp. 216-255, at 227-231; Kelyn Bacon, *European Union Law of State Aid*, 3rd
edition (OUP, 2017), pp. 69-83.

84. It is settled case-law that electricity constitutes a good under EU law. *See* 6/64 *Costa v ENEL*
[1964] ECR 585; C-393/92 *Almelo* [1994] ECR I-1477, para. 28.
85. *See*, for example, SA.39621 *French country-wide capacity mechanism*, C(2016) 7086 final, para.
57; SA.42011 *Italian capacity mechanism*, C(2018) 617 final, para. 119; SA.46100 *Planned Polish
capacity mechanism*, C(2018) 601 final, paras 120-123; SA.44464 *Irish Capacity Mechanism:
reliability option scheme*, C(2017)7789 final, para. 79.
86. Bartlomiej Kurcz and Dimitri Vallindas, 'Can General Measures Be ... Selective? Some Thoughts
on the Interpretation of a State Aid Definition', 45(1) *Common Market Law Review* (2008), pp.
159-182; Kelyn Bacon, *European Union Law of State Aid*, 3rd edition (OUP, 2017), p. 70.
87. C-143/99 *Adria-Wien* [2001] ECR I-8365, paras 35-36. In legal literature, *see* Michael Honore,
'Selectivity', in Philipp Werner and Vincent Verouden (eds), *EU State Aid Control: Law and
Economics* (Wolters Kluwer, 2017), pp. 119-168, at 127-128.
88. C-143/99 *Adria-Wien* [2001] ECR I-8365, para. 42; 173/73 *Italy v Commission* [1974] ECR 709,
para. 33; C-75/97 *Belgium v Commission* [1999] ECR I-3671, para. 33. By comparison, the
advantage was considered selective in the following cases: C-203/82 *Commission v Italy* [1983]
ECR 2525; C-241/94 *France v Commission* [1996] ECR I-4551; C-75/97 *Belgium v Commission*
[1999] ECR I-3671; C-148/04 *Unicredito Italiano* [2005] ECR I-11137; and joined cases C-393/04
and C-41/05 *Air Liquide Industries Belgium* [2006] ECR I-5293.
89. T-233/04 *Netherlands v Commission* [2008] ECR II-591.
90. N35/2003 *NOx emission trading scheme*, C(2003) 1761 final, p. 9.
91. C-75/97 *Belgium v Commission* [1999] ECR I-3671, paras 28-31; C-143/99 *Adria-Wien* [2001]
ECR I-8365, para. 41; T-233/04 *Netherlands v Commission* [2008] ECR II-591, para. 86.

comparison could not be made between undertakings to which the emissions ceiling applied and undertakings to which that ceiling did not apply.[92] The measure in question was applicable in multiple sectors to all industrial facilities with an installed capacity of more than 20 MWth.[93] The fact that there were only around 250 undertakings that were this large was not regarded as being in itself a sufficient ground on which to consider the measure selective.[94] This interpretation would not, however, be directly applicable to capacity mechanisms by analogy, because capacity remuneration does not apply multi-sectorally to all industrial undertakings but is paid to electricity undertakings alone. The criterion for selectivity under Article 107(1) TFEU is, thus, generally fulfilled in the case of capacity remuneration.[95] It is highly unlikely that an argument to the effect that a capacity mechanism is not selective would ever be accepted in a State aid evaluation by the Commission.

[D] **Distortive Impact on Competition and Effect on Trade**

In order to constitute State aid within the meaning of Article 107(1) TFEU, the measure must distort or threaten to distort competition.[96] The wording of the provision indicates that the threshold for distortive effects on competition is tremendously low – a mere threat is enough to trigger the applicability of the criterion.

The ECJ has confirmed this interpretation in its case-law, ruling that competition is distorted when aid granted by a State strengthens the competitive position of a beneficiary as compared with its competitors.[97] It has even been suggested that, as a general rule, all State aid distorts or threatens to distort competition.[98] Furthermore, the ECJ has held that it is not necessary to conduct a full analysis of market conditions in order to determine that a threat to competition exists.[99] If such a market assessment is nevertheless conducted, it can define the relevant market very broadly to extend the competitive effects of the measure in question.[100]

---

92. T-233/04 *Netherlands v Commission* [2008] ECR II-591, para. 90.
93. T-233/04 *Netherlands v Commission* [2008] ECR II-591, para. 87.
94. T-233/04 *Netherlands v Commission* [2008] ECR II-591, para. 95.
95. *See* the broad interpretation in T-55/99 *CETM* [2000] ECR II-3207, para. 40. *See also* Bartlomiej Kurcz and Dimitri Vallindas, 'Can General Measures Be ... Selective? Some Thoughts on the Interpretation of a State Aid Definition', 45(1) *Common Market Law Review* (2008), pp. 159-182, at 165-170.
96. Jacques Derenne and Vincent Verouden, 'Distortion of Competition and Effect on Trade', in Philipp Werner and Vincent Verouden (eds), *EU State Aid Control: Law and Economics* (Wolters Kluwer, 2017), pp. 169-189; Erika Szyszczak, 'Distortion of Competition and Effect on Trade between EU Member States', in Herwig Hofmann and Claire Micheau (eds), *State Aid Law of the European Union* (OUP, 2016), pp. 151-160.
97. 730/79 *Phillip Morris Holland v Commission* [1980] ECR 2671, para. 11; 295/85 *France v Commission* [1987] ECR 4393, para. 24; T-303/05 *AceaElectrabel v Commission* [2009] ECR II-137.
98. Opinion of AG Capotorti in 730/79 *Phillip Morris Holland v Commission* [1980] ECR 2671, p. 2698; Opinion of AG Léger in C-280/00 *Altmark* [2003] ECR I-7747, para. 103.
99. 730/79 *Philip Morris* [1980] ECR 2671, paras 9-12. Such a cursory evaluation can be found, for example, in SA.42011 *Italian capacity mechanism*, C(2018) 617 final, paras 121-122.
100. T-27/02 *Kronofrance v Commission* [2004] ECR II-4177, para. 42.

Finally, Article 107(1) TFEU requires that the measure in question must have an effect on trade in order to constitute State aid.[101] In a way similar to that in which the distortive effects on competition are evaluated, a very low threshold is applied in respect of this requirement. The Commission is not obliged to prove that the aid measure has a real effect on trade but rather that the aid is liable to affect trade.[102] This interpretation by the ECJ implies that the requirement in respect of trade effects is ultimately the same threat-based test as is used in respect of distortion of competition.

The low threshold for proving a potential effect on trade is further demonstrated by the way in which the Court has interpreted the extent of trade in the context of Article 107(1) TFEU. It is not necessary for the beneficiary of the aid to participate in cross-border activities in order for the measure to be deemed to have an effect on trade.[103] In other words, remuneration for solely local or regional activities may constitute State aid even if there is no trade between Member States in the sector in question.[104] Aid is liable to affect trade if the prospect of such trade is merely foreseeable.[105] The evaluation of trade effects is further broadened if the sector in question, electricity for example, is subject to harmonising legislation.[106] Public remuneration in the electricity sector, which operates as part of the internal market, is therefore always liable in principle to have an effect on trade.[107]

Traditionally, there has been no minimum monetary threshold for aid to be considered not to have an effect on trade or competition.[108] It is settled case-law that the possibility of trade being affected cannot be excluded on the basis that only a relatively small amount of aid is involved or on the basis that the undertaking receiving aid is relatively small in size.[109] It has been argued, however, that for practical reasons trade effects should be interpreted in a broader manner in this regard.[110] The legal framework has since been changed by the entry into force of Commission Regulation (EU) No 1407/2013[111] (hereinafter the 'de minimis Regulation'), which lays down de

---

101. Kelyn Bacon, *European Union Law of State Aid*, 3rd edition (OUP, 2017), pp. 83-89.
102. C-372/97 *Italy v Commission* [2004] ECR I-3679, para. 44; C-66/02 *Italy v Commission* [2005] ECR I-10901, paras 111 and 114.
103. C-66/02 *Italy v Commission* [2005] ECR I-10901, para. 117; Communication from the Commission on the application of the European Union State aid rules to compensation granted for the provision of services of general economic interest, OJ C 8, 11.1.2012, pp. 4-14, para. 38.
104. C-280/00 *Altmark* [2003] ECR I-7747, para. 82.
105. Joined cases T-447/93, T-448/93 and T-449/93 *AITEC and Others v Commission* [1995] ECR II-1971, paras 139-141; Jacques Derenne, 'Article 107 TFEU', in Weijer Ver Loren van Themaat and Berend Reuder (eds), *European Competition Law: A Case Commentary* (Edward Elgar, 2014), pp. 216-255, at 231-235.
106. C-66/02 *Italy v Commission* [2005] ECR I-10901, para. 119.
107. Similar arguments can be found in SA.46100 *Planned Polish capacity mechanism*, C(2018) 601 final, paras 124-125.
108. Conor Quigley, *European State Aid Law and Policy* (Hart Publishing, 2015), pp. 77-90.
109. C-142/87 *Belgium v Commission* [1990] ECR I-959, para. 43; C-280/00 *Altmark* [2003] ECR I-7747, para. 8; Jacques Derenne and Vincent Verouden, 'Distortion of Competition and Effect on Trade', in Philipp Werner and Vincent Verouden (eds), *EU State Aid Control: Law and Economics* (Wolters Kluwer, 2017), pp. 169-189.
110. Commission Communication, A Quality Framework for Services of General Interest in Europe, COM(2011) 900 final, p. 6.
111. Commission Regulation (EU) No 1407/2013 of 18 December 2013 on the application of Articles 107 and 108 of the Treaty on the Functioning of the European Union to de minimis aid (OJ L

minimis rules on aid comprising minimum thresholds under which aid is considered compatible with the internal market. However, since the aid limit per undertaking is set relatively low compared with the typical costs of capacity mechanisms, these rules are unlikely to apply to capacity remuneration. Nevertheless, aid schemes that grant a maximum of EUR 200,000 per undertaking per Member State within a period of three years have been held not to have any effect on trade between Member States and not to distort or threaten to distort competition.[112] In addition, the legal regime for EU State aid includes Commission Regulation (EU) No 651/2014[113] (hereinafter the 'Block Exemption Regulation'), under which certain categories of aid are declared to be compatible with the internal market. These categories, however, do not include remuneration for generation adequacy.

[E]   The Significance of Article 107(1) TFEU for Capacity Remuneration

If all the criteria laid down in Article 107(1) TFEU are fulfilled, the measure in question constitutes State aid and is, in principle, incompatible with the internal market. However, this does not mean that it is absolutely and unconditionally prohibited under the EU State aid regime.[114] The measure in question may qualify for one of the exemptions from the extensive selection set out in Article 107(2) to (3) TFEU and the State aid guidelines for energy and the environment or the *de minimis* Regulation and the Block Exemption Regulation. The measure can also be declared not to amount to aid on the basis of Article 106(2) TFEU or on the basis of settled case-law pursuant to which assistance that appears prima facie to constitute State aid may instead be classified as legitimate compensation for SGEI.[115] These exemptions and their relevance to capacity remuneration are extensively analysed in the sections that follow. However, regardless of whether a given State measure is capable of falling within the scope of application of one or more of these exemptions, fulfilling all the criteria established in Article 107(1) TFEU triggers the State aid procedure established in Article 108 TFEU. Although extensive analysis of the procedural aspects of EU State aid is beyond the scope of this book, a brief discussion of Member States' procedural obligations is necessary to establish the full extent of the effects of Article 107(1) TFEU.

352, 24.12.2013, pp. 1-8); and Commission Regulation (EU) No 360/2012 of 25 April 2012 on the application of Articles 107 and 108 of the Treaty on the Functioning of the European Union to de minimis aid granted to undertakings providing services of general economic interest (OJ L 114, 26.4.2012, pp. 8-13), which applies to services in the general economic interest. *See also* Erika Szyszczak, 'Modernising State Aid and the Financing of SGEI', 3(4) *Journal of European Competition Law & Practice* (2012), pp. 332-343.

112. Recital 3 of Commission Regulation (EU) No 1407/2013 of 18 December 2013 on the application of Articles 107 and 108 of the Treaty on the Functioning of the European Union to de minimis aid (OJ L 352, 24.12.2013, pp. 1-8).

113. Commission Regulation (EU) No 651/2014 of 17 June 2014 declaring certain categories of aid compatible with the internal market in application of Articles 107 and 108 of the Treaty (OJ L 187, 26.6.2014, pp. 1-78).

114. C-143/99 *Adria-Wien* [2001] ECR I-8365, para. 30.

115. Communication from the Commission, Guidelines on State aid for environmental protection and energy 2014-2020 (OJ C 200, 28.6.2014, pp. 1-55).

Overall, the Commission is under a general obligation to keep all aid systems operating in the Member States under constant review.[116] It can propose any appropriate measures in respect of Member States' aid schemes that are required by progressive development or the functioning of the internal market.[117] Member States are under an obligation to notify the Commission of any plans to grant State aid.[118] Based on this notification, the Commission is then obliged to initiate the procedure established in Article 108(2) TFEU if it considers that the notified measure is not compatible with the internal market pursuant to Article 107(1) TFEU. In accordance with Article 108(2) TFEU, the Commission investigates the nature of the proposed measure. If it finds that the aid in question is not compatible with the internal market or that aid is being misused, it will decide on the abolition or the alteration of the aid.[119] The Member State is not allowed to put the proposed measure into effect before this procedure has resulted in a final decision.[120]

In other words, the primary significance of whether a State measure is considered State aid is first and foremost procedural. Fulfilling the criteria under Article 107(1) TFEU triggers the procedural provisions set out in Article 108 TFEU and gives the Commission extensive competence to review a Member State's measure and determine whether or not the various exemptions can apply.[121] This procedural trigger means that national measures on supporting generation adequacy and security of supply can be reviewed by the EU institutions. It could even be argued that the prohibition of aid in Article 107(1) TFEU is not a de facto prohibition but a low threshold by which national measures are brought to the attention of the Commission and, by extension, the EU courts. This argument is supported by the existence of a broad variety of capacity mechanisms, which have not been declared incompatible with the internal market although they almost always constitute State aid. This demonstrates that the general prohibition of State aid is conditional upon the requirements established in various bases for exemption. These exemptions and their conditions are discussed in sections §4.03 and §4.04 below.

---

116. Article 108(1) TFEU; Peter Vesterdorf and Stephen Harris, *State Aid Law of the European Union* (Sweet & Maxwell, 2008), pp. 43-86; Kelyn Bacon, *European Union Law of State Aid*, 3rd edition (OUP, 2017), pp. 439-495; Leigh Hancher, 'The Administrative Procedure – The Privileged Dialogue', in Herwig Hofmann and Claire Micheau (eds), *State Aid Law of the European Union* (OUP, 2016), pp. 341-347; Leigh Hancher, Fracesco Salerno and Michael Scütte, 'The Different Stages in the State Aid Procedure', in Herwig Hofmann and Claire Micheau (eds), *State Aid Law of the European Union* (OUP, 2016), pp. 341-347; Paul Craig and Gráinne de Búrca, *EU Law: Text, Cases, and Materials*, 6th edition (OUP, 2015), pp. 1145-1152.
117. Article 108(1) TFEU.
118. Article 108(3) TFEU.
119. Kelyn Bacon, *European Union Law of State Aid*, 3rd edition (OUP, 2017), pp. 460-471.
120. Article 108(3) TFEU; Kelyn Bacon, *European Union Law of State Aid*, 3rd edition (OUP, 2017), pp. 453-454.
121. Opinion of AG Léger in C-280/00 *Altmark* [2003] ECR I-7747, para. 92; Opinion of AG Jacobs in C-379/98 *PreussenElektra* [2001] ECR I-2099, paras 110-111.

§4.03 COMPENSATION FOR PSOs

[A] The Interplay Between Electricity Market Legislation and EU State Aid Law

The legal grounds on which generation adequacy can constitute a public service under EU electricity legislation are analysed above in Chapter 3. As identified in that analysis, imposing PSOs on undertakings requires, *inter alia*, that the market would not perform the service without State intervention.[122] In simple terms, in those circumstances the market does not enable an undertaking to recover the costs associated with providing that service and to make a reasonable profit. In practice, this means that imposing PSOs involves paying compensation to cover the expenses caused by an obligation to perform otherwise unprofitable services. This type of compensation is the focus of this section.

As a general rule, compensation for public services does not constitute a ground for granting exemption from State aid rules. The connection between PSOs and Treaty rules is included in the wording of Article 3(2) of the Electricity Directive. It states that Member States may impose PSOs on undertakings operating in the electricity sector *having full regard to the relevant provisions of the Treaty* and Article 106 TFEU in particular. A direct reference to State aid is made in Recital 49 of the Electricity Directive, which highlights the procedural obligation to notify aid to the Commission insofar as it constitutes aid within the meaning of Article 107 TFEU. Similar references to the applicability of Treaty law are included in the Security of Supply Directive.[123]

Public services and compensation for an obligation to perform such services are directly addressed in the Electricity Directive, which states that financial compensation, other forms of compensation and exclusive rights granted by the Member State to fulfil PSOs should be non-discriminatory and transparent.[124] If generation capacity or other forms of ensuring generation adequacy are procured through a tender or an equivalent procedure, Article 8(3) of the Electricity Directive requires that in order to ensure transparency and non-discrimination, the pre-published tender specifications must also include an exhaustive list of incentives, such as subsidies, which are covered by the tender.[125]

This close connectivity between secondary internal electricity market provisions and the State aid provisions of the Treaty demonstrates that these two groups of provisions are intended to complement each other and be interpreted together.[126] If a

---

122. Wolf Sauter, *Public Services in EU Law* (Cambridge University Press, 2015), pp. 153-154; Ramona Ianus and Massimo Francesco Orzan, 'Aid Subject to Discretionary Assessment under Article 107(3) TFEU', in Herwig Hofmann and Claire Micheau (eds), *State Aid Law of the European Union* (OUP, 2016), pp. 240-307, at 292-293.
123. Recital 12 and Article 5(2) of the Security of Supply Directive.
124. Article 3(6) of the Electricity Directive.
125. For further discussion of the interpretation of Article 8, *see* Chapter 3 above.
126. This close connection between sector-specific electricity market legislation and the EU State aid regime is likely to continue, as the applicability of State aid rules to capacity mechanisms is explicitly confirmed in the proposal for a Recast Electricity Regulation. *See* Article 23 of the Recast Electricity Regulation.

Member State imposes PSOs to ensure sufficient generation capacity, it has to ensure that such obligations and the compensation paid in respect of them fulfil the criteria laid down in not only the Electricity Directive but also in the Treaty. The case-by-case treatment of capacity remuneration under the EU State aid rules will then depend upon the nature and characteristics of the capacity mechanism in question. Depending on these characteristics, capacity remuneration can be declared compatible with the internal market on different grounds. These grounds are next discussed.

First, Commission Regulation (EU) No 360/2012 sets a *de minimis* limit for aid granted to undertakings providing an SGEI.[127] Aid granted to undertakings for providing an SGEI is not considered State aid within the meaning of Article 107(1) TFEU if it does not exceed EUR 500,000 over any period of three fiscal years.[128] The level of aid associated with capacity mechanisms, however, is typically much greater than the threshold set in this Regulation. For example, the Finnish strategic reserve for only 299 MW cost EUR 13.4 million in the period from 2015 to 2017.[129] The aid was shared between three power facilities.[130] Due to the unlikelihood of capacity remuneration falling under the *de minimis* threshold laid down in Regulation (EU) No 360/2012, analysis of the Regulation is outside the scope of this book.

Second, a Member State can procure services relating to generation adequacy without them constituting State aid. This requires that the procured service fulfils the criteria established in *Altmark*, which is a landmark case in the area of State aid and PSOs.[131] Third, remuneration for a capacity mechanism can fall within the application of Article 106(2) TFEU in the event that the *Altmark* criteria are not met.[132] These elements of EU State aid rules are next analysed from the perspective of capacity mechanisms.

---

127. Commission Regulation (EU) No 360/2012 of 25 April 2012 on the application of Articles 107 and 108 of the Treaty on the Functioning of the European Union to de minimis aid granted to undertakings providing services of general economic interest (OJ L 114, 26.4.2012, pp. 8-13).
128. Article 2 of Commission Regulation (EU) No 360/2012 of 25 April 2012 on the application of Articles 107 and 108 of the Treaty on the Functioning of the European Union to de minimis aid granted to undertakings providing services of general economic interest (OJ L 114, 26.4.2012, pp. 8-13).
129. Energy Authority, Decision no 389/451/2015 on the procurement of a strategic reserve (Energiaviraston päätös, Tehoreservikapasiteetin hankinta, 389/451/2015), 23 April 2015.
130. *Ibid.*
131. C-280/00 *Altmark* [2003] ECR I-7747.
132. *See* Recital 5 of Commission Decision 2012/21/EU of 20 December 2011 on the application of Article 106(2) of the Treaty on the Functioning of the European Union to State aid in the form of public service compensation granted to certain undertakings entrusted with the operation of services of general economic interest (notified under document C(2011) 9380) (OJ L 7, 11.1.2012, pp. 3-10).

[B]   Escaping State Aid Status

[1]   The Altmark Criteria

PSOs are requirements imposed on undertakings in the general economic interest to ensure the performance of a service that the market would not otherwise deliver.[133] Consequently, compensation for these services is not intended as an economic advantage but as remuneration for services performed. Therefore, EU State aid rules for SGEI do not aim to prevent such remuneration but to ensure that the remuneration for public services reflects the input needed on the part of an undertaking to perform its PSOs. In other words, the role of EU State aid control is to ensure that remuneration for a PSO does not amount to covert distribution of excessive State resources.[134]

The 2003 Altmark case is a landmark ruling on the distinction between State aid and remuneration for public services.[135] Compensation for PSOs had been previously discussed in case-law but there were no well-established criteria pursuant to which remuneration for PSOs could avoid having State aid status.[136] The decision in Altmark established four cumulative criteria based on which compensation for a public service does not constitute State aid.[137]

First, the recipient undertaking must actually be required to discharge PSOs.[138] These obligations must be clearly defined.[139] In practice, this criterion requires that an undertaking entrusted with the operation of an SGEI cannot have a mere general obligation the realisation of which would be theoretical rather than practical.[140]

---

133. On the prerequisite of market failure, see Wolf Sauter, Public Services in EU Law (Cambridge University Press, 2015), pp. 153-155.
134. C-280/00 Altmark [2003] ECR I-7747, para. 87; Leigh Hancher, Tom Ottervanger and Piet Jan Slot, EU State Aids, 5th edition (Sweet & Maxwell. 2016), pp. 259-261; Aindrias Ó Caoimh and Wolf Sauter, 'Criterion of Advantage', in Herwig Hofmann and Claire Micheau (eds), State Aid Law of the European Union (OUP, 2016), pp. 84-128, at 84-100.
135. C-280/00 Altmark [2003] ECR I-7747; Juan Jorge Piernas López, The Concept of State Aid Under EU Law: From Internal Market to Competition and Beyond (OUP, 2015), pp. 87-90; Wolf Sauter, Public Services in EU Law (Cambridge University Press, 2015), pp. 140-142; Heike Schweitzer, 'Services of General Economic Interest: European Law's Impact on the Role of Markets and of Member States', in Marise Cremona (ed.), Market Integration and Public Services in the European Union (OUP, 2011), pp. 11-62, at 27-31; Leigh Hancher and Pierre Larouche, 'The Coming of Age of EU Regulation of Network Industries and Services of General Economic Interest', in Paul Craig and Gráinne de Búrca, The Evolution of EU Law (OUP, 2011), pp. 743-781, at 759-766; Natalia Fiedziuk, 'Towards a More Refined Economic Approach to Services of General Economic Interest', 16(2) European Public Law (2010), pp. 271-288.
136. For earlier case-law, see 240/83 ADBHU [1985] ECR 531; T-46/97 SIC v Commission [2000] ECR II-2125; T-106/95 FFSA and Others v Commission [1997] ECR II-229 and, finally, C-53/00 Ferring [2001] ECR I-9067, which identified some of the key features involved in the provision of compensation for public services.
137. For further analysis in legal literature, see Erika Szyszczak, The Regulation of the State in Competitive Markets in the EU (Hart Publishing, 2007), pp. 228-235; Giuseppe Conte and James Kavanagh, 'Advantage', in Philipp Werner and Vincent Verouden (eds), EU State Aid Control: Law and Economics (Wolters Kluwer, 2017), pp. 66-86, at 69-70.
138. C-280/00 Altmark [2003] ECR I-7747, para. 89.
139. Ibid.
140. C-451/03 Servizi Ausiliari Dottori Commercialisti [2006] ECR I-2941, para. 62 and C-206/06 Essent Netwerk Noord and Others [2008] ECR I-5497, para. 82.

As noted in Chapter 3 above, Member States still have a wide margin of discretion in determining what they regard as SGEIs in the electricity sector. However, in order to fulfil the first *Altmark* criterion the obligation to discharge the service in question must be explicitly conferred upon one or more undertakings. The task must be assigned by the State through legislation or by contractual means.[141] The Commission's approach requires such legislation or contracts to specify, *inter alia*, the content and duration of the obligations, the applicable territory and the parameters for calculating, controlling and potentially recovering compensation for the services.[142] An undertaking cannot, therefore, fulfil this criterion by, for example, being generally responsible for ensuring generation adequacy in a Member State.

The second *Altmark* criterion requires that the parameters on the basis of which the compensation is calculated must be established in advance in an objective and transparent manner. The objective of this criterion is to avoid the conferral of an economic advantage that would favour the recipient undertaking over competing undertakings.[143] This criterion does not mean that the compensation must be calculated on the basis of a specific formula but rather that the methodology for determining the level of compensation be generally made available.[144] This requirement applies not only to the compensation but also to the reasonable profit allowed in addition to the compensation itself.[145]

The third *Altmark* criterion requires that the compensation cannot exceed that necessary to cover all or part of the costs incurred in the discharge of the PSOs.[146] The calculation of necessary costs should take into account not only the cost of performing the services in question but also reasonable profit for the activity.[147] The objective of this criterion is to ensure that the recipient undertaking is not given any advantage that

---

141. Communication from the Commission on the application of the European Union State aid rules to compensation granted for the provision of services of general economic interest, OJ C 8, 11.1.2012, pp. 4-14, paras 51-52.
142. Communication from the Commission on the application of the European Union State aid rules to compensation granted for the provision of services of general economic interest, OJ C 8, 11.1.2012, pp. 4-14, para. 52.
143. C-280/00 *Altmark* [2003] ECR I-7747, para. 90; Erika Szyszczak, 'Modernising State Aid and the Financing of SGEI', 3(4) *Journal of European Competition Law & Practice* (2012), pp. 332-343, at 338-339.
144. Communication from the Commission on the application of the European Union State aid rules to compensation granted for the provision of services of general economic interest, OJ C 8, 11.1.2012, pp. 4-14, paras 54-55.
145. Communication from the Commission on the application of the European Union State aid rules to compensation granted for the provision of services of general economic interest, OJ C 8, 11.1.2012, pp. 4-14, para. 57.
146. C-280/00 *Altmark* [2003] ECR I-7747, para. 92.
147. C-280/00 *Altmark* [2003] ECR I-7747, para. 92; Wolf Sauter, 'Case T–289/03, British United Provident Association Ltd (BUPA), BUPA Insurance Ltd, BUPA Ireland Ltd v. Commission of the European Communities, Judgement of the Court of First Instance of 12 February 2008, nyr', 46(1) *Common Market Law Review* (2009), pp. 269-286, at 278-279.

distorts or threatens to distort competition by strengthening that undertaking's competitive position.[148] The wording of this criterion clearly indicates that it is intended as a condition for controlling the proportionality of the remuneration.[149]

What constitutes an acceptable amount of remuneration can be calculated by reference either to expected costs and revenues or to actual costs and revenues.[150] The methodology can also contain efficiency incentives. The Commission's interpretative stance is that the calculation of reasonable profit should be based on rate-of-return on capital.[151] The rate should be determined by comparison to that involved in discharging similar services in competitive conditions or by analogy to comparable undertakings in other Member States or even other comparable sectors.[152] The calculations for reasonable profit should take into account the level of risk associated with performing the services in question.[153] The risk is dependent upon the sector concerned.

The fourth and last *Altmark* criterion concerns the procedure for acquiring the public services. The preferred method for selecting a service provider is a public procurement procedure, which allows for the selection of the tenderer capable of providing those services at the least cost.[154] If, however, the service provider is not selected pursuant to a tender, the level of compensation paid must be determined on the basis of an analysis that evaluates the expected costs involved in discharging the services in question. This evaluation should reflect the expenses and revenues of a typical, well-run undertaking with adequate resources to meet the obligations, while allowing for a reasonable level of profit for discharging the obligations.[155] There is no established definition of a well-run undertaking. Overall, the Commission requires Member States to apply objective criteria that represent satisfactory management of the

---

148. C-280/00 *Altmark* [2003] ECR I-7747, para. 92.
149. C-451/03 *Servizi Ausiliari Dottori Commercialisti* [2006] ECR I-2941, para. 66; C-206/06 *Essent Netwerk Noord and Others* [2008] ECR I-5497, para. 84; Natalia Fiedziuk, 'Putting Services of General Economic Interest up for Tender: Reflections on Applicable EU Rules', 50(1) *Common Market Law Review* (2013), pp. 87-114.
150. Communication from the Commission, European Union framework for State aid in the form of public service compensation (2011), OJ C 8, 11.1.2012, pp. 15-22, paras 22-50.
151. Communication from the Commission on the application of the European Union State aid rules to compensation granted for the provision of services of general economic interest, OJ C 8, 11.1.2012, pp. 4-14, paras 33-36 and 61.
152. Communication from the Commission on the application of the European Union State aid rules to compensation granted for the provision of services of general economic interest, OJ C 8, 11.1.2012, pp. 4-14, para. 61.
153. *Ibid.*
154. Christopher Bovis, 'Public Procurement and State aid', Herwig Hofmann and Claire Micheau (eds), *State Aid Law of the European Union* (OUP, 2016), pp. 161-186; Heike Schweitzer, 'Services of General Economic Interest: European Law's Impact on the Role of Markets and of Member States', in Marise Cremona (ed.), *Market Integration and Public Services in the European Union* (OUP, 2011), pp. 11-62, at 29-30; Natalia Fiedziuk, 'Putting Services of General Economic Interest up for Tender: Reflections on Applicable EU Rules', 50(1) *Common Market Law Review* (2013), pp. 87-114; Philipp Kiiver, *The Practice of Public Procurement: Tendering, Selection and Award* (Intersentia, 2014).
155. C-280/00 *Altmark* [2003] ECR I-7747, para. 93; Erika Szyszczak, 'Modernising State Aid and the Financing of SGEI', 3(4) *Journal of European Competition Law & Practice* (2012), pp. 332-343, at 340.

undertaking in question when evaluating this criterion.[156] Compliance with national and EU legislation is a typical criterion for fulfilling the requirement of satisfactory management but assessments of the undertaking's productivity and quality of service can also be included.[157]

The last *Altmark* criterion can be relevant in situations where a competitive tender procedure is not an efficient option due to the absence of competition, for example. For example, this was the argument the UK government put forward to justify non-selection of the beneficiary of the support scheme for a new nuclear facility pursuant to a competitive tender or an equivalent procedure.[158]

If all four of the cumulative criteria specified in the *Altmark* case are fulfilled, the State resource granted does not fall within Article 107(1) TFEU and, therefore, does not have to be notified to the Commission in accordance with Article 108 TFEU.[159] It follows from this conclusion that a measure that does not comply with one or more of these criteria constitutes State aid within the meaning of Article 107(1) TFEU.

[2]   Applying the Altmark Criteria to Capacity Remuneration

The first well-known case in which the Commission applied the *Altmark* criteria to the electricity sector concerned an Irish support scheme for new electricity generation capacity.[160] In 2003, the Irish TSO reported that Ireland would suffer from significant generation inadequacy if no measures were taken to ensure additional generation capacity. To address this concern, the Irish government introduced a mechanism to compensate for additional capacity to facilitate the construction of 531 MW of new generation capacity.[161]

As a result, ten-year Capacity and Differences Agreements (hereinafter 'CADAs') were granted to successful bidders to undertake the construction of this new capacity.[162] The CADAs allowed generators guaranteed payments for their available capacity, which they had to reimburse in the event that the market-based price exceeded the

---

156. Communication from the Commission on the application of the European Union State aid rules to compensation granted for the provision of services of general economic interest, OJ C 8, 11.1.2012, pp. 4-14, para. 71.
157. Communication from the Commission on the application of the European Union State aid rules to compensation granted for the provision of services of general economic interest, OJ C 8, 11.1.2012, pp. 4-14, paras 72-73.
158. SA.34947 *Support to Hinkley Point C Nuclear Power Station*, C(2014) 7142 final; Filip Černoch and Veronika Zapletalová, 'Hinkley Point C: A New Chance for Nuclear Power Plant Construction in Central Europe?' 83 *Energy Policy* (2015), pp. 165-168.
159. C-280/00 *Altmark* [2003] ECR I-7747, para. 94; Peter Vesterdorf and Stephen Harris, *State Aid Law of the European Union* (Sweet & Maxwell, 2008), pp. 43-86; Kelyn Bacon, *European Union Law of State Aid*, 3rd edition (OUP, 2017), pp. 439-495; Leigh Hancher, 'The Administrative Procedure – The Privileged Dialogue', in Herwig Hofmann and Claire Micheau (eds), *State Aid Law of the European Union* (OUP, 2016), pp. 341-347; Leigh Hancher, Fracesco Salerno and Michael Scütte, 'The Different Stages in the State Aid Procedure', in Herwig Hofmann and Claire Micheau (eds), *State Aid Law of the European Union* (OUP, 2016), pp. 341-347.
160. N475/2003 *Irish CADA*, 16 December 2003.
161. N475/2003 *Irish CADA*, 16 December 2003, paras 2 and 6.
162. N475/2003 *Irish CADA*, 16 December 2003, para. 7.

reference price set in the contract. The measure, therefore, was similar to that of a reliability option.[163]

The Commission applied the *Altmark* criteria to the Irish scheme. It began by considering compliance with the first *Altmark* criterion by evaluating generation adequacy as an objective of general economic interest and by analysing possible less interventionist measures to ensure such an objective.[164] It established that the urgent need for additional capacity was well founded but did not explicitly discuss whether the obligations to be discharged were clearly defined. Instead, the Commission highlighted the distinction between 'normal' capacity and 'reserve' capacity, the latter being the additional capacity that is not spontaneously provided by the market but nevertheless considered necessary to meet peak demand. The CADA was to be used only to procure this 'reserve' capacity, the necessity for which had been clearly demonstrated by Ireland.[165]

The second *Altmark* criterion was considered fulfilled as the bidding had been organised in a competitive manner and the conditions for awarding the CADA were published ex ante.[166] To determine compliance with the third *Altmark* criterion, the Commission emphasised the fact that the contracted generators were not prevented from trading in the energy-only market and that the remuneration was for capacity only and not for energy.[167] Because of this separation and the liberalisation of the Irish electricity market, the Commission argued that it was unlikely that beneficiaries could be overcompensated for capacity.[168] Furthermore, the fourth *Altmark* criterion was considered fulfilled because the CADA had been awarded as a result of a transparent, objective and competitive procedure.[169]

A similar case concerning Slovenia involved a State aid assessment of two Slovenian measures.[170] The first was a support scheme for the generation of electricity from renewable energy sources and combined heat and power. The second involved compensation to secure a reliable supply of energy from indigenous sources.[171] The Commission assessed the notified aid schemes separately but declared the second of them, a support scheme for a brown coal power plant, as legitimate compensation for the costs of an SGEI to ensure security of electricity supply.

The Commission declared both the *Irish CADA* and the Slovenian scheme compatible with the *Altmark* criteria. However, more recent cases have departed from the evaluation made in them as to what is required of capacity mechanisms in order to

---

163. For more on reliability options, *see* Chapter 2 above.
164. N475/2003 *Irish CADA*, 16 December 2003, paras 21-34.
165. N475/2003 *Irish CADA*, 16 December 2003, para. 35.
166. N475/2003 *Irish CADA*, 16 December 2003, paras 13-17 and 46-48.
167. N475/2003 *Irish CADA*, 16 December 2003, para. 11.
168. N475/2003 *Irish CADA*, 16 December 2003, paras 49-55.
169. N475/2003 *Irish CADA*, 16 December 2003, paras 56-64.
170. Commission Decision of 24 April 2007 on the State aid scheme implemented by Slovenia in the framework of its legislation on qualified energy producers (OJ L 219, 24.8.2007, pp. 9-24).
171. *Ibid.*

comply with the *Altmark* criteria.[172] In fact, it seems that capacity mechanisms are no longer likely to fulfil all the *Altmark* criteria. This has been demonstrated in recent case-law concerning remuneration for capacity as a public service, in which a stricter approach has been taken as to the application of the *Altmark* criteria than in *Irish CADA*.[173]

The Commission continues to maintain that the clear definition of 'reserve' capacity rather than 'normal' (i.e., market-driven) capacity was the distinctive element that separates the decision in *Irish CADA* from some of the more recent cases.[174] However, this distinction has not been applied in an entirely consistent manner. Although the capacity mechanisms currently in existence do not all physically hold capacity in 'reserve', Member States are still required to prove that the capacity for which they are compensating would not be generated through 'normal' market conditions. Furthermore, the content of the first *Altmark* criterion is wider than that of market failure. The first *Altmark* criterion calls for the definition and discharge of a PSO. One criterion of a legitimate PSO is that the market would not deliver the service by itself without intervention. Therefore, the first *Altmark* criterion should not be interpreted as being satisfied by the mere occurrence of a market failure, although such a failure is needed.[175] It seems that in following the distinction made in *Irish CADA*, the Commission clings unnecessarily to a narrow and very case-specific distinction that is of doubtful applicability to current capacity mechanisms.

Despite the evolution in the threshold for capacity remuneration to meet the *Altmark* criteria, some elements of the *Irish CADA* decision are still present in more recent cases concerning capacity mechanisms. In particular, the argument as to the need for market failure, which was strongly present in the argumentation in *Irish CADA*, remains a key element of the justification of capacity mechanisms.[176] Capacity remuneration is typically introduced to address national concerns over the adequacy of existing or future capacity to produce electricity. In this context, it would be counter-intuitive to allow remuneration for investment that can be satisfactorily generated by the energy-only market.

This logic was applied and tested in the support scheme for a new nuclear power plant in the UK.[177] In *Hinkley Point C*, the Commission questioned the UK's argument that State-financed investment in a new power plant would not take place on commercial terms. The Commission took this approach, in particular, because it was

---

172. *See* similar conclusions in Elisabetta Righini and Juan Carlos González Fernández, 'Capacity Mechanisms and State Aid: Between PSOs, Market Liberalisation, and Security of Supply', 7(10) *Journal of European Competition Law & Practice* (2016), pp. 661-675.
173. *See*, for example, SA.34947 SA.34947 *Support to Hinkley Point C Nuclear Power Station*, C(2014) 7142 final and SA.45852 *German capacity reserve*, C(2018) 612 final, particularly at paras 30-31. In legal literature, *see* Filip Černoch and Veronika Zapletalová, 'Hinkley Point C: A New Chance for Nuclear Power Plant Construction in Central Europe?', 83 *Energy Policy* (2015), pp. 165-168.
174. SA.34947 *Support to Hinkley Point C Nuclear Power Station*, C(2013) 9073 final, paras 104-105.
175. SA.45852 *German capacity reserve*, C(2018) 612 final, para. 31.
176. N475/2003 *Irish CADA*, 16 December 2003, para. 35. This element was also the underlying idea in the distinction between 'normal', i.e., market-based, and 'reserve' capacity in *Irish CADA*.
177. SA.34947 *Support to Hinkley Point C Nuclear Power Station*, C(2013) 9073 final.

clear that the power plant, once constructed, would compete against other, commercially operated plants.[178] Furthermore, the Commission argued that the nuclear technologies chosen are generally considered to be commercially viable.[179] The UK disagreed with this, stating that there were three market failures that affected incentives to invest in nuclear generation: decarbonisation, market failure in terms of security and diversity of supply, and the imperfections of the financial markets.[180] In its final decision, the Commission disagreed with only some of the UK's arguments but acknowledged that certain market failures affect nuclear energy uniquely and, therefore, merit resorting to State intervention.[181] The Commission's analysis had further confirmed that there was a high degree of uncertainty over whether the market would generate the necessary investment in new nuclear capacity within a realistic timeframe.[182] It seems, therefore, that high uncertainty as to future investment is enough to trigger the existence of a market failure. There were, however, multiple appeals in respect of the *Hinkley Point C* decision, which demonstrates that the elements of the case – particularly the approval for the aid – were not accepted without criticism.[183]

The first *Altmark* criterion was also evaluated in the case concerning the French country-wide capacity mechanism.[184] In the French scheme, electricity suppliers and, to some extent, network operators and consumers were under an obligation to contribute to security of electricity supply in France in line with their own and their customers' power and energy consumption.[185] This was done by acquiring tradable capacity guarantees in relation to customers' peak demand.[186] The Commission did not consider the first *Altmark* criteria to be fulfilled because the PSO was not clearly defined. It took the view that there were too many obligations and that these differed between the various actors involved.[187] The fact that these obligations were established under French law was not sufficient to comply with the first criterion.

Similar conclusions were reached in *Hinkley Point C*, albeit not because of a lack of well-defined obligations but because the measure did not constitute an SGEI.[188] The UK argued that the aim of the measure was to incentivise investment in new nuclear generation. It considered this a legitimate objective of general economic interest in accordance with the broad margin of discretion afforded to Member States.[189] However, the Commission noted that the measure did not involve any procurement of

---

178. SA.34947 *Support to Hinkley Point C Nuclear Power Station*, C(2013) 9073 final, paras 107-111.
179. SA.34947 *Support to Hinkley Point C Nuclear Power Station*, C(2013) 9073 final, paras 107.
180. SA.34947 *Support to Hinkley Point C Nuclear Power Station*, C(2014) 7142 final, para. 273.
181. SA.34947 *Support to Hinkley Point C Nuclear Power Station*, C(2014) 7142 final, paras 375-392.
182. SA.34947 *Support to Hinkley Point C Nuclear Power Station*, C(2014) 7142 final, para. 390.
183. Cases include T-382/15 *Greenpeace Energy and Others v Commission* [2016], order of the General Court of 26 September 2016, published in the electronic Reports of Cases and T-356/15 *Austria v Commission* [2018], judgment of the General Court of 12 July 2018, published in the electronic Reports of Cases.
184. SA.39621 *French country-wide capacity mechanism*, C(2016) 7086 final.
185. SA.39621 *French country-wide capacity mechanism*, C(2016) 7086 final, para. 7.
186. *Ibid.*
187. SA.39621 *French country-wide capacity mechanism*, C(2016) 7086 final, para. 56.
188. SA.34947 *Support to Hinkley Point C Nuclear Power Station*, C(2014) 7142 final, paras 305-313.
189. SA.34947 *Support to Hinkley Point C Nuclear Power Station*, C(2014) 7142 final, para. 308.

supply, works or services for the benefit of the UK government.[190] The beneficiary of the aid was not factually obliged to construct the nuclear plant[191] nor was there any obligation to produce electricity after construction.[192] The UK government had no legal means to enforce these obligations, only the possibility to terminate the contract.[193] Here, the mere fact that the contractual terms were detailed did not in itself constitute a well-defined objective of general economic interest. As the first *Altmark* criterion was not fulfilled, the Commission did not analyse the remaining three criteria.

The challenges in fulfilling the *Altmark* criteria in terms of capacity remuneration raise questions concerning the relationship between State aid provisions, rules on PSOs and Article 8 of the Electricity Directive. It is clear that a competitive tender or an equally competitive procedure in accordance with Article 8 is the preferred method for selecting undertakings to perform PSOs such as guarantees to construct new generation capacity.[194] It has been argued that if the criteria for launching a tender or an equivalent procedure under Article 8 of the Electricity Directive are followed carefully, the subsidies granted are likely to satisfy the *Altmark* criteria and hence escape being classified as State aid.[195] This certainly holds true in terms of the fourth *Altmark* criterion.[196] However, based on close reading of a number of cases on capacity remuneration, it is not entirely clear whether capacity mechanisms can sufficiently fulfil the other *Altmark* criteria.[197]

As noted above, the way in which the *Altmark* criteria are evaluated has undergone evolution since *Irish CADA*. As a result, a higher threshold for compliance with the well-established criteria now seems to be in place. The ECJ has also adopted a strict approach to the application of the *Altmark* criteria, although it has yet to apply them to capacity remuneration.[198] The Commission has very rarely declared compensation for PSOs to be compatible with the *Altmark* criteria, but has instead taken an extremely strict approach to the interpretation of the ECJ's judgment in that case.[199] In the likely event that the capacity remuneration scheme is not compatible with the

---

190. SA.34947 *Support to Hinkley Point C Nuclear Power Station*, C(2014) 7142 final, para. 310.
191. SA.34947 *Support to Hinkley Point C Nuclear Power Station*, C(2014) 7142 final, para. 312.
192. SA.34947 *Support to Hinkley Point C Nuclear Power Station*, C(2014) 7142 final, para. 313.
193. SA.34947 *Support to Hinkley Point C Nuclear Power Station*, C(2014) 7142 final, para. 312.
194. Communication from the Commission on the application of the European Union State aid rules to compensation granted for the provision of services of general economic interest, OJ C 8, 11.1.2012, pp. 4-14, paras 63-70.
195. Angus Johnston and Guy Block, *EU Energy Law* (OUP, 2012), p. 264.
196. Communication from the Commission on the application of the European Union State aid rules to compensation granted for the provision of services of general economic interest, OJ C 8, 11.1.2012, pp. 4-14, paras 63-70.
197. *See*, for example, T-57/11 *Castelnou Energía v Commission* [2014], judgment of the General Court of 3 December 2014, published in the electronic Reports of Cases; SA.34947 *Support to Hinkley Point C Nuclear Power Station*, C(2014) 7142 final; SA.39621 *French country-wide capacity mechanism*, C(2016) 7086 final; SA.45852 *German capacity reserve*, C(2018) 612 final, paras 30-32.
198. C-34/01 *Enirisorse* [2003] ECR I-14243.
199. For an analysis, *see* Max Klasse, 'The Impact of Altmark: The European Commission Case Law Responses', in Erika Szyszczak and Johan Willem van de Gronden (eds), *Financing Services of General Economic Interest: Reform and Modernisation* (T.M.C. Asser Press, 2013), pp. 35-52, at 36.

Altmark criteria, it can still be considered compatible with EU law under Article 106(2) TFEU. This provision is analysed below with reference to capacity remuneration.

[C] Article 106(2) TFEU and State Aid

Article 106(2) TFEU provides that undertakings entrusted with the operation of SGEIs are subject to the rules contained in the Treaties. However, this only applies insofar as the application of such rules does not obstruct the performance of the particular tasks assigned to these undertakings.[200] The provision grants Member States limited ability to balance national interests against the prohibitions laid down in Treaty law and, in particular, competition law.[201] This possibility to derogate from the rules contained in the Treaties under Article 106(2) TFEU can also be invoked to justify exemption from the prohibition of State aid under Article 107(1) TFEU.[202]

It is established case-law that the scope of the *Altmark* criteria and Article 106(2) TFEU largely overlap as exemptions from the prohibition of aid.[203] First, the requirement for market failure is present in both the *Altmark* criteria and Article 106(2) TFEU. It would be unreasonable to attach specific PSOs to services that are already provided or can be provided satisfactorily by the market alone. Therefore, the approval of a State scheme under both assessments requires that the market has been or will be unable to provide services that the Member State considers essential.[204]

Second, both the first *Altmark* criterion and well-established interpretation of Article 106(2) TFEU require that the SGEI is well defined.[205] It follows from the wording of Article 106(2) TFEU that the undertaking has to be *entrusted* with the operation of SGEIs in order to be granted exemption from the application of the rules contained in the Treaties. An exemption granted on the grounds of Article 106(2) TFEU must not affect the development of trade to an extent that would be contrary to the interests of

---

200. Article 106(2) TFEU. In case-law, *see* C-158/94 *Commission v Italy* [1997] ECR I-5789, para. 36.
201. Julian Nowag, *Competition Law, State Aid Law and Free-Movement Law: The Case of the Environmental Integration Obligation* (University of Oxford, PhD thesis 2014), pp. 116-117.
202. *See* generally Philipp Werner and Vincent Verouden, 'Services of General Economic Interest', in Philipp Werner and Vincent Verouden (eds), *EU State Aid Control: Law and Economics* (Wolters Kluwer, 2017), pp. 439-465; Natalia Fiedziuk, 'Towards a More Refined Economic Approach to Services of General Economic Interest', 16(2) *European Public Law* (2010), pp. 271-288.
203. T-289/03 *BUPA* [2008] ECR II-81, para. 160; Nuno Albuquerque Matos, 'The Role of the BUPA Judgement in the Legal Framework for Services of General Economic Interest', 16(1) *Tilburg Law Review* (2011), pp. 83-104.
204. Communication from the Commission, European Union framework for State aid in the form of public service compensation (2011), OJ C 8, 11.1.2012, pp. 15-22, paras 12-14.
205. T-289/03 *BUPA* [2008] ECR II-81, para. 165; Opinion of AG Léger in C-280/00 *Altmark* [2003] ECR I-7747, para. 87; Communication from the Commission on the application of the European Union State aid rules to compensation granted for the provision of services of general economic interest, OJ C 8, 11.1.2012, pp. 4-14, para. 47; Recital 13 of Commission Decision 2012/21/EU of 20 December 2011 on the application of Article 106(2) of the Treaty on the Functioning of the European Union to State aid in the form of public service compensation granted to certain undertakings entrusted with the operation of services of general economic interest (notified under document C(2011) 9380) (OJ L 7, 11.1.2012, pp. 3-10).

the Union.[206] This wording implies the requirement for proportionality.[207] A review of such proportionality is limited to assessing whether the compensation provided is necessary in order for the SGEI to be performed under economically acceptable conditions and whether the service is manifestly inappropriate to address the objective in question.[208]

Third, any compensation that goes beyond that necessary to fulfil the PSO constitutes State aid regardless of whether a legitimate general economic interest is involved.[209] This requirement applies equally to measures assessed under the *Altmark* criteria and under Article 106(2) TFEU.

Finally, regardless of the legal basis used to seek exemption from the application of State aid rules, compliance with the Electricity Directive is required in the case of capacity remuneration. A Member State that grants financial compensation, other forms of compensation and exclusive rights for the fulfilment of PSOs must do so in a non-discriminatory and transparent way.[210] Furthermore, it is established case-law that Member States continue to have a wide margin of discretion in determining what they regard as PSOs, as long as these obligations comply with Article 3 of the Electricity Directive and the conditions laid down in the seminal *Federutility* case.[211]

Despite these overlapping elements between the evaluation criteria in Article 106(2) TFEU and the cumulative *Altmark* criteria, there are practical, substantial and procedural differences in applying these two exemptions.

First, both the Commission and the Court have applied the four cumulative *Altmark* criteria very strictly. As a result, very few State measures have been able to escape the State aid classification on the basis of being compensation for PSOs.

---

206. *See* analysis in the Opinion of AG Rozès in 78/82 *Commission v Italy* [1983] ECR 1955, point VI-C; Opinion of AG Cosmas in cases C-157/94 *Commission v Netherlands* [1997] ECR I-5699, C-158/94 *Commission v Italy* [1997] ECR I-5789; C-159/94 *Commission v France* [1997] ECR I-5815 and C-160/94 *Commission v Spain* [1997] ECR I-5851; Heike Schweitzer, 'Services of General Economic Interest: European Law's Impact on the Role of Markets and of Member States', in Marise Cremona (ed.), *Market Integration and Public Services in the European Union* (OUP, 2011), pp. 11-62, at 29.
207. C-320/91 *Corbeau* [1993] ECR I-2533, para. 14; C-393/92 *Almelo* [1994] ECR I-1477, para. 49.
208. T-289/03 *BUPA* [2008] ECR II-81, para. 222; Nuno Albuquerque Matos, 'The Role of the BUPA Judgement in the Legal Framework for Services of General Economic Interest', 16(1) *Tilburg Law Review* (2011), pp. 83-104; C-157/94 *Commission v Netherlands* [1997] ECR I-5699, para. 53; C-67/96 *Albany* [1999] ECR I-5751, paras 107 and 111; joined cases T-125/96 and T-152/96 *Boehringer v Council and Commission* [1999] ECR II-3427, paras 73-74.
209. C-53/00 *Ferring* [2001] ECR I-9067, para. 32. *See also* Recitals 15 and 16 of Commission Decision 2012/21/EU of 20 December 2011 on the application of Article 106(2) of the Treaty on the Functioning of the European Union to State aid in the form of public service compensation granted to certain undertakings entrusted with the operation of services of general economic interest (notified under document C(2011) 9380) (OJ L 7, 11.1.2012, pp. 3-10).
210. Article 3(6) of the Electricity Directive. In case-law, *see* SA.45852 *German capacity reserve*, C(2018) 612 final, para. 31.
211. C-265/08 *Federutility* [2010] ECR I-03377 and more recently C-242/10 *Enel Produzione SpA v Autorità per l'energia elettrica e il gas* [2011] ECR I-13665; and C-36/14 *Commission v Poland* [2015], judgment of the Court of 10 September 2015, published in the electronic Reports of Cases. For an analysis of the *Federutility* case and Article 3 of the Electricity Directive, *see* Chapter 3 above.

Conversely, the Commission and the Court have interpreted Article 106(2) TFEU more broadly.[212]

For example, in *Castelnou*, the Commission declared a Spanish measure supporting indigenous coal to be compatible with the internal market on the basis of Article 106(2) TFEU even though the measure failed to meet the fourth *Altmark* criterion.[213] The case concerned electricity power plants which were required to source coal of Spanish origin at prices higher than that of other fuels. These power plants were then obliged to produce certain volumes of electricity from that coal.[214] In order to mitigate the higher costs arising from this obligation, the power plants received compensation equal to the difference between the additional production costs that they had incurred and the sale price on the daily electricity market.[215] Furthermore, the electricity they produced from the indigenous coal benefited from a preferential dispatch mechanism, which, in practice, guaranteed the sale of the electricity produced using that coal.[216] The electricity produced by the contracted power plants was bought in preference to the electricity produced by other power plants using imported coal – a clear protectionist measure.[217]

The Commission and, on appeal, the General Court accepted Spain's argument that the measure was adopted to address a legitimate security of supply concern over the ability of the Spanish electricity system to supply electricity in the long term.[218] The General Court even confirmed that Member States are not required to demonstrate specific and imminent threats to the security of their electricity supply but the identification of more general issues suffices.[219]

The Commission listed several reasons for why the fourth *Altmark* criterion was not fulfilled. The operation of the SGEI had not been awarded as a result of a public procurement procedure, nor had Spain provided the necessary analysis of the costs of meeting the public service requirements.[220] The contested measure was nevertheless

---

212. *See*, for example T-289/03 *BUPA* [2008] ECR II-81, para. 307; Julian Nowag, *Competition Law, State Aid Law and Free-Movement Law: The Case of the Environmental Integration Obligation* (University of Oxford, PhD thesis 2014), p. 122; Leigh Hancher and Pierre Larouche, 'The Coming of Age of EU Regulation of Network Industries and Services of General Economic Interest', in Paul Craig and Gráinne de Búrca, *The Evolution of EU law* (OUP, 2011), pp. 743-781, at 761-762.
213. N178/2010 *Preferential dispatch of indigenous coal plants*, C(2010) 4499, paras 106-108; and the case that followed, T-57/11 *Castelnou Energía v Commission* [2014], judgment of the General Court of 3 December 2014, published in the electronic Reports of Cases.
214. T-57/11 *Castelnou Energía v Commission* [2014], judgment of the General Court of 3 December 2014, published in the electronic Reports of Cases, paras 2-5.
215. *Ibid.*
216. *Ibid.*
217. T-57/11 *Castelnou Energía v Commission* [2014], judgment of the General Court of 3 December 2014, published in the electronic Reports of Cases, para. 3. Priority dispatch for indigenous sources was then governed by Article 11(4) of Directive 2003/54/EC of the European Parliament and of the Council of 26 June 2003 concerning common rules for the internal market in electricity and repealing Directive 96/92/EC, OJ L 176, 15.7.2003, pp. 37-56.
218. T-57/11 *Castelnou Energía v Commission* [2014], judgment of the General Court of 3 December 2014, published in the electronic Reports of Cases, paras 143-144.
219. T-57/11 *Castelnou Energía v Commission* [2014], judgment of the General Court of 3 December 2014, published in the electronic Reports of Cases, para. 131.
220. N178/2010 *Preferential dispatch of indigenous coal plants*, C(2010) 4499, para. 108.

declared compatible with the internal market on the basis of Article 106(2) TFEU, because the objective of security of supply was considered a legitimate SGEI, the measure was necessary to achieve the objective and the compensation for the measure was considered appropriate.[221]

Second, Article 106(2) TFEU does not require or even prioritise a competitive tendering procedure to procure SGEI, nor does it require that the parameters on the basis of which the compensation is granted are published in advance.[222] This difference is insignificant from the point of view of capacity remuneration. The reason for this is that PSOs must fulfil the requirements for transparency and non-discrimination on the basis of Article 3 of the Electricity Directive, so regardless of the legal basis for exemption from the EU State aid regime, the parameters for granting compensation must be made public.[223] Furthermore, as noted in Chapter 3 above, the competitive tendering procedure established in Article 8 of the Electricity Directive is the preferred method for procuring generation capacity.

Third, there is a procedural obligation to notify a State measure as aid on the grounds of Article 108 TFEU even if the measure is later declared compatible with the internal market on the basis of Article 106(2) TFEU. A State measure that fulfils the *Altmark* criteria entirely escapes being classified as State aid and, therefore, does not have to be notified to the Commission. However, the Commission has laid down specific rules under which certain aid in the form of public service compensation is compatible with the internal market and exempt from the notification requirement laid down in Article 108(3) of the Treaty.[224] These rules may be applied to capacity mechanisms provided that the criteria laid down in Article 106(2) TFEU are fulfilled, the compensation does not exceed EUR 15 million annually and the operation of the SGEI does not exceed ten years.[225] As mentioned in section §4.03[A] above, capacity remuneration is generally very costly and, therefore, unlikely to fall below these minimum thresholds.

Although the interpretation of Article 106(2) TFEU allows for broader derogations from the application of State aid rules, it should not be understood as providing unrestricted exemption from the EU State aid regime.[226] It is established case-law that

---

221. N178/2010 *Preferential dispatch of indigenous coal plants*, C(2010) 4499, paras 130-148.
222. Henrik Bjørnebye, *Investing in EU Energy Security: Exploring the Regulatory Approach to Tomorrow's Electricity Production* (University of Oslo, PhD thesis 2009), p. 244.
223. Particularly Article 3(2) and (6) of the Electricity Directive.
224. Commission Decision 2012/21/EU of 20 December 2011 on the application of Article 106(2) of the Treaty on the Functioning of the European Union to State aid in the form of public service compensation granted to certain undertakings entrusted with the operation of services of general economic interest (notified under document C(2011) 9380) (OJ L 7, 11.1.2012, pp. 3-10); Wolf Sauter, 'Public Services and the Internal Market: Building Blocks or Persistent Irritant?', 21(6) *European Law Journal* (2015), pp. 738-757.
225. Article 2 of Commission Decision 2012/21/EU of 20 December 2011 on the application of Article 106(2) of the Treaty on the Functioning of the European Union to State aid in the form of public service compensation granted to certain undertakings entrusted with the operation of services of general economic interest (notified under document C(2011) 9380) (OJ L 7, 11.1.2012, pp. 3-10).
226. Conor Quigley, *European State Aid Law and Policy* (Hart Publishing, 2015), pp. 231-254.

Article 106(2) TFEU should also be interpreted objectively and strictly to ensure that Member States cannot easily escape the application of EU rules on State aid.[227]

§4.04 AID COMPATIBLE WITH THE INTERNAL MARKET

[A] Aid to Facilitate the Development of Certain Economic Activities or Certain Economic Areas

The criteria for assessing whether a Member State measure may avoid classification as State aid and those for assessing whether a Member State measure may constitute aid but still be declared compatible with the internal market based on Article 106(2) TFEU are analysed above. If neither of these options is available due to the lack of a legitimate general economic interest, for example, the EU State aid regime provides other possibilities for derogation from the general prohibition laid down in Article 107(1) TFEU. These are discussed in this section.

Article 107(2) TFEU contains an exhaustive list of situations in which State aid is compatible with the internal market.[228] These include, *inter alia*, social aid granted to individual consumers, aid to repair damage caused by natural disasters or exceptional occurrences. None of the situations specified apply to capacity remuneration.

Article 107(3) TFEU, however, provides a more legitimate legal basis under which capacity remuneration can be assessed. Article 107(3)(c) TFEU provides that aid to facilitate the development of certain economic activities or of certain economic areas may be considered compatible with the internal market. It is well established that capacity remuneration is caught by this provision and may, therefore, be declared compatible with the internal market.[229] However, such aid may only be provided if it has no adverse effects on trading conditions to an extent contrary to the common interest.[230] This clear requirement for proportionality is the only element in Article 107(3)(c) TFEU that explicitly limits the application of this provision.

The wording of Article 107(3)(c) TFEU is broad. Taken by itself, it would allow for extensive interpretation of what amounts to compatible aid.[231] In order to provide interpretative guidance to this end, the Commission regularly adopts sector-specific guidelines with a rather broad margin of discretion. Although these guidelines are not legally binding on Member States,[232] the Court has consistently held that they do bind

---

227. C-157/94 *Commission v Netherlands* [1997] ECR I-5699, para. 37; C-242/95 *GT-Link* [1997] ECR I-4449, para. 50; T-289/03 *BUPA* [2008] ECR II-81, para. 99.
228. Massimo Francesco Orzan, '*De Jure* Compatible Aid under Article 107(2) TFEU', in Herwig Hofmann and Claire Micheau (eds), *State Aid Law of the European Union* (OUP, 2016), pp. 234-239.
229. Communication from the Commission, Guidelines on State aid for environmental protection and energy 2014-2020 (OJ C 200, 28.6.2014, pp. 1-55).
230. Article 107(3)(c) TFEU.
231. Ramona Ianus and Massimo Francesco Orzan, 'Aid Subject to Discretionary Assessment under Article 107(3) TFEU', in Herwig Hofmann and Claire Micheau (eds), *State Aid Law of the European Union* (OUP, 2016), pp. 240-307.
232. In case-law, *see* C-526/14 *Kotnik* [2016], judgment of the Court of 19 July 2016, published in the electronic Reports of Cases.

the Commission itself.[233] Therefore, they provide legal certainty for Member States in relation to the planning of their State interventions. Furthermore, the assessment of the compatibility of aid measures with the internal market falls within the exclusive competence of the Commission, subject to review by the EU Courts.[234] The Commission's significant competence further emphasises the practical importance of the guidelines.

In terms of generation adequacy, the Guidelines on State aid for environmental protection and energy 2014-2020 (hereinafter 'EEAG') concretise the scope of Article 107(3)(c) TFEU.[235] After the entry into force of the EEAG, most capacity mechanisms in the EU have been approved on the basis of them.[236] To fall within the scope of the EEAG, the mechanism in question has to constitute a measure to ensure generation adequacy.[237] The Commission has had to draw a line between capacity mechanisms themselves and ancillary services, the provision of which is the responsibility of a TSO.[238] The EEAG and their contribution to the evaluation of capacity mechanisms are analysed below.

[B]   Commission Guidelines on State Aid for Environmental Protection
        and Energy

The Commission published the EEAG in 2014.[239] These guidelines lay down the conditions based on which the Commission will consider State aid measures compatible with the internal market within the meaning of Article 107(3)(c) TFEU. The EEAG

---

233. 310/85 *Deufil v Commission* [1987] ECR 901, para. 22; C-313/90 *CIRFS v Commission* [1993] ECR I-1125, paras 32-36; C-311/94 *Ijssel-Vliet* [1996] ECR I-5023, para. 42; and T-59/02 *Archer Daniels Midland v Commission* [2006] ECR II-3627, para. 43. This approach is also highlighted from the electricity market perspective in the Opinion of the European Economic and Social Committee on the communication from the Commission, Delivering the internal electricity market and making the most of public intervention C(2013) 7243 final, OJ C 226, 16.7.2014, pp. 28-34, para. 2.7.
234. C-284/12 *Deutsche Lufthansa* [2013], judgment of the Court of 21 November 2013, published in the electronic Reports of Cases, para. 28; C-526/14 *Kotnik* [2016], judgment of the Court of 19 July 2016, published in the electronic Reports of Cases, para. 37.
235. Communication from the Commission, Guidelines on State aid for environmental protection and energy 2014-2020 (OJ C 200, 28.6.2014, pp. 1-55); Kelyn Bacon, *European Union Law of State Aid*, 3rd edition (OUP, 2017), p. 233.
236. Most recently, SA.44464 *Irish Capacity Mechanism: reliability option scheme*, C(2017)7789 final; SA.45852 *German capacity reserve*, C(2018) 612 final; SA.46100 *Planned Polish capacity mechanism*, C(2018) 601 final; SA.48490 *Specific demand response tender in France*, C(2018) 588 final; SA.48648 *Belgian Strategic Reserve*, C(2018) 589 final; SA.48780 *Prolongation of the Greek interruptibility scheme*, C(2018) 604 final.
237. SA.43735 *German ABLAV Interruptibility Scheme*, C(2016) 6765 final, paras 53-55; SA.42955 *German Network Reserve*, C(2016) 8742 final, paras 47-48.
238. Article 12 of the Electricity Directive.
239. The EEAG have been the topic of wide academic discussion. *See*, for example, Leigh Hancher, Tom Ottervanger and Piet Jan Slot, *EU State Aids*, 5th edition (Sweet & Maxwell, 2016), particularly at pp. 15-16; Phedon Nicolaides and Maria Kleis, 'Critical Analysis of Environmental Tax Reductions and Generation Adequacy Provisions in the EEAG 2014-2020', 4 *European State Aid Quarterly* (2014); Marcella Giacomarra and Filippa Bono, 'European Union Commitment Towards RES Market Penetration: From the First Legislative Acts to the Publication of the Recent Guidelines on State Aid 2014/2020', 47 *Renewable and Sustainable Energy Reviews*

establish general compatibility conditions applicable to all aid measures within the scope of the EEAG but also establish specific principles based on which subsidies for generation adequacy are evaluated.[240] These specific sections of the EEAG take priority over the general conditions where they specify or amend the general compatibility conditions.[241]

The EEAG concretises and substantiates the scope of Article 107(3)(c) TFEU with regard to energy and, more specifically, how the Commission interprets the scope of this provision. The wording of Article 107(3)(c) TFEU, which states that the aid may not 'adversely affect trading conditions to an extent contrary to the common interest', is the starting point for this interpretation and for the compatibility assessment. In fact, the common element in the general and the specific conditions for compatible aid is the requirement that the positive impacts of the aid exceed the potential negative effects on trade and competition and that, overall, the aid contributes to the objectives of EU energy law.[242]

The wording of Article 107(3)(c) TFEU essentially requires proportionality. The EEAG's approach to proportionality is twofold. First, the EEAG lays down conditions for the proportionality of the State measure itself. In other words, the guidelines establish criteria based on which the design of the State intervention is proportional to an extent that merits the granting of State resources. Second, they establish criteria based on which the aid itself, i.e., the amount of State resources granted, can be considered proportional.[243] By comparison, the proportionality requirements for the design of the measure itself seem much more substantial than the conditions established in relation to the amount of the aid. In addition, the Commission may require certain aid schemes to be subject to a time limitation.[244]

In practice, the proportionality requirement for the amount of aid given means that the economic advantage bestowed should be limited to that necessary to achieve the pursued objective. The price paid for availability should automatically be zero when the level of capacity supplied is expected to be adequate to meet the level of capacity required.[245] However, in a State aid case concerning the Greek flexibility scheme, the Commission held that there was no need to enforce this provision because the necessity and proportionality of the measure had been established for only one

---

(2015); Kai Struckmann and Geza Sapi, 'Energy and Environmental Aid', in Philipp Werner and Vincent Verouden (eds), *EU State Aid Control: Law and Economics* (Wolters Kluwer, 2017), pp. 663-713; Kelyn Bacon, *European Union Law of State Aid*, 3rd edition (OUP, 2017), pp. 233-247.

240. *See*, for example, SA.38968 *Transitory electricity flexibility remuneration mechanism (FRM)*, C(2016) 1791 final.

241. Communication from the Commission, Guidelines on State aid for environmental protection and energy 2014-2020 (OJ C 200, 28.6.2014, pp. 1-55), para. 25.

242. Communication from the Commission, Guidelines on State aid for environmental protection and energy 2014-2020 (OJ C 200, 28.6.2014, pp. 1-55), paras 23 and 26.

243. Communication from the Commission, Guidelines on State aid for environmental protection and energy 2014-2020 (OJ C 200, 28.6.2014, pp. 1-55), para. 27.

244. *See*, for example, SA.35980 *GB capacity mechanism*, C(2014) 5083 final, para. 162.

245. Communication from the Commission, Guidelines on State aid for environmental protection and energy 2014-2020 (OJ C 200, 28.6.2014, pp. 1-55), para. 231; SA.48648 *Belgian Strategic Reserve*, C(2018) 589 final, para. 146; Kelyn Bacon, *European Union Law of State Aid*, 3rd edition (OUP, 2017), p. 245.

year, which was considered a relatively short and predictable period of time.[246] Additionally, the aid granted should not allow for windfall profits, nor should it allow for unreasonably high rates of return.[247] The Commission has argued, for example, that when the maximum available budget for a capacity mechanism is lower than the system's opportunity costs and the remuneration paid to the main providers of the capacity service is lower than the cost of providing the service, the aid can be considered proportional.[248]

In order to be declared proportional and, thus, compatible with the internal market, the EEAG specifically requires that the measures to support generation adequacy fulfil the following cumulative conditions:

- they contribute to a clearly defined objective of common interest;
- they are used where there is a need for State intervention;
- they have an incentivising effect;
- they are appropriate;
- they avoid undue negative effects on competition and trade;
- they are transparent.

These requirements are analysed below with regard to generation adequacy, which the EEAG defines as 'a level of generated capacity which is deemed to be adequate to meet demand levels in the Member State in any given period'.[249] A measure to address such adequacy is referred to as 'a mechanism which has the aim of ensuring that certain generation adequacy levels are met at national level'.[250]

In order for the measure to be deemed compatible with the internal market, it must pursue a well-defined objective of common interest.[251] In addition to clearly defining the objective pursued, Member States must disclose how the planned measure is expected to contribute to it.[252]

In the energy sector, the primary goal of public subsidisation under EU rules is to ensure a competitive, sustainable and secure energy system in a functioning internal

---

246. SA.38968 *Transitory electricity flexibility remuneration mechanism (FRM)*, C(2016) 1791 final, para. 87; Leigh Hancher and Christoph Riechmann, 'Capacity Mechanisms and Auctions', in Leigh Hancher, Adrien de Hautecloque and Francesco Maria Salerno (eds), *State Aid and the Energy Sector* (Hart Publishing, 2018), pp. 145-177, at 168.
247. Communication from the Commission, Guidelines on State aid for environmental protection and energy 2014-2020 (OJ C 200, 28.6.2014, pp. 1-55), paras 228 and 230; SA.48648 *Belgian Strategic Reserve*, C(2018) 589 final, para. 142; SA.42011 *Italian capacity mechanism*, C(2018) 617 final, paras 179-180.
248. SA.38968 *Transitory electricity flexibility remuneration mechanism (FRM)*, C(2016) 1791 final, para. 98.
249. Communication from the Commission, Guidelines on State aid for environmental protection and energy 2014-2020 (OJ C 200, 28.6.2014, pp. 1-55), para. 19.
250. *Ibid.*
251. Communication from the Commission, Guidelines on State aid for environmental protection and energy 2014-2020 (OJ C 200, 28.6.2014, pp. 1-55), para. 27; and analysis in SA.43735 *German ABLAV Interruptibility Scheme* C(2016) 6765 final, paras 57-62; and SA.42955 *German Network Reserve*, C(2016) 8742 final, paras 50-59.
252. Communication from the Commission, Guidelines on State aid for environmental protection and energy 2014-2020 (OJ C 200, 28.6.2014, pp. 1-55), para. 31.

market.[253] State aid for generation adequacy undoubtedly contributes to the security of the energy system, despite often resulting in higher prices, but should also avoid conflicting with the objective of phasing out environmentally harmful subsidies.[254] This latter requirement is problematic in the sense that capacity mechanisms tend to favour conventional generation capacities, which are often more suited to respond to variations in demand.[255] The tendency to favour conventional generation capacities is addressed in the Clean Energy for All Europeans package, which imposes a 550 g CO_2/kWh limit for any capacity participating in a capacity mechanism.[256]

Despite the difficulties in balancing the sometimes conflicting objectives of EU energy law, the EEAG recognises that generation adequacy is a legitimate common interest that may warrant public financial support.[257] However, Member States should be adequately aware of the precise generation adequacy challenges they face and choose the measure that is best suited to addressing them.[258] Different capacity mechanism designs can address generation adequacy in the short term or in the long term or they can be best suited to address a local shortage of capacity rather than a market-wide challenge.[259] Consequently, Member States should choose a design that best addresses the specificities of their electricity market.[260] A Member State's analysis of the perceived generation inadequacies should also be in line with the generation adequacy analysis carried out by the ENTSO-E.[261] For example, the Commission raised doubts as to the necessity of the French capacity market, because the generation adequacy analysis conducted by ENTSO-E had not identified a security of supply

---

253. Article 194 TFEU; Communication from the Commission, Guidelines on State aid for environmental protection and energy 2014-2020 (OJ C 200, 28.6.2014, pp. 1-55), para. 30.
254. Communication from the Commission, Guidelines on State aid for environmental protection and energy 2014-2020 (OJ C 200, 28.6.2014, pp. 1-55), para. 220.
255. See approved support scheme for indigenous coal in T-57/11 Castelnou Energía v Commission [2014], judgment of the General Court of 3 December 2014, published in the electronic Reports of Cases.
256. Article 23(4) of the Recast Electricity Regulation. This limitation would effectively exclude coal from participation in capacity mechanisms. For the Clean Energy for All Europeans package in general, see Communication from the Commission to the European Parliament, the Council, the European Economic and Social Committee, the Committee of the Regions and the European Investment Bank, Clean Energy For All Europeans, COM(2016) 860 final.
257. Kai Struckmann and Geza Sapi, 'Energy and Environmental Aid', in Philipp Werner and Vincent Verouden (eds), EU State Aid Control: Law and Economics (Wolters Kluwer, 2017), pp. 663-713, at 683-684.
258. Communication from the Commission, Guidelines on State aid for environmental protection and energy 2014-2020 (OJ C 200, 28.6.2014, pp. 1-55), para. 221.
259. Report from the Commission, Final Report of the Sector Inquiry on Capacity Mechanisms, COM(2016) 752 final.
260. Communication from the Commission, Guidelines on State aid for environmental protection and energy 2014-2020 (OJ C 200, 28.6.2014, pp. 1-55), para. 219.
261. Required by Article 8 of Regulation (EC) No 714/2009 of the European Parliament and of the Council of 13 July 2009 on conditions for access to the network for cross-border exchanges in electricity and repealing Regulation (EC) No 1228/2003 (OJ L 211, 14.8.2009, pp. 15-35). This requirement is further strengthened in the Clean Energy for All Europeans package, since Article 23(5) of the Recast Electricity Regulation states that Member States may not apply a capacity mechanism where the European resource adequacy assessment has not identified a resource adequacy concern.

problem in France before 2025.[262] In this case, France was able to demonstrate that its national generation adequacy assessment was more recent and more detailed than the ENTSO-E's deterministic assessment.[263]

In connection with the well-defined objective of common interest, the EEAG requires that there is a need for intervention. In other words, it is not sufficient for there to be a legitimate objective of common interest. It must also be the case that this objective cannot be satisfactorily achieved by the market alone.[264] The Commission has stressed that there are various ways of facilitating a well-functioning investment climate, not all of which involve State aid.[265] Furthermore, the measure in question has to have an incentivising effect on the behaviour of undertakings in the sense that the aid leads them to engage in activities in which they would not otherwise engage or at least not to a sufficient extent.[266] The measure should also be limited in duration so that the measure can be immediately withdrawn when the market can deliver the adequate resources on its own.[267]

There is no common European methodology for measuring generation adequacy or any definite threshold for proving a legitimate threat to generation adequacy. Because of this, Member States have significant margin of discretion in determining when intervention is necessary. Despite this lack of a common methodology, Member States have to clearly demonstrate the reasons for the perceived generation inadequacy and why the market alone cannot be expected to resolve this issue.[268] In evaluating a Member State's defence of its public intervention, the Commission will take into account the expected market and technological developments, impacts of variable generation, demand side participation and the potential of interconnecting capacity as well as any elements that might cause or exacerbate the generation adequacy problem, such as capped wholesale electricity prices.[269]

---

262. SA.39621 *French country-wide capacity mechanism*, C(2016) 7086 final, para. 60.
263. SA.39621 *French country-wide capacity mechanism*, C(2016) 7086 final, para. 222.
264. This is essentially a requirement for market failure. *See* Communication from the Commission, Guidelines on State aid for environmental protection and energy 2014-2020 (OJ C 200, 28.6.2014, pp. 1-55), pp. 1-55, paras 27 and 36. *See also* Ramona Ianus and Massimo Francesco Orzan, 'Aid Subject to Discretionary Assessment under Article 107(3) TFEU', in Herwig Hofmann and Claire Micheau (eds), *State Aid Law of the European Union* (OUP, 2016), pp. 240-307, at 292-293; Wolf Sauter, 'Public Services and the Internal Market: Building Blocks or Persistent Irritant?', 21(6) *European Law Journal* (2015), pp. 738-757, at 743-744.
265. SA.43735 *German ABLAV Interruptibility Scheme*, C(2016) 6765 final, para. 67.
266. Communication from the Commission, Guidelines on State aid for environmental protection and energy 2014-2020 (OJ C 200, 28.6.2014, pp. 1-55), para. 27; and analysis in SA.43735 *German ABLAV Interruptibility Scheme*, C(2016) 6765 final, paras 85-87; and SA.42955 *German Network Reserve*, C(2016) 8742 final, paras 106-109.
267. Communication from the Commission, Guidelines on State aid for environmental protection and energy 2014-2020 (OJ C 200, 28.6.2014, pp. 1-55), paras 28 and 242; and analysis in SA.42955 *German Network Reserve*, C(2016) 8742 final, para. 105.
268. Communication from the Commission, Guidelines on State aid for environmental protection and energy 2014-2020 (OJ C 200, 28.6.2014, pp. 1-55), para. 223. In case-law, *see* SA.48648 *Belgian Strategic Reserve*, C(2018) 589 final, paras 108-115; SA.46100 *Planned Polish capacity mechanism*, C(2018) 601 final, paras 137-140.
269. Communication from the Commission, Guidelines on State aid for environmental protection and energy 2014-2020 (OJ C 200, 28.6.2014, pp. 1-55), para. 224.

In the State aid case concerning the Greek flexibility mechanism, the Commission evaluated the need for intervention to pursue a well-defined objective of common interest.[270] It concluded that Greek generation adequacy concerns had been clearly identified through quantifiable indicators, which demonstrated the need for intervention.[271] Similarly in the State aid assessment for the German network reserve, the Commission considered the German methodology for measuring generation adequacy to be appropriate because it utilised detailed and partly probabilistic calculations.[272] On the basis of this methodology, Germany argued that there was a generation capacity shortage in southern Germany, which was likely to continue in the coming years.[273] Furthermore, due to anticipated investment in transmission capacity between the north and the south, the issue was argued to be transitional. Because of this, there were no incentives to keep existing capacity operational or build new capacities.[274]

The task of proving that the market will fail to deliver the investment needed is not entirely unproblematic in the case of capacity mechanisms. As noted above in various different connections, the internal market in electricity is fundamentally built upon the assumption that a well-functioning, liberalised and deregulated energy-only market is the most efficient way to ensure generation adequacy at competitive prices. Many economists support this approach and argue that the energy-only market is the only realistic and cost-efficient approach to ensure sufficient generation capacity.[275] Others emphasise that the lack of sufficient levels of capacity is an inherent part of an electricity market that results from the physical characteristics of electricity and, in particular, from the lack of flexibility in demand.[276] Even those who agree that market failure is a genuine concern are unsure as to whether capacity mechanisms are the most appropriate instruments through which to address this issue.[277] Because of the lack of consensus on the existence and causes of, and the remedies for, market failure, the Commission's evaluation of Member States' generation inadequacy is conducted on a case-by-case basis and by individually assessing each Member State's market specificities.[278] This approach can be defended by reference to the subsidiarity principle: Member States are responsible for ensuring security of supply within their

270. SA.38968 *Transitory electricity flexibility remuneration mechanism (FRM)*, C(2016) 1791 final.
271. SA.38968 *Transitory electricity flexibility remuneration mechanism (FRM)*, C(2016) 1791 final, paras 65-66.
272. SA.42955 *German Network Reserve*, C(2016) 8742 final, para. 67.
273. SA.42955 *German Network Reserve*, C(2016) 8742 final, para. 61.
274. *Ibid.*
275. Commission Staff Working Document, Generation adequacy in the internal electricity market – guidance on public interventions, SWD(2013) 438 final, p. 30.
276. Henrik Bjørnebye, *Investing in EU Energy Security: Exploring the Regulatory Approach to Tomorrow's Electricity Production* (University of Oslo, PhD thesis 2009), pp. 35-43.
277. Laurens De Vries and Petra Heijnen, 'The Impact of Electricity Market Design upon Investment under Uncertainty: The Effectiveness of Capacity Mechanisms', 16(3) *Utilities Policy* (2008), pp. 215-227.
278. Report from the Commission, Final Report of the Sector Inquiry on Capacity Mechanisms, COM(2016) 752 final, p. 7.

territories and have the most accurate, real-time information on the potential challenges involved in ensuring the uninterrupted availability of affordable electricity.[279]
The challenge remains that, in the absence of a harmonised and comparable approach,
it is easy for Member States to exaggerate their capacity deficits and even defend
protectionist measures on the grounds of security of supply.[280]

The requirement for market failure in the interpretation of Article 107(3)(c) TFEU
was in place even before the 2014-2020 EEAG. In a State aid case concerning a tender
for new capacity in Latvia, the Commission argued that Member States have to
demonstrate that the market incentives for new investment are not functioning and
that the lack of capacity is due to a structural market failure which cannot be repaired
by other means.[281] To fulfil this requirement, the Latvian authorities provided information that demonstrated the unwillingness of investors to undertake the construction
of new capacity that would sufficiently cover expected demand.[282] The Latvian
authorities also argued that the EU directives to liberalise the energy markets had been
fully implemented and no legal or administrative barriers were in place that would
prevent new market entry.[283]

In a recent case concerning the nuclear power station at Hinkley Point C, the
General Court made a distinction between the necessity requirement in Article
107(3)(c) TFEU and the requirement of market failure.[284] It concluded that while the
existence of a market failure may be a relevant for declaring State aid compatible with
the internal market, the absence of such a failure does not necessarily mean that the
conditions laid down in Article 107(3)(c) TFEU are not satisfied.[285] In other words, the
necessity requirement extends beyond market failure. For example, State intervention
may be considered necessary if the pursued objective cannot be achieved in sufficient
time, even if the market itself cannot be considered failing as such.[286] However, the

---

279. Article 5 TEU. In respect of State aid evaluation, see SA.39621 French country-wide capacity
    mechanism, C(2016) 7086 final, para. 222; Thomas Horsley, 'Subsidiarity and the European
    Court of Justice: Missing Pieces in the Subsidiarity Jigsaw?', 50(2) Journal of Common Market
    Studies (2012), pp. 267-282; Tim Koopmans, 'Subsidiarity, Politics and the Judiciary Articles
    EC 5, Draft Convention I-9; Protocol on the Application of the Principles of Subsidiarity and
    Proportionality', 1(1) European Constitutional Law Review (2005), pp. 112-116; Robert
    Schütze, 'Subsidiarity after Lisbon: Reinforcing the Safeguards of Federalism?', 68(3) The
    Cambridge Law Journal (2009), pp. 525-536.
280. Additionally, Member States have a tendency to grant aid to undertakings operating in their
    respective territories only. See Ben Clift, 'Economic Patriotism, the Clash of Capitalisms, and
    State Aid in the European Union', 13(1) Journal of Industry, Competition and Trade (2013), pp.
    101-117.
281. N675/2009 Tender for Aid for New Electricity Generation Capacity (LV), C(2010) 4146.
282. N675/2009 Tender for Aid for New Electricity Generation Capacity (LV), C(2010) 4146, paras
    32-36.
283. Ibid.
284. T-356/15 Austria v Commission [2018], judgment of the General Court of 12 July 2018,
    published in the electronic Reports of Cases. For an extensive analysis, see Leigh Hancher,
    'State Aid to the Nuclear Power Sector: The General Court's Ruling on the UK Reactor at
    Hinkley Point C', OGEL (2018), pp. 7-8.
285. T-356/15 Austria v Commission [2018], judgment of the General Court of 12 July 2018,
    published in the electronic Reports of Cases, para. 151.
286. T-356/15 Austria v Commission [2018], judgment of the General Court of 12 July 2018,
    published in the electronic Reports of Cases, para. 151.

General Court confirms that the core of the necessity test is to find out whether the objective pursued by the Member State would be attained without that Member State's intervention.[287]

It is not in itself sufficient for there to be a legitimate need for a State aid measure. In addition, the EEAG requires that the Member State measure must be appropriate to address the well-defined objective of common interest.[288] This requirement essentially means that a measure cannot be considered compatible with the market if the same common objective could be achieved through less interventionist or less distortive measures.[289] In its State aid assessment for the German network reserve, the Commission evaluated the appropriateness of the German measure by identifying the actions Germany had taken or would take in order to ensure that the market could function without public subsidisation of a strategic reserve. These actions to improve the market design, including the introduction of scarcity pricing and the improvement of short-term markets, were considered sufficient to ensure that the need for the network reserve would only be transitional. Therefore, the measure was considered appropriate to address the issue.[290]

In relation to capacity mechanisms, the requirement for appropriateness also means that the design of the mechanism should not allow compensation for electricity but for capacity only.[291] The remunerated capacity, furthermore, should not be limited to certain technologies, but should provide incentives for both existing and future generation and for both supply and demand side measures.[292] Additionally, the mechanisms should allow both domestic and imported capacities to bid into the scheme.[293] In other words, the eligibility criteria should be formulated in a non-discriminatory way that allows all technologies to bid into the capacity mechanism. The concept of non-discrimination, when interpreted together with Article 8 of the Electricity Directive, requires that the eligibility criteria do not discriminate directly or

---

287. T-356/15 *Austria v Commission* [2018], judgment of the General Court of 12 July 2018, published in the electronic Reports of Cases, para. 150.
288. Communication from the Commission, Guidelines on State aid for environmental protection and energy 2014-2020 (OJ C 200, 28.6.2014, pp. 1-55), para. 27; and analysis in SA.38968 *Transitory electricity flexibility remuneration mechanism (FRM)*, C(2016) 1791 final, paras 73-81.
289. Communication from the Commission, Guidelines on State aid for environmental protection and energy 2014-2020 (OJ C 200, 28.6.2014, pp. 1-55), para. 40; and analysis in a State aid case SA.42955 *German Network Reserve*, C(2016) 8742 final, paras 74-105.
290. SA.42955 *German Network Reserve*, C(2016) 8742 final, para. 104; and similar argumentation in SA.35980 *GB capacity mechanism*, C (2014) 5083 final, paras 88-94.
291. Communication from the Commission, Guidelines on State aid for environmental protection and energy 2014-2020 (OJ C 200, 28.6.2014, pp. 1-55), para. 225; Kai Struckmann and Geza Sapi, 'Energy and Environmental Aid', in Philipp Werner and Vincent Verouden (eds), *EU State Aid Control: Law and Economics* (Wolters Kluwer, 2017), pp. 663-713, at 705.
292. Communication from the Commission, Guidelines on State aid for environmental protection and energy 2014-2020 (OJ C 200, 28.6.2014, pp. 1-55), paras 226 and 232; Kai Struckmann and Geza Sapi, 'Energy and Environmental Aid', in Philipp Werner and Vincent Verouden (eds), *EU State Aid Control: Law and Economics* (Wolters Kluwer, 2017), pp. 663-713, at 706.
293. Communication from the Commission, Guidelines on State aid for environmental protection and energy 2014-2020 OJ C 200, 28.6.2014, pp. 1-55, paras 226 and 232; SA.45852 *German capacity reserve*, C(2018) 612 final, para. 31. For further discussion of the cross-border elements, *see* Chapter 5 on capacity mechanisms and the free movement rules.

indirectly. Indirect discrimination in the form of very short lead times, for example, can in practice exclude technologies that could otherwise significantly contribute to generation adequacy.[294] The Commission has, however, permitted temporary discrimination for interconnecting capacity in its State aid decisions in respect of capacity mechanisms.[295]

Allowing non-discriminatory access to a capacity remuneration scheme also contributes to ensuring that the measure does not cause undue negative effects on competition and trade.[296] In parallel with ensuring that all capacities can participate, the design of the mechanism should also ensure that the introduction of public financing does not negatively affect investment in interconnecting capacity or cause the withdrawal of generation investment decisions made prior to the introduction of a capacity mechanism.[297] The Commission has considered this requirement fulfilled when the capacity mechanism is open to existing and future capacity providers that meet the technical eligibility criteria. The exclusion of demand response and imports over interconnectors has been considered justified by the Commission if they cannot technically provide the needed service.[298] These types of exclusions should, however, be interpreted extremely narrowly in the light of the objectives of EU energy law and the rules on free movement of goods.[299] Furthermore, the mechanism should be designed in a way that does not undermine market coupling or strengthen market dominance.[300] The Commission has considered this condition fulfilled even when a single undertaking owns the majority of all eligible capacity and will therefore be the beneficiary in respect of most of the capacity remuneration.[301]

The prohibition of negative effects on trade is a challenge for a Member State in designing a capacity mechanism because the market impacts of such schemes are very difficult to predict comprehensively.[302] In the French market-wide capacity mechanism, for example, the Commission raised concerns over the impact of the measure on

---

294. Communication from the Commission, Guidelines on State aid for environmental protection and energy 2014-2020 (OJ C 200, 28.6.2014, pp. 1-55), para. 226.
295. SA.39621 *French country-wide capacity mechanism*, C(2016) 7086 final; and SA.35980 *GB capacity mechanism*, C (2014) 5083 final. It is clear that such discrimination will no longer be possible if the new provisions set out in the Clean Energy for All Europeans package enter into force. *See*, in particular, Article 21 of the Recast Electricity Regulation.
296. Communication from the Commission, Guidelines on State aid for environmental protection and energy 2014-2020 (OJ C 200, 28.6.2014, pp. 1-55), para. 27; SA.48648 *Belgian Strategic Reserve*, C(2018) 589 final, para. 151.
297. Communication from the Commission, Guidelines on State aid for environmental protection and energy 2014-2020 (OJ C 200, 28.6.2014, pp. 1-55), para. 233.
298. SA.38968 *Transitory electricity flexibility remuneration mechanism (FRM)*, C(2016) 1791 final, para. 100.
299. For further discussion of capacity mechanisms and the rules on free movement, *see* Chapter 5 below. For the interrelationship between the objectives of EU energy law and capacity mechanisms, *see* Chapter 6.
300. Communication from the Commission, Guidelines on State aid for environmental protection and energy 2014-2020 (OJ C 200, 28.6.2014, pp. 1-55), para. 233.
301. SA.38968 *Transitory electricity flexibility remuneration mechanism (FRM)*, C(2016) 1791 final, para. 103.
302. Laurens De Vries Petra Heijnen, 'The Impact of Electricity Market Design upon Investment under Uncertainty: The Effectiveness of Capacity Mechanisms', 16(3) *Utilities Policy* (2008), pp. 215-227.

increasing market concentration.[303] It argued that because of the incumbent's market power, the capacity mechanism would enable the withholding of capacity and capacity guarantees and that there was a significant risk of a price squeeze.[304] The French authorities were forced to modify their capacity mechanism design to address the risks identified by the Commission.

The EEAG also emphasises the requirement for transparency. In its State aid case decisions, the Commission has held that this requirement is fulfilled when all essential information regarding the aid is published. This information includes the identity of the individual beneficiaries, the form and amount of aid granted to each beneficiary, the date on which it is granted, the type of undertaking to which it has been granted, the region in which the beneficiary is located and the principal economic sector in which it is active.[305] This information is to be available to the general public without restrictions.[306]

It is clear that competitive tender is the preferred method of procuring capacity to achieve non-discrimination, transparency and the most efficient price levels.[307] This is clear not only from the EEAG and the findings of the State aid sector inquiry but also from Article 8 of the Electricity Directive,[308] all of which highlight the importance of ensuring non-discrimination and transparency in achieving the objective pursued in the most cost-effective way.[309] However, non-competitive allocation of capacity remuneration can be approved if, for example, there are not enough relevant undertakings that could participate in a competitive tender.[310] In these situations, bilateral negotiations have been approved by the Commission.[311]

Prior to the 2014-2020 EEAG, there were no specific rules in place concerning the evaluation of capacity mechanisms under Article 107(3)(c) TFEU. The proportionality principle laid down in Article 107(3)(c) TFEU was interpreted in a less well-defined manner, resulting in greater legal uncertainty over which aid schemes could be declared compatible with the internal market. Before the EEAG, the compatibility of

---

303. SA.39621 *French country-wide capacity mechanism*, C(2016) 7086 final, paras 275-288.
304. SA.39621 *French country-wide capacity mechanism*, C(2016) 7086 final, para. 275.
305. SA.38968 *Transitory electricity flexibility remuneration mechanism (FRM)*, C(2016) 1791 final, para. 106; SA.42955 *German Network Reserve*, C(2016) 8742 final, para. 126.
306. SA.38968 *Transitory electricity flexibility remuneration mechanism (FRM)*, C(2016) 1791 final, para. 106; *see also* SA.39621 *French country-wide capacity mechanism*, C(2016) 7086 final, paras 259-269.
307. Communication from the Commission, Guidelines on State aid for environmental protection and energy 2014-2020 (OJ C 200, 28.6.2014, pp. 1-55), para. 229; SA.48648 *Belgian Strategic Reserve*, C(2018) 589 final, para. 140; Kai Struckmann and Geza Sapi, 'Energy and Environmental Aid', in Philipp Werner and Vincent Verouden (eds), *EU State Aid Control: Law and Economics* (Wolters Kluwer, 2017), pp. 663-713, at 700-701; Leigh Hancher and Pierre Larouche, 'The Coming of Age of EU Regulation of Network Industries and Services of General Economic Interest', in Paul Craig and Gráinne de Búrca, *The Evolution of EU Law* (OUP, 2011), pp. 743-781, at 763-765.
308. European Commission, Interim Report of the Sector Inquiry on Capacity Mechanisms, C(2016) 2107 final, p. 14.
309. Communication from the Commission, Guidelines on State aid for environmental protection and energy 2014-2020 (OJ C 200, 28.6.2014, pp. 1-55), paras 27 and 99.
310. SA.42955 *German Network Reserve*, C(2016) 8742 final, paras 114-115.
311. *Ibid.*

capacity mechanisms under Article 107(3)(c) TFEU was based on a general proportionality assessment that sought to assess whether the overall balance of the aid measure was positive and whether the distortion of competition and effect on trade were limited.[312]

Although the existence of the EEAG provides for legal predictability in the interpretation of Article 107(3)(c) TFEU, the legitimacy of carrying out such detailed control via a legally non-binding instrument has been questioned.[313] In *European Renewable Energies Federation*, an association applied for the annulment of the EEAG on three bases.[314] First, it argued that the Commission did not have the competence to adopt such rules. Second, it stated that the adoption of the EEAG violated the principle of proportionality and the duty to state reasons for action. Third, the applicant argued that the Commission had misused its powers and had used the EEAG as a means of wresting from the Member States their competence to organise their energy markets.[315] The General Court dismissed the claim as inadmissible because, first, Member States were obliged neither in law nor in fact to amend their legislation to bring it into line with EEAG and, second, because the legal situation of the represented undertakings was not directly affected by the EEAG.[316] However, ECJ case-law suggests that the validity of Commission Communications can be challenged in the context of preliminary rulings.[317]

§4.05   THE RELATIONSHIP BETWEEN THE STATE AID EXEMPTIONS

It is well established that capacity mechanisms are unlikely to escape the concept of State aid within the meaning of Article 107(1) TFEU. The analysis above demonstrates that despite the broad prohibition of aid laid down in Article 107(1) TFEU, Member States can invoke a variety of exemptions that enable them to adopt measures that would otherwise be declared incompatible with the internal market.

It seems, however, that the legal bases for exemption from the prohibition in Article 107(1) TFEU have similar requirements. First, the compatibility criteria require that the compensated service could not be delivered under normal market conditions, regardless of whether the Member State invokes the *Altmark* criteria, Article 106(2) TFEU or Article 107(3)(c) TFEU and, by extension, the EEAG. This requirement for market failure is logical when assessed together with the principles based on which the internal market in electricity is built – it would be counterintuitive to grant public funds

---

312. N675/2009 *Tender for Aid for New Electricity Generation Capacity (LV)*, C(2010) 4146, para. 50.
313. Leigh Hancher, Tom Ottervanger and Piet Jan Slot, *EU State Aids*, 5th edition (Sweet & Maxwell, 2016), pp. 15-16.
314. T-694/14 *European Renewable Energies Federation v Commission* [2015], order of the General Court of 23 November 2015.
315. T-694/14 *European Renewable Energies Federation v Commission* [2015], order of the General Court of 23 November 2015, para. 12.
316. T-694/14 *European Renewable Energies Federation v Commission* [2015], order of the General Court of 23 November 2015, para. 38.
317. C-526/14 *Kotnik* [2016], judgment of the Court of 19 July 2016, published in the electronic Reports of Cases.

to support activities that can be delivered by the markets alone.[318] Second, all the legal bases require that the measure adopted by a Member State pursues a legitimate general economic interest or a common interest. This requirement emphasises the importance of adequately demonstrating the causes and scope of the security of supply concerns. Third, it seems that the *Altmark* criteria, Article 106(2) TFEU and Article 107(3)(c) TFEU all indicate a preference for the competitive allocation of remuneration through tendering.[319] In relation to capacity mechanisms, this interpretation is fully aligned with secondary legislation, in particular Article 8 of the Electricity Directive. Finally, there is a general requirement for proportionality irrespective of the legal basis used. The methodology for evaluating proportionality differs from one legal basis to another but the key common element is that the positive outcomes of the measure must outweigh the negative.

These similarities between the assessment criteria for different legal bases raise the question of what the relevant differences between these legal bases constitute.

The first and the most obvious difference is procedural in nature. If remuneration for capacity were to fulfil all the cumulative *Altmark* criteria, it would escape being classified State aid under Article 107(1) TFEU and, therefore, escape the obligation to be notified to the Commission on the basis of Article 108 TFEU.[320] Measures approved under Articles 106(2) TFEU or Article 107(3)(c) TFEU, conversely, have to be notified to the Commission and are thus subject to EU-level review.

Second, the analysis outlined above indicates that the *Altmark* criteria impose a higher standard of scrutiny than is the case under Article 107(3)(c) TFEU and the EEAG. Both the *Altmark* criteria and the interpretation of Article 107(3)(c) TFEU require that the capacity mechanism pursues a well-defined or a clearly defined objective of common interest or general economic interest. However, based on the Commission's body of decisions, a capacity mechanism is not likely to meet this requirement under the *Altmark* criteria, but it has been fulfilled in a number of cases under Article 107(3)(c) TFEU and the EEAG. For example, the French country-wide capacity mechanism could not constitute compensation for a PSO because it was not clearly defined enough, but it was ultimately held to fulfil all the conditions under Article 107(3)(c) TFEU and the EEAG.[321] This tendency to apply the *Altmark* criteria more strictly than the similar conditions under the EEAG is apparent from the application of the EEAG but also from State aid cases decided before the adoption of the

---

318. *See* Chapter 2 above.
319. Christopher Bovis, 'Public Procurement and State Aid', Herwig Hofmann and Claire Micheau (eds), *State Aid Law of the European Union* (OUP, 2016), pp. 161-186; Heike Schweitzer, 'Services of General Economic Interest: European Law's Impact on the Role of Markets and of Member States', in Marise Cremona (ed.), *Market Integration and Public Services in the European Union* (OUP, 2011), pp. 11-62, at 29-30; Natalia Fiedziuk, 'Putting Services of General Economic Interest up for Tender: Reflections on Applicable EU rules', 50(1) *Common Market Law Review* (2013), pp. 87-114; Philipp Kiiver, *The Practice of Public Procurement: Tendering, Selection and Award* (Intersentia, 2014).
320. The obligation to notify does not apply to aid schemes that do not exceed the *de minimis* thresholds. However, the relevance of these thresholds to capacity mechanisms is limited in practice. Communication from the Commission, Guidelines on State aid for environmental protection and energy 2014-2020 (OJ C 200, 28.6.2014, pp. 1-55), para. 20.
321. SA.39621 *French country-wide capacity mechanism*, C(2016) 7086 final, para. 56.

EEAG.[322] This observation indicates that the evaluation carried out under the EEAG is, in fact, less stringent than that carried out pursuant to the conditions established in *Altmark*. This is the case despite the fact that the criteria laid down in *Altmark* are less detailed than those under the EEAG. Such a tendency to assess capacity mechanisms on the basis of legally non-binding Guidelines is not entirely unproblematic. On the other hand, the evaluation of complex instruments, such as capacity mechanisms, does require that the assessment criteria are adaptive, if needed, and that there is scope for context-sensitive interpretation.

In practice, Member States do not choose one legal basis to invoke to escape the prohibition on the provision of State aid. Instead, they commonly invoke all possible legal bases to ensure that a nationally designed measure can pass the EU-level assessment. It is not uncommon for a Member State first to argue that the measure does not fall within the scope of Article 107(1) TFEU because it does not meet one of the cumulative criteria for constituting aid. If this argument is not successful, the Member State then proceeds to argue that the measure is compensation for PSOs and not State aid on the basis of the *Altmark* criteria. As established above, it is unlikely that a capacity mechanism will fulfil these conditions. Therefore, the Member State may argue that the measure is compatible with the internal market on the basis of Article 106(2) TFEU despite the fact that it does not fulfil one or more of the *Altmark* criteria.[323] Finally, the Member State is likely to invoke Article 107(3)(c) TFEU and the EEAG, based on which it will submit that the measure constitutes State aid but is nevertheless compatible with the internal market.[324]

The UK's argumentation in the State aid assessment of the support for the nuclear facility in *Hinkley Point C* provides an illustrative example of a Member State invoking all the legal bases open to it.[325] The remuneration for capacity was finally approved under Article 107(3)(c) TFEU.[326] Germany used a similar approach in defending its network reserve.[327] It argued first that the measure in question only governed an exchange of funds between private parties and that the remuneration itself was not financed from State resources. Second, Germany claimed that the measure did not confer a selective advantage on its beneficiaries, because the remuneration granted was based on actual costs and did not improve the beneficiaries' competitive position. It argued, furthermore, that the measure did not impact on cross-border trade given

---

322. SA.34947 *Support to Hinkley Point C Nuclear Power Station*, C(2014) 7142 final.
323. Heike Schweitzer, 'Services of General Economic Interest: European Law's Impact on the Role of Markets and of Member States', in Marise Cremona (ed.), *Market Integration and Public Services in the European Union* (OUP, 2011), pp. 11-62, at 29; Natalia Fiedziuk, 'Towards a More Refined Economic Approach to Services of General Economic Interest', 16(2) *European Public Law* (2010), pp. 271-288.
324. Analysis in Leigh Hancer and Wolf Sauter, 'Public Services and EU Law', in Catherine Barnard and Steve Peers (eds), *European Union Law* (OUP, 2013), pp. 539-566, at 546-553; Leigh Hancher, 'Capacity Mechanisms and State Aid Control: A European Solution to the "Missing Money" Problem?', in Leigh Hancher, Adrien de Hautecloque and Malgorzata Sadowska (eds), *Capacity Mechanisms in the EU Energy Market* (OUP, 2015), pp. 157-181, at 166 and 176.
325. SA.34947 *Support to Hinkley Point C Nuclear Power Station*, C(2013) 9073 final, paras 90-92.
326. SA.34947 *Support to the Hinkley Point C Nuclear Power Station*, C(2014) 7142 final cor, para. 550.
327. SA.42955 *German Network Reserve*, C(2016) 8742 final.

that the capacities were held outside the electricity market and the remuneration did not go beyond the mere reimbursement of costs.[328] The Commission rejected these arguments, but nevertheless declared the measure compatible with the internal market on the grounds of Article 107(3)(c) TFEU and the EEAG.

---

328. SA.42955 *German Network Reserve*, C(2016) 8742 final, paras 26-27.

CHAPTER 5
Capacity Mechanisms and the EU Rules on Free Movement

---

§5.01 FREE MOVEMENT RULES IN THE ELECTRICITY SECTOR AND CAPACITY MECHANISMS

[A] The Challenges in Ensuring Compliance with Free Movement Rules in Capacity Mechanism Designs

The EU internal market is founded on the idea that an area without internal frontiers in which the free movement of goods, persons, services and capital is ensured guarantees the lowest prices and the best quality goods and services for European citizens.[1] The most essential instrument with which primary EU law facilitates the existence of the internal market is the legal framework for free movement, which is the focus of this Chapter.[2]

The internal market is an instrument through which to pursue not only the economic goals of price stability and economic growth but also societal objectives such as full employment, social progress and environmental protection.[3] The internal market in electricity has been developed with the very same idea in mind. The internal electricity market, where energy is allowed to cross borders without hindrances, is

---

1. Article 26 TFEU and Article 3 TEU.
2. The sector-specific electricity legislation also establishes that Member States are forbidden from discriminating between cross-border contracts and national contracts when taking exceptional measures to ensure security of supply. *See* Article 4(3) of the Security of Supply Directive and Article 16 of Regulation (EC) No 714/2009 of the European Parliament and of the Council of 13 July 2009 on conditions for access to the network for cross-border exchanges in electricity and repealing Regulation (EC) No 1228/2003 (OJ L 211, 14.8.2009, pp. 15-35).
3. Friedl Weiss and Clemens Kaupa, *European Union Internal Market Law* (Cambridge University Press, 2014), pp. 1-3.

intended to achieve not only efficiency gains through competition but also high quality services, security of supply and a sustainably maintained system.[4]

For many Member States, the internal market approach to security of electricity supply has meant setting aside the national pursuit of energy independence in exchange for lower prices that have been enabled by increased competition through cross-border trade.[5] This shift towards greater interdependence between Member States requires mutual trust and solidarity between them in a sector that has traditionally been subject to strong national protection and national security interests.[6] This need for mutual trust is well demonstrated in the dynamics concerning national capacity mechanisms.[7] If national generation capacity is not sufficient to cover national demand, a Member State is expected to trust in the ability of the neighbouring Member State's market to produce and sell the needed electricity. The internal market operates on the idea that this arrangement is mutually beneficial to the trading Member States. However, what if both Member States face generation inadequacy simultaneously? Will one Member State interfere with the functioning of the internal market by restricting exports of electricity on grounds of national security? What happens to the security of supply of the other Member State if it relies on imports to some extent to ensure its generation adequacy? These sorts of questions concerning Member States' national interests lie at the heart of the discussion on capacity mechanisms and the internal market in electricity. Sharing the benefits of the internal market in electricity is not difficult for Member States but sharing the insecurities and the potential downsides of an efficient internal market is not in their national interest.

Capacity mechanisms, as instruments to protect Member States' national security of supply interests, tend to be problematic from the point of view of EU free movement rules in various ways.[8] Capacity mechanisms have been identified as particularly problematic in terms of electricity market integration because they tend either to prohibit the participation of foreign capacities or interconnecting capacities or merely ignore the contribution of imports when calculating the severity of national generation adequacy concerns.[9] As a result, the remuneration provided for participating in a

---

4. Recital 1 of the Electricity Directive.
5. Kaisa Huhta, 'Too Important to Be Entrusted to Neighbours? The Dynamics of Security of Electricity Supply and Mutual Trust in EU law', 43(6) *European Law Review* (2018), pp. 920-933.
6. Angus Johnston and Guy Block, *EU Energy Law* (OUP, 2012), p. 10; cases 25/88 *Bouchara* [1989] ECR 1105, para. 18; C-5/94 *Hedley Lomas* [1996] ECR I-2553, paras 19-20; C-1/96 *Compassion in World Farming* [1998] ECR I-1251, para. 47; Opinion of AG Ruiz-Jarabo Colomer delivered on 19 September 2002 in joined cases C-187/01 and C- 385/01 *Gözütok and Brügge* [2003] ECR I-1345, para. 124; European Court of Justice, opinion 2/13 of 18 December 2014, para. 191; and joined cases C-404/15 and C-659/15 *PPU, Aranyosi and Caldararu* [2016], judgment of the Court of 5 April 2016, published in the electronic Reports of Cases, para. 78.
7. Kaisa Huhta, 'Too Important to Be Entrusted to Neighbours? The Dynamics of Security of Electricity Supply and Mutual Trust in EU law', 43(6) *European Law Review* (2018), pp. 920-933.
8. Paolo Mastropietro, Pablo Rodilla and Carlos Batlle, 'National Capacity Mechanisms in the European Internal Energy Market: Opening the Doors to Neighbours', 82 *Energy Policy* (2015), pp. 38-47; Elisabetta Righini and Juan Carlos González Fernández, 'Capacity Mechanisms and State Aid: Between PSOs, Market Liberalisation, and Security of Supply', 7(10) *Journal of European Competition Law & Practice* (2016), pp. 661-675, at 661.
9. The latter is also referred to as implicit participation. Report from the Commission, Final Report of the Sector Inquiry on Capacity Mechanisms, COM(2016) 752 final; Commission Staff Working

capacity mechanism may also be available for domestic capacity providers only.[10] Both approaches reflect a desire to protect national security of supply rather than to allow the energy-only design of the internal market to ensure that the sale of electricity takes place where it is most economically beneficial. In fact, many Member States continue to reserve the right to limit cross-border trade if domestic security of supply is threatened.[11]

Overall, public security matters lie at the heart of national sovereignty.[12] Securing the uninterrupted availability of affordable energy is a crucial element of modern-day public security and is accordingly subject to strong national protection. Security of supply is, therefore, a highly political subject, a fact that cannot be dismissed in legal assessments of the matter.[13] Geopolitical issues and external dependence on a significant source of energy, for example, have been brought up in the context of justifying exemptions from free movement rules on the grounds of public security.[14] This dynamic between national security interests and the fundamental EU objective of market integration is the broader discussion to which this chapter contributes.

Although capacity mechanisms have been identified as being potentially restrictive of free movement and the functioning of the internal market, there is no case-law on the direct application of free movement rules to capacity mechanisms. In 2015, a case concerning the compatibility of the French capacity mechanism with free movement rules was referred to the ECJ after the French national association for retail energy providers (hereinafter 'ANODE') brought an action for annulment of the national capacity mechanism design on the basis that it was contrary to EU law.[15] The referring French court sought a ruling on whether the existing prohibition of quantitative restrictions on imports should be interpreted as precluding national legislation that restricted the participation of foreign capacity and whether such a measure was capable of being justified on grounds of public security. However, ANODE withdrew its

---

Document accompanying the document Report from the Commission Interim Report of the Sector Inquiry on Capacity Mechanisms, SWD(2016) 119 final, pp. 80-84; SA.35980 *GB Capacity Mechanism*, C(2014) 5083 final, para. 20; SA.45852 *German Capacity Reserve*, C(2018) 612 final, paras 123-126; Graeme Hawker, Keith Bell and Simon Gill, 'Electricity security in the European Union – The conflict between national Capacity Mechanisms and the Single Market', 24 *Energy Research & Social Science* (2017), pp. 51-58, at 56-57.

10. Commission Staff Working Document accompanying the document Report from the Commission Interim Report of the Sector Inquiry on Capacity Mechanisms, SWD(2016) 119 final, pp. 80-84.

11. Paolo Mastropietro, Pablo Rodilla and Carlos Batlle, 'National Capacity Mechanisms in the European Internal Energy Market: Opening the Doors to Neighbours', 82 *Energy Policy* (2015), pp. 38-47, at 38-40.

12. John Agnew, *Globalization and Sovereignty* (Rowman & Littlefield Publishers, 2009), pp. 97-142; Steffen Hindelang, *The Free Movement of Capital and Foreign Direct Investment: The Scope of Protection in EU Law* (OUP, 2009), p. 3.

13. Panos Koutrakos, 'Public Security Exceptions and EU Free Movement Law', in Panos Koutrakos, Niamh Nic Shuibhne and Phil Syrpis (eds), *Exceptions from EU Free Movement Law: Derogation, Justification and Proportionality* (Hart Publishing, 2016), pp. 190-217, at 218.

14. 72/83 *Campus Oil* [1984] ECR 2727, p. 2737. On the role of geopolitics in energy security, *see* Graeme Hawker, Keith Bell and Simon Gill, 'Electricity Security in the European Union – The Conflict Between National Capacity Mechanisms and the Single Market', 24 *Energy Research & Social Science* (2017), pp. 51-58.

15. C-543/15 *ANODE* [2016], order of the President of the Court of 12 Apr. 2016.

application for annulment in 2016. Consequently, the French court withdrew its request for a preliminary ruling and, as a result, the president of the ECJ ordered the case to be removed from the court register.[16] Therefore, the ECJ never had the opportunity to determine the compatibility of capacity mechanisms with EU free movement rules.

This chapter first explains why capacity mechanisms are likely to constitute quantitative restrictions or measures having equivalent effect. Second, it analyses the conditions under which capacity mechanisms may be exempted from the prohibition on quantitative restrictions or measures having equivalent effect. Due to the lack of case-law on the application of free movement rules to capacity mechanisms, this analysis will draw, on an analogous basis, on case-law that uses security of supply as a justification for derogation from the free movement rules.

At Treaty level, the free movement rules most relevant to capacity mechanisms are enshrined in Articles 34 and 35 TFEU, which concern the prohibition of quantitative restrictions on imports and exports and all measures having equivalent effect. Furthermore, capacity mechanisms may fall within the scope of application of Articles 30 and 110 TFEU, which concern the prohibition of customs duties on imports and exports and the imposition of discriminatory internal taxing. The objective of these provisions is to prohibit measures that restrict the completion and maintenance of the internal market. The detrimental effects that capacity mechanisms may have upon the internal market make it of paramount importance to analyse the interpretation of the existing justification regime. Before proceeding to the interpretation of these rules in the context of ensuring generation adequacy, the role of electricity and capacity in the framework of the free movement of goods and services is first analysed.

[B]   Generation Capacity As a Good

The EU rules on the free movement of goods and their applicability to energy have been interpreted by the EU courts on various occasions. The Court has, in general, established a very broad definition for goods in the context of free movement rules.[17] Goods must be understood as products that can be valued in money and which are capable of being the subject of commercial transactions.[18]

Electricity has been considered to be a good since the Court's seminal ruling in *Costa v ENEL,* where the Court implicitly established energy as a good by applying

---

16. *Ibid.*
17. Morten Broberg and Nina Holst-Christensen, *Free Movement in the European Union,* 3rd edn. (DJØF, 2010), pp. 109-114; C-2/90 *Commission of the European Communities v Kingdom of Belgium* [1992] ECR I-4431.
18. 7/68 *Commission of the European Communities v Italian Republic* [1968] ECR 423, para. 2. On the concept of goods, *see* Laurence Gormley, *EU Law of Free Movement of Goods and Customs Union* (OUP, 2009), pp. 399-403.

Article 37 TFEU to electricity.[19] This interpretation was later explicitly confirmed in *Almelo* and has been applied consistently in subsequent case-law.[20]

The Court has also rejected Member States' arguments to the effect that the free movement rules do not apply to energy because of its vital importance to modern society.[21] It has held that the Treaty applies the principle of free movement to all goods irrespective of their importance to the functioning of a Member State.[22] In other words, electricity cannot be exempted from the application of Treaty rules simply because it is of particular importance for the economy of a Member State.[23] An exemption is only permissible where specifically provided for in the Treaty. This interpretation is in line with established case-law confirming that exceptions to fundamental rules of the Treaty should be interpreted strictly.[24] Furthermore, the free movement rules benefit all goods directly and thus do not, for example, permit distinctions on the basis of their owner's nationality.[25]

It would be overly simplistic to consider the different elements of trade in electricity as only falling within the scope of the rules on the free movement of *goods*. In addition to the physical movement of energy across borders, electricity trade and investment in the electricity sector involve significant capital transactions, which raise questions with regard to the free movement of capital.[26] However, the direct challenges

---

19. 6/64 *Costa v ENEL* [1964] ECR 585.
20. Cases C-393/92 *Almelo* [1994] ECR I-1477, paras 27-28; C-157/94 *Commission v Netherlands* [1997] ECR I-5699; C-159/94 *Commission v France* [1997] ECR I-5815; C-158/94 *Commission v Italy* [1997] ECR I-5789, para. 17; joined cases C-105/12 to C-107/12 *Essent and Others* [2013], judgment of the Court 22 October 2013, published in the electronic Reports of Cases, para. 59. In legal literature, *see* Malcolm Jarvis, 'Scope: Subject Matter', in Peter Oliver (ed), *Oliver on Free Movement of Goods in the European Union* (Hart Publishing, 2010), pp. 15-22.
21. Case 72/83 *Campus Oil* [1984] ECR 2727, para. 14.
22. *Ibid.*, para. 17.
23. *Ibid.*, para. 17; Stephen Weatherill, *The Internal Market as a Legal Concept* (OUP, 2017), pp. 33-48.
24. Cases 36/75 *Rutili v Minister for the Interior* [1975] ECR 1219, para. 27; 30/77 *R v Bouchereau* [1977] ECR -1999, para. 30; C-157/94 *Netherlands* [1997] ECR I-5699, para. 37; C-159/94 *Commission v France* [1997] ECR I-5815, paras 53-55; C-54/99 *Église de scientologie* [2000] ECR I-1335 para. 17; C-326/07 *Commission v Italy* [2009] ECR I-2291, para. 70; C-503/99 *Commission v Belgium* [2002] ECR I-4809, para. 47; C-463/00 *Commission v Spain* [2003] ECR I-4581, para. 34; C-483/99 *Commission v France* [2002] ECR I-4781, para. 48.
25. Joined cases 2 and 3-69 *Sociaal Fonds voor de Diamantarbeiders v S.A. Ch. Brachfeld & Sons and Chougol Diamond Co* [1969] ECR 211, paras 24-26; and C-441/04 *A-Punkt Schmuckhandel* [2006] ECR I-2093. *See also* Malcolm Jarvis, 'Scope: Subject Matter', in Peter Oliver (ed), *Oliver on Free Movement of Goods in the European Union* (Hart Publishing, 2010), pp. 27-28; and Laurence Gormley, *EU Law of Free Movement of Goods and Customs Union* (OUP, 2009), pp. 104-105.
26. *See* Golden Shares cases C-367/98 *Commission v Portugal* [2002] ECR I-4731; C-483/99 *Commission v France* [2002] ECR I-4781; C-503/99 *Commission v Belgium* [2002] ECR I-4809; C-463/00 *Commission v Spain* [2003] ECR I-4581; C-98/01 *Commission v Great Britain* [2003] ECR I-4641; C-174/04 *Commission v Italy* [2005] ECR I-4933; C-274/06 *Commission v Spain* [2008] ECR I-165; C-326/07 *Commission v Italy* [2009] ECR I-2291; Steffen Hindelang, *The Free Movement of Capital and Foreign Direct Investment: The Scope of Protection in EU Law* (OUP, 2009); Sirja-Leena Penttinen, 'The Growing Impact of Free Movement Provisions in the EU Energy Market', in Raphael J. Heffron and Gavin F. M. Little, *Delivering Energy Law and Policy in the EU and the US. A Reader* (Edinburgh University Press, 2016), pp. 116-120, at 117; Steffen Hindelang, *The Free Movement of Capital and Foreign Direct Investment: The Scope of Protection in EU Law* (OUP, 2009); Jukka Snell, 'Free Movement of Capital: Evolution as a Non-linear

regarding free movement law and capacity mechanisms emerge from the restrictions on offering foreign capacity to participate in a capacity mechanism.[27] Consequently, free movement law and capacity remuneration revolve around the physical movement of electricity and not capital transactions.

The case-law establishing electricity as a good dates back to the period prior to liberalisation.[28] It has been argued that the impacts of the extensive sector-specific requirements on unbundling may have changed the status of electricity as a good.[29] Separating network operations from the generation and supply of electricity could create a situation where generation and supply would be considered goods but the transmission and distribution of electricity would be regarded as a service.[30] Similarly, it is possible that the provision of capacity could be considered a service rather than a good. The reason for this is that the provision of the availability of capacity rather than the physical delivery of electricity is what amounts to the capacity product being sold.[31] The Court has discussed this separation with regard to television broadcasting.[32] It has held that the transmission of television signals is a service, but that trade in material, sound recordings, films, apparatus and other products used for the diffusion of television signals are goods.[33]

The TFEU defines a service as an activity that is normally provided for remuneration, particularly an activity of an industrial or commercial character or an activity of craftsmen or of the professions.[34] An activity is considered a service only insofar as it is not governed by the Treaty provisions relating to the free movement of goods, capital

---

Process', in Paul Craig and Gráinne De Búrca, *The Evolution of EU Law* (OUP, 2011), pp. 547-574; Paul Craig and Gráinne de Búrca, *EU Law: Text, Cases, and Materials*, 6th edn. (OUP, 2015), pp. 721-743.

27. Pradyumna Bhagwat, Jörn Richstein, Emile Chappin, Kaveri Iychettira and Laurens De Vries, 'Cross-Border Effects of Capacity Mechanisms in Interconnected Power Systems', 46 *Utilities Policy* (2017), pp. 33-47.

28. Cases 6/64 *Costa v ENEL* [1964] ECR 585 and C-393/92 *Almelo* [1994] ECR I-1477.

29. Martha Roggenkamp and François Boisseleau, 'The Liberalization of the EU Electricity Market and the Role of Power Exchanges', in Martha Roggenkamph and François Boisseleau (eds), *The Regulation of Power Exchanges in Europe* (Intersentia, 2005), p. 5; and Sirja-Leena Penttinen, 'The Growing Impact of Free Movement Provisions in the EU Energy Market', in Raphael J. Heffron, Gavin F. M. Little, *Delivering Energy Law and Policy in the EU and the US. A Reader* (Edinburgh University Press, 2016), pp. 116-120, at 117.

30. This is the case under WTO rules. *See* WTO, 'Energy Services', Background Note by the Secretariat, S/C/W/52, 9 September 1998. On EU case-law on services, *see* Vassilis Hatzopoulos, 'The Court's Approach to Services (2006-2012): From Case Law to Case Load?' 50(2) *Common Market Law Review* (2013), pp. 459-501.

31. This is typically the case for capacity payments and strategic reserves, for example. *See* Graeme Hawker, Keith Bell and Simon Gill, 'Electricity security in the European Union – The Conflict Between National Capacity Mechanisms and the Single Market', 24 *Energy Research & Social Science* (2017), pp. 51-58, at 52.

32. C-155/73 *Sacchi* [1974] ECR 409.

33. C-155/73 *Sacchi* [1974] ECR 409, paras 6-7. This ruling was later confirmed in C-52/79 *Procureur du Roi v Debauve* [1980] ECR 833. On free movement of services, *see* Vassilis Hatzopoulos, *Regulating Services in the European Union* (OUP, 2012); Mads Andenæs and Wulf-Henning Roth, *Services and Free Movement in EU Law* (OUP, 2002).

34. Article 57 TFEU. C-55/94 *Reinhard Gebhard v Consiglio dell'Ordine degli Avvocati e Procuratori di Milano* [1995] ECR I-4165.

and persons.[35] Therefore, the provisions on free movement of services are secondary to those on free movement of goods.[36]

Despite these possibilities to interpret different elements of electricity trade under different free movement provisions, the EU courts have not changed their approach to electricity as a good but have continued to interpret the concept of goods broadly compared to the concept of services. In the absence of case-law that would change this approach, a logical approach is to consider capacity and generation resources as also falling within the scope of the definition of a good.[37] This approach, therefore, serves as the starting point for this chapter, which evaluates generation capacity in relation to the rules on free movement of goods.

§5.02   RULES ENSURING THE FREE MOVEMENT OF GOODS

[A]   Prohibition of Quantitative Restrictions on Imports and Exports

The rules on free movement of goods, persons, services and capital lie at the core of ensuring a functional European internal market.[38] The Court has consistently held that the concept of the internal market involves the elimination of obstacles to intra-EU trade in an effort to merge national markets into a single market.[39] This objective finds expression in Articles 34 and 35 TFEU, which prohibit quantitative restrictions on imports and exports as well as all measures having equivalent effect.[40] As the provisions on the free movement of goods are fundamental to the functioning of the EU, they have traditionally been interpreted broadly to involve an extensive variety of measures. Any deviation from the rules laid down in Articles 34 and 35, even minor, is prohibited.[41]

The wording and well-established interpretation of Articles 34 and 35 TFEU make them directly applicable EU law that can, therefore, be directly invoked by individuals

---

35. Article 57 TFEU. *See also* Alina Kaczorowska-Ireland, *European Union Law* (Routledge, 2009), p. 784.
36. Vassilis Hatzopoulos, 'The Court's Approach to Services (2006-2012): From Case Law to Case Load?' 50(2) *Common Market Law Review* (2013), pp. 459-501; Vassilis Hatzopoulos, *Regulating Services in the European Union* (OUP, 2012); Mads Andenæs and Wulf-Henning Roth, *Services and Free Movement in EU Law* (OUP, 2002), pp. 69-139.
37. For an opposing view, *see* Fabien Roques, Charles Verhaeghe and Guillaume Dezobry, 'Cross-Border Participation in Capacity Mechanisms: Legal and Economic Issues', in Leigh Hancher, Adrien de Hauteclocque and Francesco Maria Salerno (eds), *State Aid and the Energy Sector* (Hart Publishing, 2018), pp. 179-199, at 184.
38. Article 26 TFEU.
39. C-15/81 *Schul* [1982] ECR 1409, para. 33.
40. For a contextual interpretation of the full effect of the Treaty, *see* C-347/88 *Commission v Greece* [1990] ECR I-4747, para. 42.
41. C-49/89 *Corsica Ferries France v Direction générale des douanes* [1989] ECR-4441, para. 8; joined cases 177 and 178/82 *Jan van de Haar and Kaveka de Meern BV* [1984] ECR-1797; C-67/97 *Bluhme* [1998] ECR I-8033; Peter Oliver, 'Measures of Equivalent Effect I: General', in Peter Oliver (ed), *Oliver on Free Movement of Goods in the European Union* (Hart Publishing, 2010), pp. 84-156, at 91.

in the court systems of the EU and the Member States.[42] The prohibitions these articles lay down are addressed to Member States and accordingly catch all national laws, regulations, administrative provisions and practices, as well as recommendations that conflict with them.[43] Measures enacted by independent professional bodies on which certain powers have been conferred under national legislation also fall within the scope of Articles 34 and 35 TFEU.[44] Measures enacted by TSOs through powers conferred upon them under national laws fall within this category.

In practice, Articles 34 and 35 TFEU contain two mutually supportive prohibitions, which have been separately interpreted in case-law. First, they prohibit quantitative restrictions, which cover any total or partial bans on imports, exports or goods in transit or the imposition of quotas.[45] Second, they prohibit measures of equivalent effect to quantitative restrictions.

In accordance with the well-established *Dassonville* formula, measures of equivalent effect under Article 34 TFEU refer to all trading rules enacted by Member States which are capable of hindering, directly or indirectly, actually or potentially, intra-EU trade.[46] The approach to measures having equivalent effect is thus an effects-based interpretation.[47] In other words, the Member State measure does not need to have a discriminatory intent in order to be prohibited by Article 34 TFEU, nor does it have to actually discriminate between domestic and imported goods – the potential to do so suffices.[48] Even a national measure whose purpose is to promote domestic goods over imported ones falls within the scope of application of Article 34 TFEU.[49] Other

---

42. C-26/62 *Van Gend en Loos v Administratie der Belastingen* [1963] ECR 3; C-74/76 *Ianelli v Meroni* [1977] ECR 557, para. 13; Alina Kaczorowska-Ireland, *European Union Law* (Routledge, 2009), pp. 352-360; Nigel Foster, *Foster on EU Law* (OUP, 2015), pp. 170-171.
43. Laurence Gormley, *EU Law of Free Movement of Goods and Customs Union* (OUP, 2009), p. 396; Alina Kaczorowska-Ireland, *European Union Law* (Routledge, 2009), pp. 580-629; Nigel Foster, *Foster on EU Law* (OUP, 2015), pp. 273-277.
44. Joined cases 266 and 267/87 *R v Royal Pharmaceutical Society of Great Britain, ex p. Association of Pharmaceutical Importers* [1998] ECR 1295.
45. 2/73 *Riseria Luigi Geddo v Ente Nazionale Risi* [1973] ECR 865, para. 5; 154/85 *Commission v Italy* [1987] ECR 2717; 53/76 *Procureur de la République de Besançon v Les Sieurs Bouhelier and others* [1977] ECR 843; Malcolm Jarvis, 'Quantitative Restrictions', in Peter Oliver (ed), *Oliver on Free Movement of Goods in the European Union* (Hart Publishing, 2010), pp. 79-83; Laurence Gormley, *EU Law of Free Movement of Goods and Customs Union* (OUP, 2009), pp. 396 and 414-443.
46. C-8/74 *Dassonville* [1974] ECR 837, para. 5; Paul Craig and Gráinne de Búrca, *EU Law: Text, Cases, and Materials*, 6th edn. (OUP, 2015), pp. 665-686.
47. *See* discussion in C-322/01 *Deutscher Apothekerverband* [2003] ECR I-14887, paras 64-67; Opinion of AG Jacobs in C-379/98 *PreussenElektra* [2001] ECR I-2099, para. 201 and the case-law cited therein. In legal literature, *see* Paul Craig and Gráinne de Búrca, *EU Law: Text, Cases, and Materials*, 6th edn. (OUP, 2015), pp. 666-668; Peter Oliver, 'Measures of Equivalent Effect I: General', in Peter Oliver (ed), *Oliver on Free Movement of Goods in the European Union* (Hart Publishing, 2010), pp. 84-156, at 95.
48. The *Dassonville* formula is reiterated in almost every case concerning the free movement of goods. However, *see* C-142/05 *Mickelsson and Roos* [2009] ECR I-4273. Peter Oliver and Martín Martínez Navarro, 'Free Movement of Goods', in Catherine Barnard and Steve Peers (eds), *European Union Law* (OUP, 2014), pp. 325-355, at 334.
49. C-249/81 *Commission v Ireland* [1982] ECR 4005. In legal literature, *see* Peter Oliver, 'Measures of Equivalent Effect I: General', in Peter Oliver (ed), *Oliver on Free Movement of Goods in the European Union* (Hart Publishing, 2010), pp. 84-156, at 87-88.

prohibited measures include, for example, price fixing that makes it more difficult to market imported goods[50] or measures that make importing more difficult or imported goods more costly.[51]

The expansive *Dassonville* approach to measures having equivalent effect was reviewed in the seminal *Keck* judgment, which sought to re-evaluate and clarify the scope of measures having equivalent effect.[52] The *Keck* judgment excluded certain selling arrangements from the scope of measures having equivalent effect, as long as these arrangements fulfilled two criteria. First, they had to apply to all relevant traders operating within the national territory and, second, they had to affect the marketing of domestic and foreign products in the same way both in law and in fact.[53]

The *Keck* judgment was widely criticised by Advocates General and legal scholars because it failed to clarify the concept of measures having equivalent effect but instead established the additional unclear concept of selling arrangements.[54] The concept of selling arrangements has since been further elaborated.[55] Selling arrangements that are excluded from the prohibition in Article 34 TFEU now comprise national measures that determine *who* can sell certain goods and *where* these goods can be sold or how they can be advertised.[56]

Capacity mechanisms often directly limit the participation of foreign capacity and are consequently more likely to constitute quantitative restrictions than measures

---

50. 82/77 *Openbaar* [1978] ECR 25.
51. 50/85 *Schloh v Auto Contrôle Technique* [1986] ECR 1855.
52. Joined cases C-267/91 and C-268/91 *Keck Mithouard* [1993] ECR I-6097, paras 14-18. Laurence Gormley, *EU Law of Free Movement of Goods and Customs Union* (OUP, 2009), p. 408; José Luís Da Cruz Vilaça, *EU Law and Integration: Twenty Years of Judicial Application of EU Law* (Hart Publishing, 2014), pp. 306-320; Paul Craig and Gráinne de Búrca, *EU Law: Text, Cases, and Materials*, 6th edn. (OUP, 2015), pp. 665-686.
53. Joined cases C-267/91 and C-268/91 *Keck Mithouard* [1993] ECR I-6097, para. 17.
54. Opinion on AG Jacobs in C-412/93 *Leclerc-Siplec v TF1 and M6* [1995] ECR I-179; Opinion of AG Poiares Maduro in C-158/04 *Alfa Vita Vassilopoulos* [2006] ECR I-8135; Stephen Weatherill, 'After Keck: Some Thoughts on How to Clarify the Clarification', 33(5) *Common Market Law Review* (1996), pp. 887-908; Laurence Gormley, 'Reasoning Renounced? The Remarkable Judgment in Keck & Mithouard?', 5(3) *European Business Law Review* (1994), pp. 63-67; and later Peter Pecho, 'Good-Bye Keck?: A Comment on the Remarkable Judgment in Commission v. Italy, C-110/05', 36(3) *Legal Issues of Economic Integration* (2009), pp. 257-272; Peter Oliver and Stefan Enchelmaier, 'Free Movement of Goods: Recent Developments in the Case Law', 44(3) *Common Market Law Review* (2007), pp. 649-704.
55. C-110/05 *Commission v Italy* [2009] ECR I-519; C-142/05 *Mickelsson and Roos* [2009] ECR I-4273; Stefan Enchelmaier, 'Moped Trailers, Mickelsson and Roos, Gysbrechts: The ECJ's Case Law on Goods Keeps on Moving', 190(29) *Yearbook of European Law* (2010), pp. 190-223; Peter Oliver, 'Measures of Equivalent Effect II: Specific Measures', in Peter Oliver (ed), *Oliver on Free Movement of Goods in the European Union* (Hart Publishing, 2010), pp. 157-214, at 206; Laurence Gormley, 'Silver Threads Among the Gold ... 50 Years of the Free Movement of Goods', 31(6) *Fordham International Law Journal* (2008), pp. 1637-1691.
56. Laurence Gormley, *EU Law of Free Movement of Goods and Customs Union* (OUP, 2009), pp. 409-410; Peter Oliver, 'Measures of Equivalent Effect I: General', in Peter Oliver (ed), *Oliver on Free Movement of Goods in the European Union* (Hart Publishing, 2010), pp. 84-156, at 116 and the abundant case-law cited by both authors.

having equivalent effect. Due to the abundant legal literature on the general interpretation and application of EU law regarding the free movement of goods, the focus here is on how these rules impact upon capacity mechanisms.[57]

Both Articles 34 and 35 TFEU can be significant for capacity mechanisms. As noted above, national capacity mechanisms restrict the participation of foreign capacity providers, thus creating a restriction on imports within the meaning of Article 34 TFEU. However, the protection of domestic security of supply is a common rationale for Member States to impose restrictions on exports.[58] Therefore, a Member State is also liable to restrict domestic capacity providers' ability to deliver to a foreign capacity mechanism scheme if there is an ongoing domestic scarcity situation at the time that another Member State's capacity mechanism is activated.[59]

The quantitative import and export restrictions laid down in Articles 34 and 35 TFEU are applied without distinction. However, the measures of equivalent effect laid down in Article 35 TFEU have not been interpreted as broadly as those laid down in Article 34 TFEU.[60] In particular, goods intended purely for a domestic market do not fall within the scope of application of Article 35 TFEU.[61] This distinction, however, does not concern electricity, the internal and interconnected market for which ensures that producing electricity purely for domestic use is not an option. Furthermore, as noted above, the typical restrictive elements of capacity mechanisms are generally caught directly by the concept of quantitative restriction and not by that of equivalent effect. Because of this, the apparent interpretational differences between Articles 34 and 35 TFEU with regard to measures having equivalent effect are not further discussed below.[62]

57. Peter Oliver (ed), *Oliver on Free Movement of Goods in the European Union* (Hart Publishing, 2010); Paul Craig and Gráinne De Búrca, *The Evolution of EU Law* (OUP, 2011); Morten Broberg and Nina Holst-Christensen, *Free Movement in the European Union*, 3rd edn. (DJØF, 2010); Scott Siegel, *The Political Economy of Noncompliance: Adjusting to the Single European Market* (Routledge, 2011); Nigel Foster, *Foster on EU Law* (OUP, 2015); Ettore Recchi, *Mobile Europe: The Theory and Practice of Free Movement in the EU* (Palgrave Macmillan, 2015); Pedro Caro de Sousa, *The European Fundamental Freedoms: A Contextual Approach* (OUP, 2015); Niamh Nic Shuibhne, *The Coherence of EU Free Movement Law: Constitutional Responsibility and the Court of Justice* (OUP, 2014); Gareth Davies, *EU Internal Market Law* (Cavendish Pub. Ltd, 2003); Stephen Weatherill, *The Internal Market as a Legal Concept* (OUP, 2017); Panos Koutrakos and Jukka Snell, *Research Handbook on the Law of the EU's Internal Market* (Edward Elgar Publishing, 2017).
58. 68/76 *Commission of the European Communities v French Republic* [1977] ECR-515.
59. This was also acknowledged with regard to capacity mechanisms in the 2016 Clean Energy for All Europeans -proposals.
60. *See* distinction in cases C-15/79 *Groenveld* [1979] ECR 3409; 155/80 *Oebel* [1981] ECR -1993; C-388/95 *Belgium v Spain* [2000] ECR I-3123; and discussion in legal literature in Peter Oliver, 'Measures of Equivalent Effect I: General', in Peter Oliver (ed), *Oliver on Free Movement of Goods in the European Union* (Hart Publishing, 2010), pp. 84-156, at 133-140.
61. C-15/79 *Groenveld* [1979] ECR 3409; Peter Oliver, 'Measures of Equivalent Effect I: General', in Peter Oliver (ed), *Oliver on Free Movement of Goods in the European Union* (Hart Publishing, 2010), pp. 84-156, at 133-140; Niamh Nic Shuibhne, *The Coherence of EU Free Movement Law: Constitutional Responsibility and the Court of Justice* (OUP, 2014), pp. 115-156; Marek Szydło, 'Export Restrictions within the Structure of Free Movement of Goods: Reconsideration of an Old Paradigm', 47(3) *Common Market Law Review* (2010), pp. 753-789.
62. Marek Szydło, 'Export Restrictions within the Structure of Free Movement of Goods: Reconsideration of an Old Paradigm', 47(3) *Common Market Law Review* (2010), pp. 753-789.

The tensions between the aim of securing the national electricity supply and the aims of free movement law were touched upon in a case concerning a Spanish scheme where certain power plants were required to produce certain volumes of electricity from indigenous coal.[63] The Spanish government compensated these power plants for the additional costs caused by procuring coal the price of which was higher than that of other fuels. In addition, the electricity produced from the indigenous coal benefited from a preferential dispatch mechanism. Proceedings for annulment of the scheme were brought before the General Court after the Commission had approved the scheme under Article 106(2) TFEU.

The applicant argued, *inter alia*, that the Spanish measure infringed Article 34 TFEU by making it difficult to import primary energy sources from other Member States for electricity production.[64] The Commission, however, contended that the Spanish measure could not be considered a measure having equivalent effect simply because it benefited national electricity and coal production.[65]

The Court rejected the applicant's argument on the infringement of Article 34 TFEU. However, it did not go into depth in its analysis concerning the nature of the Spanish measure in relation to Article 34 TFEU. Instead, it relied on established case-law on the relationship between the free movement provisions and State aid.[66] The Court had previously stated that aid does not constitute a measure having equivalent effect simply because certain national undertakings or products benefit from it and, conversely, make the importation of similar or competing products less favourable.[67] Moreover, the General Court referred to the potential justification of the Spanish measure rather than deciding on whether it hindered intra-EU trade.[68] Finally, the General Court stated that the applicant had failed to provide detailed evidence to support its claim that an infringement of Article 34 TFEU had taken place but had only referred to general unfavourable effects of the measure under consideration.[69]

As noted above, the scope of Articles 34 and 35 TFEU is broad and likely to catch capacity mechanisms or elements of capacity mechanisms if cross-border participation is restricted with the effect that intra-EU trade is or could be hindered. The scope of these provisions, however, is not as broad as to include measures that are caught by other Treaty provisions.[70] It is therefore possible that capacity mechanisms may also fall within the application of Article 110 TFEU, which concerns internal taxation, and Article 30 TFEU, which concerns customs duties. These provisions are analysed below with regard to capacity mechanisms.

---

63. Case T-57/11 *Castelnou Energía v Commission* [2014], judgment of the General Court of 3 December 2014, published in the electronic Reports of Cases.
64. *Ibid.*, para. 194.
65. *Ibid.*, para. 195.
66. *Ibid.*, paras 194-197. For further discussion of this topic, *see* section 4 below. *See also* Jacques Derenne, 'Article 107 TFEU', in Weijer Ver Loren van Themaat and Berend Reuder (eds), *European Competition Law: A Case Commentary* (Edward Elgar, 2014), pp. 216-255, at 237.
67. C-74/76 *Ianelli v Meroni* [1977] ECR 557, para. 10.
68. T-57/11 *Castelnou Energía v Commission* [2014], judgment of the General Court of 3 December 2014, published in the electronic Reports of Cases, para. 197.
69. *Ibid.*, paras 199-200.
70. C-74/76 *Ianelli v Meroni* [1977] ECR 557, para. 9.

[B]   Prohibition on Customs Duties, Charges and Taxes

Articles 34 and 35 TFEU seek to ensure that goods and products are able to cross EU's internal borders without being limited by quotas or other quantitative limitations.[71] In addition to prohibiting limitations on the movement of goods or products, the Treaty also prohibits certain monetary obligations attached to these export and import activities.[72] These prohibitions are laid down in Articles 30 and 110 TFEU. These provisions are an integral element in ensuring the free movement of goods.[73]

Article 30 TFEU prohibits customs duties on imports and exports between Member States as well as customs duties of a fiscal nature. The prohibition laid down in Article 30 applies to all charges regardless of their size.[74] As with Articles 34 and 35 TFEU, there is therefore no *de minimis* threshold.[75] Article 30 TFEU also prohibits all charges having equivalent effect to customs duties. The objective of this extension to the scope of Article 30 TFEU is to complement the prohibition of obstacles to trade by increasing the efficiency of the provision.[76] Aligned with this approach, the interpretation of Article 30 TFEU is traditionally broad.[77] It includes any pecuniary charges regardless of their designation or mode of application if imposed on domestic or foreign goods because they cross a border.[78]

It is has been established in case-law that Articles 30 and 110 TFEU do not apply simultaneously.[79] However, Article 110 TFEU further complements the objectives of Article 30 TFEU by prohibiting the imposition of direct or indirect internal taxation of any kind on the products of other Member States in excess of the direct or indirect internal taxation imposed on similar domestic products.[80] Furthermore, Article 110 TFEU contains a prohibition on the imposition of internal taxation on the products of

---

71. Nigel Foster, *Foster on EU Law* (OUP, 2015), pp. 257-258.
72. Alina Kaczorowska-Ireland, *European Union Law* (Routledge, 2009), pp. 541-579.
73. Peter Oliver, 'Free Movement of Goods in the Labyrinth of Energy Policy and Capacity Mechanisms', in Leigh Hancher, Adrien de Hauteclocque and Malgorzata Sadowska (eds), *Capacity Mechanisms in the EU Energy Market* (OUP, 2015), pp. 201-223, at 205; Paul Craig and Gráinne de Búrca, *EU Law: Text, Cases, and Materials*, 6th edn. (OUP, 2015), pp. 638-664.
74. Nigel Foster, *Foster on EU Law* (OUP, 2015), pp. 264-269; Alina Kaczorowska-Ireland, *European Union Law* (Routledge, 2009), pp. 541-579.
75. Joined cases 2 and 3-69 *Sociaal Fonds voor de Diamantarbeiders v S.A. Ch. Brachfeld & Sons and Chougol Diamond Co* [1969] ECR 211, paras 15/18–19/21; Laurence Gormley, *EU Law of Free Movement of Goods and Customs Union* (OUP, 2009), pp. 381-394.
76. Joined cases 2 and 3-69 *Sociaal Fonds voor de Diamantarbeiders v S.A. Ch. Brachfeld & Sons and Chougol Diamond Co* [1969] ECR 211, paras 15/18–19/21.
77. Joined cases 2/62 and 3/62 *Commission v Luxembourg and Belgium* [1962] ECR 0813.
78. Case 24/68 *Commission v Italian Republic* [1969] ECR 193, para. 9; Paul Craig and Gráinne de Búrca, *EU Law: Text, Cases, and Materials*, 6th edn. (OUP, 2015), pp. 639-646.
79. C-383/01 *De Danske Bilimportører* [2003] ECR I-6065; 10/65 *Deutschmann v Germany* [1965] ECR 469, pp. 473-474; 57/65 *Lütticke v Hauptzollamt Saarlouis* [1966] ECR 205, p. 211; C-266/91 *Celbi v Fazenda Pública* [1993] ECR I-4337, para. 9; C-90/94 *Haahr Petroleum Ltd* [1997] ECR I-4085, para. 19.
80. Laurence Gormley, *EU Law of Free Movement of Goods and Customs Union* (OUP, 2009), pp. 381-394; Nigel Foster, *Foster on EU Law* (OUP, 2015), pp. 264-269; Alina Kaczorowska-Ireland, *European Union Law* (Routledge, 2009), pp. 541-579.

other Member States the purpose of which is to indirectly protect other products.[81] It is established case-law that EU law does not restrict the freedom of each Member State to maintain a tax system that differentiates between products.[82] However, EU law does require such differentiation to be compatible with the objectives laid down in EU primary and secondary law and not contain any form of direct or indirect discrimination.[83]

The Commission examined a potential infringement of Articles 30 and 110 TFEU in a State aid case concerning the UK capacity mechanism in 2014.[84] The capacity market, adopted by the UK, is based on centrally managed auctions that are held every four years to procure capacity necessary to ensure generation adequacy in Great Britain.[85] The capacity providers that are successful in the auctions commit to delivering electricity during the contracted delivery year.[86] Eligible capacity providers include both existing and forthcoming capacities as well as demand-side measures. However, interconnected capacity was not eligible in the first auction, which excluded the participation of foreign capacities.[87] The UK scheme is financed by a levy imposed on all licensed electricity suppliers and scaled in relation to the suppliers' market share based on electricity volumes sold. The proceeds of this levy are then reallocated to the capacity providers.[88] The Commission considered this to be very similar to a tax on the electricity consumed.[89]

The potential infringement of EU law was brought up by the Commission in connection with the EEAG, which provides that if a State aid measure or the conditions attached to it entail a non-severable violation of Union law, the aid cannot be declared compatible with the internal market.[90] The EEAG specifically refer to case-law where it is established that a levy financing a State aid measure has to comply with Articles 30

---

81. *See* interpretation in C-132/78 *Denkavit Loire* [1979] ECR 1923, para. 8 and C-15/81 *Schul* [1982] ECR 1409, paras 31-32.
82. C-213/96 *Outokumpu* [1998] ECR I-1777, para. 30.
83. *Ibid.*
84. SA.35980 *GB Capacity Mechanism*, C(2014) 5083 final.
85. The Commission's decision to approve the UK capacity market was annulled by the General Court in T-793/14 *Tempus Energy and Tempus Energy Technology v Commission* [2018], judgment of the General Court of 15 November 2018, published in the electronic Reports of Cases. On 21 February 2019, the Commission opened an in-depth investigation into the UK capacity market. The UK capacity market is suspended while the Commission makes its decision. *See* European Commission, State aid: Commission opens in-depth investigation into British Capacity Market scheme, 21 February 2019, available at http://europa.eu/rapid/press-release_IP-19-1348_en.htm (last accessed 5.3.2019).
86. For an analysis of the elements of the UK capacity market, *see* Pradyumna Chaitanya Bhagwat, *Security of Supply During the Energy Transition: The Role of Capacity Mechanisms* (Technische Universiteit Delft, Phd thesis 2016), pp. 61-72; and Kaisa Huhta, 'Prioritising Energy Efficiency and Demand Side Measures over Capacity Mechanisms under EU Energy Law', 35(1) *Journal of Energy & Natural Resources Law* (2017), pp. 7-24, at 23-24.
87. SA.35980 *GB Capacity Mechanism*, C(2014) 5083 final, para. 20.
88. *Ibid.*, para. 111.
89. *Ibid.*, para. 158.
90. Communication from the Commission, Guidelines on State aid for environmental protection and energy 2014-2020 (OJ C 200, 28.6.2014, pp. 1-55), para. 29; SA.35980 *GB Capacity Mechanism*, C(2014) 5083 final, para. 157; C-156/98 *Germany v Commission* [2000] ECR I-6857, para. 78; joined cases C-128/03 and C-129/03 *AEM and AEM Torino* [2005] ECR I-2861, paras 38-51;

and 110 TFEU.[91] Furthermore, it is established case-law that a charge that is collected from all undertakings, but reallocated for the benefit of domestic undertakings only, may infringe Article 110 TFEU.[92]

The Commission concluded that the UK capacity market did not violate Article 30 or, in particular, Article 110 TFEU. It took the view that the exclusion of interconnecting capacity and the resulting discriminatory taxation was in fact objectively justified on grounds of physical constraints that prevented the equal treatment of foreign and domestic capacity.[93] The Commission also opined that the objective of ensuring national generation adequacy could therefore only be provided by capacity located within the national territory.[94] It further emphasised that the discriminatory arrangement was temporary and that the UK was committed to including interconnecting capacity in future auctions after technical and legal limitations had been solved.[95]

The Commission's conclusion in this respect has been justifiably criticised.[96] The decision seems to interpret the scope of Article 110 TFEU less strictly than the established case-law referred to above. It can even be argued that in the light of the established expansive interpretation of the scope of Articles 30 and 110 TFEU the Court is unlikely to uphold an interpretation that dilutes the objectives and established interpretation of these provisions.[97] Nevertheless, the Commission has since given a similar decision on Greek flexibility services that allowed only domestic capacities to

---

C-333/07 *Régie Networks v Rhone Alpes Bourgogne* [2008] ECR I-10807, paras 94-116. For further discussion of the relationship between free movement law and EU State aid control, *see* section 4 below.

91. C-206/06 *Essent Netwerk Noord* [2008] ECR I-5497, paras 40-59; Communication from the Commission, Guidelines on State aid for environmental protection and energy 2014-2020 (OJ C 200, 28.6.2014, pp. 1-55), para. 29.
92. C-206/06 *Essent Netwerk Noord* [2008] ECR I-5497, para. 57
93. SA.35980 *GB Capacity Mechanism*, C(2014) 5083 final, paras 160-161.
94. *Ibid.*
95. *Ibid.*, para. 160; Annex 2 to Commission Staff Working Document accompanying the document Report from the Commission Final Report of the Sector Inquiry on Capacity Mechanisms, SWD(2016) 385 final, p. 184. The final report of the 2016 State aid sector inquiry shows that, although the UK mechanism was opened to interconnectors, it was still not open to participation by foreign capacity. *See* Commission Staff Working Document accompanying the document Report from the Commission Final Report of the Sector Inquiry on Capacity Mechanisms, SWD(2016) 385 final, para. 186. *See* similar argumentation in cases SA.42011 *Italian Capacity Mechanism*, C(2018) 617 final, particularly paras 204-217, and SA.46100 *Planned Polish Capacity Mechanism*, C(2018) 601 final, paras 188-191.
96. Leigh Hancher, 'Capacity Mechanisms and State Aid Control: A European Solution to the "Missing Money" Problem?', in Leigh Hancher, Adrien de Hautecloque and Malgorzata Sadowska (eds), *Capacity Mechanisms in the EU Energy Market* (OUP, 2015), pp. 157-181, at 179-180.
97. Two appeals were submitted to the General Court on the UK capacity market decision, but neither sought annulment of the decision on the grounds of Articles 30 and 110 TFEU. It has been rightly noted, however, that free movement provisions have been interpreted with varying consistency and that the Court 'tends to recognize the retention of large areas of policy discretion by both governments and the Commission, and is given to accepting the policy compromises hammered out between the Commission, Member States, and other influential forces, instead of trying to interfere with them'. *See* Kim Talus, *EU Energy Law and Policy: A Critical Account* (OUP, 2013), pp. 159-160.

participate in the capacity mechanism.[98] The Commission resorted to very similar reasoning as it used in the case concerning the UK capacity market.[99]

There is no exemption regime that would apply to Article 30 or 110 TFEU.[100] In practice, this means that deviation from the prohibitions laid down in these provisions cannot be justified on the grounds set out in Treaty provisions but rather requires the modification of the national scheme in such a way as to remove the discriminatory effect.[101] The prohibition on quantitative restrictions, however, is subject to a well-established exemption regime founded in both Treaty law and case-law. These exemptions establish grounds to justify the prima facie restrictive elements of capacity mechanisms.

§5.03   JUSTIFICATIONS FOR RESTRICTIONS ON THE FREE MOVEMENT OF GOODS

[A]   Capacity Mechanisms in the Justification Regime

Ensuring investment in sufficient generation capacity through State intervention rather than through market mechanisms constitutes an exemption to the rule on which the EU electricity market is founded. Because of this exceptional role of capacity mechanisms within the context of EU electricity legislation, some elements of many of these mechanisms are in principle prohibited by various legal instruments, such as EU State aid rules and, as seen above, Articles 34 and 35 TFEU. Although capacity mechanisms are easily caught by these prohibitions, their increasing usage by Member States indicates that despite the adverse effect they are known to have on the internal market, the available justifications can be interpreted in favour of national security of supply measures. This section assesses the justifications for restricting the free movement of goods in the context of ensuring generation adequacy through capacity mechanisms.

Security of supply has been established as a legitimate justification for derogation from the rules regarding free movement of goods.[102] However, security of supply is a concept that has no single established definition, let alone a legally binding one. Furthermore, the complex and multi-influential nature of capacity mechanisms does not allow them to be categorised as purely beneficial in terms of fulfilling the objective of security of supply or, *a fortiori*, fulfilling other EU energy policy objectives. It is well established that capacity mechanisms increase the price of electricity and can, thus,

---

98. SA.38968 *Transitory Electricity Flexibility Remuneration Mechanism (FRM)*, C(2016) 1791 final, paras 108-109.
99. *Ibid.*
100. *See* discussion in the Opinion of AG Jacobs in C-383/01 *De Danske Bilimportører* [2003] ECR I-6065, para. 28.
101. Nigel Foster, *Foster on EU Law* (OUP, 2015), pp. 264-269; Alina Kaczorowska-Ireland, *European Union Law* (Routledge, 2009), pp. 541-579.
102. 72/83 *Campus Oil* [1984] ECR 2727.

even have an adverse effect on certain elements of security of supply.[103] Capacity mechanisms also tend to favour conventional generation capacity for the simple reason that conventional power plants are often more suited to responding to peak demand. This tendency is inconsistent with the objectives of phasing out environmentally harmful subsidies and decreasing carbon emissions.[104] Finally, and with particular relevance to this chapter, the competitive advantages achieved through European market integration are undermined when cross-border trade is restricted, even if such restriction is adopted to achieve security of supply within a Member State.[105]

The nature of capacity mechanisms is not the only challenge in interpreting the established justifications for restricting the free movement of goods. The Treaty grounds for exemptions are general and broadly worded and, thus, leave extensive room for interpretation.[106] This broad margin of discretion allows not only legal but also political and technical issues to be taken into account.[107] Therefore, the evolving body of case-law on the justification of restrictions on free movement varies in its consistency and is subject to compromises between European integration and national interests.

Another challenge in analysing the justifications available for capacity mechanisms is the lack of case-law on free movement and measures to ensure national generation adequacy. It is possible to draw upon, on an analogous basis, the case-law on other national security of supply measures and, to a very limited extent, cases concerning environmental justifications in the electricity sector.[108] The reason for the limited analogous applicability of environmental justifications to capacity mechanisms lies in the apparent divergence in the Court's argumentation regarding environmental justifications on the one hand and security of supply justifications on the other. The Court seems to allow for narrower exemptions in the interests of security of supply than for environmental reasons and to settle for less scrutiny before granting an exemption on environmental grounds.[109] Talus has rightly pointed out that the greater value

---

103. International experience of capacity mechanisms shows that their existence can cost up to 10%–20% of wholesale electricity prices. *See* Commission Staff Working Document, Generation Adequacy in the internal electricity market – guidance on public interventions accompanying the document Communication from the Commission Delivering the internal electricity market and making the most of public intervention, SWD(2013) 438 final, p. 32.
104. For more on this objective, *see* Communication from the Commission, Guidelines on State aid for environmental protection and energy 2014-2020 (OJ C 200, 28.6.2014, pp. 1-55), para. 220.
105. Paolo Mastropietro, Pablo Rodilla and Carlos Batlle, 'National Capacity Mechanisms in the European Internal Energy Market: Opening the Doors to Neighbours', 82 *Energy Policy* (2015), pp. 38-47, at 38-41.
106. Kim Talus, *EU Energy Law and Policy: A Critical Account* (OUP, 2013), p. 159; Alina Kaczorowska-Ireland, *European Union Law* (Routledge, 2009), pp. 630-656; Nigel Foster, *Foster on EU Law* (OUP, 2015), pp. 278-284.
107. Kim Talus, *EU Energy Law and Policy: A Critical Account* (OUP, 2013), pp. 159-160. In case-law, *see* SA.42011 *Italian Capacity Mechanism*, C(2018) 617 final, para. 59.
108. *See*, for example, C-379/98 *PreussenElektra* [2001] ECR I-2099; and C-573/12 *Ålands Vindkraft AB v Energimyndigheten* [2014] ECR II-2037.
109. *See*, for example, C-379/98 *PreussenElektra* [2001] ECR I-2099, paras 68-81, where instead of scrutinising the applicability of the grounds for justification, the Court simply declared the contested measure to be 'not incompatible' with Article 34 TFEU. Similar arguments on the leeway afforded to environmental justifications can be found in Henrik Bjørnebye, *Investing in EU Energy Security: Exploring the Regulatory Approach to Tomorrow's Electricity Production*

accorded to environmental objectives means that 'protectionism will increasingly seek environmental camouflage'.[110] This inevitably also applies to capacity mechanisms, particularly if they are adopted to protect purely national interests rather than to safeguard legitimate concerns over security of supply.

Finally, due to the variation in capacity mechanism designs, some elements of these mechanisms can be more problematic in terms of free movement than others. Therefore, it is not realistic to attempt to formulate a definitive interpretation of the justification regime by which capacity mechanisms could always be exempted from the prohibition on quantitative restrictions. Rather, the purpose here is to demonstrate the potential framework within which it is possible for capacity mechanisms to be caught by the justification regime.

The legal point of departure for derogation from Articles 34 and 35 TFEU is Article 36 TFEU.[111] Article 36 TFEU establishes that the restrictions prohibited in Articles 34 and 35 TFEU can be justified on grounds of, *inter alia*, public morality, public policy, public security and the protection of health and life of humans, animals or plants. Such restrictions cannot, however, constitute arbitrary discrimination or a disguised restriction on trade between Member States.[112]

In addition to the explicit derogation established in Article 36 TFEU, the Court has established a non-exhaustive list of so-called mandatory requirements, which have been developed to protect other legitimate interests that are not caught by Article 36 TFEU.[113] Most importantly for (renewable) electricity, protection of the environment has been established as a mandatory requirement that can be invoked to justify derogation from the prohibitions laid down in Articles 34 and 35 TFEU.[114] It is established law that the exhaustive list of justifications set out in Article 36 TFEU and the mandatory requirements established in case-law are the only grounds on which Member States may deviate from the prohibitions laid down in Articles 34 and 35

(University of Oslo, PhD thesis 2009), pp. 63, 65 and 92-99; and Kim Talus, EU *Energy Law and Policy: A Critical Account* (OUP, 2013), pp. 167-174. On a general level, *see* Tim Rusche, *EU Renewable Electricity Law and Policy: From National Targets to a Common Market* (Cambridge University Press, 2015).

110. Kim Talus, *EU Energy Law and Policy: A Critical Account* (OUP, 2013), p. 174.
111. Panos Koutrakos, 'Public Security Exceptions and EU Free Movement Law', in Panos Koutrakos, Niamh Nic Shuibhne and Phil Syrpis (eds), *Exceptions from EU Free Movement Law: Derogation, Justification and Proportionality* (Hart Publishing, 2016), pp. 190-217; Laurence Gormley, *EU Law of Free Movement of Goods and Customs Union* (OUP, 2009), pp. 463-465; Paul Craig and Gráinne de Búrca, *EU Law: Text, Cases, and Materials*, 6th edn. (OUP, 2015), pp. 698-699; Alina Kaczorowska-Ireland, *European Union Law* (Routledge, 2009), pp. 630-656; Nigel Foster, *Foster on EU Law* (OUP, 2015), pp. 278-284.
112. Article 36 TFEU.
113. The concept of mandatory requirements was first established in case 120/78 *Rewe-Zentral AG v Bundesmonopolverwaltung für Branntwein 'Cassis de Dijon'* [1979] ECR 649. For a list of cases in which mandatory requirements have been applied, *see* Friedl Weiss and Clemens Kaupa, *European Union Internal Market Law* (Cambridge University Press, 2014), p. 33, and the case-law cited therein. *See also* Henrik Bjørnebye, *Investing in EU Energy Security: Exploring the Regulatory Approach to Tomorrow's Electricity Production* (University of Oslo, PhD thesis 2009), pp. 64-65.
114. 302/86 *Commission v Denmark* [1988] ECR 4607, para. 9. *See* the discussion on environmental protection as a mandatory requirement in the Opinion of AG Jacobs in C-379/98 *PreussenElektra* [2001] ECR I-2099, paras 190-238.

TFEU. This also applies to the exemption provided for in Article 106(2) TFEU, which is extensively discussed above.[115] In other words, even a legitimately established PSO that is in the general economic interest must be justifiable under Article 36 TFEU if the measure in question infringes Article 34 or 35 TFEU. In practice, however, general economic interests within the meaning of Article 106(2) TFEU largely overlap with the protected interests established in Article 36 TFEU.[116] Nevertheless, Article 106(2) TFEU cannot be invoked to justify non-compliance with Articles 34 and 35 TFEU.[117]

Security of supply has traditionally been assessed under the head of public security provided for in Article 36 TFEU.[118] This is also the starting point for assessing the justifiability of capacity mechanisms. Regardless of the extent to which national interests and needs are involved, a public security exemption should be interpreted narrowly as an exemption from a fundamental rule of EU law. The objective is to avoid extending the scope of the exemption further than necessary to protect public security.[119] Furthermore, a Member State that invokes Article 36 TFEU to justify a restriction must prove that the restriction is justified.[120]

---

115. *See* Chapter 3 above.
116. For a discussion on the relationship between Article 106 TFEU and the free movement provisions, *see* C-157/94 *Commission v Netherlands* [1997] ECR I-5699, paras 27-33, and the very same arguments in almost the same formulation in C-158/94 *Commission v Italy* [1997] ECR I-5789, paras 38-44 and C-159/94 *Commission v France* [1997] ECR I-5815, paras 44-50. *See* also Wolf Sauter, 'Public Services and the Internal Market: Building Blocks or Persistent Irritant?', 21(6) *European Law Journal* (2015), pp. 738-757, at 747-750.
117. 72/83 *Campus Oil* [1984] ECR 2727, para. 19.
118. However, other grounds for justifying security of supply measures have been suggested in legal literature. *See* Henrik Bjørnebye, *Investing in EU Energy Security: Exploring the Regulatory Approach to Tomorrow's Electricity Production* (University of Oslo, PhD thesis 2009), pp. 82-85, which suggests security of supply could be reviewed on public health grounds, also provided for in Article 36 TFEU.
119. On free movement rules, *see* 72/83 *Campus Oil* [1984] ECR 2727, para. 37; C-54/99 *Église de scientologie* [2000] ECR I-1335, para. 17; C-503/99 *Commission v Belgium* [2002] ECR I-4809, para. 47; 13/78 *Eggers* [1978] ECR I-1935, para. 30. On other Treaty provisions, *see* C-157/94 *Netherlands* [1997] ECR I-5699, para. 37; and C-159/94 *Commission v France* [1997] ECR I-5815, paras 53-55.
120. C-251/78 *Denkavit Futtermittel* [1979] ECR 3369, para. 28; C-297/05 *Commission v Netherlands* [2007] ECR I-7467, para. 76; C-420/01 *Commission v Italy* [2003] ECR I-6445, paras 30-31; and C-270/02 *Commission v Italy* [2004] ECR I-1559, para. 22. For further discussion of this topic, *see* Niamh Nic Shuibhne, 'Exceptions to the Free Movement Rules', in Catherine Barnard and Steve Peers (eds), *European Union Law* (OUP, 2014), pp. 473-503, at 489-490. Conversely, the Commission or an undertaking invoking an infringement of Article 34 or 35 must prove that a Member State measure infringes these articles. On the failure to do so, *see* case T-57/11 *Castelnou Energía v Commission* [2014], judgment of the General Court of 3 December 2014, published in the electronic Reports of Cases, paras 194-201.

[B]   Security of Supply As a Justification under Article 36 TFEU

[1]   *The Historical Point of Reference for Interpreting Article 36 TFEU:* Campus Oil

The well-established point of departure for interpreting the scope of Article 36 TFEU with regard to security of energy supply is the seminal 1984 *Campus Oil* case.[121] This landmark ruling has been the topic of extensive discussion not only in the literature on EU energy law but also in the literature concerning general EU law, particularly free movement law.[122] The case still continues to be the Court's main point of reference when discussing security of supply and justifying restrictions on free movement.[123]

The *Campus Oil* case concerned a measure enacted by the Irish government to pursue security of energy supply in Ireland in the 1980s. To ensure this objective, the Irish government established a State-owned oil company Irish National Petroleum Corporation (hereinafter 'INPC'), the purpose of which was to meet a significant proportion of Ireland's oil demand.[124] In the early 1980s, the INPC purchased Ireland's only operational refinery, in Whitegate, to prevent it from closing down and Ireland from becoming entirely dependent on external supplies of oil.[125] To ensure the continuance of operations at the refinery, the government adopted a measure by which all those importing petroleum products into Ireland had to purchase a certain proportion of their requirements from the INPC and the Whitegate refinery.[126] The price of these products was determined by the government on the basis of costs incurred by the INPC, and was usually above market price.[127]

The Irish measure was brought before a national court on the basis that it constituted a violation of EU law. The case was referred to the ECJ to inquire, first, whether the Irish measure was contrary to Article 34 TFEU and, second, whether it could nevertheless be justified on the basis of Article 36 TFEU and, in particular, public security or public policy.

Without hesitation, both the Court and the Advocate General declared the Irish measure to fall within the scope of application of prohibited measures having equivalent effect to a quantitative restriction.[128] However, the continuing relevance of the

---

121. 72/83 *Campus Oil* [1984] ECR 2727.
122. Panos Koutrakos, 'Public Security Exceptions and EU Free Movement Law', in Panos Koutra- kos, Niamh Nic Shuibhne and Phil Syrpis (eds), *Exceptions from EU Free Movement Law: Derogation, Justification and Proportionality* (Hart Publishing, 2016), pp. 190-217; Laurence Gormley, *EU Law of Free Movement of Goods and Customs Union* (OUP, 2009), pp. 463-465; Paul Craig and Gráinne de Búrca, *EU Law: Text, Cases, and Materials*, 6th edn. (OUP, 2015), pp. 698-699; Nigel Foster, *Foster on EU Law* (OUP, 2015), p. 280.
123. C-503/99 *Commission v Belgium* [2002] ECR I-4809; C-398/98 *Commission v Greece* [2001] ECR I-7915; C-347/88 *Commission v Greece* [1990] ECR I-4747; C-463/00 *Commission v Spain* [2003] ECR I-4581; C-483/99 *Commission v France* [2002] ECR I-4781; C-326/07 *Commission v Italy* [2009] ECR I-2291.
124. 72/83 *Campus Oil* [1984] ECR 2727, p. 2731.
125. *Ibid.*, paras 3-5.
126. *Ibid.*, p. 2732.
127. *Ibid.*
128. *Ibid.*, para. 20; and Opinion of AG Slynn in 72/83 *Campus Oil* [1984] ECR 2727, p. 2761.

case lies in the guidance it provides as to the extent to which Member States may successfully invoke public security as justification for national measures ensuring security of supply, as in this case the Court first made the connection between the two. On this basis, the Irish measure was held to be justified on the grounds of Article 36 TFEU.[129]

The Court's decision in *Campus Oil* is regarded as exceptional as it permitted a clearly protectionist measure to stand on the basis of the exemptions provided for in Article 36 TFEU.[130] It is nevertheless consistently referenced in case-law on security of supply and free movement under EU law.[131] However, the Court seems to refer to *Campus Oil* primarily to distinguish the case at hand from it and to indicate why the criteria established in *Campus Oil* do not apply analogously.[132] This approach has led inevitably to the Court narrowing of the scope of the public security justification for ensuring security of supply.

Arguably a lot has changed since *Campus Oil*. In particular, numerous political, technical, economic and legal changes have taken place. There have also been significant developments in the role of the State in providing important societal services. Taken cumulatively, these changes offer a strong body of argument as to why the reasoning used in *Campus Oil* cannot be analogously applied to capacity mechanisms.

First, *Campus Oil* should be viewed in its historical and geopolitical context. Ireland took steps to secure its energy supply at a time when the 1973-1974 oil crisis had triggered Europe-wide action to ensure that dependence on external oil supplies did not threaten national and European security.[133] As an island State with no domestic supply of oil, Ireland was particularly vulnerable to external political turmoil.[134] Had

---

129. This connection has since made its way into legal instruments as well. *See* recital 2 of Commission Regulation (EU) 2015/1222 of 24 Jul. 2015 establishing a guideline on capacity allocation and congestion management (OJ L 197, 25.7.2015, pp. 24-72) (hereinafter the 'Regulation on Capacity Allocation and Congestion Management').

130. Opinion of AG Jacobs in C-379/98 *PreussenElektra* [2001] I-2099, para. 209. However, some suggest that the public security criteria established in *Campus Oil* are, in fact, strict. *See* Henrik Bjørnebye, *Investing in EU Energy Security: Exploring the Regulatory Approach to Tomorrow's Electricity Production* (University of Oslo, PhD thesis 2009), p. 81.

131. For example, C-398/98 *Commission v Greece* [2001] ECR I-7915, para. 29; C-503/99 *Commission v Belgium* [2002] ECR I-4809, paras 27 and 46; C-347/88 *Commission v Greece* [1990] ECR I-4747, paras 47-50; joined cases C-105/12 to C-107/12 *Essent and Others* [2013], judgment of the Court of 22 October 2013, published in the electronic Reports of Cases, para. 59; C-174/04 *Commission v Italy* [2005] ECR I-4933.

132. For example, C-347/88 *Commission v Greece* [1990] ECR I-4747, paras 47-50; C-463/00 *Commission v Spain* [2003] ECR I-4581; C-483/99 *Commission v France* [2002] ECR I-4781; C-326/07 *Commission v Italy* [2009] ECR I-2291; and in contrast C-503/99 *Commission v Belgium* [2002] ECR I-4809.

133. The obligation to maintain minimum oil stocks first found expression in Council Directive 68/414/EEC of 20 December 1968 imposing an obligation on Member States of the EEC to maintain minimum stocks of crude oil and/or petroleum products (OJ L 308, 23.12.1968, pp. 14-16). These requirements were further extended in the early 1970s through Council Directive 72/425/EEC of 19 December 1972 amending the Council Directive of 20 December 1968 imposing an obligation on Member States of the EEC to maintain minimum stocks of crude oil and/or petroleum products (OJ L 291, 28.12.1972, pp. 154-154).

134. On the relationship between energy dependence and State exposure to externally unfavourable developments, *see* Daniel Yergin, 'Energy Security and Markets', in Jan H. Kalicki and David L.

the Whitegate refinery been allowed to close down, Ireland would have been entirely dependent on foreign supplies of petroleum products, 80% of which would have come from a single source.[135] Although Ireland's geographical location continues to impose certain limitations, it is no longer as isolated as it was in the 1980s. In 2014, approximately 9% of the country's installed electricity generation capacity was interconnected with other Member States.[136]

Second, the significance of petroleum products to fulfil energy demand is decreasing within the context of the energy transition. Although it remains dependent on oil to a remarkable extent, Europe is in the process of diversifying and decarbonising its energy mix, which will lead to decreased dependence on conventional energy sources.[137] Because of this shift, the nature of security of supply concerns has also changed and evolved to include other issues, such as generation inadequacy. This development demonstrates the fact that security of supply is an ever-evolving, multidimensional concept that is anchored to ever-developing political, legal, technical and market realities.

Finally, the changing economic approach to markets and the legal requirements imposed by the EU on Member States have fundamentally reshaped the structure of the European electricity markets and the roles of the players operating within those markets. The State is no longer the provider of all services but rather the facilitator of non-discriminatory competition, which is believed to ensure security of supply at least cost to the consumer. In practice, this is well demonstrated by the aftermath of *Campus Oil*. The refinery that Ireland had considered so indispensable was closed down by the State in the mid-1990s, thus entrusting the task of guaranteeing security of supply to the market.[138] Aligned with this new approach to market forces, legal changes followed. European electricity markets have since been subjected to extensive legal requirements aimed at achieving a competitive internal market in electricity.[139] This ever-increasing body of harmonising law that applies to electricity markets and security of supply is discussed below with regard to capacity mechanisms.

Goldwyn (eds), *Energy & Security*, 2nd edn. (John Hopkins University Press, 2013), pp. 69-87, at 73-74; Elisabetta Righini and Juan Carlos González Fernández, 'Capacity Mechanisms and State Aid: Between PSOs, Market Liberalisation, and Security of Supply', 7(10) *Journal of European Competition Law & Practice* (2016), pp. 661-675, at 664.

135. 72/83 *Campus Oil* [1984] ECR 2727, para. 5. *See also* paras 30-31, where it is noted that this single supplier, the UK, would be able to restrict exports to Ireland.

136. Communication from the Commission to the European Parliament and the Council, Achieving the 10% electricity interconnection target Making Europe's electricity grid fit for 2020, COM(2015) 82 final, p. 5.

137. Communication from the Commission to the European Parliament and the Council, European Energy Security Strategy, COM(2014) 330 final.

138. Kim Talus, *EU Energy Law and Policy: A Critical Account* (OUP, 2013), p. 163.

139. Recital 1 of the Electricity Directive.

[2]   The Relevance of Existing Harmonisation

It is established case-law that when a matter is extensively harmonised, recourse to Article 36 TFEU is no longer possible.[140] The rationale of this rule is that harmonising legislation is expected to sufficiently protect the interests mentioned in Article 36 TFEU and, therefore, remove the need to invoke the general justification grounds established in that article.[141]

Even in *Campus Oil*, it was argued that the existing Community measures provided sufficient guarantees of security of supply and made recourse to Article 36 TFEU no longer possible.[142] This was despite the fact that the applicable Community measures were significantly less comprehensive than the current legislative framework for security of electricity supply.[143] The Court agreed that Community measures provided certain guarantees for countries whose supplies of petroleum products *depended totally or almost totally* on deliveries from other countries.[144] However, it concluded that the security of supply guarantees contained in Community legislation did not provide *unconditional assurance* that supplies would be maintained at a level that would ensure that Ireland's minimum energy needs would be met.[145] Because of this, Ireland was able to successfully invoke Article 36 TFEU and justify its national legislation on grounds of public security.

Since *Campus Oil*, the body of law that governs EU electricity markets and, in particular, security of supply has grown extensively. Ensuring a minimum level of oil stocks in Member States is no longer at the core of EU security of supply requirements. Instead, the emphasis is on ensuring security of supply in the long term by increasing energy efficiency, pursuing ambitious climate goals, diversifying the energy mix and ensuring sufficient generation of electricity within the EU.[146] Most importantly in

---

140. 120/78 *Rewe-Zentral v Bundesmonopolverwaltung fuer Branntwein* [1979] ECR 649; joined cases C-267/91 and C-268/91 *Keck Mithouard* [1993] ECR I-6097, para. 15; 148/78 *Ratti* [1979] ECR 1629; 251/78 *Denkavit* [1979] ECR 3369; C-190/87 *Oberkreisdirektor des Kreises Borken and Others v Moormann* [1988] ECR 4689; C-102/96 *Commission v Germany* [1998] ECR I-6871; C-473/98 *Toolex* [2000] ECR I-5681, para. 25; C-5/94 *Hedley Lomas* [1996] ECR I-2553, para. 18; C-573/12 *Ålands Vindkraft AB v Energimyndigheten* [2014] ECR II-2037, para. 58; Paul Craig and Gráinne de Búrca, *EU Law: Text, Cases, and Materials*, 6th edn. (OUP, 2015), pp. 703-704; Nina Boeger, 'Minimum Harmonisation, Free Movement and Proportionality', in Phil Syrpis (ed), *The Judiciary, the Legislature and the EU Internal Market* (Cambridge University Press, 2012), pp. 62-91.
141. Cases 5/77 *Carlo Tedeschi* [1977] ECR 1555, paras 34-35; and 72/83 *Campus Oil* [1984] ECR 2727, para. 27.
142. The legal instrument in force at the time was Council Directive 72/425/EEC of 19 December 1972 amending the Council Directive of 20 December 1968 imposing an obligation on Member States of the EEC to maintain minimum stocks of crude oil and/or petroleum products (OJ L 291, 28.12.1972, pp. 154-154). *See* the Commission's argumentation on the sufficiency of the minimum stocking obligations in C-483/99 *Commission v France* [2002] ECR I-4781, paras 24-26.
143. For an analysis of the existing legislative framework for security of supply, *see* Chapter 3 above.
144. 72/83 *Campus Oil* [1984] ECR 2727, para. 32.
145. *Ibid.*, para. 31.
146. Communication from the Commission to the European Parliament and the Council, European Energy Security Strategy, COM(2014) 330 final.

respect of capacity mechanisms, the emphasis is on the facilitation of necessary investment in both network and generation capacity.[147]

However, it is questionable whether any legal framework could genuinely provide *unconditional* assurances in respect of such a multidimensional and complex objective as security of supply.[148] The key to approaching this question in terms of capacity mechanisms lies in the market-based approach to electricity markets. The prevailing EU legal approach does not require a State to unilaterally guarantee the supply of electricity during all hours of the year but expects the balance between supply and demand to incentivise the level of generation capacity that final consumers are willing to pay for. The price of guaranteeing an absolutely reliable system within which no supply disruptions could take place would be absurdly high. In other words, the market-based approach to generation investment adopted in EU electricity law is not expected to guarantee unconditional assurances as to security of supply but only to guarantee the level of security of supply for which the market is prepared to pay. In fact, security of supply guarantees are very much conditional on the market price of electricity and the corresponding economic incentives. Furthermore, the internal market ideology is governed by the notion that electricity should be produced where the cost of doing so is lowest and sold where the price is the highest. This approach implies that Member States are expected to be *dependent* on other countries to supply energy when needed.[149]

The EU's electricity market legislation contains harmonising provisions under which Member States may take exceptional measures to ensure security of supply. In addition to the specific legal grounds for introducing capacity mechanisms,[150] Article 15(4) of the Electricity Directive provides that a Member State may, for reasons of security of supply, direct that priority access be given to the dispatch of generating installations using indigenous primary energy fuel sources. This exception is limited to a maximum of 15% of the overall primary energy necessary to produce the electricity consumed in a Member State within any calendar year.[151] Member States may also take temporary safeguard measures in the event of a sudden crisis in the energy market and where the physical safety or security of persons, apparatus or installations or system integrity is threatened.[152] The question arises, however, as to whether the matter of capacity mechanisms can be considered harmonised to such an extent as would preclude the application of Article 36 TFEU to capacity mechanisms.

As noted in Chapter 3 above, security of electricity supply is not addressed in detail in secondary electricity legislation. In particular, State intervention to facilitate investment in generation capacity is directly and substantially governed only by a

---

147. *Ibid.*
148. Henrik Bjørnebye, *Investing in EU Energy Security: Exploring the Regulatory Approach to Tomorrow's Electricity Production* (University of Oslo, PhD thesis 2009), p. 70.
149. Kaisa Huhta, 'Too Important to Be Entrusted to Neighbours? The Dynamics of Security of Electricity Supply and Mutual Trust in EU law', 43(6) *European Law Review* (2018), pp. 920-933.
150. Analysed in Chapter 3 above.
151. Article 15(4) of the Electricity Directive.
152. Article 42 of the Electricity Directive.

fragmentary body of both primary and secondary law, the systematic application of which has not yet been tested by the EU courts. If the electricity sector legislation is assessed in its entirety, the harmonising measures seem indeed extensive. However, if the legislative measures concerning capacity mechanisms alone are analysed, the level of detail and legal direction is much more ambiguous. In determining the existing level of harmonisation, the Court has taken a fairly restricted approach to the subject matter at hand. For example, in *Ålands Vindkraft*, the Court determined the level of harmonisation by looking at the harmonisation of support schemes for green electricity and not the production of renewable energy as a whole.[153] It stated that because EU law had not harmonised national support schemes for green electricity, it was still possible, in principle, for Member States to limit access to such schemes located in their territory.[154] Therefore, asking whether the security of supply defence under Article 36 TFEU is still relevant in the electricity sector is not really the right question.[155] Rather than looking at the harmonisation of security of supply alone, the focus should be specifically on the harmonisation of capacity mechanisms. Aligned with this analysis, the harmonisation of capacity mechanisms cannot be considered sufficiently exhaustive to preclude the application of Article 36 TFEU.

However, remuneration for capacity at national level will be the subject of future EU legislation, which will considerably limit Member States' ability to invoke Article 36 TFEU.[156] The position of the EU is clear in this regard: it is no longer sufficient to set general objectives and leave the measures to ensure security of supply to Member States' individual discretion. Instead, a coordinated approach, which reflects the needs of an interconnected electricity market, is needed.[157] When the legislation proposed for capacity mechanisms in 2016 enters into force, the threshold for exhaustive harmonisation with regard to Article 36 TFEU will be reached.[158] Overall, such exhaustive harmonisation would result in assessing Member States' capacity mechanism designs in the light of the harmonising provisions and not those contained in the Treaty.[159]

---

153. C-573/12 *Ålands Vindkraft AB v Energimyndigheten* [2014] ECR II-2037, para. 94.
154. *Ibid.*
155. Opinion of AG Jacobs in C-379/98 *PreussenElektra* [2001] ECR I-2099, para. 209; Kim Talus, *EU Energy Law and Policy: A Critical Account* (OUP, 2013), p. 165.
156. *See*, in particual, the Recast Electricity Regulation.
157. Proposal for a Regulation of the European Parliament and of the Council on risk-preparedness in the electricity sector and repealing Directive 2005/89/EC, COM(2016) 862 final, pp. 2-3 and recitals 5 and 6 of the Proposal for a Regulation of the European Parliament and of the Council, Establishing a European Union Agency for the Cooperation of Energy Regulators, COM(2016) 863 final.
158. For an analysis, *see* Chapter 7 below.
159. C-37/92 *Vanacker and Lesage* [1993] ECR I-4947, para. 9; C-324/99 *DaimlerChrysler* [2001] ECR I-9897, para. 32; C-322/01 *Deutscher Apothekerverband* [2003] ECR I-14887, para. 64. For further discussion of this topic, *see* Niamh Nic Shuibhne, 'Exceptions to the free movement rules', in Catherine Barnard and Steve Peers (eds), *European Union Law* (OUP, 2014), pp. 473-503, at 475.

[3]   The Public Security Defence and Capacity Mechanisms

As noted above, the Court first made the connection between security of supply and the public security defence in *Campus Oil*.[160] The availability of petroleum product was the key element in justifying the validity of security of supply as a facet of public security in that case. Since *Campus Oil*, the public security defence has been invoked to defend restrictions on free movement on the basis of different elements of security of supply.[161]

It is well established that the public security defence can be applied in relation to petroleum products. This was confirmed not only in *Campus Oil* but also in two subsequent cases in which Greece defended its restrictive national measures on public security grounds.[162] Although Greece was unsuccessful in its arguments, the Court confirmed in both cases that maintaining sufficient supplies of petroleum products was, in principle, capable of constituting a public security interest.

The Court has since extended its interpretation of the scope of the public security defence still further. In *Commission v Belgium*, it held that safeguarding energy supplies in the event of a crisis falls undeniably within the scope of 'a legitimate public interest'.[163] The General Court has referred to achieving security of electricity supply as a reason capable of justifying restrictions on free movement on grounds of public security.[164] As a fundamental element of uninterrupted availability of electricity, adequate generation capacity is implicitly included within the scope of this reason.

Extending the scope of the public security justification from petroleum products to electricity is in line with Member States' increasing reliance on electricity. The more the European economy is dependent on electricity, the stronger the public security justification for security of electricity supply becomes. The special economic role of petroleum products at the time the case was decided constituted the critical reason for the Court taking the view in *Campus Oil* that their availability amounted to a legitimate

---

160. 72/83 *Campus Oil* [1984] ECR 2727.
161. C-347/88 *Commission v Greece* [1990] ECR I-4747; C-398/98 *Commission v Greece* [2001] ECR I-7915; C-503/99 *Commission v Belgium* [2002] ECR I-4809; C-463/00 *Commission v Spain* [2003] ECR I-4581; C-483/99 *Commission v France* [2002] ECR I-4781; C-326/07 *Commission v Italy* [2009] ECR I-2291; joined cases C-105/12 to C-107/12 *Essent and Others* [2013], judgment of the Court of 22 October 2013, published in the electronic Reports of Cases, para. 59; C-174/04 *Commission v Italy* [2005] ECR I-4933.
162. C-347/88 *Commission v Greece* [1990] ECR I-4747, para. 48; C-398/98 *Commission v Greece* [2001] ECR I-7915, para. 29.
163. C-503/99 *Commission v Belgium* [2002] ECR I-4809, para. 46. This case concerned the free movement of capital, which is not governed by Articles 34 and 36 TFEU. However, the rules on free movement of capital also include justifications on grounds of public security and are, therefore, relevant here. *See* Articles 63 and 65 TFEU. *See also* C-393/92 *Almelo* [1994] ECR I-1477, paras 46-50; and C-463/00 *Commission v Spain* [2003] ECR I-4581, para. 70.
164. T-57/11 *Castelnou Energía v Commission* [2014], judgment of the General Court of 3 December 2014, published in the electronic Reports of Cases, para. 197.

public security interest.[165] The economic role of electricity today is not unlike that of petroleum products in the 1980s.[166]

In principle, Member States are free to determine the content of their public security requirements in accordance with their domestic needs.[167] Overall, the concept of public security has been established to cover matters of both internal and external security.[168] However, the application of the public security defence to ensuring generation adequacy must be carried out in a manner that observes the boundaries established by EU law.

As an exemption from a fundamental EU rule, the public security justification should be interpreted strictly.[169] In practice, this means that Member States cannot unilaterally determine the scope of their public security requirements without control by EU institutions.[170] This interpretation is also in line with the *telos* of Article 36 TFEU, which is not to reserve certain matters to the exclusive jurisdiction of Member States. Rather, its purpose is to allow derogation from the principle of free movement to the extent that is necessary in order to protect the interests mentioned in Article 36 TFEU.[171] Reserving those matters to the exclusive jurisdiction of the Member States would also be contrary to the competence provisions of the Treaty, which determine the scope of the EU's competence in different sectors and define energy as an area in which shared competences apply.[172] Any Member State invoking a public security justification must be able to demonstrate that grounds for such justification exist.[173]

---

165. The Opinion of AG Jacobs in C-379/98 *PreussenElektra* [2001] ECR I-2099, para. 209.
166. Similar argumentation in Henrik Bjørnebye, *Investing in EU Energy Security: Exploring the Regulatory Approach to Tomorrow's Electricity Production* (University of Oslo, PhD thesis 2009), pp. 65-81.
167. C-326/07 *Commission v Italy* [2009] ECR I-2291, para. 70; C-54/99 *Église de scientologie* [2000] ECR I-1335 para. 17; C-83/94 *Leifer and Others* [1995] ECR I-3231, para. 35.
168. C-367/89 *Richardt and 'Les Accessoires Scientifiques'* [1991] ECR I-4621, para. 22; C-83/94 *Leifer and Others* [1995] ECR I-3231, para. 26; and discussion in the Opinion of AG Slynn in 72/83 *Campus Oil* [1984] ECR 2727, p. 2764.
169. Cases 36/75 *Rutili v Minister for the Interior* [1975] ECR 1219, para. 27; 30/77 *R v Bouchereau* [1977] ECR -1999, para. 30; C-157/94 *Commission v Netherlands* [1997] ECR I-5699, para. 37; C-159/94 *Commission v France* [1997] ECR I-5815, paras 53-55; C-54/99 *Église de scientologie* [2000] ECR I-1335, para. 17; C-326/07 *Commission v Italy* [2009] ECR I-2291, para. 70; C-503/99 *Commission v Belgium* [2002] ECR I-4809, para. 47; C-483/99 *Commission v France* [2002] ECR I-4781, para. 48; C-463/00 *Commission v Spain* [2003] ECR I-4581, para. 72.
170. C-326/07 *Commission v Italy* [2009] ECR I-2291, para. 70; C-54/99 *Eglise de scientologie* [2000] ECR I-1335, para. 17; C-463/00 *Commission v Spain* [2003] ECR I-4581, para. 34; C-483/99 *Commission v France* [2002] ECR I-4781, para. 48; 36/75 *Rutili v Minister for the Interior* [1975] ECR 1219, para. 27.
171. C-106/77 *Amministrazione delle finanze dello Stato v Simmenthal* [1978] ECR 629, para. 14; 153/78 *Commission v Germany* [1979] ECR 2555, para. 5; 72/83 *Campus Oil* [1984] ECR 2727, para. 32.
172. Article 4 TFEU. *See also* Panos Koutrakos, 'Public Security Exceptions and EU Free Movement Law', in Panos Koutrakos, Niamh Nic Shuibhne and Phil Syrpis (eds), *Exceptions from EU Free Movement Law: Derogation, Justification and Proportionality* (Hart Publishing, 2016), pp. 190-217; Laurence Gormley, *EU Law of Free Movement of Goods and Customs Union* (OUP, 2009), pp. 463-465; Paul Craig and Gráinne de Búrca, *EU Law: Text, Cases, and Materials*, 6th edn. (OUP, 2015), pp. 698-699; Alina Kaczorowska-Ireland, *European Union Law* (Routledge, 2009), pp. 630-656; Nigel Foster, *Foster on EU Law* (OUP, 2015), pp. 278-284.
173. C-251/78 *Denkavit Futtermittel* [1979] ECR 3369, para. 28. *See*, for example, cases C-297/05 *Commission v Netherlands* [2007] ECR I-7467, para. 76; C-420/01 *Commission v Italy* [2003]

In interpreting the scope of Member States' legitimate public security interest, the Court has sought to balance Member States' interests against the need to prevent an ever-widening interpretation that would undermine the objectives of the internal market. In *Campus Oil*, the legitimacy of the Irish measure was evaluated against the facts and background circumstances. First, petroleum products were of fundamental importance to the functioning of a modern economy and, second, Ireland had no domestic supply of crude oil.[174] It was, therefore, heavily reliant on external suppliers.[175] In this context, the Court stated as follows:

> 'because of their exceptional importance as an energy source in the modern economy, [petroleum products] are of fundamental importance for a country's existence since not only its economy but above all its institutions, its essential public services and even the survival of its inhabitants depend upon them. An interruption of supplies of petroleum products, with the resultant dangers for the country's existence, could therefore seriously affect the public security that Article 36 allows States to protect.'[176]

In other words, the Court evaluated the legitimacy of a Member State's public security interests in relation not only to its *dependence on others* in ensuring an interest but also in relation to the *importance of the protected interest*.

The Court applied the dependence approach in its analysis of a Greek security of supply measure in 1990.[177] The purpose of the measure was to ensure the supply of crude oil and petroleum products by reserving the right to import crude oil and petroleum products exclusively to the State.[178] The Court confirmed that total or partial dependence on external supplies was, in principle, an argument in favour of a legitimate public service interest.[179] However, it concluded that the State's exclusive right to import and market crude oil and petroleum products had the effect of excluding competition and, thus, preventing rather than ensuring the continued operation of other refineries.[180]

Defining and scoping the importance of a protected interest is a difficult task, not least because the definition must be capable of being interpreted in a national context. This risks the objectivity of the concept and may allow an exemption to be given an unnecessarily wide interpretation. The Court has consistently held that while safeguarding energy supplies in the event of a crisis is a legitimate public security interest, it can be relied on as a justification only if there is *a genuine and sufficiently serious*

ECR I-6445, paras 30 and 31; and C-270/02 *Commission v Italy* [2004] ECR I-1559, para. 22. For further discussion of this topic, *see* Niamh Nic Shuibhne, 'Exceptions to the Free Movement Rules', in Catherine Barnard and Steve Peers (eds), *European Union Law* (OUP, 2014), pp. 473-503, at 489-490.

174. 72/83 *Campus Oil* [1984] ECR 2727, p. 2731.
175. *Ibid.*
176. *Ibid.*, paras 32-34.
177. C-347/88 *Commission v Greece* [1990] ECR I-4747.
178. *Ibid.*
179. *Ibid.*, paras 47-48.
180. *Ibid.*

threat to a fundamental interest of society.[181] Even in those circumstances the restrictions should only aim to ensure *a minimum supply* of petroleum products.[182]

The Court's references to crises and serious threats are particularly pronounced in the relevant case-law. However, this choice of wording should be viewed as pursuing a narrow interpretation of Article 36 TFEU and not as an effort to restrict the application of public security defences to unpredictable and chaotic crisis events. This interpretation is supported by the fact that the Treaty contains separate *lex specialis* provisions covering such events. Article 122 TFEU, for example, establishes that the Council may decide upon measures appropriate to the economic situation, in particular if severe difficulties arise in the supply of certain products, notably in the area of energy.[183] Furthermore, Article 347 TFEU addresses measures a Member State may be called upon to take in the event of serious internal disturbances affecting the maintenance of law and order.[184] Similar events are addressed through sector-specific legislation. Under Article 42 of the Electricity Directive, Member States may take temporary safeguard measures in the event of a sudden crisis in the energy market and where the physical safety or security of persons, apparatus or installations or system integrity is threatened. The purpose of these provisions is to address sudden, severe and exceptional circumstances that have been difficult or impossible to predict. These circumstances should not be confused with the public security defence, which is intended for the protection of essential interests but in considerably less exceptional circumstances.

It should not be forgotten that the events that led to *Campus Oil* and the case concerning Greek supplies of petroleum products took place over three decades ago.[185] A great deal has changed since then in terms of European integration both on an ideological and on a legal level. The legislative framework covering the energy sector is now much more extensive than it used to be and security of supply has been identified as one of the key objectives of EU energy law.[186] In this respect, the importance of security of supply as an interest worth protecting has strengthened. However, the ideological shift from a State-driven approach to a market-driven one means that the factual circumstances of *Campus Oil* would, in fact, argue in favour of allowing the Whitegate refinery to close as unprofitable.[187] It also means that dependence on other Member States should no longer be an argument in favour of justifying restrictions on grounds of public security. In fact, deepening European integration and the market-based approach to security of supply inevitably leads to greater dependence

181. C-54/99 *Église de scientologie* [2000] ECR I-1335 para. 17; C-483/99 *Commission v France* [2002] ECR I-4781, para. 48; C-326/07 *Commission v Italy* [2009] ECR I-2291, para. 70; C-355/98 *Commission v Belgium* [2000] ECR I-1221, para. 28.
182. 72/83 *Campus Oil* [1984] ECR 2727, para. 35. Minimum supplies were also emphasised in C-463/00 *Commission v Spain* [2003] ECR I-4581, para. 73. In legal literature, *see* Angus Johnston and Guy Block, *EU Energy Law* (OUP, 2012), p. 242.
183. Bram Delvaux, *EU Law and the Development of a Sustainable, Competitive and Secure Energy Policy: Opportunities and Shortcomings* (Intersentia, 2013), p. 283.
184. *See* discussion in the Opinion of AG Slynn in 72/83 *Campus Oil* [1984] ECR 2727, p. 2764.
185. C-347/88 *Commission v Greece* [1990] ECR I-4747.
186. Article 194 TFEU.
187. 72/83 *Campus Oil* [1984] ECR 2727, p. 2732.

between Member States.[188] In this legal setting, restricting cross-border trade would mean fewer competitors, less choice for consumers, higher prices and, ultimately, reduced security of supply.[189] With specific regard to capacity mechanisms, the evidence shows that allowing foreign capacities to bid into a national mechanism lowers the price of capacity and thus contributes to security of supply.[190] Because of the altered legal setting, the dependence argument is no longer likely to win the Court's approval. A Member State's ability to restrict cross-border trade on the grounds of Article 36 TFEU would not actually facilitate security of supply in the current legal and ideological setting – quite the opposite.[191] That is, unless there is *a genuine and sufficiently serious threat to a fundamental interest of society*.

It is established above that, particularly in the current legal setting, the availability of affordable electricity is a fundamental interest of society. However, can a failure of the market to deliver sufficient and appropriately timed investment in generation capacity constitute a genuine and sufficiently serious threat?

If capacity mechanisms are examined either as PSOs or tenders for capacity, it is clear that introducing such measures requires the Member State in question to demonstrate that market failure has occurred.[192] Similarly, remunerating capacity under prevailing State aid rules requires that the objective in question cannot be achieved by the market alone.[193] Furthermore, the analysis of both sector-specific provisions and State aid rules indicates that, even in the event of a recognised market failure, interventionist State measures can only be used to the extent that other, less restrictive measures cannot achieve the pursued objective. If this legislative framework for capacity mechanisms is interpreted systematically, the approach to capacity mechanisms should preclude restrictions in the public security interest if generation adequacy can be achieved through market-based approaches. This interpretation is also in line with the judgment in *Campus Oil*, in which it was held that restrictions on grounds of public security could be used to ensure only *a minimum supply* of petroleum products.[194] A minimum supply, in the context of capacity mechanisms, should be interpreted as an amount of capacity that is needed but not delivered by the market.

---

188. Kaisa Huhta, 'Too Important to Be Entrusted to Neighbours? The Dynamics of Security of Electricity Supply and Mutual Trust in EU law', 43(6) *European Law Review* (2018), pp. 920-933.
189. This was, in fact, a decisive factor in C-347/88 *Commission v Greece* [1990] ECR I-4747, para. 49.
190. Commission Staff Working Document accompanying the document Report from the Commission Final Report of the Sector Inquiry on Capacity Mechanisms, SWD(2016) 385 final, paras 335 and 345. On cross-border effects of capacity mechanisms, *see* Pradyumna Bhagwat, Jörn Richstein, Emile Chappin, Kaveri Iychettira and Laurens De Vries, 'Cross-Border Effects of Capacity Mechanisms in Interconnected Power Systems', 46 *Utilities Policy* (2017), pp. 33-47.
191. Similar arguments were made by the Commission in C-503/99 *Commission v Belgium* [2002] ECR I-4809, paras 23-24.
192. For further discussion of this topic, *see* Chapter 3 above.
193. *Ibid.*, *see* Chapter 4 above.
194. 72/83 *Campus Oil* [1984] ECR 2727, para. 35. Minimum supplies are also emphasised in C-463/00 *Commission v Spain* [2003] ECR I-4581, para. 73. In legal literature, *see* Angus Johnston and Guy Block, *EU Energy Law* (OUP, 2012), p. 242.

In the context of the relevant case-law analysed above, it seems clear that a failure of the market to deliver sufficient and appropriately timed investment in generation capacity may constitute a genuine and sufficiently serious threat to the availability of affordable electricity as a fundamental interest of a society. However, the systematic interpretation of the relevant legal framework for capacity mechanisms leads one to question whether these mechanisms are the appropriate instrument through which to address a societal interest of this kind. In other words, the objective of ensuring generation adequacy may well be caught by the public security justification but capacity mechanisms, as instruments to pursue such an objective, may not be declared compatible with the internal market. Determining whether capacity mechanisms can be justified on the basis of public security ultimately boils down to two factors. The first of these is deciding whether capacity mechanisms have been adopted to genuinely pursue security of supply objectives or rather to achieve protectionist interests of a purely economic nature. The second is that the compatibility of capacity mechanisms with the internal market under Article 36 TFEU is a matter of proportionality. These issues are analysed below.

[4]   Purely Economic Considerations

As established above in Chapter 4, financing capacity mechanisms typically involves large amounts of public funding. To support their domestic economies, Member States have a natural incentive to direct that funding toward domestic undertakings and domestic capacity rather than to all potential capacity providers across the internal market. If Member States were able to invoke Article 36 TFEU to justify the protection of the national economy or State budget, the whole concept of internal market integration would be undermined.[195] In order to ensure that Member States pursue legitimate security of supply interests rather than protectionist ones, it has been established in case-law that Article 36 TFEU cannot be invoked to defend measures that pursue purely economic objectives.[196] For example, the public security defence cannot be successfully invoked to increase domestic tax income,[197] to protect a Member State's general financial interests or to pursue a Member State's national economic policy.[198] In particular, Member States cannot defend a public security exemption by pleading that the process of European integration is causing them economic difficulties.[199] For example, in *Duphar v The Netherlands*, the Court ruled that Article 36 TFEU could not

---

195. Niamh Nic Shuibhne, 'Exceptions to the Free Movement Rules', in Catherine Barnard and Steve Peers (eds), *European Union Law* (OUP, 2014), pp. 473-503, at 487.
196. Cases 7/61 *Commission v Italy* [1961] ECR 317; 72/83 *Campus Oil* [1984] ECR 2727, para. 35; C-398/98 *Commission v Greece* [2001] ECR I-7915, para. 30; C-54/99 *Église de scientologie* [2000] ECR I-1335, para. 17; C-120/95 *Decker v Caisse de Maladie des Employés Privés* [1998] ECR I-1831, para. 39; C-158/96 *Kohll v Union des Caisses de Maladie* [1998] ECR I-1931, para. 41; C-463/00 *Commission v Spain* [2003] ECR I-4581, para. 35; C-367/98 *Commission v Portugal* [2002] ECR I-4731, para. 52; C-35/98 *Verkooijen* [2000] ECR I-4071, para. 48; C-265/95 *Commission v France* [1997] ECR I-6959, para. 62.
197. However, *see* C-290/04 *FKP Scorpio Konzertproduktionen* [2006] ECR I-9461.
198. C-367/98 *Commission v Portugal* [2002] ECR I-4731, para. 52.
199. 95/81 *Commission v Italy* [1982] ECR 2187.

justify national legislation whose objective was to reduce the operational costs of an insurance scheme.[200] In terms of capacity mechanisms, this means that a restriction on the participation of cross-border capacities cannot be justified merely on grounds of an increase in the cost of operating the capacity mechanism.

One of the reasons Member States have rarely been successful in invoking the public security defence in the interests of security of supply after *Campus Oil* is that their national measures have been held to pursue economic objectives rather than legitimate security of supply objectives. The case of *Commission v Greece*, for example, concerned a Greek measure to ensure national security of supply.[201] Greek law required petroleum marketing companies to hold minimum stocks of petroleum products.[202] These companies were entitled to transfer the supply obligation to Greek refineries from which they had bought products during the previous calendar year.[203] Such transfers could only be made to refineries established in Greece and, as a result, the measure was contrary to Article 34 TFEU.

The Greek government argued, primarily, that the measure did not create any discrimination against imports of petroleum products and, secondarily, that it was nevertheless justified on the basis of ensuring security of supply in Greece.[204] It also argued that the refineries' fundamental right to economic freedom would be excessively restricted if they were required to store minimum stocks of petroleum products in the absence of an obligation for the marketing companies to purchase from them.[205] The Court rejected both arguments. It took the view that the factors on which Greece had based its measure were, in fact, purely economic in nature and could not, therefore, justify a quantitative restriction.[206]

Nonetheless, there is a distinct line of cases that deviate from this principle.[207] These cases, however, seem to relate exclusively to medical services or access to healthcare and are not, therefore, relevant to discussion of capacity mechanisms.[208] Nevertheless, it is possible to identify energy-specific case-law in which the advancement of economic objectives has been accepted because such advancement is an inevitable consequence of pursuing legitimate security of supply objectives. In particular, in *Campus Oil*, it was acknowledged that restrictions on imports inevitably arise in an economic context.[209] The Court concluded that due to the severity of the consequences of energy supplies being interrupted, a quantitative restriction on imports

---

200. C-238/82 *Duphar v The Netherlands* [1984] ECR 523, para. 23.
201. C-398/98 *Commission v Greece* [2001] ECR I-7915, para. 5.
202. *Ibid.*
203. *Ibid.*, para. 6.
204. *Ibid.*, paras 19-20.
205. *Ibid.*, para. 21.
206. *Ibid.*, para. 30.
207. C-141/07 *Commission v Germany* [2008] ECR I-6935, para. 60; C-158/96 *Kohll v Union des Caisses de Maladie* [1998] ECR I-1931, para. 50; C-368/98 *Vanbraekel and Others* [2001] ECR I-5363, para. 47.
208. Niamh Nic Shuibhne, 'Exceptions to the Free Movement Rules', in Catherine Barnard and Steve Peers (eds), *European Union Law* (OUP, 2014), pp. 473-503, at 487.
209. Opinion of AG Slynn in 72/83 *Campus Oil* [1984] ECR 2727, p. 2763.

transcends purely economic considerations.[210] In other words, the favourable economic ends achieved by the Irish measure in *Campus Oil* were only secondary and
could therefore be allowed in order to ensure that security of supply was not
compromised.[211]

[5]   Proportionality Assessment

In addition to setting out specific grounds for justifying restrictions on the free
movement of goods, Article 36 TFEU provides that restrictions on imports or exports
permitted under it may not constitute a means of arbitrary discrimination or a disguised
restriction on trade between Member States.[212] The objective of this wording is to avoid
unnecessary widening of the scope of the article.[213] In particular, it seeks to prevent
abuse of the justification grounds through discrimination against foreign goods or the
provision of protection for certain national goods.[214] An arbitrary assessment of similar
products by a national court, for example, would constitute a disguised restriction of
trade.[215] Such Member State practice, however, is only caught by the second sentence
of Article 36 TFEU if the discrimination cannot be objectively justified.[216]

A number of cases have shaped the scope of interpretation of arbitrary discrimination and disguised restrictions of trade under Article 36 TFEU.[217] A measure taken by
a Member State essentially constitutes arbitrary discrimination if it exceeds the scope
of that Member State's right to exercise its powers in relation to the subject matter in
question, i.e., it cannot go beyond what is necessary to protect the interests laid down
in Article 36 TFEU.[218] The principle of proportionality, therefore, underlies the last

---

210. 72/83 *Campus Oil* [1984] ECR 2727, para. 35.
211. This distinction was later confirmed in C-118/86 *Openbaar Ministerie v Nertsvoederfabriek
    Nederland* [1987] ECR 3883.
212. Article 36 TFEU. *See also* Panos Koutrakos, 'Public Security Exceptions and EU Free Movement
    Law', in Panos Koutrakos, Niamh Nic Shuibhne and Phil Syrpis (eds), *Exceptions from EU Free
    Movement Law: Derogation, Justification and Proportionality* (Hart Publishing, 2016), pp.
    190-217; Laurence Gormley, *EU Law of Free Movement of Goods and Customs Union* (OUP,
    2009), pp. 463-465; Paul Craig and Gráinne de Búrca, *EU Law: Text, Cases, and Materials*, 6th
    edn. (OUP, 2015), pp. 698-699; Alina Kaczorowska-Ireland, *European Union Law* (Routledge,
    2009), pp. 630-656; Nigel Foster, *Foster on EU Law* (OUP, 2015), pp. 278-284.
213. Cases 13/78 *Eggers* [1978] ECR 1935; 42/82 *Commission v France* [1983] ECR 1013; 72/83
    Campus Oil [1984] ECR 2727, para. 37; Nina Boeger, 'Minimum Harmonisation, Free Move-
    ment and Proportionality', in Phil Syrpis (ed), *The Judiciary, the Legislature and the EU Internal
    Market* (Cambridge University Press, 2012), pp. 62-91.
214. 34/79 *Henn and Darby* [1979] ECR 3795, paras 20-22; C-317/91 *Deutsche Renault v AUDI*
    [1993] ECR I-6227, para. 19.
215. C-9/93 *IHT Internationale Heiztechnik v Ideal-Standard* [1994] ECR I-2789, para. 19; Stephen
    Weatherill, *The Internal Market as a Legal Concept* (OUP, 2017), p. 101.
216. Stefan Enchelmaier, 'Article 36 TFEU: General', in Peter Oliver (ed), *Oliver on Free Movement
    of Goods in the European Union* (Hart Publishing, 2010), pp. 215-312, at 223.
217. 78/70 *Deutsche Grammophon Gesellschaft mbH v Metro-SB-Großmärkte GmbH & Co. KG* [1971]
    ECR 487; 152/78 *Commission v French Republic* [1980] ECR 2299; 53/76 *Procureur de la
    République de Besançon v Les Sieurs Bouhelier and others* [1977] ECR 197; 104/75 *Adriaan de
    Peijper* [1976] ECR 613; C-317/91 *Deutsche Renault v AUDI* [1993] ECR I-6227.
218. 78/70 *Deutsche Grammophon Gesellschaft mbH v Metro-SB-Großmärkte GmbH & Co. KG* [1971]
    ECR 487, para. 10; 104/75 *Adriaan de Peijper* [1976] ECR 613, paras 14-17.

sentence of Article 36 TFEU.[219] In other words, a national measure must be necessary to achieve the objective protected by Article 36 TFEU in order to be justified and compatible with the second sentence of Article 36 TFEU.[220] Member States must demonstrate that their national measures comply with the requirement of proportionality. However, the burden of proof in this regard does not extend to requiring a Member State to show that no other conceivable measure could achieve the objective pursued.[221]

The interpretation of the second sentence of Article 36 TFEU is particularly relevant with regard to capacity mechanisms. As noted above, ensuring generation adequacy can constitute a legitimate public security interest. In fact, it would be contradictory to argue that an objective pursued by primary EU law, such as security of supply, could not be protected by Article 36 TFEU when the matter is not fully harmonised.[222] However, capacity mechanisms are not the objective per se. They are only the vehicle for achieving the objective of generation adequacy. Therefore, the proportionality assessment should be directed towards evaluating two intertwined issues. The first of these is whether capacity mechanisms provide assurance that there is a *minimum* supply of electricity in the event of a genuine and serious threat to generation adequacy or whether they go beyond what is necessary to ensure that minimum supply.[223] The second issue is whether capacity mechanisms that restrict cross-border trade offer a necessary, appropriate and proportional (*proportionality stricto sensu*) means by which to pursue generation adequacy in the internal electricity market.[224]

Assessing the proportionality of a restrictive measure involves weighing the protected interest and the circumstances threatening the protection of that interest against the negative effects caused by adopting a restrictive measure. Because of this, it cannot be generally determined that all capacity mechanisms fail to be proportionate or that a certain design may always be regarded as proportional. The ability of a capacity mechanism to ensure a minimum supply of energy depends on the particular generation adequacy issue addressed through that mechanism. Hence, the proportionality of a capacity mechanism design is dependent on the severity of a Member State's generation inadequacy and, in particular, on the extent to which that Member State is able to demonstrate that this issue is best addressed by means of a capacity mechanism.

---

219. C-174/82 *Sandoz* [1983] ECR 2445, para. 18; C-227/82 *Van Bennekom* [1983] ECR 3883, para. 39; 247/84 *Motte* [1985] ECR 3898, para. 23.
220. On the limits of proportionality, *see* C-483/99 *Commission v France* [2002] ECR I-4781; C-367/98 *Commission v Portugal* [2002] ECR I-4731. In legal literature, *see* Peter Oliver and Martín Martínez Navarro, 'Free Movement of Goods', in Catherine Barnard and Steve Peers (eds), *European Union Law* (OUP, 2014), pp. 325-355, at 343-344.
221. C-157/94 *Commission v Netherlands* [1997] ECR I-5699, para. 58; C-110/05 *Commission v Italy* [2009] ECR I-519, para. 66.
222. Article 194 TFEU.
223. C-463/00 *Commission v Spain* [2003] ECR I-4581, para. 73.
224. 72/83 *Campus Oil* [1984] ECR 2727, para. 26; C-55/94 *Reinhard Gebhard v Consiglio dell'Ordine degli Avvocati e Procuratori di Milano* [1995] ECR I-4165, para. 37; C-19/92 *Kraus v Land Baden-Wuerttemberg* [1993] ECR I-1663, para. 32; Friedl Weiss and Clemens Kaupa, *European Union Internal Market Law* (Cambridge University Press, 2014), pp. 34-35.

The Court has been particularly vigilant in testing whether a national measure is necessary to pursue the objective protected by Article 36 TFEU. In essence, the national measure may not go beyond what is necessary to achieve the objective.[225] In particular, other equally effective measures that have a less restrictive impact on cross-border trade should first be utilised.[226] In *Greece v Commission*, for example, the Court declared the Greek measure incompatible with the Treaty because it considered that security of supply could have been ensured using measures that were less restrictive of cross-border trade.[227] In particular, the Greek government had failed to demonstrate that security of supply would be compromised in the absence of the adopted measure.[228] Market-based approaches or other less restrictive measures to address generation adequacy should first be exhausted before a capacity mechanism may be introduced. The Court may even explicitly specify alternative measures that would better comply with the principle of proportionality.[229] Within a capacity mechanism, these alternative measures may relate to the design of the capacity mechanism and may involve widening the eligibility criteria for participating capacity. These alternative measures should be assessed in the light of the overall objectives of EU energy law. This contextual approach and the prioritisation of different types of measures to ensure generation adequacy are analysed in Chapter 6.

The case-law on the interpretation of Article 36 TFEU indicates that the necessity assessment includes a review of how well the objective of the measure is defined. The lack of precisely and objectively defined criteria has in the past been used as a basis on which to declare that a restrictive measure goes beyond what is necessary to achieve the objective of the national legislation.[230]

---

225. 72/83 *Campus Oil* [1984] ECR 2727, para. 44; C-483/99 *Commission v France* [2002] ECR I-4781, para. 45; C-205/07 *Gysbrechts and Santurel Inter* [2008] ECR I-9947, para. 53; C-54/99 *Église de Scientologie* [2000] ECR I-1335, para. 18; joined cases C-163/94, C-165/94 and C-250/94 *Lucas Emilio Sanz de Lera, Raimundo Díaz Jiménez and Figen Kapanoglu* [1995] ECR I-4821, para. 23; C-451/05 *ELISA* [2007] ECR I-8251, para. 82; C-522/04 *Commission v Belgium* [2007] ECR I-5701, para. 47; C-100/01 *Oteiza Olazabal* [2002] ECR I-10981, para. 43; C-527/06 *Renneberg* [2008] ECR I-7735, para. 81; joined cases C-155/08 and C-157/08 *X and Passenheim-van Schoot* [2009] ECR I-5093, para. 47; C-169/08 *Presidente del Consiglio dei Ministri* [2009] ECR I-10821, para. 42; C-384/08 *Attanasio Group* [2010] ECR I-2055, para. 51. *See also* Norbert Reich, Annette Nordhausen Scholes and Jeremy Scholes, *Understanding EU Internal Market Law* (Intersentia, 2015), p. 72.
226. C-205/07 *Gysbrechts and Santurel Inter* [2008] ECR I-9947, para. 53; C-54/99 *Église de scientologie* [2000] ECR I-1335, para. 18; C-165/94 and C-250/94 *Lucas Emilio Sanz de Lera, Raimundo Díaz Jiménez and Figen Kapanoglu* [1995] I-4821, para. 23; 261/81 *Walter Rau Lebensmittelwerke v De Smedt PVBA* [1982] ECR 3961, para. 12; C-443/10 *Bonnarde* [2011] ECR I-9327, para. 35; C-463/00 *Commission v Spain* [2003] ECR I-4581, para. 68; C-367/98 *Commission v Portugal* [2002] ECR I-4731, para. 49; C-483/99 *Commission v France* [2002] ECR I-4781, para. 45; C-503/99 *Commission v Belgium* [2002] ECR I-4809, para. 45; 104/75 *Adriaan de Peijper* [1976] ECR 613, paras 16-17.
227. C-398/98 *Commission v Greece* [2001] ECR I-7915, para. 31.
228. C-347/88 *Commission v Greece* [1990] ECR I-4747, paras 47-49 and 58-61.
229. C-387/99 *Commission v Germany* [2004] ECR I-3751, para. 81; and Peter Oliver, 'Free Movement of Goods in the Labyrinth of Energy Policy and Capacity Mechanisms', in Leigh Hancher, Adrien de Hautecloque and Malgorzata Sadowska (eds), *Capacity Mechanisms in the EU Energy Market* (OUP, 2015), pp. 201-223, at 211.
230. C-483/99 *France* [2002] ECR I-4781, para. 53; C-463/00 *Commission v Spain* [2003] ECR I-4581, paras 71-84.

In addition to a review of necessity, the overall proportionality of the national measure is assessed. This involves carrying out a balancing act between the objectives of European integration on the one hand and protecting interests vital to Member States on the other. In practice, and particularly in the absence of harmonisation, Member States have a significant margin of discretion in determining the desired level of protection of the pursued interest.[231] In relation to generation adequacy, this means that Member States may independently determine the level of capacity and resources they consider adequate to ensure national security of supply.[232] As a result, generation adequacy assessments and the methodologies underlying them are not mutually comparable, thus potentially preventing cross-border capacities from being taken effectively into consideration.[233]

Finally, the proportionality review includes a suitability assessment to ascertain whether the selected measure is appropriate to achieve the objective pursued.[234] The Court's assessment of suitability is often brief and shallow.[235] Determining the appropriateness of a measure only requires that there is a causal link between the measure and the objective in question.[236] Demonstrating causality between capacity mechanisms and increasing levels of generation capacity is rather straightforward. However, it was established in *Campus Oil* that the quantity of petroleum products governed by the Irish system must not exceed that necessary to ensure security of supply.[237] By analogy, this means that a capacity mechanism should increase the level of generation capacity only to the extent necessary to ensure a minimum supply of electricity.[238] Furthermore, remuneration for capacity should automatically be zero if the necessary generation capacity is delivered or expected to be delivered without a

---

231. C-158/04 *Alfa Vita Vassilopoulos* [2006] ECR I-8135, paras 21-22 and the case-law cited therein. For examples of national approaches to defining the pursued level of security of supply, *see* SA.48648 *Belgian Strategic Reserve*, C(2018) 589 final, paras 10-11 and SA.46100 *Planned Polish Capacity Mechanism*, C(2018) 601 final, paras 29-32. In legal literature, *see* Henrik Bjørnebye, *Investing in EU Energy Security: Exploring the Regulatory Approach to Tomorrow's Electricity Production* (University of Oslo, PhD thesis 2009), pp. 85-92.
232. In case-law, *see* SA.48648 *Belgian Strategic Reserve*, C(2018) 589 final, paras 10-11.
233. Commission Staff Working Document accompanying the document Report from the Commission Final Report of the Sector Inquiry on Capacity Mechanisms, SWD(2016) 385 final, para. 234.
234. C-443/10 *Bonnarde* [2011] ECR I-9327, para. 35; C-100/01 *Oteiza Olazabal* [2002] ECR I-10981, para. 43; C-527/06 *Renneberg* [2008] ECR I-7735, para. 81; joined cases C-155/08 and C-157/08 *X and Passenheim-van Schoot* [2009] ECR I-5093, para. 47; C-169/08 *Presidente del Consiglio dei Ministri* [2009] ECR I-10821, para. 42; C-384/08 *Attanasio Group* [2010] ECR I-2055, para. 51; C-451/05 *ELISA* [2007] ECR I-8251, para. 82;
235. Niamh Nic Shuibhne, 'Exceptions to the Free Movement Rules', in Catherine Barnard and Steve Peers (eds), *European Union Law* (OUP, 2014), pp. 473-503, at 495.
236. C-436/01 *Commission v Germany* [2004] ECR I-11705, para. 78; C-483/99 *Commission v France* [2002] ECR I-4781, para. 45; Henrik Bjørnebye, *Investing in EU Energy Security: Exploring the Regulatory Approach to Tomorrow's Electricity Production* (University of Oslo, PhD thesis 2009), p. 86.
237. 72/83 *Campus Oil* [1984] ECR 2727, para. 48.
238. *See* argumentation on the minimum level of supplies in 72/83 *Campus Oil* [1984] ECR 2727, para. 58; and, in subsequent case-law, C-483/99 *Commission v France* [2002] ECR I-4781, para. 49.

capacity mechanism.[239] These requirements are typically not fulfilled in the mechanisms adopted within the EU Member States. It is widely acknowledged that capacity mechanisms tend to lead to overcapacity in the market and, thus, deliver much more than a minimum level of generation capacity.[240]

Based on the analysis contained in this section, it is likely that if a restrictive element in a capacity mechanism is declared incompatible with Article 36 TFEU, it is not due to failure to demonstrate a legitimate public security interest. Rather, it seems probable that, as a means through which to pursue generation adequacy, a capacity mechanism will not be considered a proportional approach within the meaning of the second sentence of Article 36 TFEU. The reasons for this may be derived from the existing case-law. First, capacity mechanisms may go beyond what is necessary to ensure generation adequacy because the objectives pursued are not defined precisely and objectively or because generation adequacy could be ensured without restricting cross-border trade at all. It is highly unlikely that the Court would accept a restriction on cross-border trade if generation adequacy could be ensured without such restrictions. Furthermore, the Court is unlikely to accept an argument that a restriction on cross-border trade is necessary due to the fact that allowing cross-border capacities to participate in a capacity mechanism typically increases the available capacity and hence, security of supply.[241] Second, the tendency of capacity mechanisms to generate overcapacity conflicts with the suitability assessment mentioned above. If capacity is remunerated beyond that needed to ensure a minimum supply in the event of a crisis, the measure may be deemed disproportionate to the objective pursued.[242]

§5.04   THE RELATIONSHIP BETWEEN THE RULES ON FREE MOVEMENT OF GOODS AND STATE AID

At EU level, capacity mechanisms are governed by a fragmentary body of both primary and secondary legal instruments. As noted at various points above, the adoption of capacity mechanisms typically requires the application of exemptions from this legislation, which includes, *inter alia*, rules such as the prohibition of State aid and the prohibition of quantitative restrictions as well as provisions governing the market-based approach to investment in generation capacity. The fragmentary nature of the

---

239. Communication from the Commission, Guidelines on State aid for environmental protection and energy 2014-2020 (OJ C 200, 28.6.2014, pp. 1-55), para. 231; SA.48648 *Belgian Strategic Reserve*, C(2018) 589 final, para. 146; Kelyn Bacon, *European Union Law of State Aid*, 3rd edn. (OUP, 2017), p. 245.
240. Commission Staff Working Document accompanying the document Report from the Commission Final Report of the Sector Inquiry on Capacity Mechanisms, SWD(2016) 385 final, paras 345 and 452-455.
241. Pradyumna Bhagwat, Jörn Richstein, Emile Chappin, Kaveri Iychettira and Laurens De Vries, 'Cross-Border Effects of Capacity Mechanisms in Interconnected Power Systems', 46 *Utilities Policy* (2017), pp. 33-47.
242. C-483/99 *Commission v France* [2002] ECR I-4781, paras 45-48 and the case-law cited therein. Similar argumentation in Henrik Bjørnebye, *Investing in EU Energy Security: Exploring the Regulatory Approach to Tomorrow's Electricity Production* (University of Oslo, PhD thesis 2009), p. 100.

body of legislation governing capacity mechanisms raises questions as to the relationships between its different elements. If one provision permits but another prohibits the adoption of capacity mechanisms, it is essential to determine which provision takes priority. Against this background, this section analyses the relationship between the rules on the free movement of goods and EU State aid rules.

In practice there is often overlap in the scope of application of EU State aid rules and free movement rules.[243] An aid system that benefits domestic products over foreign ones is also likely to make the importation of foreign goods less competitive than under normal market conditions. This effect is capable of hindering, at least indirectly, cross-border trade within the EU and may accordingly be caught by the prohibition laid down in Article 34 TFEU.[244]

This overlap was directly addressed in *Ianelli v Meroni*, a seminal case heard in 1977, which established that the effect a national aid system might have in hindering cross-border trade is not in itself sufficient to permit the categorisation of such aid as having an effect equivalent to a quantitative restriction.[245] Regardless of legitimate grounds for granting aid, however, an aid scheme cannot be declared compatible with the internal market if the State aid system or the conditions attached to it involve a non-severable violation of EU law.[246] This applies equally to the financing method used in respect of a State aid scheme. Therefore, a levy collected from the final users of electricity to finance a capacity mechanism must comply with the rules on free movement.[247] The fact that a national scheme is caught by Article 107 TFEU does not mean that it is automatically exempt from the rules on free movement.[248] In the field of energy law, this interpretation of the relationship between State aid and free movement provisions was confirmed in the EEAG and applied in the Commission's State aid decisions regarding capacity mechanisms.[249]

---

243. Andrea Biondi and Martin Farley, 'The Relationship Between State Aid and the Single Market', in Erika Szyszczak (ed), *Research Handbook on European State Aid Law* (Edward Elgar 2011), pp. 277-292.
244. C-8/74 *Dassonville* [1974] ECR 837, para. 5.
245. C-74/76 *Ianelli v Meroni* [1997] ECR 557, para. 10. In subsequent case-law, *see* C-225/91 *Matra v Commission* [1993] ECR I-3203, paras 41-45; and in the energy-sector T-57/11 *Castelnou Energía v Commission* [2014], judgment of the General Court of 3 December 2014, published in the electronic Reports of Cases, para. 196.
246. 73/79 *Commission v Italy* [1980] ECR 1533, para. 11; C-225/91 *Matra v Commission* [1993] ECR I-3203, para. 41; C-156/98 *Germany v Commission* [2000] ECR I-6857, para. 78; C-333/07 *Régie Networks v Rhone Alpes Bourgogne* [2008] ECR I-10807, paras 94-116; joined cases C-128/03 and C-129/03 *AEM and AEM Torino* [2005] ECR I-2861, paras 38-51; SA.42011 *Italian Capacity Mechanism*, C(2018) 617 final, paras 204-217.
247. Case C-206/06 *Essent* [2008] ECR I-5497.
248. 103/84 *Commission v Italy* [1986] ECR 1759; C-263/85 *Commission of the European Communities v Italian Republic* [1991] ECR I-2457; C-21/88 *Du Pont de Nemours Italiana SpA v Unità sanitaria locale N° 2 di Carrara* [1990] ECR I-889, para. 20; Jacques Derenne, 'Article 107 TFEU', in Weijer Ver Loren van Themaat and Berend Reuder (eds), *European Competition Law: A Case Commentary* (Edward Elgar, 2014), pp. 216-255, at 237.
249. Communication from the Commission, Guidelines on State aid for environmental protection and energy 2014-2020 (OJ C 200, 28.6.2014, pp. 1-55), para. 29; SA.35980 *GB Capacity Mechanism*, C (2014) 5083 final, paras 157-161.

CHAPTER 6

The Hierarchy Between Different Measures to Address Generation Adequacy

§6.01 CAPACITY MECHANISMS IN THE CONTEXT OF THE OBJECTIVES OF EU ENERGY LAW

Ensuring the functioning of the internal market and security of supply, while promoting energy efficiency, energy savings, renewable energy and interconnection between energy networks, is a complex operation. It has been fittingly stated that the achievement of these goals precludes the possibility of addressing different objectives in isolation from one another.[1] When designing national measures to address these objectives, Member States are expected to avoid conflict between different objectives by planning holistically and by taking into account the cross-effects of pursuing one objective over another.[2]

It has been rightly argued that the means of overcoming security of supply and environmental challenges, for example, often largely overlap.[3] However, the plurality of EU energy law objectives and the wide margin of discretion that remains with Member States make it difficult to proactively address one objective without undermining the drive to achieve other objectives of EU energy law.[4] Capacity mechanisms offer an excellent example of this challenge. In addition to deviating from the

---

1. Articles 194 and 170 TFEU. In legal literature, *see* Leigh Hancher and Francesco Maria Salerno, 'Energy Policy After Lisbon', in Andrea Biondi, Piet Eeckhout and Stefanie Ripley (eds), *EU Law After Lisbon* (OUP, 2012), pp. 367-402 and Bram Delvaux, *EU Law and the Development of a Sustainable, Competitive and Secure Energy Policy: Opportunities and Shortcomings* (Intersentia, 2013), pp. 328-368.
2. Communication from the Commission Delivering the internal electricity market and making the most of public intervention, C(2013) 7243 final, p. 8.
3. Bjørnebye, Henrik, *Investing in EU Energy Security: Exploring the Regulatory Approach to Tomorrow's Electricity Production* (University of Oslo, PhD thesis, 2009), p. 31.
4. Philipp Ringler, Dogan Keles and Wolf Fichtner, 'How to Benefit from a Common European Electricity Market Design', 101 *Energy Policy* (2017), pp. 629-643, at 629.

market-based approach to investment, capacity mechanisms are likely to have a negative impact upon the pursuit of a functioning and interconnected internal market characterised by high shares of renewable penetration and energy efficiency, and they may even conflict with certain vital elements of security of supply.

In terms of the objectives of EU energy law, one specific problem with capacity mechanisms is that their impact on security of supply is not solely positive. By hedging the risks on investments, they ensure necessary (and potentially excessive) investment in generation adequacy and, therefore, clearly contribute to ensuring security of electricity supply.[5] However, capacity mechanisms also always increase the cost of the electricity system, which is typically reflected in the electricity price.[6] This inevitably makes electricity less affordable – and therefore less available – for those already struggling with rising energy bills.[7]

Furthermore, capacity mechanisms have been identified as problematic in terms of internal market integration because they may distort price signals and often fail to fully take into account the contribution of foreign capacities as a result of which they may distort cross-border trade.[8] These distortions can reduce incentives to invest in interconnection capacity.[9] This tendency is particularly harmful in situations where interconnection investment could ensure security of supply to the same extent as a capacity mechanism while better complementing the objectives of market and renewable integration, pooling risks and allowing consumers access to the cheapest resources.

Finally, capacity mechanisms have a tendency to favour conventional generation capacity, thus undermining the objectives of decarbonising the economy and phasing out environmentally harmful subsidies.[10] This tendency to favour generation capacity

---

5. Pradyumna Chaitanya Bhagwat, *Security of Supply During the Energy Transition: The Role of Capacity Mechanisms* (Technische Universiteit Delft, PhD thesis 2016), pp. 73-83.
6. Commission Staff Working Document, Generation Adequacy in the internal electricity market – guidance on public interventions accompanying the document Communication from the Commission Delivering the internal electricity market and making the most of public intervention, SWD(2013) 438 final, p. 32; Communication from the Commission Delivering the internal electricity market and making the most of public intervention, C(2013) 7243 final, p. 4.
7. Despoina Mantzari, 'The Quest for Reasonable Retail Energy Prices in Europe: Positive and Normative Dimensions', 36(1) *Yearbook of European Law* (2017), pp. 599-627.
8. Report from the Commission, Final Report of the Sector Inquiry on Capacity Mechanisms, COM(2016) 752 final; Commission Staff Working Document accompanying the document Report from the Commission Interim Report of the Sector Inquiry on Capacity Mechanisms, SWD(2016) 119 final, pp. 80-84; Commission Staff Working Document accompanying the document Report from the Commission Final Report of the Sector Inquiry on Capacity Mechanisms, SWD(2016) 385 final, paras 83 and 186; SA.35980 *GB Capacity Mechanism*, C(2014) 5083 final, para. 20; Graeme Hawker, Keith Bell and Simon Gill, 'Electricity security in the European Union – The conflict between national Capacity Mechanisms and the Single Market', 24 *Energy Research & Social Science* (2017), pp. 51-58, at 56-57; Roland Meyer and Olga Gore, 'Cross-Border Effects of Capacity Mechanisms: Do Uncoordinated Market Design Changes Contradict the Goals of the European Market Integration?', 51 *Energy Economics* (2015), pp. 9-20.
9. Communication from the Commission, Guidelines on State aid for environmental protection and energy 2014-2020 (OJ C 200, 28.6.2014, pp. 1-55), paras 232-233.
10. Communication from the Commission, Guidelines on State aid for environmental protection and energy 2014-2020 (OJ C 200, 28.6.2014, pp. 1-55), para. 220; Communication from the Commission to the European Parliament, the Council, the European Economic and Social Committee and the Committee of the Regions Making the internal energy market work

based on fossil fuels, or generation capacity over resources in general, also implicitly means that the potential contribution of energy efficiency, energy savings and demand-side management is marginalised. The introduction of capacity mechanisms should not, however, prevent the full implementation of the 2020 and 2030 objectives.[11]

If capacity mechanisms are examined within the broader context of EU energy objectives, it is clear that the availability of generation capacity should not be viewed as a value in its own right but should only be considered as having instrumental value in ensuring security of electricity supply.[12] In this context, it seems uncontroversial to argue that if security of supply can be ensured through measures that are considered more in line with the objectives of EU energy law, these measures should be prioritised over State intervention that tends to allocate public resources predominantly to generation capacity.[13]

However, the lack of harmonisation on capacity mechanisms means that many of the legal issues relevant to their adoption and operation are left to the Member States to determine. For example, the scope of PSOs under the Electricity Directive or the measures to protect public security under free movement rules are characteristically matters that the State defines and defends. Furthermore, compensation for the performance of PSOs or the granting of State aid requires that the remunerated service could not be achieved by the market alone. The provision of evidence for the existence of market failure is also a responsibility that falls to the Member State. Likewise, each Member State must decide upon the level of generation adequacy to be pursued through national measures.[14]

However, there are a number of issues, all of which are extensively analysed in the chapters above, that can and should be decided at EU level. One of the key legal criteria for the evaluation of the appropriateness and necessity of capacity mechanisms

---

COM(2012) 663 final, p. 15; Communication from the Commission Delivering the internal electricity market and making the most of public intervention, C(2013) 7243 final, p. 4.

11. Communication from the Commission, Delivering the internal electricity market and making the most of public intervention, C(2013) 7243 final, p. 14.
12. Communication from the Commission to the European Parliament, the Council, the European Economic and Social Committee, the Committee of the Regions and the European Investment Bank, a Framework Strategy for a Resilient Energy Union with a Forward-Looking Climate Change Policy, COM(2015) 80 final, p. 12.
13. In case-law, *see* SA.42011 *Italian Capacity Mechanism*, C(2018) 617 final, para. 132; SA.46100 *Planned Polish Capacity Mechanism*, C(2018) 601 final, para. 137; SA.44464 *Irish Capacity Mechanism: Reliability Option Scheme*, C(2017) 7789 final, para. 93. For an opposing argument, *see* Henrik Bjørnebye, 'Electricity Generation Capacity Tenders in the Security of Supply Interest: EU Regulation of Internal Electricity Market Facilitation and Intervention', 4 *OGEL* (2007), pp. 23-24, albeit this view was presented before the third energy package entered into force in 2009. Since then, the Court has rightly opined, in C-573/12 *Ålands Vindkraft AB v Energimyndigheten* [2014] ECR II-2037, paras 85-86, that 'the finding made by the Court in para. 78 of the judgment in PreussenElektra – that Directive 96/92/EC of the European Parliament and of the Council of 19 December 1996 concerning common rules for the internal market in electricity (OJ 1997 L 27, p. 20), then in force, merely marked a phase in the liberalisation of the electricity market and left in place some barriers to trade in electricity between Member States – no longer holds true'.
14. For further discussion of these issues, *see* Chapters 3-5 above.

at EU level is the principle of proportionality.[15] It is required by the existing sector-specific rules on the internal electricity market as well as under the rules governing State aid and exemptions from the prohibition of restrictions on the free movement of goods. Because of this dynamic, there is a good case for arguing that, in relation to these provisions, proportionality should be interpreted in the light of the objectives of EU energy law.[16] From this perspective, the principle of proportionality means that if the objective of security of supply can be achieved through measures that serve the purposes of EU energy law objectives better than remuneration for capacity, then these measures should first be exhausted when addressing concerns over generation adequacy.

In other words, after a Member State has demonstrated the inability of the energy-only markets to deliver sufficient generation capacity, it faces a choice as to how to address this market failure. Remunerating capacity is one option, but Member States may also, depending on the circumstances, choose to address generation adequacy through demand side measures; for example, by incentivising flexibility and improving energy efficiency. They may also seek to facilitate investment in more interconnections with other Member States. In general, the legal framework for ensuring generation adequacy and introducing capacity mechanisms should be interpreted in such a way as to prioritise measures that complement rather than conflict with the overall objectives of EU energy law.

Against this background, this chapter analyses the relationships between capacity mechanisms as instruments that primarily compensate generation capacity and other measures that could be used to address generation adequacy in a manner that better complements the objectives of EU energy law.

This argument for prioritising different measures to address generation adequacy is analysed below in three parts. The first part takes the form of a proportionality assessment, which is required by all the legal bases on which capacity mechanisms can be introduced. In the context of the objectives of EU energy law, the proportionality assessment facilitates identification of the measures that could and should be prioritised over remuneration for generation capacity. The second part provides a contextual interpretation of the legal framework within which the proportionality assessment is carried out. The third part assesses the extent to which the hierarchy of the different instruments used to ensure generation adequacy is legally binding.

---

15. Wolf Sauter, 'Proportionality in EU Law: A Balancing Act?', 15(2) *Cambridge Yearbook of European Legal Studies* (2012), pp. 439-466; Tor-Inge Harbo, *The Function of Proportionality Analysis in European Law* (Brill Nijhoff, 2015); Nigel Foster, *Foster on EU Law* (OUP, 2015), pp. 88-89; Jürgen Kühling, 'Fundamental Rights', in Armin von Bogdandy and Jürge Bast (eds), *Principles of European Constitutional Law*, revised 2nd edn. (Hart Publishing, 2011), pp. 479-514, at 505-511.
16. Article 194 TFEU. On the interpretation of this article, *see* Leigh Hancher and Francesco Maria Salerno, 'Energy Policy After Lisbon', in Andrea Biondi, Piet Eeckhout and Stefanie Ripley (eds), *EU Law After Lisbon* (OUP, 2012), pp. 367-402. On balancing capacity mechanisms with other objectives of EU energy law, *see* Communication from the Commission – Guidelines on State aid for environmental protection and energy 2014-2020, OJ C 200, 28.6.2014, pp. 1-55, paras 40 and 43.

§6.02   THE REQUIREMENT OF PROPORTIONALITY IN STATE INTERVENTION TO ENSURE GENERATION ADEQUACY

[A]   Approaching Proportionality from Different Directions

As identified above in Chapters 3-5, all the legal bases under which capacity mechanisms may be evaluated require a proportionality assessment in one form or another. The rationale of this approach lies in the fact that a State-driven procurement of generation capacity is an exception to the market-based rule on which the internal market in electricity is founded.[17] Consequently, procuring capacity under sector-specific electricity market rules, remunerating the availability of generation capacity and restricting free movement of goods to protect public security all require that the interventionist measure adopted is proportional in relation to the objective pursued.

The proportionality requirement for imposing PSOs in the electricity sector is clear not only from the wording of Article 106(2) TFEU but also from the interpretation of Article 3 of the Electricity Directive adopted by the Court and by the Commission.[18] A proportionality assessment is also required if remuneration is offered for such services.[19] Moreover, if remuneration for capacity does not comply with the well-established *Altmark* criteria or Article 106(2) TFEU, it is typically evaluated under Article 107(3)(c) TFEU, the wording of which underlines proportionality. The interpretation of Article 107(3)(c) TFEU with regard to subsidising generation adequacy is further specified in the EEAG, which addresses the relationship between measures to incentivise investment in generation capacity and measures to ensure generation

---

17. Article 7 of the Electricity Directive. *See* recitals 6 and 56 of the Electricity Directive; William W. Hogan, 'On an "Energy Only" Electricity Market Design for Resource Adequacy', Harvard University papers, 2005, available at hwww.hks.harvard.edu/fs/whogan/ Hogan_Energy_Only_092305.pdf (last accessed 5.3.2019), p. 7. On the economics of a functioning energy-only market, *see* Paul Joskow and Jean Tirole, 'Reliability and Competitive Electricity Markets', 38(1) RAND *Journal of Economics* (2007), pp. 60-84; Paul Joskow, 'Capacity Payments in Imperfect Electricity Markets: Need and Design', 16(3) *Utilities Policy* (2008), pp. 159-170, at 160-161; and Philipp Ringler, Dogan Keles and Wolf Fichtner, 'How to Benefit from a Common European Electricity Market Design', 101 *Energy Policy* (2017), pp. 629-643.
18. C-265/08 *Federutility and Others v Autorità per l'energia elettrica e il gas* [2010] ECR I-3377; Communication from the Commission, Services of general interest in Europe, OJ C 17, 19.1.2001, pp. 4-23, para. 23; and for capacity mechanisms, Case T-57/11 *Castelnou Energía v Commission* [2014], judgment of the General Court of 3 December 2014, para. 148; Heike Schweitzer, 'Services of General Economic Interest: European Law's Impact on the Role of Markets and of Member States', in Marise Cremona (ed), *Market Integration and Public Services in the European Union* (OUP, 2011), pp. 11-62, at 38-42.
19. C-280/00 *Altmark* [2003] ECR I-7747; Juan Jorge Piernas López, *The Concept of State Aid Under EU Law: From Internal Market to Competition and Beyond* (OUP 2015), pp. 87-90; Wolf Sauter, *Public Services in EU Law* (Cambridge University Press, 2015), pp. 140-142; Heike Schweitzer, 'Services of General Economic Interest: European Law's Impact on the Role of Markets and of Member States', in Marise Cremona (ed), *Market Integration and Public Services in the European Union* (OUP, 2011), pp. 11-62, at 27-31; Leigh Hancher and Pierre Larouche, 'The Coming of Age of EU Regulation of Network Industries and Services of General Economic Interest', in Paul Craig and Gráinne De Búrca (eds), *The Evolution of EU Law* (OUP, 2011), pp. 743-781, at 759-766; Natalia Fiedziuk, 'Towards a More Refined Economic Approach to Services of General Economic Interest', 16(2) *European Public Law* (2010), pp. 271-288.

adequacy through other means.[20] The EEAG recognises that a failure to adequately balance different objectives of EU energy law may lead to a situation where the negative effects of one measure counteract the positive effects of another.[21] Specifically, an aid measure will not be considered compatible with the internal market if the same objective could be achieved through less distortive aid instruments.[22]

Finally, the rules on free movement emphasise the notion that derogation from the rules on free movement is compatible with the Treaty only to the extent that it is necessary to achieve the objective pursued.[23] The well-established interpretation of Article 36 TFEU requires that Member States should choose the instrument that least restricts the free movement of goods and cross-border trade.[24]

In the light of the proportionality requirements laid down in the provisions identified above, it can be argued that if generation adequacy could be ensured through measures that better complement the objectives of ensuring the functioning of the internal market while promoting energy efficiency, energy savings, renewable energy and interconnection between energy networks, these measures should first be exhausted before adopting a supply-oriented capacity mechanism.

In this context, attention should be directed towards two groups of measures. The first of these are measures on the demand side, such as demand response, energy efficiency and energy savings.[25] The second group of measures comprises instruments

---

20. Communication from the Commission – Guidelines on State aid for environmental protection and energy 2014-2020 (OJ C 200, 28.6.2014, pp. 1-55).
21. *Ibid.*, paras 6, 43, 99 and 220.
22. *Ibid.*, para. 40; and in case-law SA.42011 *Italian Capacity Mechanism*, C(2018) 617 final, para. 132.
23. *See* the second sentence of Article 36 TFEU and cases 13/78 *Eggers* [1978] ECR 1935; 42/82 *Commission v France* [1983] ECR 1013; 72/83 *Campus Oil* [1984] ECR 2727, paras 37 and 44; 104/75 *Adriaan de Peijper* [1976] ECR 613, para. 16; C-483/99 *Commission v France* [2002] ECR I-4781, para. 45; C-205/07 *Gysbrechts and Santurel Inter* [2008] ECR I-9947, para. 53; C-54/99 *Église de Scientologie* [2000] ECR I-1335, para. 18; joined cases C-163/94, C-165/94 and C-250/94 *Lucas Emilio Sanz de Lera, Raimundo Díaz Jiménez and Figen Kapanoglu* [1995] ECR I-4821, para. 23; C-451/05 *ELISA* [2007] ECR I-8251, para. 82; C-522/04 *Commission v Belgium* [2007] ECR I-0000, para. 47; C-100/01 *Oteiza Olazabal* [2002] ECR I-10981, para. 43; C-527/06 *Renneberg* [2008] ECR I-7735, para. 81; joined cases C-155/08 and C-157/08 *X and Passenheim-van Schoot* [2009] ECR I-0000, para. 47; C-169/08 *Presidente del Consiglio dei Ministri* [2009] ECR I-0000, para. 42; C-384/08 *Attanasio Group* [2010] ECR I-2055, para. 51. *See also* Norbert Reich, Annette Nordhausen Scholes and Jeremy Scholes, *Understanding EU Internal Market Law* (Intersentia, 2015), p. 72.
24. C-205/07 *Gysbrechts and Santurel Inter* [2008] ECR I-9947, para. 53; C-54/99 *Église de scientologie* [2000] ECR I-1335, para. 18; joined cases C-163/94, C-165/94, and C-250/94 *Lucas Emilio Sanz de Lera, Raimundo Díaz Jiménez and Figen Kapanoglu* [1995] I-4821, para. 23; 261/81 *Walter Rau Lebensmittelwerke v De Smedt PVBA* [1982] ECR 3961, para. 12; C-443/10 *Bonnarde* [2011] ECR I-9327, para. 35; C-463/00 *Commission v Spain* [2003] ECR I-4581, para. 68; C-367/98 *Commission v Portugal* [2002] ECR I-4731, para. 49; C-483/99 *Commission v France* [2002] ECR I-4781, para. 45; C-503/99 *Commission v Belgium* [2002] ECR I-4809, para. 45; 104/75 *Adriaan de Peijper* [1976] ECR 613, paras 16-17; C-387/99 *Commission v Germany* [2004] ECR I-3751, para. 81; 382/87 *Buet v Ministère Public* [1989] ECR 1235, para. 11; C-315/92 *Verband Sozialer Wettbewerb v Clinique Laboratories and Estée Lauder* [1994] ECR I-317, para. 16.
25. Communication from the Commission, Guidelines on State aid for environmental protection and energy 2014-2020 (OJ C 200, 28.6.2014, pp. 1-55), paras 220, 226 and 232-233.

to ensure investment in networks and interconnectors between networks.[26] The potential contribution of these measures to generation adequacy is analysed in the sections that follow.

[B] Addressing Generation Adequacy Through Demand-Side Solutions

Capacity mechanisms aim to ensure generation adequacy, typically by providing remuneration for new or existing generation capacity. Many capacity mechanisms are open to demand-side participation, but in practice the share of contributions from the demand side is small.[27] Because of this, capacity mechanisms are typically considered to fall within the category of supply-side measures. The overall reduction of or shift in electricity demand in the form of energy efficiency or demand response, on the other hand, are characteristically demand-side measures. Although these measures are physically different, both can be used to pursue generation adequacy.[28] The relationship between them is considered a key component in determining the compatibility of capacity mechanisms with EU law.[29]

Defining energy efficiency and demand-side measures as means to address energy demand on the one hand and defining capacity mechanisms as purely supply-side measures on the other is, however, an overly simplistic approach. For example, interruptibility schemes are often characterised as capacity mechanisms and can constitute an integral part of a strategic reserve, for example, but are predominantly demand-side measures.[30] For the purposes of examining the legal relationship between different measures to achieve generation adequacy, this chapter views capacity mechanisms as measures that primarily compensate for generation capacity only.

---

26. *Ibid.*, paras 220, 226 and 232-233; SA.39621 *French Country-Wide Capacity Mechanism*, C(2016) 7086 final, paras 238-239.
27. On the reasons as to why demand played such a marginal role in the actual bids, *see* Yingqi Liu, 'Demand Response and Energy Efficiency in the Capacity Resource Procurement: Case Studies of Forward Capacity Markets in ISO New England, PJM and Great Britain', 100 *Energy Policy* (2017), pp. 271-282.
28. *See* Xian He et al. 'How to Engage Consumers in Demand Response: A Contract Perspective', 27 *Utilities Policy* (2013), pp. 108-122; and Commission Q&A, Consultation paper on generation adequacy, capacity mechanisms and the internal market in electricity, February 2013, available at https://ec.europa.eu/energy/sites/ener/files/documents/20130207_generation_adequacy_question_answers.pdf (last accessed 5.3.2019), p. 1.
29. Communication from the Commission to the European Parliament and the Council, Energy Efficiency and its contribution to energy security and the 2030 Framework for climate and energy policy, COM(2014) 520 final; Capacity Mechanisms Working Group, The Participation of Non-Generation Activities, Demand-Side, and Storage in Generation Adequacy Measures, 22 January 2015, available at http://ec.europa.eu/competition/sectors/energy/capacity_mechanisms_working_group_4.pdf (last accessed 5.3.2019).
30. *See* Commission Staff Working Document accompanying the document Report from the Commission Interim Report of the Sector Inquiry on Capacity Mechanisms, SWD(2016) 119 final, pp. 40 and 46-47. *See* cases SA.38968 *Greece Transitory Electricity Flexibility Remuneration Mechanism (FRM)* and SA.38711 *Greece Interruptibility Service for the Electric System in Greece.*

As demonstrated above in Chapter 2, the role and status of demand-side measures in achieving EU energy policy objectives of security of supply and sustainability have increased in the context of the latest policy initiatives.[31] Many demand-side elements are viewed and emphasised as independent resources whose potential has not yet been fully exploited.[32]

In this context, demand-side measures are considered to include, *inter alia*, measures to achieve energy efficiency, energy savings and demand-side response. Article 2 of the Energy Efficiency Directive provides that energy efficiency refers to the ratio of output of performance, services, goods or energy, to input of energy.[33] Under the same article, 'energy efficiency improvement' is defined as an increase in energy efficiency as a result of technological, behavioural and/or economic changes;[34] while 'energy savings' is defined as an amount of saved energy determined by measuring and/or estimating consumption before and after implementation of an energy efficiency improvement measure, while ensuring normalisation for external conditions that affect energy consumption.[35]

Furthermore, as noted in Chapter 2 above, the Electricity Directive defines energy efficiency/demand-side management as a global or integrated approach aimed at influencing the amount and timing of electricity consumption in order to reduce primary energy consumption and peak loads.[36] Under the EU legal framework for energy efficiency, demand response is seen as an important instrument for improving energy efficiency because it significantly increases opportunities to reduce or shift consumption, resulting in energy savings in both final consumption and, through more optimal use of networks and generation assets, in energy generation, transmission and

---

31. Communication from the Commission to the European Parliament and the Council, Energy Efficiency and its contribution to energy security and the 2030 Framework for climate and energy policy, COM(2014) 520 final; Communication from the Commission to the European Parliament, the Council, the European Economic and Social Committee, the Committee of the Regions and the European Investment Bank, Clean Energy For All Europeans, COM(2016) 860 final; Communication from the Commission to the European Parliament, the Council, the European Economic and Social Committee, the Committee of the Regions and the European Investment Bank, a Framework Strategy for a Resilient Energy Union with a Forward-Looking Climate Change Policy, COM(2015) 80 final.
32. Communication from the Commission to the European Parliament, the Council, the European Economic and Social Committee, the Committee of the Regions and the European Investment Bank, Clean Energy For All Europeans, COM(2016) 860 final, p. 4; Communication from the Commission to the European Parliament, the Council, the European Economic and Social Committee, the Committee of the Regions and the European Investment Bank, a Framework Strategy for a Resilient Energy Union with a Forward-Looking Climate Change Policy, COM(2015) 80 final, p. 12; Communication from the Commission, Delivering the internal electricity market and making the most of public intervention, C(2013) 7243 final, p. 5; Commission Staff Working Document, Incorporing demand-side flexibility, in particular demand response, in electricity markets, SWD(2013) 442 final; Benjamin K. Sovacool and Michael H. Dworkin, *Global Energy Justice: Problems, Principles, and Practices* (Cambridge University Press, 2014), pp. 113-116.
33. Article 2(4) of the Energy Efficiency Directive.
34. Article 2(6) of the Energy Efficiency Directive.
35. Article 2(5) of the Energy Efficiency Directive.
36. Article 2(29) of the Electricity Directive. For a broader definitional approach, *see* Communication from the Commission – Guidelines on State aid for environmental protection and energy 2014-2020, OJ C 200, 28.6.2014, pp. 1-55, para. 19.

distribution.[37] From a legal point of view, demand-side response can be considered to include a large variety of measures, such as smart distribution networks, smart meters and appliances, electricity storage, dynamic pricing, interruptible contracts, participation in balancing markets as well as services aggregating and optimising demand for households.[38]

Within the context of the debate on generation adequacy and electricity market design in the EU, strong emphasis has been placed on developing the role of demand-side measures and energy efficiency.[39] The importance of energy efficiency, and moderating demand in general, can clearly be seen in relation not only to Article 194 TFEU but also the 2020 and the 2030 targets and the objective of ensuring energy security.[40]

The need to take into account the potential for energy efficiency and demand-side response has been explicitly underlined in the EU level discussion concerning capacity mechanisms.[41] The overall EU message strongly encourages measures aimed at reducing or shifting demand over investment in new generation.[42]

---

37. Recital 44 of the Energy Efficiency Directive.
38. *See* Communication from the Commission Delivering the internal electricity market and making the most of public intervention, C(2013) 7243 final, pp. 5-6. Generally, however, the concept of demand-side measures is in itself subject to definitional challenge. For further discussion, *see* Lorna Greening, 'Demand Response Resources: Who is Responsible for Implementation in a Deregulated Market?', 35(4) *Energy* (2010), pp. 1518-1525, at 1518-1520; Masood Parvania, Mahmud Fotuhi-Firuzabad and Mohammad Shahidehpour, 'Optimal Demand Response Aggregation in Wholesale Electricity Markets', 4(4) *IEEE Transactions on Smart Grid* (2013), pp. 1957-1965; Hesamoddin Marzooghi, Gregor Verbič, and David J. Hill, 'Aggregated Demand Response Modelling for Future Grid Scenarios', 5 *Sustainable Energy, Grids and Networks* (2016), pp. 94-104.
39. Communication from the Commission to the European Parliament, the Council, the European Economic and Social Committee, the Committee of the Regions and the European Investment Bank, Clean Energy For All Europeans, COM(2016) 860 final.
40. Communication from the Commission to the European Parliament, the Council, the European Economic and Social Committee, the Committee of the Regions and the European Investment Bank, a Framework Strategy for a Resilient Energy Union with a Forward-Looking Climate Change Policy, COM(2015) 80 final, p. 4; Commission Staff Working Document, Generation Adequacy in the internal electricity market – guidance on public interventions accompanying the document, Communication from the Commission Delivering the internal electricity market and making the most of public intervention, SWD(2013) 438 final, p. 21 and Communication from the Commission to the European Parliament and The Council, European Energy Security Strategy, COM(2014) 330 final, p. 3.
41. Communication from the Commission to the European Parliament, the Council, the European Economic and Social Committee, the Committee of the Regions and the European Investment Bank, a Framework Strategy for a Resilient Energy Union with a Forward-Looking Climate Change Policy, COM(2015) 80 final, p. 6 and 12 and Communication from the Commission to the European Parliament, the Council, the European Economic and Social Committee and the Committee of the Regions, Making the internal energy market work, COM(2012) 663 final, p. 15; Communication from the Commission to the European Parliament, the Council, the European Economic and Social Committee and the Committee of the Regions, Progress towards completing the Internal Energy Market, COM(2014) 634 final, p. 6; ENTSO-E, Communication Paper on Capacity Remuneration Mechanisms, available at www.entsoe.eu/fileadmin/user_upload/_library/position_papers/120510_MC_TOP_11_CRM_memorandum_external.pdf (last accessed 5.3.2019), p. 3.
42. Communication from the Commission to the European Parliament, the Council, the European Economic and Social Committee, the Committee of the Regions and the European Investment Bank, a Framework Strategy for a Resilient Energy Union with a Forward-Looking Climate

Demand-side measures could play an important role in ensuring generation adequacy particularly because they have the potential to flatten demand peaks and, as a result, reduce the need for peak-load units.[43] Furthermore, the activation of the demand side plays an integral part in facilitating the integration of intermittent renewable generation in the overall energy mix.[44]

Despite the importance of demand-side measures in ensuring generation adequacy, capacity mechanisms may directly or indirectly disregard their potential contribution.[45] The potential of the demand side is recognised to be underutilised and, in practice, the majority of remuneration in capacity mechanisms is directed towards generation capacity.[46]

[C]   Addressing Generation Adequacy Through Cross-Border Solutions

As noted at various points above, capacity mechanisms are problematic with regard to electricity market integration because they tend to exclude the participation of interconnectors and foreign capacities either implicitly or even explicitly.[47] This results in

---

Change Policy, COM(2015) 80 final, p. 6 and 12; Communication from the Commission Delivering the internal electricity market and making the most of public intervention, C(2013) 7243 final, p. 9.
43. Commission Staff Working Document accompanying the document Report from the Commission Interim Report of the Sector Inquiry on Capacity Mechanisms, SWD(2016) 119 final, p. 32.
44. Communication from the Commission Delivering the internal electricity market and making the most of public intervention, C(2013) 7243 final, p. 9; Commission Staff Working Document accompanying the document Report from the Commission Interim Report of the Sector Inquiry on Capacity Mechanisms, SWD(2016) 119 final, p. 32; Expert Group for Regulatory Recommendations for Smart Grids deployment, Regulatory Recommendations for the Deployment of Flexibility, January 2015, available at https://ec.europa.eu/energy/sites/ener/files/documents /EG3%20Final%20-%20January%202015.pdf (last accessed 5.3.2019).
45. Report from the Commission, Interim Report of the Sector Inquiry on Capacity Mechanisms, C(2016) 2107 final, p. 3.
46. Communication from the Commission Delivering the internal electricity market and making the most of public intervention, C(2013) 7243 final, pp. 5-6; Benjamin K. Sovacool and Michael H. Dworkin, *Global Energy Justice: Problems, Principles, and Practices* (Cambridge University Press, 2014), pp. 113-116; Commission Staff Working Document accompanying the document Report from the Commission Final Report of the Sector Inquiry on Capacity Mechanisms, SWD(2016) 385 final.
47. Report from the Commission, Final Report of the Sector Inquiry on Capacity Mechanisms, COM(2016) 752 final; Commission Staff Working Document accompanying the document Report from the Commission Interim Report of the Sector Inquiry on Capacity Mechanisms, SWD(2016) 119 final, pp. 80-84; Report from the Commission Interim Report of the Sector Inquiry on Capacity Mechanisms, C(2016) 2107 final, pp. 14-15; Communication from the Commission Delivering the internal electricity market and making the most of public intervention, C(2013) 7243 final, p. 8; Annex 2 to Commission Staff Working Document accompanying the document Report from the Commission Final Report of the Sector Inquiry on Capacity Mechanisms, SWD(2016) 385 final, p. 177 and 179; SA.35980 *GB Capacity Mechanism*, C(2014) 5083 final, para. 20; Graeme Hawker, Keith Bell and Simon Gill, 'Electricity Security in the European Union – The Conflict Between National Capacity Mechanisms and the Single Market', 24 *Energy Research & Social Science* (2017), pp. 51-58, at 56-57; Paolo Mastropietro, Pablo Rodilla, Carlos Batlle, 'National Capacity Mechanisms in the European Internal Energy Market: Opening the Doors to Neighbours', 82 *Energy Policy* (2015), pp. 38-47, at 39; Roland Meyer and

disregarding the potential contribution of cross-border trade and the increased competition to security of supply. In this context, an interconnector is defined as equipment used to link different electricity systems.[48]

The pursuit of an internal market as a cornerstone of the European integration project is embedded within EU energy law. Achieving an increase in the number and capacity of interconnections is not only the physical prerequisite for ensuring the functioning of the internal market in electricity under Article 194(1)(a) TFEU but also an objective in its own right under Article 194(1)(d) TFEU. Furthermore, the establishment and development of trans-European networks in energy infrastructures is provided for in Article 170 TFEU. In 2002, the EU set the target of interconnecting a minimum of 10% of all installed generation capacity in the EU.[49] This target was reviewed in 2015 and the current objective is to reach 15% by 2030.[50]

The importance of competitive cross-border trade, and interconnectors as facilitators of such trade, is also established throughout secondary electricity legislation. The significance of cross-border trade in relation to ensuring security of supply at least cost to consumers is particularly emphasised throughout the relevant legal and policy documents.[51] Cross-border solutions are also established as having a vital role in integrating the increasing shares of intermittent renewable generation into the electricity mix.[52] The available evidence indicates that increasing interconnecting capacity can

---

Olga Gore, 'Cross-Border Effects of Capacity Mechanisms: Do Uncoordinated Market Design Changes Contradict the Goals of the European Market Integration?', 51 *Energy Economics* (2015), pp. 9-20.

48. Article 2(13) of the Electricity Directive.
49. European Council, Presidency Conclusions, 15-16 March 2002, available at http://ec.europa.eu /invest-in-research/pdf/download_en/barcelona_european_council.pdf   (last   accessed 5.3.2019); Communication from the Commission to the European Parliament and the Council, European Energy Security Strategy, COM(2014) 330 final, p. 10 and 20.
50. Communication from the Commission to the European Parliament, the Council, the European Economic and Social Committee, the Committee of the Regions and the European Investment Bank, a Framework Strategy for a Resilient Energy Union with a Forward-Looking Climate Change Policy, COM(2015) 80 final, p. 8. On recent developments, *see* Peter Cameron, 'Introduction', in Peter Cameron and Raphael Heffron (eds), *Legal Aspects of EU Energy Regulation: The Consolidation of Energy Law Across Europe* (OUP, 2016), pp. 3-31, at 29.
51. For example, Article 3(10) of the Electricity Directive; Article 4(3) of the Security of Supply Directive; recitals 12-15 of the Security of Supply Directive; recitals 1 and 2 of the Regulation on Capacity Allocation and Congestion Management; Communication from the Commission – Guidelines on State aid for environmental protection and energy 2014-2020, OJ C 200, 28.6.2014, pp. 1-55, paras 201-215; Commission Staff Working Document accompanying the document Report from the Commission Interim Report of the Sector Inquiry on Capacity Mechanisms, SWD(2016) 119 final, p. 131; and discussion in Graeme Hawker, Keith Bell and Simon Gill, 'Electricity Security in the European Union – The Conflict Between National Capacity Mechanisms and the Single Market', 24 *Energy Research & Social Science* (2017), pp. 51-58, at 52; C-573/12 *Ålands Vindkraft AB v Energimyndigheten* [2014] ECR II-2037, paras 85-86; Lionel Kapff and Jacques Pelkmans, 'Interconnector Investment for a Well-functioning Internal Market: What EU Regime of Regulatory Incentives?', *Bruges European Economic Research Papers* 2010, available at http://aei.pitt.edu/58594/ (last accessed 5.3.2019), pp. 4-5.
52. For example, recitals 1 and 2 of the Regulation on Capacity Allocation and Congestion Management; Communication from the Commission – Guidelines on State aid for environmental protection and energy 2014-2020, OJ C 200, 28.6.2014, pp. 1-55, paras 201-215; Muireann Á. Lynch, Richard S.J. Tol and Mark J. O'Malley, 'Optimal Interconnection and Renewable Targets for North-West Europe', 51 *Energy Policy* (2012), pp. 605-617; Lionel Kapff and Jacques

lead to making electricity significantly more affordable[53] while significantly improving generation adequacy and achieving better integration of intermittent generation.[54] In comparison, using a national capacity mechanism that does not take into account the contribution of imported electricity can result in significant overcapacity and increase the price of electricity, whilst allocating public funding to high-carbon technologies.[55]

There are, however, significant challenges in achieving the objective of interconnecting the internal market in electricity. When the 10% interconnection target was originally set in 2002, the idea was that the investment required to achieve this objective would be financed by the private sector. However, the interconnection percentage was still below 10% in 2016.[56] Various reasons for this can be identified: lengthy and bureaucratic permitting processes, disagreement on cost allocation between Member States as well as uncertainties about investment recovery and an overall lack of economic incentives.[57] Furthermore, the 10% target has generally been criticised as constituting an overly simplistic approach to a complex issue and for failing to take into account the varying needs of different Member States.[58]

Pelkmans, 'Interconnector Investment for a Well-functioning Internal Market: What EU Regime of Regulatory Incentives?' Bruges *European Economic Research Papers* 2010, available at http://aei.pitt.edu/58594/ (last accessed 5.3.2019), pp. 4-5; András Mezősi, Zsuzsanna Pató and László Szabó, 'Assessment of the EU 10% Interconnection Target in the Context of CO_2 Mitigation', 16(5) *Climate Policy* (2016), pp. 658-672.

53. Federico Boffa, Viswanath Pingali and Davide Vannoni, 'Increasing Market Interconnection: An Analysis of the Italian Electricity Spot Market', 28(3) *International Journal of Industrial Organization* (2010), pp. 311-322.
54. Mauricio Cepeda, Marcelo Saguan, Dominique Finon and Virginie Pignon, 'Generation Adequacy and Transmission Interconnection in Regional Electricity Markets', 37(12) *Energy Policy* (2009), pp. 5612-5622, at 5613; Philipp Ringler, Dogan Keles and Wolf Fichtner, 'How to Benefit from a Common European Electricity Market Design', 101 *Energy Policy* (2017), pp. 629-643, at 630; Muireann Á. Lynch, Richard S. J. Tol and Mark J. O'Malley, 'Optimal Interconnection and Renewable Targets for North-West Europe', 51 *Energy Policy* (2012), pp. 605-617.
55. Lionel Kapff and Jacques Pelkmans, Interconnector Investment for a Well-functioning Internal Market: What EU regime of regulatory incentives? Bruges *European Economic Research Papers* 2010, available at http://aei.pitt.edu/58594/ (last accessed 5.3.2019), pp. 4-5; Capacity Mechanisms Working Group, Enabling the Participation of Interconnectors and/or Foreign Capacity Providers in Capacity Mechanisms, 30 June 2015, available at http://ec.europa.eu/competition /sectors/energy/capacity_mechanisms_working_group_6_draft.pdf (last accessed 5.3.2019). International experience concerning capacity mechanisms shows that their existence can cost up to 10%-20% of wholesale electricity prices. Commission Staff Working Document, Generation Adequacy in the internal electricity market – guidance on public interventions accompanying the document Communication from the Commission Delivering the internal electricity market and making the most of public intervention, SWD(2013) 438 final, p. 32.
56. Conclusions of the European Council, Barcelona, March 2002, p. 15.
57. Graeme Hawker, Keith Bell and Simon Gill, 'Electricity Security in the European Union – The Conflict Between National Capacity Mechanisms and the Single Market', 24 *Energy Research & Social Science* (2017), pp. 51-58, at 52; Mari Makkonen, *Cross-Border Transmission Capacity Development – Experiences from the Nordic Electricity Markets* (Lappeenranta University of Technology, PhD thesis 2015). Network capacity is not only congested across Member State borders but also within Member States. See SA.42011 *Italian Capacity Mechanism*, C(2018) 617 final, para. 5.
58. Matti Supponen, *Influence of National and Company Interests on European Electricity Transmission Investments* (Aalto University, PhD thesis 2011), pp. 42-43.

The overall estimated investment needed for European energy infrastructures amounts to around EUR 200 billion for the period to 2020.[59] Although tariffs are still anticipated to be the primary form of investment recovery, the current EEAG recognises that these infrastructure projects will need to be partly funded from State resources.[60] Aligned with the prevailing interpretation of Article 107(1) TFEU, State aid may be granted only when the market alone cannot to generate the investment incentives required.[61]

§6.03 CONTEXTUAL INTERPRETATION OF THE RELEVANT LEGAL FRAMEWORK

The EU legal framework for electricity is built upon the assumption that the market will deliver the most efficient, sustainable and economic balance between supply and demand. This underlying assumption explains why there are no specific EU-level legal obligations to invest in specific volumes of specific technologies. The general role of the Member States is to ensure a level playing field for competition and facilitate an investment climate that ensures the continuity of electricity supplies.[62] For example, Member States should take the necessary steps to remove regulatory and non-regulatory barriers to energy efficiency.[63] Furthermore, they should establish a legal framework that provides investment signals for the development of transmission and distribution networks to meet market demand.[64] The Electricity Directive places the responsibility for ensuring adequate transmission capacity and the system reliability of their networks on TSOs.[65]

However, to fill the gap between capacity generated through market-based investment and capacity required to ensure security of supply, Member States may resort to intervention to ensure that the necessary investment in generation adequacy is made. These measures are extensively analysed in earlier chapters.

As explained in Chapter 3 above, Member States must ensure that it is possible to provide for new capacity or energy efficiency/demand-side management measures through a tendering procedure or any procedure equivalent in terms of transparency and non-discrimination, on the basis of published criteria and in the interests of security of supply.[66] However, the interpretation of the wording of Article 8(1) together with Articles 8(4) and 2(24) of the Electricity Directive makes it clear that tendering or

---

59. Commission Staff Working Document, Energy infrastructure investment needs and financing requirements, SEC(2011) 755, p. 2.
60. Communication from the Commission – Guidelines on State aid for environmental protection and energy 2014-2020, OJ C 200, 28.6.2014, pp. 1-55, paras 201-215.
61. *Ibid.*
62. Article 3 of the Security of Supply Directive.
63. Article 19 of the Energy Efficiency Directive.
64. Article 6 of the Security of Supply Directive.
65. Article 12(c) of the Electricity Directive.
66. Article 8 of the Electricity Directive. For the interpretation of Article 8, *see* Chapter 3 above. In case-law, *see* SA.34947 *Support to Hinkley Point C Nuclear Power Station*, C(2014) 7142 final, particularly paras 359-362.

equivalent procedures are intended not only for new but also for existing capacity.[67] In accordance with Article 8(4) of the Electricity Directive, the tenders must also consider electricity supply offers with long-term guarantees from existing generating units, provided that the established additional requirements can be met in this way. This interpretation is in line with the underlying efforts to make sure that the balance between supply and demand is cost efficient. In fact, it would be disproportionate to require the construction of new generation capacities if existing capacities or energy efficiency and demand-side approaches could resolve the issue by themselves. It could even be argued that despite its title ('Tendering for new capacity'), Article 8 of the Electricity Directive establishes the conditions for procuring generation adequacy and not new capacity alone. However, the wording of this article alone provides an apparent choice for Member States to determine whether to ensure security of supply through generation capacity or demand-side measures.[68]

The procedure under Article 8 of the Electricity Directive may only be launched if the market-based authorisation procedure under Article 7 has failed to deliver generation adequacy either through new generation capacity, existing guarantees or measures to reduce and shift demand. Again, the wording of Articles 7 and 8 taken in isolation seems to provide a choice for Member States to determine whether supply-side or demand-side measures have failed to deliver adequate capacity on the basis of the authorisation procedure.

As noted in Chapter 3 above, generation adequacy may also constitute a public service.[69] In addition to imposing PSOs in the interests of security of supply, such obligations may also be introduced to ensure energy efficiency.[70] Furthermore, Member States should implement measures to achieve the objectives of social and economic cohesion and environmental protection.[71] These measures include energy efficiency/demand-side management measures and the provision of adequate economic incentives for the maintenance and construction of the necessary network infrastructure, including interconnection capacity.[72] Again, the wording of Article 3 of the Electricity Directive alone does not establish a hierarchy between PSOs introduced to serve different objectives.

Overall, it is clear that the wording of the existing legal framework provides a choice for Member States to decide whether to pursue generation adequacy through generation capacity, demand-side efforts or through the construction of networks in an

---

67. Peter Cameron, *Competition in Energy Markets* (OUP, 2007), p. 134.
68. Angus Johnston and Guy Block, *EU Energy Law* (OUP, 2012), p. 263.
69. For a discussion on the development of capacity mechanisms as services in the general economic interest, *see* Leigh Hancher, 'Capacity Mechanisms and State Aid Control: A European Solution to the 'Missing Money' Problem?', in Leigh Hancher, Adrien de Hautecloque and Malgorzata Sadowska (eds), *Capacity Mechanisms in the EU Energy Market* (OUP, 2015), pp. 162-163.
70. The wording of Article 3 of the Electricity Directive clearly indicates that the provision should be read together with Article 106(2) TFEU.
71. Article 3(10) of the Electricity Directive.
72. *Ibid.*

effort to pool generation capacity on a larger scale.[73] In other words, the secondary legal provisions do not establish a hierarchy between investment in national generation capacity, investment in demand-side measures and investment in interconnecting capacity.[74]

However, based upon the nature of EU law and established case-law by the ECJ, EU law should not be interpreted purely on the basis of its wording but must be placed in its context and interpreted in the light of the provisions and objectives of EU law as a whole.[75] This seems particularly relevant in relation to the energy sector, where securing adequate energy supplies has to be balanced against other objectives, which carry equal weight from a legal point of view. The Commission has emphasised that when designing public intervention such as capacity mechanisms, Member States should avoid addressing different public policy objectives in isolation from each other in order to avoid conflicts between these objectives.[76] Member States should aim to plan holistically taking into account not only these potentially conflicting energy policy objectives but also the need to coordinate the various instruments of public intervention, such as capacity mechanisms.[77]

This contextual approach established in EU law illustrates that the introduction of capacity mechanisms does not take place in a near-vacuum populated by a few isolated provisions but must be examined in the wider context of electricity market legislation and even from the broader perspective of EU energy law and policy. The need for this type of contextual approach is well illustrated by the relationship between capacity mechanisms as measures that remunerate capacity on the one hand and alternative measures to address generation adequacy on the other. This approach also follows from the requirement for proportionality, which is present in all the legal bases used to evaluate the compatibility of capacity mechanisms with EU law.

---

73. Kaisa Huhta, 'Prioritising Energy Efficiency and Demand Side Measures over Capacity Mechanisms under EU Energy Law', 35(1) *Journal of Energy & Natural Resources Law* (2017), pp. 1-18; Mauricio Cepeda, Marcelo Saguan, Dominique Finon and Virginie Pignon, 'Generation Adequacy and Transmission Interconnection in Regional Electricity Markets', 37(12) *Energy Policy* (2009), pp. 5612-5622, at 5614.
74. Henrik Bjørnebye, 'Electricity Generation Capacity Tenders in the Security of Supply Interest: EU Regulation of Internal Electricity Market Facilitation and Intervention', 4 *OGEL* (2007), pp. 23-24; Angus Johnston and Guy Block, *EU Energy Law* (OUP 2012), p. 263.
75. C-283/81 *CILFIT v Ministero della Sanità* [1982] ECR 3415, para. 20; C-337/82 *St. Nikolaus Brennerei v Hauptzollamt Krefeld* [1984] ECR 1051, para. 10; C-223/98 *Adidas AG* [1999] ECR I-7099, para. 23; C-391/05 *Jan De Nul* [2007] ECR I-1793, para. 20 and C-76/06 *P Britannia Alloys & Chemicals Ltd v Commission of the European Communities* [2007] ECR I-4443 para. 21; and for energy, *see* C-17/03 *VEMW and Others* [2005] I-4983, para. 41. *See also* Paul Craig and Gráinne de Búrca, *EU Law: Text, Cases, and Materials*, 6th edn. (OUP, 2015), pp. 266-315; Matej Avbelj, 'Supremacy or Primacy of EU Law—(Why) Does it Matter?', 17(6) *European Law Journal* (2011), pp. 744-763; Nigel Foster, *Foster on EU Law*, 6th edn. (OUP, 2017), pp. 66-68; Norbert Reich, Annette Nordhausen Scholes and Jeremy Scholes, *Understanding EU Internal Market Law* (Intersentia, 2015), pp. 44-45.
76. Communication from the Commission, Delivering the internal electricity market and making the most of public intervention, C(2013) 7243 final, p. 8.
77. *Ibid.*

A broader approach to the legal hierarchy between measures to address genera-tion adequacy is also supported by the fact that capacity mechanisms are characteris-tically national measures. Ensuring a functioning internal market in electricity, pro-moting the interconnection of energy networks and integrating renewable generation are objectives established at the Treaty level. In contrast, capacity mechanisms are merely nationally adopted legal instruments utilised to address one element of national security of supply, whilst potentially contradicting other elements of security of supply. It follows from this Treaty context and the primacy of EU law that if generation adequacy can be achieved through measures that are better suited to achieve the objectives of EU energy law, these measures should in most circumstances be exhausted before resorting to measures that clearly contradict fundamental objectives of EU law.[78]

This interpretation is also supported by the definition of energy efficiency/demand-side management set out in Article 2(29) of the Electricity Direc-tive. The reduction of primary energy consumption and peak loads mentioned in that definition is achieved by giving precedence to investment in energy efficiency mea-sures, or other measures such as interruptible supply contracts, over investment to increase generation capacity.[79] Such precedence should only be given if the energy efficiency measures are the most effective and economic option, taking into account the positive environmental impact of reduced energy consumption and the related security of supply and distribution cost aspects.[80] A similar argument can be made with regard to interconnection investment. In *Irish CADA*, for example, it was argued that developing new interconnection infrastructure between Member States or increasing the capacity of existing interconnections is generally a more rational solution since it complements the functioning of the internal market, reduces market distortions and gives Member States the possibility to share reserve capacity.[81] Furthermore, Article 25(7) of the Electricity Directive states that when planning the development of the distribution network, energy efficiency/demand-side management measures or distrib-uted generation that might supplant the need to upgrade or replace electricity capacity should be considered by the distribution system operator.

The contextual interpretation as to the hierarchy between different measures to address generation adequacy should be viewed together with the criteria established

---

78. 6/64 *Costa v ENEL* [1964] ECR 585; Nigel Foster, *Foster on EU Law*, 6th edn. (OUP, 2017), pp. 143-157; Christoph Grabenwarter, 'National Constitutional Law Relating to the European Union', in Armin von Bogdandy and Jürge Bast (eds), *Principles of European Constitutional Law*, revised 2nd edn. (Hart Publishing, 2011), pp. 83-129; Karl Riesenhuber, 'Interpretation of EU Secondary Law', in Karl Riesenhuber (ed), *European Legal Methodology* (Intersentia, 2017), pp. 231-260, at 245; and, with regard to capacity mechanisms, Kaisa Huhta, 'Prioritising Energy Efficiency and Demand Side Measures over Capacity Mechanisms under EU Energy Law', 35(1) *Journal of Energy & Natural Resources Law* (2017), pp. 1-18.
79. Article 3(29) of the Electricity Directive.
80. *Ibid.*
81. N475/2003 *Irish CADA*, 16 December 2003, para. 32. In legal literature, *see* Yann Rebours, Marc Trotignon, Vincent Lavier, Thibault Derbanne and François Meslier, 'How Much Electric Interconnection Capacities are Needed Within Western Europe?', *7th International Conference on the European Energy Market*, 23-25 June 2010.

for the market-based authorisation procedure, which further supports the interpretation presented above.[82] Under Article 7 of the Electricity Directive, Member States must
lay down criteria for granting authorisations for the construction of generation capacity
in their territory. In determining these criteria, Member States must consider issues
such as the protection of the environment, energy efficiency, the contribution of the
generation capacity to meeting the EU's renewable targets and the contribution of
generation capacity to reducing emissions.[83] When Article 7 is the primary rule by
which investment in generation capacity should be made, exceptions to this rule
should be as narrow as possible. This means that even if there are legitimate grounds
for exemption from Article 7, Member States should still aim to protect the interests laid
down in Article 7(2) if this is reasonably possible.

In this broader context of EU energy law, it is possible to identify legal requirements that need to be fulfilled in order to justify State intervention to secure generation
adequacy through measures that compensate for generation capacity. First, and before
the introduction of any intervention on the supply side, a Member State concerned
about generation adequacy has to assess the existing market structure and examine
whether there is a legitimate need for intervention or whether the markets could be
expected to deliver the investment or flexibility required on their own.[84] Instead of
capacity remuneration, the first priority should normally be to ensure that policies are
in place to control growth in demand.[85] The measure should also take into account the
extent to which interconnection capacity could be used to address generation adequacy.[86] A Member State should consider State intervention to ensure adequate
generation capacity only after it has shown that the potential of market-based
instruments has been exhausted.[87]

Second, it seems that a separate assessment is required, once the need for
intervention has been assessed, to scope the potential of alternative policies or
measures and to evaluate whether using these policies and measures alone would be
inadequate to achieve a sufficient level of generation adequacy.[88] This requirement
was evaluated in *Irish CADA*, where the Commission argued that one of the reasons for
accepting the Irish capacity mechanism was that Ireland had presented convincing
evidence not only of the insufficiency of generation capacity but also of their efforts to

---

82. Article 7 of the Electricity Directive.
83. *Ibid.*
84. Commission Staff Working Document, Generation Adequacy in the internal electricity market –
    guidance on public interventions accompanying the document, Communication from the
    Commission Delivering the internal electricity market and making the most of public interven-
    tion, SWD(2013) 438 final, pp. 18-19, 21 and 34-36.
85. *Ibid.*; N 475/2003 *Irish CADA*, 16 December 2003, paras 31 and 35; and N675/2009 *Tender for
    Aid for New Electricity Generation Capacity (LV)*, C(2010) 4146, para. 38.
86. Communication from the Commission, Guidelines on State aid for environmental protection and
    energy 2014-2020 (OJ C 200, 28.6.2014, pp. 1-55), para. 226.
87. N 475/2003 *Irish CADA*, 16 December 2003, para. 31; and N675/2009 *Tender for Aid for New
    Electricity Generation Capacity (LV)*, C(2010) 4146, para. 38; and more recently SA.42011 *Italian
    Capacity Mechanism*, C(2018) 617 final, para. 150.
88. Communication from the Commission, Guidelines on State aid for environmental protection and
    energy 2014-2020 (OJ C 200, 28.6.2014, pp. 1-55), paras 224, 226 and 232.

manage demand.[89] Furthermore, Ireland was unable to rely on interconnectors to address generation adequacy due to its geographical isolation.[90] Similarly, a Latvian call for tenders was accepted as a measure to ensure generation adequacy because Latvia had successfully argued that energy efficiency and demand-side measures in Latvia were essentially limited to improving the effectiveness of heat supply systems and promoting the energy efficiency of public housing. Furthermore, it was argued that the Latvian economy was still in the process of catching up with the European average and this development made growth in energy demand inevitable.[91] Therefore, measures to moderate demand would not have been sufficient to ensure security of electricity supply in the Latvian situation.[92] Furthermore, Latvia argued that although it was relatively well connected with other Baltic States, it remained isolated from the rest of the EU. Therefore, in respect of the majority of the Member States, it was unable to access the generation capacity located in them.[93] In *German Network Reserve*, the strategic reserve scheme adopted by Germany was defended precisely because a transmission line was about to be constructed, which made market-based investment in generation capacity unprofitable.[94] Therefore, Germany considered temporary capacity remuneration necessary.[95] In fact, even in *Campus Oil*, the fact that alternative measures had been explored to a sufficient extent was used as one of the arguments to justify restrictions on free movement of goods.[96]

In addition to the adequate assessment of alternative solutions being available as an argument justifying intervention, a Member State's failure to sufficiently assess the potential of alternative measures has been used as an argument for initiating State aid investigations in accordance with Article 108 TFEU. For example, an invitation to submit comments pursuant to Article 108(2) TFEU was initiated after France notified a call for tenders for additional capacity in Brittany.[97] The Commission argued that it was doubtful whether the tender was appropriate to achieve its objective since security of supply in Brittany could be achieved by instruments less distortive than the measure in question.[98] Similarly, in its decision to initiate investigations in the French country-wide capacity mechanism, the Commission underlined its doubts as to whether the capacity mechanism was appropriate to address French generation adequacy concerns. These doubts were raised because the capacity scheme established a distinction between explicit and implicit demand response and did not allow interconnections or foreign capacity to participate directly in the mechanism.[99]

---

89. N 475/2003 *Irish CADA*, 16 December 2003, para. 38.
90. *Ibid.*, para. 37.
91. N675/2009 *Tender for Aid for New Electricity Generation Capacity (LV)*, C(2010) 4146, para. 39.
92. *Ibid.*
93. *Ibid.*, paras 5-6.
94. SA.42955 *German Network Reserve*, C(2016) 8742 final, para. 61.
95. *Ibid.*
96. 72/83 *Campus Oil* [1984] ECR 2727, written observations by the plaintiff in the main action, p. 2735.
97. SA.40454 Call for tenders for additional capacity in Brittany, Invitation to submit comments pursuant to Article 108(2) of the Treaty on the Functioning of the European Union, OJ C 46, 5.2.2016, pp. 69-88.
98. *Ibid.*
99. SA.39621 *French Country-Wide Capacity Mechanism*, C(2015) 7805 final.

In *Hinkley Point C*, State aid investigation was initiated because it was unclear whether the UK had considered the potential and future development of demand response, which could significantly impact upon security of supply.[100] This step was taken despite the fact that the UK had provided an assessment of the state of generation adequacy and the potential of measures on the demand side.[101] However, the UK had not taken into account future interconnection capacity when modelling its capacity projections.[102]

In other words, alternative measures to address generation adequacy are relevant even if a Member State considers these measures inadequate and then decides to introduce a mechanism that increases generation capacity.[103] When evaluating the acceptability of a supply-side measure, the assessment of the impacts and potential of alternative instruments will be taken into consideration, including a Member State's description of the measures it has taken to encourage responses on the demand-side or to increase interconnecting capacity.[104] A Member State should be able not only to clearly demonstrate why the market cannot be expected to deliver sufficient generation adequacy without State intervention but also why remuneration for capacity is required in preference to less invasive measures such as demand-side participation or increasing interconnections.[105]

Third, and only if the Member State has been able to prove that the alternative measures assessed have been, or would be, unsuccessful in securing electricity supply, the Member State is allowed, under specific conditions, to introduce a capacity mechanism.[106] This capacity mechanism should be open to both demand and supply solutions and must, therefore, promote and reward demand-side solutions to the same extent as existing or forthcoming generation capacity.[107] The measure should also

---

100. SA.34947 *Support to Hinkley Point C Nuclear Power Station*, C(2013) 9073 final.
101. OFGEM, 'Electricity Capacity Assessment Report 2013', available at www.ofgem.gov.uk/sites /default/files/docs/2013/06/electricity-capacity-assessment-report-2013_0.pdf (last accessed 5.3.2019) and Department of Energy and Climate Change, 'Overarching National Policy Statement for Energy (EN-1)', 2011, available at www.gov.uk/government/uploads/system/ uploads/attachment_data/file/47854/1938-overarching-nps-for-energy-en1.pdf (last accessed 5.3.2019).
102. SA.34947 *Support to Hinkley Point C Nuclear Power Station*, C(2013) 9073 final, para. 259.
103. *See* assessment in N675/2009 *Tender for Aid for New Electricity Generation Capacity (LV)*, C(2010) 4146, para. 8.
104. Communication from the Commission, Guidelines on State aid for environmental protection and energy 2014-2020 (OJ C 200, 28.6.2014, pp. 1-55), para. 220. In case-law, *see* SA.48648 *Belgian Strategic Reserve*, C(2018) 589 final, paras 17-24; SA.42011 *Italian Capacity Mechanism*, C(2018) 617 final, paras 17-26.
105. *Ibid. See also* argumentation in SA.39621 *French Country-Wide Capacity Mechanism*, C(2015) 7805 final and SA.42011 *Italian Capacity Mechanism*, C(2018) 617 final, paras 17-26.
106. For further discussion of these criteria, *see* Chapters 3-5 above. In case-law, *see* SA.48648 *Belgian Strategic Reserve*, C(2018) 589 final, para. 116.
107. *See* Article 15(8) and recital 47 of the Energy Efficiency Directive and Communication from the Commission to the European Parliament, the Council, the European Economic and Social Committee and the Committee of the Regions, Progress towards completing the Internal Energy Market, COM(2014) 634 final, p. 14; Communication from the Commission, Guidelines on State aid for environmental protection and energy 2014-2020 (OJ C 200, 28.6.2014, pp. 1-55), para. 232; and Communication from the Commission, Delivering the internal electricity market and making the most of public intervention, C(2013) 7243 final, p. 14.

allow the participation of operators from other Member States where such participation is physically possible, i.e., capacity can be physically delivered to the Member State implementing the measure and the obligations set out in the measure can be enforced.[108] Furthermore, capacity remuneration should be designed in a such a way that it can be withdrawn immediately if the generation adequacy problem ceases to exist or could be resolved through measures that better complement the objectives of EU energy law, such as demand response deployment or interconnection capacity.[109]

Demand-side measures and network solutions should, in other words, be allowed to bid into capacity markets on an equal basis to generation capacity.[110] In fact, capacity mechanisms should not reduce incentives to invest in interconnection capacity.[111] They should also give preference to low carbon generators if the technical and economic parameters are the same.[112] This criterion is in line with the EU approach in which demand-side measures and an interconnected market form an inseparable package, together with investment in new generation capacity, and all play a vital role in ensuring European generation adequacy.[113] Allowing demand-side measures and interconnections in a tendering procedure, for example, ensures that the end result fulfils the criterion of non-discrimination under Article 8(1) of the Electricity Directive.[114] The process is to be technologically neutral in the sense that bidding for new capacity should allow for the participation of different technologies or measures that offer equivalent technical performance.[115] Restrictions on participation can only be justified if the technical performance required is insufficient to address the generation adequacy problem.[116] However, the technical performance criteria can be formulated in a variety of ways and are, in practice, often utilised to circumvent the requirement to exhaust alternative measures first. This problem leads one to question whether other restrictions exist in relation to the priority of alternative measures established in this section. This issue is analysed below.

---

108. Communication from the Commission, Guidelines on State aid for environmental protection and energy 2014-2020 (OJ C 200, 28.6.2014, pp. 1-55), para. 232.
109. Communication from the Commission, Delivering the internal electricity market and making the most of public intervention, C(2013) 7243 final, p. 14; Communication from the Commission, Guidelines on State aid for environmental protection and energy 2014-2020 (OJ C 200, 28.6.2014, pp. 1-55), para. 231; SA.48648 *Belgian Strategic Reserve*, C(2018) 589 final, para. 146; Kelyn Bacon, *European Union Law of State Aid*, 3rd edn. (OUP, 2017), p. 245.
110. European Commission, Consultation Paper on generation adequacy, capacity mechanisms and the internal market in electricity, 15.11.2012, p. 13.
111. Communication from the Commission, Guidelines on State aid for environmental protection and energy 2014-2020 (OJ C 200, 28.6.2014, pp. 1-55), para. 233.
112. *Ibid.*
113. European Commission, Consultation Paper on generation adequacy, capacity mechanisms and the internal market in electricity, 15.11.2012.
114. This is also supported by the results of the State aid sector inquiry on capacity mechanisms and individual State aid cases on capacity remuneration. *See* Commission Staff Working Document accompanying the document Report from the Commission Final Report of the Sector Inquiry on Capacity Mechanisms, SWD(2016) 385 final, pp. 82-111 and SA.45852 *German Capacity Reserve*, C(2018) 612 final, paras 31 and 89-90.
115. Communication from the Commission, Guidelines on State aid for environmental protection and energy 2014-2020 (OJ C 200, 28.6.2014, pp. 1-55), para. 232.
116. *Ibid.*; and in case-law SA.42011 *Italian Capacity Mechanism*, C(2018) 617 final, para. 59 and SA.46100 *Planned Polish Capacity Mechanism*, C(2018) 601 final, para. 51.

§6.04 EVALUATING THE LEGALLY BINDING NATURE OF THE HIERARCHY BETWEEN MEASURES TO ADDRESS GENERATION ADEQUACY

[A] Problems with Contextual Interpretation

The contextual interpretation presented above identifies that priority should be given to demand-side measures and network solutions, as measures to address generation adequacy, in preference to generation capacity. However, this priority is not absolute. It comes with a number of problems, including restrictions of a physical, legal and practical nature.

The first and most apparently physical problem limiting the deployment of alternative measures in preference to generation capacity is that network capacity and demand-side measures can never altogether replace generation capacity. They are inherently complementary measures to address deficiencies in an already functional electricity system. Furthermore, the existing legal framework allows the limitation of demand-side measures and network solutions to generation adequacy in circumstances where their technical performance is insufficient to address the national generation adequacy concerns.[117] For example, the completion of a new interconnection line is likely to take significantly more time than the construction of a new generation facility, which makes the latter a more appealing option if the generation adequacy problem is acute. Interconnections may only solve the issue if the capacity can be physically provided and the obligations set out in the measure can be enforced.[118]

The second problem is legal is nature. The existing legal framework provides Member States with a significant margin of discretion in defining the scope of their national security of supply needs. This broad margin of discretion is present in all the legal provisions based on which capacity mechanisms can be scrutinised under EU law and which include a security of supply element. For example, in order to be compatible with State aid rules the adopted measure must contribute to a clearly defined objective of common interest, the scope of which is to be defined by the Member State in question.[119] Similarly, the content of public security justifications under free movement rules is largely defined by the Member States themselves.[120] Finally, Member

---

117. Article 8(4) of the Electricity Directive; Peter Cameron, *Competition in Energy Markets* (OUP, 2007), p. 134; Communication from the Commission, Guidelines on State aid for environmental protection and energy 2014-2020 (OJ C 200, 28.6.2014, pp. 1-55), para. 232.
118. Therefore, it may be necessary to de-rate the contribution of interconnectors or foreign capacity in relation to their ability to physically deliver capacity. See Annex 2 to Commission Staff Working Document accompanying the document Report from the Commission Final Report of the Sector Inquiry on Capacity Mechanisms, SWD(2016) 385 final, p. 184; Capacity Mechanisms Working Group, Enabling the Participation of Interconnectors and/or Foreign Capacity Providers in Capacity Mechanisms, 30 Jun. 2015, available at http://ec.europa.eu/competition /sectors/energy/capacity_mechanisms_working_group_6_draft.pdf (last accessed 5.3.2019), p. 4.
119. For further discussion of this topic, *see* Chapter 4 above.
120. *Ibid.*, *see* Chapter 5 above.

States have a broad margin of discretion in defining what they consider to be SGEIs and how they establish the threshold by which tendering procedures may be introduced to safeguard security of supply.[121] In accordance with the subsidiarity principle, the Member States are responsible for defining PSOs, whereas the EU is only responsible for ensuring that the PSOs do not entail a manifest error or affect the development of trade to such an extent as would be contrary to the interests of the Union.[122]

This broad margin of discretion left to Member States in defining the scope of security of supply or the existence of market failure is likely to have a considerable impact on the contextual interpretation identified above. Effectively, this means that Member States have significant leeway in determining the severity of their generation adequacy concerns and, in particular, in determining the necessary measures through which to address these concerns. As a result, the compatibility of capacity mechanisms with EU law greatly depends on the market structure of the Member State in question, the design of the capacity remuneration measure and the arguments the Member State can muster to defend the measure against the Commission.

Finally, the deployment of alternative measures in preference to compensation solely for generation capacity involves further practical issues, which differ for demand-side measures and network solutions. In general, the deployment of flexibility through demand-side response in the electricity market remains restricted due to the limited roll-out of demand-side technologies. Furthermore, the fact that household consumers, in particular, still typically have little information on how and when to reduce demand and little options to participate in the market as providers of flexibility poses a problem.[123] Specific challenges also exist with regard to demand-side response that affect the potential contribution of these measures to capacity mechanism schemes in particular. For example, a demand response unit can only deliver capacity for a limited number of consecutive hours. Furthermore, the need to establish a consumption baseline from which to measure the amount of energy delivered by demand

---

121. *Ibid.*, *see* Chapter 3 above. *See also* cases T-106/95 *FFSA and Others v Commission* [1997] ECR II-229, para. 99; T-17/02 *Fred Olsen v Commission* [2005] ECR II-2031, para. 216; T-289/03 *BUPA* [2008] ECR II-81, para. 166; and discussion in Francisco Enrique Gonzáles-Díaz, 'EU Policy on Capacity Mechanisms', in Leigh Hancher, Adrien de Hauteclocque and Malgorzata Sadowska (eds), *Capacity Mechanisms in the EU Energy Market* (OUP, 2015), pp. 3-31, at 24.

122. Article 3(14) of the Electricity Directive; T-106/95 *FFSA and Others v Commission* [1997] ECR II-229, paras 98-100; T-17/02 *Fred Olsen v Commission* [2005] ECR II-2031, paras 209 and 216; T-289/03 *BUPA* [2008] ECR II-81, paras 101, 148 and 164-66.

123. SA.48648 *Belgian Strategic Reserve*, C(2018) 589 final, para. 13. Peter Cramton, Axel Ockenfels and Steven Stoft, 'Capacity Market Fundamentals', 2(2) *Economics of Energy & Environmental Policy* (2013), pp. 27-46; Dominique Finon and Virginie Pignon, 'Electricity and Long-Term Capacity Adequacy: The Quest for Regulatory Mechanism Compatible with Electricity Market', 16(3) *Utilities Policy* (2008), pp. 143-158, at 143; Lawrence Ausubel and Peter Cramton, 'Using Forward Markets to Improve Electricity Market Design', 18(2) *Utilities Policy* (2010), pp. 195-200, at 196. This was also acknowledged in Commission, Interim Report of the Sector Inquiry on Capacity Mechanisms, C(2016) 2107 final, p. 9; Expert Group for Regulatory Recommendations for Smart Grids deployment, Regulatory Recommendations for the Deployment of Flexibility, January 2015, available at https://ec.europa.eu/energy/sites/ener/files/documents/EG3%20Final%20-%20January%202015.pdf (last accessed 5.3.2019), p. 7.

response presents challenges for the utilisation of demand-side response in capacity mechanisms.[124]

Network solutions to the challenge of achieving generation adequacy are hindered by difficulties related to the ability of interconnectors to contribute in practice to security of supply and by challenges related to the construction of electricity infrastructures.[125] The lack of investment incentives in cross-border transmission lines combined with complex and time-consuming cross-border permit processes lie at the core of the challenges concerning investment in new interconnections.[126] Issues with cost allocation between Member States continue to pose challenges for the achievement of interconnector projects. For example, a transmission line between Member States X and Y may be necessary for the security of supply of Member State Z but not for States X and Y themselves. This raises the question of who should then shoulder the risk involved in investing in the proposed project. Overall, uncertainty about investment recovery continues to hinder the development of intra-EU networks.[127] In practice, constructing the existence of a legal priority through a contextual approach is little more than an ideological stance if, in reality, demand-side measures and network solutions cannot respond to generation adequacy concerns in the short and medium term.[128]

[B]   Legal Priority in Theory but How About in Practice?

As identified in §6.03 above, the wording of the legal provisions that govern the introduction and design of capacity mechanisms provides a choice between measures on the supply side on the one hand and alternative measures such as network solutions or demand-side measures on the other.[129] However, when these rules are examined in the broader context of the objectives of EU energy law, a recommendation to prioritise demand-side measures and network solutions can be distinguished. This interpretation is further supported by various policy documents published by the Commission, which, although not legally binding, are representative of how the Commission interprets EU law and are binding on the Commission itself.[130] The Commission has a

---

124. Commission Staff Working Document accompanying the document Report from the Commission Final Report of the Sector Inquiry on Capacity Mechanisms, SWD(2016) 385 final, pp. 136-137.
125. Annex 2 to Commission Staff Working Document accompanying the document Report from the Commission Final Report of the Sector Inquiry on Capacity Mechanisms, SWD(2016) 385 final, pp. 186-187; *see* argumentation in SA.675/2009 *Tender for Aid for New Electricity Generation Capacity (LV)*, C(2010) 4146, para. 6.
126. DG Energy, Permitting procedures for energy infrastructure projects in the EU: evaluation and legal recommendations, July 2011.
127. Mari Makkonen, *Cross-Border Transmission Capacity Development – Experiences from the Nordic Electricity Markets* (Lappeenranta University of Technology, PhD thesis 2015).
128. Francisco Enrique González-Díaz, 'EU Policy on Capacity Mechanisms', in Leigh Hancher, Adrien de Hauteclocque and Malgorzata Sadowska (eds), *Capacity Mechanisms in the EU Energy Market* (OUP, 2015), pp. 3-31, at 8-10.
129. Angus Johnston and Guy Block, *EU Energy Law* (OUP 2012), p. 263.
130. Opinion of the European Economic and Social Committee on the communication from the Commission on 'Delivering the internal electricity market and making the most of public

central institutional role in enforcing internal market and State aid rules in particular. Therefore, its interpretation of EU law is significant in practice.

Since the alternative measures to address generation adequacy complement the objectives of EU energy law better than the provision of generation capacity alone, these measures should be prioritised over purely supply-side measures. This follows not only from the contextual approach to the legal framework but also from the requirement of proportionality.[131]

If justification for a restrictive element of a capacity mechanism is evaluated under the rules on free movement, it is clear that national rules do not fall within the application of Article 36 TFEU if the public security interest identified can be effectively protected by measures that do not restrict cross-border to the same extent.[132] Furthermore, if the appropriateness of a capacity mechanism is assessed under State aid rules, the Commission will evaluate the potential for less interventionist measures in accordance with established proportionality criteria.[133] If that evaluation establishes that the Member State in question could secure generation adequacy through demand-side measures, for example, it seems highly unlikely that such a State aid measure would be declared compatible with EU law. In other words, while it is not explicitly stated in legally binding documents, under which capacity mechanisms are typically introduced, that demand-side measures or network solutions have priority, the systematic interpretation of the role of these alternative measures demonstrates that the priority identified is likely to have relevance in legal practice.

It is well established that there is significant potential in addressing generation adequacy through demand-side measures or cross-border solutions. It has been estimated that the potential of demand-side response could be as much as 60 GW within the EU, which amounts to approximately 10% of the EU's peak demand.[134] Considerable advancements have also been made in expanding the EU network of electricity transmission lines in recent years to achieve the 10% and 15% targets for

---

intervention' C(2013) 7243 final, OJ C 226, 16.7.2014, pp. 28-34, para. 2.7. On the usage of guidelines as instruments to substantiate EU State aid law, *see* Leigh Hancher, Tom Ottervanger and Piet Jan Slot, *EU State Aids*, 5th edn. (Sweet & Maxwell, 2016), pp. 15-16. *See also* cases C-526/14 *Kotnik* [2016], judgment of the Court of 19 July 2016, published in the electronic Reports of Cases; 310/85 *Deufil v Commission* [1987] ECR 901, para. 22; C-313/90 *CIRFS v Commission* [1993] ECR I-1125, paras 32-36; and C-311/94 *Ijssel-Vliet* [1996] ECR I-5023, para, 42.

131. *See* assessment in C-265/08 *Federutility and Others v Autorità per l'energia elettrica e il gas* [2010] ECR I-3377, paras 33-47.
132. Cases 104/75 *Adriaan de Peijper* [1976] ECR 613, paras 16-17; 261/81 *Walter Rau Lebensmittelwerke v De Smedt PVBA* [1982] ECR 3961, para. 12.
133. Communication from the Commission, Guidelines on State aid for environmental protection and energy 2014-2020 (OJ C 200, 28.6.2014, pp. 1-55), paras 69-80 and 228-231. The Commission applied these criteria in SA.35980 *GB Capacity Mechanism*, C(2014) 5083 final, paras 144-147.
134. Commission Staff Working Document, Generation adequacy in the internal electricity market – guidance on public interventions, SWD(2013) 438 final, p. 9; Communication from the Commission, Delivering the internal electricity market and making the most of public intervention, C(2013) 7243 final, p. 6; Hans Christian Gils, 'Assessment of the Theoretical Demand Response Potential in Europe', 67 *Energy* (2014), pp. 1-18.

interconnecting installed generation capacity.[135] The overall benefits and the potential of these alternative measures are considered to be high.[136]

However, it is also widely acknowledged that economically rational investments to deploy the demand-side are not being made.[137] Furthermore, it is known that the structure of the electricity market and consumers' lack both of real-time market information and of knowledge of how to use this information place demand-side measures at a disadvantage.[138] It would seem that the legal framework for prioritising demand-side measures has been put in place prematurely in the sense that, although the technology exists, the roll-out of these technologies has not advanced enough to achieve short-term advantages. Similar observations can be made with regard to interconnection infrastructure. The objective of interconnecting at least 10% of all installed generation capacity within the EU had still not been reached in 2017 despite the strong policy emphasis on this target.[139] The unavoidable fact is that cross-border infrastructure projects are complex undertakings burdened by regulatory and economic issues that take time to resolve.[140]

In conclusion, it seems that although alternative measures have significant potential to address generation adequacy, they cannot completely obviate the need for remuneration for generation capacity.[141] The identified challenges in using alternative measures to address generation adequacy were addressed in the Clean Energy for All Europeans package, which aims to put energy efficiency first, achieve global leadership

135. Peter Cameron, 'Introduction', in Peter Cameron and Raphael Heffron (eds), *Legal Aspects of EU Energy Regulation: The Consolidation of Energy Law Across Europe* (OUP, 2016), pp. 3-31, at 29.
136. Commission Staff Working Document, Incorporing demand-side flexibility, in particular demand response, in electricity markets, SWD(2013) 442 final. *See also* Benjamin K. Sovacool and Michael H. Dworkin, *Global Energy Justice: Problems, Principles, and Practices* (Cambridge University Press, 2014), pp. 113-116.
137. Communication from the Commission to the European Parliament, the Council, the European Economic and Social Committee and the Committee of the Regions, Making the internal energy market work, COM(2012) 663 final, p. 3.
138. Keynote speech by European Commissioner for Competition Margrethe Vestager, Securing electricity supply in the EU: How to optimise public support, at *Capacity mechanisms in Europe: The fundamental issues behind the ongoing sector inquiry*, 29 September 2015, Brussels, available at http://ec.europa.eu/competition/sectors/energy/state_aid_to_secure_electricity_supply_en.html (last accessed 5.3.2019); Lorna Greening, 'Demand Response Resources: Who is Responsible for Implementation in a Deregulated Market?', 35(4) *Energy* (2010), pp. 1518-1525, at 1520-1521; Rita Pereira et al. 'A Fuzzy Clustering Approach to a Demand Response Model', 81 *Electrical Power and Energy Systems* (2016), pp. 184-192, at 185; Jacopo Torriti, Mohamed G. Hassan and Matthew Leach, 'Demand Response Experience in Europe: Policies, Programmes and Implementation', 35(4) *Energy* (2010), pp. 1575-1583, at 1575-1576.
139. Annex 2 to the Communication from the Commission to the European Parliament, the Council, the European Economic and Social Committee, the Committee of the Regions and the European Investment Bank, Third Report on the State of the Energy Union, COM(2017) 688 final, p. 2. Originally suggested in Conclusions of the European Council, Barcelona, March 2002, p. 15.
140. Communication from the Commission to the European Parliament and the Council Achieving the 10% electricity interconnection target Making Europe's electricity grid fit for 2020, COM(2015) 82 final.
141. Francisco Enrique González-Díaz, 'EU Policy on Capacity Mechanisms', in Leigh Hancher, Adrien de Hautecloque and Malgorzata Sadowska (eds), *Capacity Mechanisms in the EU Energy Market* (OUP, 2015), pp. 3-31, at 8-10 and 21-22.

in renewable energies and provide a fair deal for consumers.[142] It remains to be seen how this objective will be achieved in practice in the upcoming legal reform.

The restricted practical potential of alternative measures to address generation adequacy and the broad margin of discretion left to Member States in defining their national security needs limit the concrete legal obligations that can be imposed on Member States to prioritise demand-side measures and network solutions in practice over generation capacity. Due to these practical and legal limitations, it seems that the threshold is relatively low for demonstrating that alternative measures have been duly considered but nevertheless remain insufficient.[143] As a result, the remaining concrete obligation imposed on Member States is that of ensuring that, when designing and implementing a capacity mechanism, demand-side measures and interconnection capacity are able to compete equally with generation capacity.[144] In other words, these alternative measures appear to be complementary rather than real substitutes for generation capacity.

---

142. Communication from the Commission to the European Parliament, the Council, the European Economic and Social Committee, the Committee of the Regions and the European Investment Bank, Clean Energy For All Europeans, COM(2016) 860 final.
143. In case T-793/14 *Tempus Energy and Tempus Energy Technology v Commission* [2018], judgment of the General Court of 15 November 2018, published in the electronic Reports of Cases, the inadequate assessment of demand-side response is being used to challenge a State aid decision made by the Commission.
144. Article 15(8) of the Energy Efficiency Directive.

CHAPTER 7

Forthcoming Changes to the EU Legal Framework for Generation Adequacy

§7.01   A NEW APPROACH TO GENERATION ADEQUACY

In late November 2016, the Commission published an extensive legislative proposal for the energy sector.[1] This Clean Energy for All Europeans package addresses energy efficiency, renewable energy, the design of the electricity market, security of supply and governance rules in the Energy Union.[2] The legislative proposal aims to facilitate and accelerate the European clean energy transition and to address some of the issues emerged and emphasised during this transition.[3] Political agreement on the content of this package was reached in December 2018. Therefore, the proposal is, at present, being processed in accordance with the ordinary legislative procedure and may still be altered before entering into force.

Among other things, the Clean Energy for All Europeans legislative package aims to create a common European approach to capacity mechanisms. The proposed key changes to the legal *status quo* are the focus of this chapter.

---

1. Communication from the Commission to the European Parliament, the Council, the European Economic and Social Committee, the Committee of the Regions and the European Investment Bank, Clean Energy For All Europeans, COM(2016) 860 final. *See* all proposals and impact assessments on the Clean Energy for All Europeans Package in European Commission, 'Commission proposes new rules for consumer centred clean energy transition', 30 November 2016, available at https://ec.europa.eu/energy/en/news/commission-proposes-new-rules-consumer-centred-clean-energy-transition (last accessed 5.3.2019).
2. Communication from the Commission to the European Parliament, the Council, the European Economic and Social Committee, the Committee of the Regions and the European Investment Bank, Clean Energy for All Europeans, COM(2016) 860 final, p. 3.
3. Communication from the Commission to the European Parliament, the Council, the European Economic and Social Committee, the Committee of the Regions and the European Investment Bank, Clean Energy for All Europeans, COM(2016) 860 final, particularly pp. 3-4, 8 and 12; Recital 2 of the Proposal for a Directive of the European Parliament and of the Council on common rules for the internal market in electricity, COM(2016) 864 final.

The Commission's proposed legislative package is a revision of the third energy package adopted in 2009 and contributes to the objectives laid down through the 2015 Energy Union initiative.[4] The proposals address renewable energy, energy efficiency, the redesign of the electricity market and security of supply. The objective of the package is to put energy efficiency first, to achieve global leadership in renewable energies and to provide a fair deal for all consumers.[5]

The Clean Energy for All Europeans package includes three legal instruments that have particular relevance in terms of security of supply. First, the Commission's proposal includes a recast of the directive concerning common rules for the internal market in electricity (hereinafter the 'Recast Electricity Directive').[6] Second, the proposal repeals the existing Security of Supply Directive and replaces it with a regulation of the on risk-preparedness in the electricity sector (hereinafter the 'Security of Supply Regulation').[7] Third, the proposal includes a recast of the regulation on conditions for access to the network for cross-border exchanges in electricity (hereinafter the 'Electricity Regulation' and the 'Recast Electricity Regulation').[8]

The new proposals approach security of supply from two temporal points of view. First, there are instruments available to address emergency shortfalls in electricity supply as a result of unpredictable, sudden events. These short-term instruments are largely included in the proposed Security of Supply Regulation.[9] Instead of merely managing emergencies, this regulation highlights the importance of preparing for and preventing such situations.[10] Secondly, there are instruments to address long-term security of supply, which are particularly relevant in terms of capacity mechanisms. This long-term approach is more emphasised in the Recast Electricity Directive and the Recast Electricity Regulation.

Capacity mechanisms are explicitly addressed in the Recast Electricity Regulation, which adopts entirely new provisions on assessing the need for capacity mechanisms and the required design features of any capacity mechanism that is adopted, including rules on cross-border participation.[11] Article 8 of the Electricity Directive is consequently repealed in the Recast Electricity Directive. As regulations are not

---

4. Proposal for a Regulation of the European Parliament and of the Council on risk-preparedness in the electricity sector and repealing Directive 2005/89/EC, COM(2016) 862 final, Recital 3 and p. 3; Communication from the Commission to the European Parliament, the Council, the European Economic and Social Committee, the Committee of the Regions and the European Investment Bank, A Framework Strategy for a Resilient Energy Union with a Forward-Looking Climate Change Policy, COM(2015) 80 final.
5. Communication from the Commission to the European Parliament, the Council, the European Economic and Social Committee, the Committee of the Regions and the European Investment Bank, Clean Energy for All Europeans, COM(2016) 860 final, p. 3.
6. Proposal for a Directive of the European Parliament and of the Council on common rules for the internal market in electricity, COM(2016) 864 final.
7. Proposal for a Regulation of the European Parliament and of the Council on risk-preparedness in the electricity sector and repealing Directive 2005/89/EC, COM(2016) 862 final.
8. Regulation (EC) No 714/2009 of the European Parliament and of the Council of 13 July 2009 on conditions for access to the network for cross-border exchanges in electricity and repealing Regulation (EC) No 1228/2003, OJ L 211, 14.8.2009, pp. 15-35; the Recast Electricity Regulation.
9. *See*, for example, Articles 4-6, 8 and 10 of the Security of Supply Regulation.
10. Security of Supply Regulation, pp. 2-3.
11. *See* Articles 18, 19, 21 and 23 of the Recast Electricity Regulation.

nationally implemented, this shift from addressing capacity mechanisms in a regulation rather than a directive gives less leeway for Member States to interpret the EU rules in their national contexts.

However, the proposed changes in the Recast Electricity Regulation are not intended to provide full harmonisation. From the point of view of capacity mechanisms, the proposed measures aim to create a level playing field for market participants and to ensure that internal market integration is not fragmented through State intervention.[12] This approach is also in line with the subsidiarity principle, which requires that the EU can only act if and in so far as the objectives of the proposed action cannot be sufficiently achieved by the Member States.[13] Given the adverse effects nationally adopted capacity mechanisms have had on the functioning of the internal market in electricity, an EU-level approach is needed to establish the scope of when and how capacity mechanisms can be used.[14] This approach is next systematised and analysed.

§7.02 MARGINALISING THE ROLE OF CAPACITY MECHANISMS

[A] From Generation Adequacy to Resource Adequacy

The proposed legislation, particularly the Recast Electricity Regulation, no longer refers to *generation* adequacy in the context of capacity mechanisms but to *resource* adequacy, i.e., the ability of the European electricity system to offer sufficient generation and flexibility to ensure reliable electricity supply at all times.[15] This terminological shift emphasises the importance of the EU efforts to, first, ensure security of supply through measures that contribute to the EU sustainability efforts and, second, to engage consumers to become active participants in the electricity market.[16] Particularly, this terminological shift explicitly brings energy efficiency, demand-side measures and imports over interconnectors up to the same level with mere generation capacity located within the territory of a Member State.[17] This shift is not only an effort to ensure that if a capacity mechanism is needed, it allows for the inclusion of all resources. It is also an effort to tap into the full potential and efficiencies of the integrated market in electricity and, hence, avoid the need for capacity mechanisms in the first place. This approach is next analysed.

---

12. Recast Electricity Regulation, p. 11.
13. Article 5(3) TEU.
14. Recast Electricity Regulation, p. 10; Security of Supply Regulation, pp. 4-5.
15. Recast Electricity Regulation, p. 5.
16. *See* Recitals 25-26, 28-29 and 65 as well as Article 3 of the Recast Electricity Directive.
17. *See*, for example, reference to 'resource providers' in Article 1(b) and pp. 5-6 of the Recast Electricity Regulation; and non-discriminatory approach to all resources in Article 3 of the Recast Electricity Regulation.

[B]   Strengthening the Market-Based Approach

The market-based approach to investment in generation capacity, which finds expression in Article 7 of the Electricity Directive, remains unaltered in the Recast Electricity Directive and thus, continues to be the starting point for any new generation investments.[18] However, the proposed legislative changes further strengthen and enforce the market-based approach by narrowing the scope of situations in which it is acceptable to introduce capacity mechanisms.

Capacity mechanisms are State interventions that deviate from the market-based approach described above and as such, risk undermining the efficiencies achieved through the liberalisation process and internal market integration. The challenge in restricting such State interventions is that, as analysed extensively in above chapters, EU energy *acquis* allows Member States to resort to tendering or equivalent procedures in the interest of security of supply in the event that the market fails to deliver a sufficient level of investment. The prerequisites for resorting to such procedures are broadly formulated in Article 8 of the Electricity Directive and leave Member States significant leeway in adopting capacity mechanisms. Furthermore, ensuring security of supply can constitute a public service under Article 3 of the Electricity Directive, which allows Member States to impose obligations on undertakings operating in the electricity sector in the general economic interest.

The proposed legislative changes aim to address the uncoordinated approach to capacity mechanisms and to encourage Member States to approach resource adequacy through market-based solutions.[19] By enforcing the market-based approach to energy investments, the proposals aim to minimise the need for State intervention and thereby to marginalise the role of capacity mechanisms to exceptional measures, used only as an instrument of 'last resort'.[20] This idea is demonstrated through repealing the possibility of introducing a tender or an equivalent procedure on the basis of Article 8 of the Electricity Directive and through proposing new provisions that aim to facilitate the functioning of the market.

First, the Recast Electricity Regulation establishes principles based on which the electricity market is supposed to function. Many of these principles have particular relevance for avoiding the introduction of capacity mechanisms. Article 3 of the Recast Electricity Regulation establishes, *inter alia*, that market rules are expected to deliver appropriate investment incentives for generation, storage, energy efficiency and demand response to ensure security of supply. All resources, including flexibility, storage, imports and energy efficiency, should be able to participate on equal footing in the market and contribute to security of supply so that State intervention can be avoided.[21] Further, any action which prevents price formation based on demand and

---

18. Article 8 of the Recast Electricity Directive.
19. Recitals 28-31 of the Recast Electricity Regulation.
20. Recast Electricity Regulation, p. 3.
21. Article 3 of the Recast Electricity Regulation.

supply, or disincentivises the development of more flexible generation, low carbon generation, or more flexible demand, should be avoided.[22]

Establishing these principles explicitly in a legally binding act is a new approach. However, none of these principles deviate from what is already understood as cornerstones of a functioning, decarbonised internal market in electricity. Many of these principles have been included in the existing legal instruments, albeit not as principles but implicitly as presumptions on which certain obligations are based.[23] What has changed, here, is the level of clarity and emphasis. Article 3 of the Recast Electricity Regulation places a shared obligation on Member States, national regulatory authorities, transmission and distribution system operators, as well as market operators to ensure that the market is operated in accordance with these principles.[24] However, given the broad formulation of this obligation and its numerous addressees, it is highly unlikely that a TSO's activity, for example, would ever be challenged based on a claimed infringement of Article 3 of the Recast Electricity Regulation.[25] Rather, including these principles in a legally binding act can be seen as an effort to highlight their importance to the functioning of the internal market in electricity and as instruments to support the market-based interpretation of other, more concrete obligations.

Second, the Recast Electricity Regulation and Recast Electricity Directive include several detailed provisions that address price formation and aim to ensure that investment signals required to generate investments are undistorted. This requires, first and foremost, that electricity prices are determined by demand and supply, and not set administratively by Member States.[26] Article 5 of the Recast Electricity Directive establishes that electricity suppliers should be free to determine the price at which they supply electricity to customers. This provision essentially restricts Member States' ability to introduce price caps and prevent prices from rising to a level that signals scarcity. Article 5 of the Recast Electricity Directive, however, does allow public intervention to protect energy poor or vulnerable household customers,[27] but this exception is narrower than the existing possibilities for introducing price regulation.[28]

In addition to establishing market-based supply pricing in the Recast Electricity Directive, the Recast Electricity Regulation aims to abolish both explicit and implicit wholesale price caps, which distort the price signals that are needed to deliver

---

22. *Ibid.*
23. For example, the principle that prices should be determined by demand and supply is the underlying assumption under Article 7 of the Electricity Directive, which sets the primary rule for the construction of new generation capacity.
24. Article 3 of the Recast Electricity Regulation.
25. For example, rather than invoking the principle that prices should be determined by demand and supply under Article 3 of the Recast Electricity Regulation, one would be more likely to invoke a provision such as Article 5 of Recast Electricity Directive, which requires that suppliers should be free to determine the price at which they supply electricity.
26. This requirement is also established as a principle under Article 3 of the Recast Electricity Regulation.
27. Article 5(3)-(4) of the Recast Electricity Directive.
28. This is based on a comparison between Article 5(3)-(4) of the Recast Electricity Directive and Article 3 of the Electricity Directive.

sufficient investments generation resources.[29] According to Article 9 of the Recast Electricity Regulation, there can be no maximum limit on wholesale electricity prices unless this price is set at the value of lost load. The value of lost load is a Member State's estimate of the maximum electricity price (€/MWh) that customers are willing to pay to avoid an electricity outage.[30] Further, Member States are to identify and eliminate policies and measures that could contribute to implicitly restricting price formation, including limiting bids relating to capacity mechanisms.[31]

[C]   A Common Threshold for the Introduction of Capacity Mechanisms

In the event that the market-based approach described above does not deliver a sufficient level of resources to meet forecasted demand, the Recast Electricity Regulation establishes a common threshold for evaluating situations in which adopting a capacity mechanism may be compatible with EU law. This common threshold for the introduction of capacity mechanisms is higher than under the existing legal framework in force. This section identifies and analyses the main provisions that contribute to the higher threshold brought forth in the proposed legislative package.

First, the Recast Electricity Regulation establishes a common definition for capacity mechanisms, which already provides a new level of clarity as to the content of these mechanisms. According to Article 2 of the Recast Electricity Regulation, capacity mechanisms refer to administrative measures, the purpose of which is to ensure the achievement of the desired level of security of supply by remunerating resources for their availability.[32] This definition excludes measures relating to ancillary services.[33]

The proposed definition for capacity mechanisms includes strategic reserves. However, strategic reserves have also been separately defined to refer to capacity mechanisms in which resources are only dispatched in case day-ahead and intraday markets have failed to clear, balancing resources have been exhausted and the dispatch price for reserve capacity is settled at the value of lost load.[34] This distinction between strategic reserves and other capacity mechanisms will prove particularly important in terms of obligatory cross-border participation under Article 21 of the Recast Electricity Regulation, which establishes different rules to strategic reserves and types of other capacity mechanisms.

Second, the Recast Electricity Regulation establishes an EU-level resource adequacy assessment and a common methodology to conduct such an assessment. This assessment is meant to provide an objective and comparable basis for Member States'

---

29. Commission Staff Working Document, Accompanying the document Report from the Commission Final Report of the Sector Inquiry on Capacity Mechanisms, SWD(2016) 385 final, pp. 34-35; Greece, for example, has a price cap at EUR 150/MWh. *See* SA.38968 *Greece Transitory Electricity Flexibility Remuneration Mechanism*, C(2016) 1791 final, para. 17.
30. Articles 2(2)(h), 10 and 19(5) of the Recast Electricity Regulation.
31. Article 9(4)-(5) of the Recast Electricity Regulation.
32. Article 2(2)(u) of the Recast Electricity Regulation.
33. *Ibid.*
34. Articles 2(2)(u)-(v) of the Recast Electricity Regulation.

resource adequacy concerns in the medium to long term.[35] This evaluation, the methodologies for which are prepared and approved on an EU level, will be used as a basis to evaluate whether there is a legitimate security of supply concern, the addressing of which may need additional remuneration for capacity.[36]

The EU resource adequacy assessment covers the overall adequacy of the electricity system to supply current and projected demands for electricity for a ten-year period.[37] This assessment is based on scenarios that include an economic review of the likelihood of retirement of existing resources, new-build of generation assets and measures to reach energy efficiency targets.[38] It should also appropriately take into account wholesale and carbon price developments.[39] The assessment should also include scenarios without existing or planned capacity mechanisms and should be based on a market model using, where applicable, the flow-based approach.[40]

The resource adequacy assessment should take into account the contribution of all resources and not just existing and future generation capacities. This means that energy storage, demand response as well as import and export possibilities are taken into account in addition to generation capacity, when assessing the adequacy of the system.[41] These assessments are to be carried out on a bidding zone level instead of a national level to allow cross-border capacities to participate and thus, to ensure that the efficiencies of integration are exhausted before resorting to State intervention.[42]

The method for evaluating the likelihood of a resource adequacy issue is based on probabilistic calculations.[43] In this context, this means that the calculations apply indicators of 'expected energy not served', and 'loss of load expectation'. Loss of load expectation refers to a calculation which indicates the expected number of hours within a year during which some level of disconnection is expected.[44] Expected energy not served, furthermore, is an indicator that determines the total shortfall in energy (MWh) that occurs during the disconnections.[45]

Lastly, the generation adequacy assessment is required to not only identify possible resource adequacy problems, but also to identify the sources of these concerns and, in particular, to determine whether it is a network or a resource constraint, or

---

35. Recitals 26 and 27 of the Recast Electricity Regulation.
36. Article 10 of the Recast Electricity Regulation.
37. Article 19(1) of the Recast Electricity Regulation.
38. Article 19(4) of the Recast Electricity Regulation.
39. Article 19(4)b) of the Recast Electricity Regulation. With regard to price developments, the provision refers to *sensitivities*, the specific meaning of which is unclear in this context: 'The European resource adequacy assessment shall be based on a methodology which shall ensure that the assessment [--] is based on [--] appropriate sensitivities on wholesale prices and carbon price developments.'
40. Article 19(4) of the Recast Electricity Regulation.
41. Articles 3 and 19(4) of the Recast Electricity Regulation.
42. Article 19(4) of the Recast Electricity Regulation.
43. *Ibid.*
44. Commission Staff Working Document, Accompanying the document Report from the Commission Final Report of the Sector Inquiry on Capacity Mechanisms, SWD(2016) 385 final, p. 73.
45. These concepts are not explicitly defined in the Recast Electricity Regulation or in the Recast Electricity Directive. Commission Staff Working Document, Accompanying the document Report from the Commission Final Report of the Sector Inquiry on Capacity Mechanisms, SWD(2016) 385 final, p. 73.

both, that is causing the projected resource inadequacy.[46] Identifying the problems and their sources, furthermore, is not sufficient to defend the necessity for capacity mechanisms, but Member States are obligated to first exhaust other available means. This obligation is set in Article 18 of the Recast Electricity Regulation.

Member States are to monitor their national resource adequacy levels based on the European resource adequacy assessment.[47] If the assessment recognises a resource adequacy concern, Member States are to identify any regulatory distortions that caused or contributed to the emergence of the concern.[48] Article 18(3) of the Recast Electricity Regulation imposes an obligation on Member States to publish a timeline for adopting measures to eliminate any identified regulatory distortions. In addition to considering the removal of the identified distortions, Member States are to consider enabling shortage pricing and developing interconnection as well as energy storage, demand-side measures and energy efficiency.[49] The resource adequacy assessment itself should be able to anticipate the likely impact of these measures.[50]

It should be noted that despite the European resource adequacy assessment, the Recast Electricity Regulation continues to allow Member States to set their own reliability standard. Member States are obligated to have a reliability standard in place indicating their desired level of security of supply. This level can then be pursued if a capacity mechanism is allowed under the proposed legislative framework. This reliability standard is set by the national regulatory authority in a transparent manner and in accordance with the methodology laid down in Article 19(5) of the Recast Electricity Regulation.[51]

In the absence of a common resource adequacy assessment, Member States have been able to defend the necessity for national capacity mechanisms based on subjective generation adequacy concerns. Because of these incomparable assessment approaches, it has not been possible to exclude the possibility that Member States are pursuing protectionist interests rather than legitimate security of supply objectives. The existing generation adequacy assessments are based on national methodologies and are, therefore, not comparable between Member States.[52] This has lead to decreased transparency, decreased possibilities for cross-border trade and, as a consequence, potentially inefficient capacity mechanisms.[53] Most significantly, the introduction of capacity mechanisms has been possible based on these national, mutually incompatible resource adequacy assessments. This possibility is blocked in the Recast Electricity Regulation. Article 23(5) of the Recast Electricity Regulation states that if the European resource adequacy assessment does not identify a resource adequacy concern, Member States are not allowed to apply capacity mechanisms. The choice of

---

46. Article 19(4) of the Recast Electricity Regulation.
47. Article 18 of the Recast Electricity Regulation.
48. Article 18(2) of the Recast Electricity Regulation.
49. Article 18 of the Recast Electricity Regulation.
50. 19(4)(d) of the Recast Electricity Regulation.
51. Article 20 of the Recast Electricity Regulation.
52. Commission Staff Working Document, Accompanying the document Report from the Commission Final Report of the Sector Inquiry on Capacity Mechanisms, SWD(2016) 385 final, pp. 77-80.
53. Ibid.

word 'apply' here is significant. It seems to indicate that Member States are allowed to adopt a capacity mechanism but not allowed to apply it in practice where there is no identified resource adequacy concern. This might not be optimal, since the mere possibility of launching a capacity mechanism can trigger opportunistic investor behaviour where, instead of investing based on market signals, investors wait for the application of a capacity mechanism to gain access to public funding and hedged risks.[54] Nevertheless, by adopting common assessment criteria, the proposed legislative package de facto establishes a common threshold for evaluating whether capacity mechanisms are necessary and limits the scope of situations in which it may be acceptable to adopt a capacity mechanism.

§7.03 A COMMON DESIGN FOR CAPACITY MECHANISMS

[A] Design Principles

As established above in §7.02, the new legislative proposal for capacity mechanisms aims to enforce the market-based approach and, in doing so, marginalise the scope of situations in which it is acceptable to adopt capacity mechanisms. This body of provisions should be interpreted as an effort to hold capacity mechanisms as exceptions to the rule.

However, Article 23 of the Recast Electricity Regulation does establish criteria based on which it is possible to adopt a capacity mechanism. The design principles established in this Article are only relevant where first, the European resource adequacy assessment has identified a resource adequacy concern and, second, the causes of this concern cannot be eliminated through the measures established in Article 18(3) of the Recast Electricity Regulation. If these criteria are fulfilled, Member States may address the residual concerns through the introduction of capacity mechanisms. This means that, even if there is a legitimate generation adequacy concern and even if this concern cannot be entirely eliminated through removing regulatory distortions, only these remaining and unsolved concerns can be addressed with a capacity mechanism. This introduction is, furthermore, subject to the design principles of Article 23 of the Recast Electricity Regulation and to EU State aid rules.[55]

These design principles for capacity mechanisms in the Recast Electricity Regulation differ from the original draft proposal, which was leaked in mid-November 2016.[56] The leaked draft included a more detailed set of criteria for the design of a

---

54. Commission Staff Working Document, Accompanying the document Report from the Commission Final Report of the Sector Inquiry on Capacity Mechanisms, SWD(2016) 385 final, p. 144; Communication from the Commission to the European Parliament and the Council, Energy Infrastructure and Security of Supply, COM(2003) 743 final, pp. 8-9; Dominique Finon and Virginie Pignonb, 'Electricity and Long-Term Capacity Adequacy: The Quest for Regulatory Mechanism Compatible with Electricity Market', 16(3) *Utilities Policy* (2008), pp. 143-158, at 150.
55. On the application of state aid rules on capacity mechanisms, *see* Chapter 4 above.
56. Leaked proposal for a Regulation of the European Parliament and of the Council on the electricity market, available at http://stollmeyer.eu/?p=473 (last accessed 5.3.2019).

capacity mechanism, including, *inter alia*, specific requirements for transparency and non-discrimination as well as obligatory penalties for non-delivery.[57]

The main proposed obligation set for the design of a capacity mechanism is the requirement for proportionality.[58] Member States are obligated to design capacity mechanisms in a way that does not create unnecessary market distortions or limitations of cross-border trade.[59] Furthermore, the amount of capacity committed in the mechanism should not go beyond what is necessary to address the residual resource adequacy concerns that cannot be addressed through market-based approaches.[60] From the point of view of effects on cross-border trade, the requirement for proportionality should be interpreted together with Article 21 of the Recast Electricity Regulation, which addresses cross-border participation in capacity mechanisms.

In practice, determining whether a capacity mechanism fulfils the proportionality criteria will be based on a case-by-case evaluation. The formulation of the provision allows for a flexible and context-sensitive interpretation that can take into account Member States' different circumstances and national objectives.[61] However, determining whether a capacity mechanism fulfils the proportionality criteria is complex. This is due to not only their exceptional nature as derogations from the market-based principle that is fundamental to the sector-specific electricity market legislation, but also because of their potentially highly distortive effects on the internal electricity market. The evaluation of proportionality in the context of the objectives of EU energy law has been analysed above in Chapter 6.

Under Article 23(2) of the Recast Electricity Regulation, Member States are to consult their electrically connected neighbouring Member States when they wish to implement a capacity mechanism. The results of this consultation have no legal binding force, so neighbouring Member States cannot prevent a Member State from adopting a capacity mechanism.

It is well-established that capacity mechanisms tend to favour conventional generation capacities and, as such, undermine the European decarbonisation efforts.[62] Article 23(4) of the Recast Electricity Regulation aims to mitigate this tendency. It establishes a maximum emissions threshold for capacity committing to a capacity mechanism. Generation capacity for which a final investment decision has been made after the entry into force of the regulation is eligible to participate in a capacity mechanism only if its emissions are below 550 gr CO_2/kWh.[63] Any generation capacity that emits CO_2 above this threshold is not allowed to commit in capacity mechanisms five years after the entry into force of the Recast Electricity Regulation. This threshold

---

57. Article 23 of the leaked proposal for a Regulation of the European Parliament and of the Council on the electricity market, available at http://stollmeyer.eu/?p=473 (last accessed 5.3.2019).
58. Article 23 of the Recast Electricity Regulation.
59. Article 23(2) of the Recast Electricity Regulation.
60. *Ibid.*
61. *See* similar argumentation for assessing the proportionality principle in the Communication from the Commission, Services of general interest in Europe OJ C 17, 19.1.2001, pp. 4-23, para. 24.
62. *See* rationale in Commission Staff Working Document, Accompanying the document Report from the Commission Final Report of the Sector Inquiry on Capacity Mechanisms, SWD(2016) 385 final, pp. 19-23.
63. Article 23(4) of the Recast Electricity Regulation.

is in line with the European sustainability efforts and would significantly reduce the adverse environmental effects of capacity mechanisms.[64]

[B]   Ensuring Cross-Border Participation

As discussed extensively in Chapter 5 above, capacity mechanisms tend to favour national capacity providers over providers located in other Member States.[65] This tendency increases prices and risks undermining the benefits achieved through a well-connected internal market in electricity.[66] Furthermore, the fragmented State interventions for security of supply distort the functioning of cross-border trade.[67] It has been established that, in order to ensure security of supply, it is no longer sufficient to set general objectives and leave Member States in charge of the measures, but a coordinated approach which reflects the needs of a connected electricity market, is necessary.[68]

Cross-border participation in a capacity mechanism is addressed in Article 21 of the Recast Electricity Regulation. In terms of the proposed legislative framework for capacity mechanisms, Article 21 of the Recast Electricity Regulation contains the most substantive obligations. It implies that the main issue identified with regard to the compatibility of capacity mechanisms with EU law is the cross-border distortions of trade they cause, and the decreased competition that follows. This argument is supported by the findings of the State aid sector inquiry.[69]

The main obligation set through Article 21 of the Recast Electricity Regulation is to design capacity mechanisms in a way that ensures these mechanisms are open to direct participation of capacity providers located in other Member States, provided that there is a network connection between that Member State and the bidding zone applying the mechanism.[70] This obligation does not apply to strategic reserves. Member States are prohibited from restricting capacity, which is located in their territory, from participating in capacity mechanisms of other Member States.[71] As a mirror image of this prohibition, Member States are further obligated to ensure that

---

64. It is, however, a provision that has gained criticism from some Member States. *See* for example, case T-57/11 *Castelnou Energía v Commission* [2014], judgment of the General Court of 3 December 2014, published in the electronic Reports of Cases, where the Spanish support scheme for indigenous coal was approved. When the proposed changes enter into force, they will effectively prohibit the participation of coal-based capacity in a national capacity mechanisms.
65. Report from the Commission, Final Report of the Sector Inquiry on Capacity Mechanisms, COM(2016) 752 final, p. 2.
66. *Ibid.*
67. Recitals 5-6 of the Proposal for a Regulation of the European Parliament and of the Council, Establishing a European Union Agency for the Cooperation of Energy Regulators, COM(2016) 863 final.
68. Security of Supply Regulation pp. 2-3 and Recitals 5-6 of the Proposal for a Regulation of the European Parliament and of the Council, Establishing a European Union Agency for the Cooperation of Energy Regulators, COM(2016) 863 final.
69. Report from the Commission, Final Report of the Sector Inquiry on Capacity Mechanisms, COM(2016) 752 final, pp. 15-16.
70. Article 21(1) of the Recast Electricity Regulation.
71. Article 21(3) of the Recast Electricity Regulation.

capacity located in other Member States has the opportunity to participate in the same competitive process as domestic capacity.[72] This obligation only applies to capacity that fulfils equivalent technical performance to domestic capacities.[73] All capacity providers should be able to participate in more than one mechanism for the same delivery period.[74]

It should be noted that although the proposals highlight the overall importance of all resources instead of just generation capacity, Article 21 of the Recast Electricity Regulation only refers to capacity and not all resources.[75] This implies that the obligation to enable cross-border participation in a capacity mechanism does not apply to demand-side measures or energy storage, for example, if these resources are located outside the territory of a Member State applying a capacity mechanism.

Article 21(4) of the Recast Electricity Regulation requires that cross-border participation in a market-wide capacity mechanism is not allowed to change, alter or otherwise impact cross-zonal schedules and physical flows between Member States. These flows will be entirely determined by the capacity allocation process laid down in Article 14 of the Recast Electricity Regulation. As demonstrated in Chapter 2 above, market-wide capacity mechanisms typically refer to market-wide capacity payments, capacity obligations, capacity auctions and reliability options.[76] Based on this distinction, tenders for new capacity as targeted mechanisms, for example, would be excluded from the application of this provision.

Regulatory tasks included in Article 21 of the Recast Electricity Regulation are shared between institutions on a national, regional and European level. Previous experience with the implementation of internal market rules has demonstrated that coordinated institutional action is needed, particularly in closely interconnected areas.[77] Article 21(6) of the Recast Electricity Regulation establishes an obligation for the regional operational centres with regard to capacity mechanisms. These centres are new institutions established by TSOs to complement their functions.[78] The centres' mission is to establish operational arrangements in order to ensure the efficient, secure and reliable operation of the interconnected transmission system.[79]

The centres' task in relation to capacity mechanisms is to annually calculate the maximum entry capacity available for the participation of foreign capacity for each

---

72. Article 21(2) of the Recast Electricity Regulation.
73. *Ibid.*
74. Article 21(5) of the Recast Electricity Regulation.
75. For example, Article 21(5) refers to 'capacity providers', and not resource providers as in Article 1 of the Recast Electricity Regulation.
76. Commission Staff Working Document, Accompanying the document Report from the Commission Final Report of the Sector Inquiry on Capacity Mechanisms, SWD(2016) 385 final, pp. 50-52; Francisco Enrique González-Díaz, 'EU Policy on Capacity Mechanisms', in Leigh Hancher, Adrien de Hauteclocque and Malgorzata Sadowska (eds), *Capacity Mechanisms in the EU Energy Market* (OUP, 2015), pp. 3-31, at 10-16.
77. Recital 4 of the Proposal for a Regulation of the European Parliament and of the Council, Establishing a European Union Agency for the Cooperation of Energy Regulators, COM(2016) 863 final.
78. Article 32(1) of the Recast Electricity Regulation.
79. Article 32(3) of the Recast Electricity Regulation.

bidding zone border.[80] This calculation should take into account the expected availability of interconnection and the likely concurrence of system stress between the system where the mechanism is applied and the system in which the foreign capacity is located.[81] Member States have to ensure that such capacity available for the participation of foreign capacity is allocated to eligible capacity providers in a transparent, non-discriminatory and market-based manner.[82] These allocated capacities are to be transferrable between eligible capacity providers.[83]

In addition to the role of regional operational centres, national TSOs have a supporting role to ensure that the capacity providers within their territory who wish to participate in a foreign capacity mechanism fulfil the technical performance requirements set in the foreign capacity mechanism.[84] Furthermore, ENTSO-E is responsible for preparing the methodology needed for calculating the maximum entry capacity, for example, and submitting this methodology for approval to ACER.[85] The role of the national regulatory authorities is to ensure that cross-border participation in capacity mechanisms is organised in an effective and non-discriminatory manner.[86]

§7.04   THE EFFECTS OF HARMONISATION ON THE APPLICATION OF
          TREATY LAW

It is established case-law that where secondary legislation is relevant, the compliance of national measures with EU law should be assessed in light of the harmonising secondary provisions and not those of the Treaty.[87] This is because the harmonising legislation can be seen as an effort to substantiate the Treaty rules in a way that takes into account the specificities of the subject matter in question. In other words, the scope of application and therefore, the practical relevance, of Treaty provisions effectively changes when harmonising measures for capacity mechanisms are introduced.

In terms of the proposed legislation for capacity mechanisms, the effects of harmonisation are potentially relevant from the point of view of number of Treaty provisions, such as the requirements set by free movement rules and state aid rules. In addition to the requirements set by these rules, the exceptions allowed from these rules have provided Member States potential justifications for derogating from fundamental

---

80. Article 21(6) of the Recast Electricity Regulation.
81. *Ibid.*
82. Article 21(7) of the Recast Electricity Regulation.
83. Article 21(13) of the Recast Electricity Regulation.
84. Article 21(9) of the Recast Electricity Regulation.
85. Article 10 of the Proposal for a Regulation of the European Parliament and of the Council, Establishing a European Union Agency for the Cooperation of Energy Regulators, COM(2016) 863 final.
86. Article 21(12) of the Recast Electricity Regulation.
87. Cases C-573/12 *Ålands Vindkraft AB v Energimyndigheten* [2014] ECR II- 2037, para. 57; C-309/02 *Radlberger Getränkegesellschaft and S. Spitz* [2004] ECR I-11763, para. 53; C-37/92 *Vanacker and Lesage* [1993] ECR I-4947, para. 9; C-324/99 *DaimlerChrysler* [2001] ECR I-9897, para. 32; and C-322/01 *Deutscher Apothekerverband* [2003] ECR I-0000, para. 64.

rules of EU law in the interest of security of supply.[88] The existence of these exceptions implies that the uninterrupted availability of affordable electricity may be considered more important than the internal market, although subject to strict proportionality assessment.[89]

In order to determine whether, and to what extent, the proposed legislation for capacity mechanisms changes the application of Treaty law, it is necessary to examine the level of harmonisation provided in the proposals. It is clear that the proposed legislation introduces a direct and a stricter approach to capacity mechanisms than the legislative framework currently in force. It introduces capacity mechanisms as measures of last resort,[90] which are subject to the principle of proportionality[91] and continue to be subjected to EU State aid rules.[92] Furthermore, these proposed changes are adopted in a regulation, whereas the body of secondary rules currently applicable to capacity mechanisms is predominantly included in a directive. The adoption of rules in a regulation rather than a directive seems like a deliberate attempt to ensure consistent application in Member States without any discretion in implementation.[93]

Overall, the Recast Electricity Regulation is not intended as a measure of full harmonisation.[94] It merely aims to provide a level playing field for market players, especially where such a platform is needed for ensuring the functioning of cross-border trade of electricity.[95] However, if the provisions of the Recast Electricity Regulation are examined on a narrower scope of capacity mechanisms alone, the level of harmonisation appears deeper. First, the threshold for introducing capacity mechanisms is raised significantly and the monitoring of and compliance with this threshold is delegated to an EU entity, particularly through the establishment of the resource adequacy assessment. Secondly, when the introduction of capacity mechanisms is allowed, the Recast Electricity Regulation entails design criteria and concrete obligations, particularly for cross-border issues.

Because of these harmonising measures, the proposed provisions on capacity mechanisms would effectively restrict the scope of situations in which certain Treaty provisions could be successfully invoked. First, it would no longer be possible to successfully invoke an exemption from the free movement rules under Article 36 TFEU on grounds of public security to introduce a capacity mechanism. Generally, justifying an exception from free movement of goods on grounds of security of supply should be narrowly interpreted because it allows for an exception from a fundamental rule of the Treaty.[96] Furthermore, the proposed secondary rules on cross-border participation are

---

88. Articles 106(2) and 36 TFEU.
89. On the failure of proportionality in national measures, *see* cases C-347/88 *Commission v Greece* [1990] ECR I-4747 and C-398/98 *Commission v Greece* [2001] ECR I-7915.
90. Article 23(1) of the Recast Electricity Regulation.
91. Article 23(3) of the Recast Electricity Regulation.
92. Article 23(1) of the Recast Electricity Regulation.
93. *See* similar argumentation in case law, C-324/99 *DaimlerChrysler* [2001] ECR I-9897, para. 34.
94. Recast Electricity Regulation, p. 11.
95. *Ibid.*
96. *See* case 72/83 *Campus Oil Ltd* [1984] ECR 2727, para. 37; and further reasoning in Opinion of AG Cosmas in Cases C-157/94 *Commission v Netherlands* [1997] ECR I-5699, C-158/94 *Commission v Italy* [1997] ECR I-5789, C-159/94 *Commission v France* [1997] ECR I-5815 and

essentially an effort to directly ensure the free movement of electricity across borders.[97] In other words, Article 21 of the Recast Electricity Regulation appears as *lex specialis* to Treaty rules on the free movement of goods in terms of capacity mechanisms. These secondary rules should therefore be primarily applied to ensure capacity mechanisms comply with the free movement of goods.

Secondly, it seems highly unlikely that the possibility to derogate from the application of competition rules under Article 106(2) TFEU could be successfully invoked when the proposed changes enter into force. It is likely that capacity mechanisms could no longer constitute PSOs under the proposed legislative regime, because they are separately and directly addressed in the Recast Electricity Regulation. This shift is particularly relevant in terms of State aid assessment as Member States would no longer be able to successfully invoke the *Altmark* criteria or Article 106(2) TFEU to escape the general prohibition of aid under 107(1) TFEU.

Based on the analysis above, the proposed legislation would significantly limit the scope of application of Treaty law on capacity mechanisms. However, this limitation only extends to capacity mechanisms as they are defined in the Recast Electricity Regulation, which refers to capacity mechanisms as administrative measures, the purpose of which is to ensure the achievement of the desired level of security of supply by remunerating resources for their availability.[98] If a national measure is not caught by this definition, the relevance of Treaty law should be separately assessed. For example, the definition for capacity mechanisms in the Recast Electricity Regulation explicitly excludes ancillary services, which can prima facie seem to fall within the category of capacity mechanisms.[99] The proposed rules for capacity mechanisms, however, would not apply to these services.

Finally, the legal basis for the proposed legal instruments is Article 194 TFEU. The measures necessary to achieve the security of supply objectives established in Article 194 TFEU are adopted in accordance with the ordinary legislative procedure.[100] These measures, however, should not affect a Member State's right to determine the conditions for exploiting its energy resources, its choice between different energy sources, and the general structure of its energy supply.[101] As discussed above in Chapter 3, §3.02[A], this provision leaves the ambiguous impression that Member States have a wide margin of discretion in independently determining measures that affect the national exploitation of energy resources and the choice between these resources as well as the structure of the energy supply. With regard to capacity mechanisms, the proposed legislation implicitly restricts the participation of coal-based capacity in a capacity mechanism and could, therefore, potentially fall within the

---

C-160/94 *Commission v Spain* [1997] ECR I-5851 and in Opinion of AG Jacobs in C-379/98 *PreussenElektra* [2001] ECR I-2099, particularly, para. 209.

97. *See* Article 21 of the Recast Electricity Regulation.
98. Article 2(2)(u) of the Recast Electricity Regulation.
99. Commission Staff Working Document, Accompanying the document Report from the Commission Final Report of the Sector Inquiry on Capacity Mechanisms, SWD(2016) 385 final, pp. 52-53.
100. Articles 194(2), 289 and 294 TFEU.
101. T-370/11 *Poland v Commission* [2013], judgment of the General Court of 7 March 2013, published in the electronic Reports of Cases.

application of Article 194(2) TFEU. The interpretation of this provision, however, has not yet been tested by the EU courts in a situation where Article 194 TFEU has been the legal basis. Because of this, there is significant uncertainty as to the potential to challenge the newly proposed provisions on the basis of Article 194(2) TFEU.

CHAPTER 8
Conclusions

---

§8.01   THE COMPLEX ROLE OF SECURITY OF SUPPLY

This book has examined Member States' capacity mechanisms in the context of EU law and the EU energy *acquis*. In particular, Chapters 2-7 above analyse capacity mechanisms in EU law in an effort to answer the research questions set out in Chapter 1. This final chapter concludes the above analysis in three sections. It begins by summarising the main findings of the legal analysis contained in Chapters 2-7 above, before setting out conclusions on various recurring issues and the dynamics between EU law and national capacity mechanisms. The book concludes with observations as to the way forward with particular reference to the proposals put forward in the 2016 Clean Energy for All Europeans package.[1]

On a fundamental level, the analysis offered by this research illustrates the process that has taken place in Europe to ensure security of electricity supply. This is well represented in the legal approaches taken at both EU and national levels: through the provisions of the Treaties, Member States have conferred significant powers on the EU to address security of supply as a key objective of EU energy law. In turn, the EU has, to a large extent, further conferred this power on the markets, which it believes will ensure security of supply in the most cost-efficient and sustainable way. Member States have interfered with this approach by means of State intervention in the form of capacity mechanisms. State intervention of this kind is an expression of distrust in the assumption on which the EU legal framework for electricity has been built: that the

---

1. Communication from the Commission to the European Parliament, the Council, the European Economic and Social Committee, the Committee of the Regions and the European Investment Bank, Clean Energy For All Europeans, COM(2016) 860 final; the Recast Electricity Regulation; Kaisa Huhta, 'A New Era for Capacity Mechanisms – Reviewing the Commission's Clean Energy for All Europeans Legislative Package', 1 *OGEL* (2018).

economics of the single market, energy-only model can, in fact, guarantee generation adequacy.[2]

In response to the first research question as to the market context from which generation adequacy concerns arise and how capacity mechanisms address these concerns, Chapter 2 analyses the market structure and the challenges that have led to the introduction of capacity mechanisms. As illustrated in Chapter 2, capacity mechanisms arise in the context of nationally drawn markets limited by network constraints, passive demand and an underlying political sensitivity to energy security that complicates decision-making on various levels. The generation adequacy concerns identified as giving rise to national capacity mechanisms are further exacerbated within the context of the energy transition. This transition places new and heavy demands on the energy sector, which is traditionally slow to change. Capacity mechanisms address the concerns that have arisen by providing incentives in addition to those provided by the markets, thereby ensuring that investment in the uninterrupted availability of affordable electricity is made at the right time and in the right volume. In general, Member States' concern over the ability of the energy-only approach to guarantee security of supply is well demonstrated in the widespread adoption of capacity mechanisms.

As for the second research question, concerning the EU legal framework that seeks to ensure generation adequacy and its interpretation in the context of national capacity mechanisms, Chapter 3 analyses the existing provisions that address State intervention in the interests of security of supply. This legal framework addresses capacity mechanisms as instruments to ensure generation adequacy through a fragmentary body of both primary and secondary norms, which were not originally designed to address the widespread adoption of capacity remuneration schemes. Nevertheless, this fragmentary body of provisions and their established interpretation on the part of the ECJ is the legal point of departure for evaluating the compatibility of capacity mechanisms with EU law, as illustrated in Chapter 3.

The main secondary legal instruments governing the adoption and design of capacity mechanisms are the Security of Supply Directive and the Electricity Directive. While the Security of Supply Directive imposes few enforceable obligations on Member States, the Electricity Directive is more concrete. Both directives emphasise and underline the primacy of the market-based approach to investment in the EU electricity market. Despite this strong emphasis on the facilitation of market-based solutions, both directives also acknowledge the need to ensure security of supply if the markets fail to do so.

Of these two directives, the Electricity Directive offers the only concrete legal means to pursue generation adequacy through State-driven interventions in the interest of security of supply, which it primarily addresses under Articles 3 and 8. These concern, respectively, the introduction of PSOs and tendering for new capacity.

---

2. For an overview of the complex division of roles between States, the EU and the markets, *see* Leigh Hancher and Pierre Larouche, 'The Coming of Age of EU Regulation of Network Industries and Services of General Economic Interest', in Paul Craig and Gráinne De Búrca, *The Evolution of EU Law* (OUP, 2011), pp. 743-781, at 744; and Talus, Kim, 'Decades of EU Energy Policy: Towards Politically Driven Markets', *Journal of World Energy Law and Business* (2017), pp. 1-9.

Tendering or equivalent procedures under Article 8 of the Electricity Directive refer to procedures through which requirements for resource adequacy are procured from new or existing capacity or demand-side resources.[3] The launching of such procedures requires that a legitimate security of supply objective exists and that the market-based approach to ensuring security of supply is insufficient. Furthermore, the procedures must fulfil the requirements of transparency and non-discrimination.

Capacity mechanisms may also constitute PSOs as defined in Article 3 of the Electricity Directive. The obligations must be clearly defined, transparent, non-discriminatory and verifiable and should guarantee equality of access for EU electricity undertakings to national consumers. Over the years, imposing PSOs in the interests of security of supply has involved measures such as securing reasonable prices or incentivising investment in peak-load generation capacity.[4] However, more recent cases before the Commission and the ECJ on granting compensation for the performance of public services indicate a growing tendency for capacity mechanisms to fail to fulfil the criteria for granting compensation for these services.[5]

Articles 3 and 8 of the Electricity Directive are highly intertwined, as the procedure established in Article 8 is also the preferred method for procuring the services established in Article 3. However, each is able to operate independently of the other. Nevertheless, the requirements established through both provisions overlap significantly. They both require the existence of a justifiable security of supply interest and a failure in the market-based approach to ensure such security. Furthermore, the requirement of non-discrimination is highlighted in the criteria set out in both provisions. In the context of capacity mechanisms, the requirement of non-discrimination essentially means that the eligibility criteria should be designed as inclusively as possible.

The Electricity Directive leaves a significant margin of discretion to Member States as to when they introduce capacity mechanisms and how they design them. This results from multiple factors. First, two constitutional issues are involved: (1) action in the energy sector is governed by shared competences, which necessarily leaves Member States with significant decision-making powers;[6] and (2) the EU's decision to address resource adequacy in the electricity sector through a directive rather than a regulation means that Member States are only bound as to the result to be achieved but the form and method of achieving these objectives is left to national authorities.[7]

---

3. Article 8 of the Electricity Directive; Natalia Fiedziuk, 'Putting Services of General Economic Interest up for Tender: Reflections on Applicable EU Rules', 50(1) *Common Market Law Review* (2013), pp. 87-114; Philipp Kiiver, *The Practice of Public Procurement: Tendering, Selection and Award* (Intersentia, 2014).
4. C-265/08 *Federutility and Others v Autorità per l'energia elettrica e il gas* [2010] ECR I-3377 and C-121/15 *ANODE* [2016], judgment of the Court of 7 September 2016, published in the electronic Reports of Cases; N475/2003 *Irish CADA*, 16 December 2003.
5. Compare N475/2003 *Irish CADA*, 16 December 2003, for instance, with SA.34947 *Support to Hinkley Point C Nuclear Power Station*, C(2013) 9073 final, SA.39621 *French Country-Wide Capacity Mechanism*, C(2016) 7086 final and SA.45852 *German Capacity Reserve*, C(2018) 612 final.
6. Article 4 TFEU.
7. Article 288 TFEU.

Second, the Member States' broad margin of discretion is made broader still by the wording and interpretation of secondary norms governing the introduction of capacity mechanisms in the EU.[8] That is to say that while both Articles 3 and 8 of the Electricity Directive require a legitimate security of supply objective that is being pursued and the failure of the markets to guarantee such security, no legally binding definitions of security of supply and market failure have been laid down to narrow the scope of Member State discretion.

In an effort to answer the third research question, Chapter 4 explores the legal conditions for subsidising generation adequacy and their interpretation with regard to the adoption of national capacity mechanisms. Compared with the provisions of the Electricity Directive, the EU State aid regime offers a stronger legal means of controlling the introduction and design of capacity mechanisms. As demonstrated in Chapter 4, it is highly unlikely that capacity mechanisms can escape being classified as State aid within the meaning of Article 107(1) TFEU. However, the extensive body of exemptions from the prohibition established in Article 107(1) TFEU make it possible for capacity mechanisms to be declared compatible with the EU State aid regime. In fact, after the entry into force of the EEAG, most capacity mechanisms in the EU have been approved under these Guidelines.[9]

If certain criteria are met, the derogations allowed from the broad prohibition of State aid extend the range of situations in which subsidising generation adequacy is compatible with EU law. All of the legal bases that can be invoked to justify an exemption share to some extent a set of criteria that need to be met for a capacity remuneration scheme to be declared compatible with the EU State aid regime. The first criterion requires that generation adequacy would not be delivered by the operation of the markets alone. This requirement of market failure applies regardless of whether the Member State invokes the *Altmark* criteria, Article 106(2) TFEU or Article 107(3)(c) TFEU and, by extension, the EEAG. Second, all of the legal bases require that the Member State in question is pursuing a legitimate objective of security of supply. As noted above, there is no legally binding definition of the concept of security of supply.

---

8. Specifically, Member States traditionally have a broad margin of discretion in defining their PSOs. Cases T-106/95 *FFSA and Others v Commission* [1997] ECR II-229, para. 99; T-17/02 *Fred Olsen v Commission* [2005] ECR II-2031, para. 216; T-289/03 *BUPA* [2008] ECR II-81, para. 166; C-265/08 *Federutility and Others v Autorità per l'energia elettrica e il gas* [2010] ECR I-3377, para. 29; C-67/96 *Albany* [1999] ECR I-5751, para. 104; Communication from the Commission, Services of general interest in Europe, OJ C 17, 19.1.2001, pp. 4-23, para. 22; Heike Schweitzer, 'Services of General Economic Interest: European Law's Impact on the Role of Markets and of Member States', in Marise Cremona (ed), *Market Integration and Public Services in the European Union* (OUP, 2011), pp. 11-62, at 32-35; Natalia Fiedziuk, 'Services of General Economic Interest and the Treaty of Lisbon: Opening Doors to a Whole New Approach or Maintaining the "status quo"', 36(2) *European Law Review* (2011), pp. 226-242, at 229-230.
9. Communication from the Commission, Guidelines on State aid for environmental protection and energy 2014-2020 (OJ C 200, 28.6.2014, pp. 1-55); Kelyn Bacon, *European Union Law of State Aid*, 3rd edn. (OUP, 2017), p. 233. Cases in which capacity mechanisms have recently been approved under the Guidelines include SA.44464 *Irish Capacity Mechanism: Reliability Option Scheme*, C(2017)7789 final; SA.45852 *German Capacity Reserve*, C(2018) 612 final; SA.46100 *Planned Polish Capacity Mechanism*, C(2018) 601 final; SA.48490 *Specific Demand Response Tender in France*, C(2018) 588 final; SA.48648 *Belgian Strategic Reserve*, C(2018) 589 final; SA.48780 *Prolongation of the Greek Interruptibility Scheme*, C(2018) 604 final.

However, the Member State in question must provide evidence of the causes and scope of its security of supply concerns. The third shared criterion connects the EU State aid regime to that of the sector-specific electricity market rules, and the Electricity Directive, in particular. The *Altmark* criteria, Article 106(2) TFEU and assessment of the type of aid described in Article 107(3)(c) TFEU all favour the competitive allocation of remuneration through tendering, which makes Article 8 of the Electricity Directive the preferred method of procuring generation adequacy.[10] Finally, there is a general requirement of proportionality irrespective of the legal basis utilised within the State aid regime. The methodology for evaluating proportionality differs from one legal basis to another but one central element remains: the positive outcomes of the measure must outweigh the negative.

In response to the fourth research question, on free movement rules and their relevance to generation adequacy, Chapter 5 examines how capacity mechanisms and the objective of generation adequacy are caught by the well-established interpretations of the free movement rules. In a similar manner to the rules on State aid, proportionality and legitimately defined security of supply objectives are also at the heart of the EU rules on free movement of goods when evaluated from the perspective of capacity mechanisms. As demonstrated in Chapter 5, capacity mechanisms are likely to fall within the application of Articles 34 and 35 TFEU if cross-border participation is restricted or if the contributions of foreign capacities are disregarded in national generation adequacy assessments.

Security of supply can, however, be utilised as a justification to restrict the free movement of goods on the basis of the public security defence established in Article 36 TFEU.[11] The existing body of case-law on the interpretation of Article 36 TFEU, however, demonstrates that there are currently three key legal issues with regard to EU free movement law and capacity mechanisms. These issues affect the scope within which Member States can successfully invoke Article 36 TFEU. The first issue has to do with a Member State's discretion to decide on the national measures to be taken and accordingly extends the scope within which Member States are able to invoke Article 36 TFEU. The second and third, conversely, significantly limit Member States' recourse to Article 36 TFEU. These three issues are discussed below with reference to the findings set out in Chapter 5.

The relatively broad scope of Member State discretion limits the control the EU can have over national efforts to achieve generation adequacy despite the protectionist tendencies of capacity mechanisms that have been identified. As noted above, the reasons for this broad margin of discretion are partly constitutional and a result of the

---

10. Christopher Bovis, 'Public Procurement and State Aid', in Herwig Hofmann and Claire Micheau (eds), *State Aid Law of the European Union* (OUP, 2016), pp. 161-186; Heike Schweitzer, 'Services of General Economic Interest: European Law's Impact on the Role of Markets and of Member States', in Marise Cremona (ed), *Market Integration and Public Services in the European Union* (OUP, 2011), pp. 11-62, at 29-30; Natalia Fiedziuk, 'Putting Services of General Economic Interest Up for Tender: Reflections on Applicable EU Rules', 50(1) *Common Market Law Review* (2013), pp. 87-114; Philipp Kiiver, *The Practice of Public Procurement: Tendering, Selection and Award* (Intersentia, 2014).
11. 72/83 *Campus Oil* [1984] ECR 2727.

shared competences in the energy sector. Furthermore, the Treaty grounds for exemption from the prohibition of restrictions on the free movement of goods are broadly worded and, therefore, allow significant room for interpretative manoeuvre. This allows for the kinds of political compromise often needed in security of supply issues as well as limitations on free movement on technical grounds, which are often invoked in arguments defending restrictions on cross-border participation in capacity mechanisms.

The second issue concerning the interpretation of Article 36 TFEU in the light of capacity mechanisms relates to the arguments used to defend capacity mechanisms. The existing interpretation precludes recourse to Article 36 TFEU if the arguments invoked to this end are purely economic in nature.[12] The pursuit of security of supply on a domestic rather than regional or European level is one of the typical elements of capacity mechanisms. Disregarding cross-border solutions to generation adequacy and only remunerating capacity located domestically conflicts with the overall pursuit of a genuine single market. Such tendencies rightly invite accusations of protectionism – due to the tendency not only to protect domestic security of supply but also to protect the national economy and State budget.

Finally, the evaluation of the principle of proportionality, which underpins the second sentence of Article 36 TFEU, may in practice limit the design of capacity mechanisms in ensuring generation adequacy, as noted in Chapter 5. The reason for this is that although safeguarding generation adequacy can constitute a legitimate public security defence, capacity mechanisms are merely the vehicle through which generation adequacy is pursued as opposed to being an end in themselves. Since the right to restrict the free movement of goods cannot extend beyond what is necessary to protect the interests mentioned in Article 36 TFEU, it seems highly likely that a capacity mechanism, as a vehicle for pursuing a legitimate public security interest, would be considered disproportionate by the ECJ if less restrictive measures were available.

These less restrictive measures connect Chapter 5 with the fifth research question, which is the focus of Chapter 6. The latter analyses the broader context of EU energy law, in which generation adequacy operates, and the interpretation of capacity mechanisms in the light of the objectives of EU energy law. Adopting a contextual approach, this analysis demonstrates that the legal framework should be interpreted to give precedence to less restrictive measures that complement rather than undermine the objectives of EU energy law. In this context, demand-side efforts and network solutions are identified as measures that could improve generation adequacy in a manner involving impacts less detrimental to the objectives of EU energy law than remuneration for capacity only.

---

12. Cases 7/61 *Commission v Italy* [1961] ECR 317; 72/83 *Campus Oil* [1984] ECR 2727, para. 35; C-398/98 *Commission v Greece* [2001] ECR I-7915, para. 30; C-54/99 *Église de scientologie* [2000] ECR I-1335, para. 17; C-120/95 *Decker v Caisse de Maladie des Employés Privés* [1998] ECR I-1831, para. 39; C-158/96 *Kohll v Union des Caisses de Maladie* [1998] ECR I-1931, para. 41; C-463/00 *Commission v Spain* [2003] ECR I-4581, para. 35; C-367/98 *Commission v Portugal* [2002] ECR I-4731, para. 52; C-35/98 *Verkooijen* [2000] ECR I-4071, para. 48; C-265/95 *Commission v France* [1997] ECR I-6959, para. 62.

The wording of the existing legal framework does not establish a hierarchy between investment in generation capacity, investment in demand-side measures and investment in interconnecting capacity. However, the contextual approach applied in Chapter 6 clearly demonstrates that the introduction and design of capacity mechanisms should not take place in a near-vacuum populated by a few disparate provisions but that a broader approach to the system of EU energy law as a whole is needed. This interpretation is further supported by the pervasive requirement for proportionality, which argues in favour of first exhausting alternative measures in preference to resorting to remuneration for generation capacity.

As acknowledged in Chapter 6, reducing or shifting demand and increasing or optimising cross-border capacities can never altogether replace the need for generation capacity. Nevertheless, the analysis demonstrates that, under the existing legal framework, capacity mechanisms should not be about remunerating capacity, but about resources. In other words, generation capacity is not a value in its own right. The emphasis should rather be on ensuring the availability of sufficient resources. The facilitation of this objective should occur primarily through legal solutions capable of supporting the pursuit of a functioning internal market, competitiveness and the EU sustainability goals.

In response to the sixth research question on the proposed new legal framework for generation adequacy, Chapter 7 examines how these new proposed rules will alter the existing legal framework for national capacity mechanisms. The analysis identifies a clear shift in the EU approach to introducing capacity mechanisms. Not only do the proposed rules explicitly harmonise the EU-level approach to capacity mechanisms, but they also aim to marginalise the role of State intervention by strengthening the market-based approach.

§8.02 RECURRING THEMES IN THE DYNAMICS OF THE EU LEGAL FRAMEWORK FOR CAPACITY MECHANISMS

[A] The Roles of the Market and Market Failure

As reiterated throughout this book, the role of the markets and market-based investment is emphasised throughout EU energy law. The internal market in electricity is based on the idea that pooling the resources of all Member States by establishing an area without internal frontiers creates benefits that the Member States cannot achieve individually.[13] The underlying assumption is that a competitive single market will provide the most cost-efficient prices and the highest standards of service and ensure that the objectives of sustainability and security of supply are guaranteed. On the basis of this market-based ideology, a competitive energy-only electricity market is expected

---

13. Kaisa Huhta, *Capacity Mechanisms in EU Law – A Comment on the Free Movement of Goods* (Oxford Institute for Energy Studies, May 2018).

to be the best vehicle for achieving EU energy policy objectives, including security of supply and generation adequacy as an element of such security.[14]

This assumption is open to criticism. Critical voices have been raised about the suitability of the energy-only model to ensure generation adequacy in practice.[15] Nevertheless, a single energy-only market is the weapon of choice in EU law to ensure objectives such as security of supply.

Due to the central role of markets in guaranteeing security of supply, justifying an exemption from the market-based approach to generation adequacy requires that market forces alone are, or would be, unable to deliver a level of security of supply that Member States consider adequate. This requirement for market failure is logical when reflected against the market-based ideology: it would be counterintuitive to grant public funds to support activities that can be delivered by the markets alone.

The requirement of market failure is a recurring theme in the legal framework for introducing capacity mechanisms. However, there is no legally binding definition of market failure, nor is there a consistent method of evaluating its existence. The EEAG generally refers to market failure as a situation in which, markets, if left to their own devices, are unlikely to produce efficient outcomes.[16] Despite the lack of precise definition, market failure is included in the legal framework as a necessary criterion for State-driven procurement of generation adequacy.[17] The existence of market failure is required for the adoption of tendering procedures, for the introduction of PSOs and for granting compensation for their performance.[18] Market failure is equally emphasised if remuneration for generation adequacy is granted as State aid under Article 107(3)(c) TFEU and the EEAG.[19] Finally, the requirement of market failure also underpins restrictions on free movement of goods. Established case-law indicates that a restriction on the free movement of goods on grounds of security of supply is compatible with EU law only if there is a genuine and sufficiently serious threat to the availability of affordable electricity.[20] It is unlikely that such a threat could be proven if the markets could guarantee security of supply even without restrictions on the free movement of goods. In other words, a Member State must always be able to demonstrate the existence of a market failure in order to introduce a capacity mechanism.

---

14. Article 194 TFEU.
15. Bram Delvaux, *EU Law and the Development of a Sustainable, Competitive and Secure Energy Policy: Opportunities and Shortcomings* (Intersentia, 2013), pp. 38-46; Mauricio Cepeda, Marcelo Saguan, Dominique Finon, and Virginie Pignon, 'Generation Adequacy and Transmission Interconnection in Regional Electricity Markets', 37(12) *Energy Policy* (2009), pp. 5612-22; Alberto Heimler and Frédéric Jenny, 'The Limitations of European Union Control of State Aid', 28(2) *Oxford Review of Economic Policy* (2012), pp. 347-367.
16. Communication from the Commission, Guidelines on State aid for environmental protection and energy 2014-2020 (OJ C 200, 28.6.2014, pp. 1-55), footnote 38.
17. Article 8 of the Electricity Directive and Chapter 3 above.
18. Article 3 of the Electricity Directive; Article 106(2) TFEU; C-280/00 *Altmark* [2003] ECR I-7747; and Chapters 3 and 4 above.
19. Communication from the Commission, Guidelines on State aid for environmental protection and energy 2014-2020 (OJ C 200, 28.6.2014, pp. 1-55).
20. 72/83 *Campus Oil* [1984] ECR 2727.

[B] The Riptide Between Rules and Exceptions

Ensuring investment in generation adequacy through State intervention rather than through the operation of market forces constitutes an exemption to the rule by which the EU electricity market is expected to operate. Because of this exceptional role of capacity mechanisms within the context of EU energy law, many of these mechanisms or typical elements of these mechanisms are in principle prohibited by various legal instruments, such as EU State aid rules or the rules on free movement of goods. This same dynamic between the market-based rule and capacity mechanisms as the exception is also identifiable in the sector-specific electricity market rules. The Electricity Directive, in particular, establishes the market-based authorisation procedure as the rule by which investment should occur and tendering or equivalent procedures, as well as PSOs, as the exceptions.

In accordance with established interpretation of EU law, exceptions should always be interpreted strictly to avoid undermining the objectives of the rules themselves.[21] This requirement is particularly emphasised in the established case-law on restricting the free movement of goods.[22] As an instrument of market integration, the Electricity Directive should be interpreted in alignment with the free movement rules. Therefore, any exceptions related to the threshold for State intervention should also be interpreted narrowly.[23]

In other words, the EU legal framework for capacity mechanisms is based on an exemption regime in which capacity mechanisms are always an exception to the rule. This dynamic applies regardless of the legal angle from which capacity mechanisms, as instruments of security of supply, are viewed. In principle, therefore, there should be a high threshold for introducing capacity mechanisms.

However, the importance of security of supply seems to significantly widen the narrow interpretation identified above. This can be seen both de jure and de facto. Security of supply is protected not only by Article 194 TFEU but also by other Treaty provisions.[24] It is also a recurring theme throughout the sector-specific electricity market legislation. In practice, furthermore, the fact that no Member State capacity mechanisms have thus far been declared entirely incompatible with the internal market in reviews by various EU institutions demonstrates that all threats to security of supply, as presented by Member States, are taken seriously. This approval of capacity remuneration schemes under EU law is a manifestation of the importance accorded to security of supply. However, it is also the result of a lack of shared rules that would

---

21. On free movement rules 72/83 *Campus Oil* [1984] ECR 2727, para. 37; C-54/99 *Église de scientologie* [2000] ECR I-1335 para. 17; C-503/99 *Commission v Belgium* [2002] ECR I-4809, para. 47; 13/78 *Eggers* [1978] ECR I-1935, para. 30; and on other Treaty provisions C-157/94 *Netherlands* [1997] ECR I-5699, para. 37; C-159/94 *Commission v France* [1997] ECR I-5815, paras 53-55.
22. *See* Chapter 5 above.
23. Norbert Reich, Annette Nordhausen Scholes, Jeremy Scholes, *Understanding EU Internal Market Law* (Intersentia, 2015), p. 44.
24. The aim of protecting the uninterrupted availability of the energy supply is present in Articles 122, 170(1) and 192(2)(c) TFEU, for example.

allow greater EU involvement in establishing the threshold for and timing of the use of capacity mechanisms, as well as their design.

[C]   Fragmentation and Definitional Ambiguity

There is no single legal instrument in force in the EU that directly, let alone exhaustively, addresses the legal issues related to capacity mechanisms. Instead, there is a fragmentary body of both primary and secondary provisions that addresses the broader objective of security of supply and applies, or may apply, to remunerating capacity, attracting investment in the electricity sector and facilitating cross-border trade. This lack of harmonisation in relation to capacity mechanisms necessarily limits the concrete legal measures available to EU institutions to address them under EU law.

Due to the lack of harmonisation mentioned above, evaluation of capacity mechanisms under EU law necessarily focuses on the content of concepts such as market failure and, even more centrally, security of supply. As noted above, neither of these concepts have legally binding definitions or common methods of evaluation. This book has analysed the concept of security of supply as constituting the uninterrupted availability of affordable electricity. As an element of security of supply, the concept of generation adequacy has been examined on the basis that it constitutes the ability of installed and expected generation capacity to meet demand at all times. Overall, however, the concepts of security of supply and market failure seem to defy attempts at exhaustive definition. This definitional ambiguity in respect of such vitally important concepts in the legal framework for capacity mechanisms further deepens the impacts of the lack of harmonisation.

However, some observations can be made about the role and dynamics of security of supply in the EU legal framework for capacity mechanisms. Regardless of the legal provision under which a capacity mechanism is reviewed, the introduction of such a mechanism requires the existence of an objective that is protected under EU law. In terms of tendering or equivalent procedures, this objective is directly referred to as security of supply. In terms of PSOs, however, it is referred to as a general economic interest.[25] In relation to exemption from the prohibition of State aid, the same protected interest is referred to as an objective of common interest. In relation to derogation from the rules on free movement of goods, it is known as public security. The preceding chapters have established that security of electricity supply – and generation adequacy as a necessary prerequisite for ensuring such security – can legitimately constitute a general economic interest, a common interest or, indeed, a public security interest.

However, capacity mechanisms themselves should be examined separately from their objective. Although generation adequacy is indisputably an objective that can be protected under EU law, capacity mechanisms as instruments to pursue generation adequacy may involve elements that are not protected by EU law. The reason for this is partly that capacity mechanisms do not necessarily always make an entirely

---

25. Article 3 of the Electricity Directive.

favourable contribution to security of supply. For example, by increasing the cost of the electricity system, they tend to decrease the affordability of energy.

The fragmentary nature of the EU legal framework for capacity mechanisms and the definitional ambiguity surrounding the key concepts relevant to it present challenges in terms of the consistent legal treatment of Member States' capacity mechanisms. However, it is possible to identify some unifying elements that alleviate the impacts of fragmentation and definitional ambiguity irrespective of the EU provision under which a capacity mechanism is reviewed.

The first of these unifying elements is the way in which Member States must define the objective that is being pursued through a capacity mechanism. This objective needs to be clearly defined in order for the payment of compensation for public services and for the provision of State aid to be justifiable. It seems that the threshold concerning the clarity of such definition is higher in respect of compensation for PSOs than for grants of State aid, but both nevertheless require that this criterion is met.[26] Furthermore, the proportionality assessment under Article 36 TFEU includes a review of how well the objective of the measure is defined. The lack of precisely and objectively defined grounds for a restriction has been used as a reason to declare that a restrictive measure goes beyond what is necessary to achieve its objective.[27]

The second element concerns the principle of proportionality. This principle and a contextual approach to the objectives of EU energy law are, overall, given greater emphasis in non-harmonised matters and, in this case, in the legal evaluation of Member States' capacity mechanisms. The importance of proportionality is underlined in reviews concerning the granting of compensation for PSOs and State aid assessments, as well as in the evaluation of measures necessary to protect public security under free movement rules. Compliance with the principle of proportionality is a matter of weighing the importance of the protected interest and the threats to it against the negative impacts of the measure in question. This review is, and ought to be, sensitive to the context from which generation adequacy concerns arise. Therefore, it is not possible to take a blanket view as to whether all capacity mechanisms are either proportionate or disproportionate under EU law. A capacity mechanism's ability to ensure security of supply depends on the particular generation adequacy issue being addressed through it. Hence, the proportionality of a capacity mechanism design is dependent upon the severity and nature of a Member State's generation adequacy issue and, in particular, upon how well a Member State is able to demonstrate that this issue

---

26. *See* Chapter 4 above. In particular, compare SA.39621 *French Country-Wide Capacity Mechanism*, C(2016) 7086 final (in which the objective being pursued was not defined clearly enough to comply with the first *Altmark* criteria) with the following cases: SA.44464 *Irish Capacity Mechanism: Reliability Option Scheme*, C(2017)7789 final; SA.46100 *Planned Polish Capacity Mechanism*, C(2018) 601 final; SA.48490 *Specific Demand Response Tender in France*, C(2018) 588 final; SA.48648 *Belgian Strategic Reserve*, C(2018) 589 final; and SA.48780 *Prolongation of the Greek Interruptibility Scheme*, C(2018) 604 final (in which the objectives being pursued were defined clearly enough to comply with the EEAG).
27. C-483/99 *France* [2002] ECR I-4781, para. 53; C-463/00 *Commission v Spain* [2003] ECR I-4581, paras 71-84.

is best addressed by means of a capacity mechanism. In evaluating the proportionality of State intervention, a contextual approach to EU energy law is needed.[28]

The fragmentation and definitional ambiguity described above incontestably leave Member States with significant leeway in deciding when and in what form to introduce capacity mechanisms. This is well illustrated by the fact that the only detailed EU rules governing specific elements of capacity mechanisms are, in fact, not legally binding.[29] Rather than explicitly establishing rules on the basis of which to approve or prohibit outright State intervention to ensure generation adequacy, the existing EU rules on capacity mechanisms offer procedural means by which to subject a national measure to evaluation by the EU's institutions.[30] This evaluation, however, is limited by a broad margin of Member State discretion, the ambiguity of key concepts governing the relevant rules and the overall lack of harmonisation. This dynamic between national and EU rules is ultimately a matter of balancing the interests of Member States against those of the EU.

[D]   Balancing National Security and the Ambitions of the EU

There is friction between the Member States and the EU. This friction is at the heart of the legal debate on capacity mechanisms. On a legal level, both the EU and the Member States agree that generation adequacy, as an element of security of supply, is an objective that needs to be safeguarded. The source of this friction lies in the different means by which the objective of generation adequacy is pursued, rather than in the objective itself. EU law has fundamentally taken the market-based approach to security of supply in order to ensure cost efficiency. Regardless of the realities affecting the electricity markets, the legal framework applicable to generation adequacy relies on the ability of the pooled resources of the energy-only market to deliver the most cost-efficient level of generation adequacy. Member States, conversely, prioritise unconditional guarantees of generation adequacy over cost efficiency.

The EU's approach to generation adequacy ultimately requires a willingness on the part of Member States to rely on interdependence instead of independence in matters of security of supply. The delicate balance of interests affecting security of supply is not influenced only by the legal framework but also by strong political drivers. In the case of the EU, it has been fittingly argued that 'an emphasis on the *telos* of market integration overshadows profound political and ideological questions concerning the relationship between law, politics and the economy'.[31] However, in the case of capacity mechanisms, this argument does not seem to apply. The reason for this is rooted in the importance of ensuring the uninterrupted availability of affordable electricity. It seems that the importance of security of supply to the functioning of

---

28. For more on this topic, *see* Chapter 6 above.
29. Communication from the Commission, Guidelines on State aid for environmental protection and energy 2014-2020 (OJ C 200, 28.6.2014, pp. 1-55).
30. Usually the Commission or the EU courts.
31. Wolf Sauter and Harm Schepel, *State and Market in European Union Law: The Public and Private Spheres of the Internal Market before the EU Courts* (Cambridge University Press, 2009), p. 12.

European societies creates political and economic pressure in Member States that, at least partially, overshadows the *telos* of market integration. As noted at the very beginning of this book, this delicate balance between Member States' security interests and EU ambitions is further complicated by the political, economic and technological issues that arise in the context of the energy transition. While certain elements of capacity mechanisms can be explicitly controlled by means of the fragmentary body of rules governing capacity mechanisms, the existing framework is not equipped to fully control the introduction and design of this type of State intervention. Instead, EU law for capacity mechanisms serves as an instrument for balancing the partially conflicting interests between the EU and its Member States.

§8.03   THE WAY FORWARD WITH GENERATION ADEQUACY IN EU LAW

The energy transition has brought security of supply issues to the forefront of European discussion of electricity markets. Overall, the analysis set out in this research shows that, although capacity mechanisms are not harmonised, the interpretation of EU law regarding State intervention to ensure generation adequacy has evolved since the national electricity markets were first subjected to EU law. While State intervention in the interest of generation adequacy was viewed as a PSO accompanied by compensation for its performance in the early 2000s, more recent case-law indicates that this no longer holds good.[32] In a similar way, the case-law on free movement seems to have evolved in a direction that allows less scope for measures that restrict the free movement of goods on grounds of public security.[33] In the electricity sector, these changes in interpretative stance may be attributed to the deepening of integration and to the enhanced role conferred on the markets through the proliferation of sector-specific rules. Under these rules, the State is no longer the provider of all services but rather the facilitator of stable market conditions and non-discriminatory competition.

Despite the overall cautiousness of the legal framework in relation to State intervention to ensure generation adequacy, capacity mechanisms have found their place in EU law through the interpretation of the State aid regime. Nevertheless, the deepening harmonisation that has taken place over the years and the approaches adopted in the context of that process have narrowed the range of legal provisions Member States may invoke to justify their capacity mechanisms. Along with the increase in the number of legal instruments adopted by the EU to further market integration and the energy-only approach, further marginalisation of the role of measures such as capacity mechanisms has taken place. This process will continue

---

32. N475/2003 *Irish CADA*, 16 December 2003; T-57/11 *Castelnou Energía v Commission* [2014], judgment of the General Court of 3 December 2014, published in the electronic Reports of Cases; SA.34947 *Support to Hinkley Point C Nuclear Power Station*, C(2013) 9073 final; SA.39621 *French Country-Wide Capacity Mechanism*, C(2016) 7086 final; and SA.45852 *German Capacity Reserve*, C(2018) 612 final.
33. 72/83 *Campus Oil* [1984] ECR 2727; C-347/88 *Commission v Greece* [1990] ECR I-4747; C-398/98 *Commission v Greece* [2001] ECR I-7915.

along the same path when the proposed changes in the Clean Energy for All Europeans package enter into force.

The Clean Energy for All Europeans package demonstrates the EU's need for a higher level of control in capacity mechanisms if these mechanisms are to be adopted and designed while pursuing other objectives of EU energy law. The package includes several legal instruments that address security of supply.[34] The only one of these that directly addresses the introduction and design of capacity mechanisms is the recast of the regulation on conditions for access to the network for cross-border exchanges in electricity, i.e., the proposal for a Recast Electricity Regulation.[35] This proposes entirely new provisions governing assessment of the need for capacity mechanisms and the required design features of any capacity mechanism that is adopted, including rules on cross-border participation.[36] In turn, the provision on tendering and equivalent procedures under the Electricity Directive would be repealed.[37] The proposed rules on capacity mechanisms aim to further strengthen the role of market-based approaches to generation adequacy at the expense of State-driven ones. The proposed rules also place greater emphasis on resources rather than generation capacity alone.[38] With regard to Treaty rules, State aid control would continue to have high relevance, whereas recourse to other Treaty provisions would be significantly narrowed and even entirely blocked in some cases. However, the emphasis on the proportionality principle in the design of capacity mechanisms would still leave room for context-sensitive interpretations in case-by-case analyses of capacity mechanisms. Nevertheless, the proposed rules together with the shift to addressing capacity mechanisms in a regulation rather than a directive further narrows Member States' margin of discretion in interpreting these rules in their national contexts.

The Clean Energy for All Europeans package addresses certain aspects of the existing legal framework that do not at present facilitate EU involvement in a way that would allow for more consistent pursuit of the objectives of EU energy law. With particular focus on the findings presented in this book, several issues can be identified that are of specific relevance to capacity mechanisms. First, the proposed provisions of the package continue the process of deepening and strengthening the role of the markets in guaranteeing security of supply. In contrast, the role of State intervention in guaranteeing generation adequacy is further marginalised. In addition, the proposal addresses the definitional ambiguity surrounding the key concepts relevant to capacity

---

34. Proposal for a Directive of the European Parliament and of the Council on common rules for the internal market in electricity, COM(2016) 864 final; Proposal for a Regulation of the European Parliament and of the Council on risk-preparedness in the electricity sector and repealing Directive 2005/89/EC, COM(2016) 862 final; the Recast Electricity Regulation.
35. Regulation (EC) No 714/2009 of the European Parliament and of the Council of 13 July 2009 on conditions for access to the network for cross-border exchanges in electricity and repealing Regulation (EC) No 1228/2003 (OJ L 211, 14.8.2009, pp. 15-35); the Recast Electricity Regulation.
36. *See* Articles 18, 19, 21 and 23 of the Recast Electricity Regulation.
37. Proposal for a Directive of the European Parliament and of the Council on common rules for the internal market in electricity (recast) COM(2016) 864 final. This document proposes the repeal of Article 8 of the Electricity Directive. However, it does not propose repeal of Article 3 of the Electricity Directive.
38. *Ibid.*

mechanisms. Most pressingly, the lack of a common methodology for assessing requirements such as market failure or a legitimate security of supply objective have allowed the varying consistency of reasons to justify intervention. The proposal seeks to address this issue by establishing the necessary methodology and a common threshold for the introduction of capacity mechanisms. It also seeks to further address the objectives of EU energy law by shifting the focus of capacity mechanisms from mere *capacity* to overall *resources*. This approach would facilitate a more holistic pursuit of the objectives of EU energy law as a whole. The proposed rules directly address capacity mechanisms as such, which would also necessarily decrease the degree of fragmentation identified in the existing rules.

However, the proposed provisions set out in the Clean Energy for All Europeans package are unlikely to solve the fundamental friction between the priority given to national security by Member States and the priority given to competition and integration of the markets by the EU. As the energy transition progresses, the amount of conventional generation capacities and related infrastructure will necessarily decrease. To protect their economies, Member States have a natural incentive to adopt State interventions to compensate for the economic losses caused by the evolving electricity markets. The complexity involved in balancing these interests is anchored in the fundamental importance of protecting security of electricity supply, which has been the overarching theme of this book. The exemptions allowed in all the legal bases under which capacity mechanisms may be evaluated in EU law are inherently instruments to mitigate the friction identified between the EU and its Member States. Because of this dynamic, the interpretation of EU law in the light of capacity mechanisms is fundamentally an evolving attempt to reconcile the interests of the Member States with those of the EU while safeguarding the objective of security of supply.

Bibliography

Agnew, John, *Globalization and Sovereignty* (Rowman & Littlefield Publishers, 2009)

Alter, Karen, *Establishing the Supremacy of European Law: The Making of an International Rule of Law in Europe* (OUP, 2003)

Andenæs, Mads and Wulf-Henning Roth, *Services and Free Movement in EU Law* (OUP, 2002)

Ausubel, Lawrence and Peter Cramton, 'Using forward markets to improve electricity market design', 18(2) *Utilities Policy* (2010), pp. 195-200

Avbelj, Matej, 'Supremacy or primacy of EU law – (why) does it matter?', 17(6) *European Law Journal* (2011), pp. 744-763

Bacon, Kelyn, *European Union Law of State Aid*, 3rd edition (OUP, 2017)

Barnard, Catherine and Okeoghene Odudu (eds.), *The Outer Limits of European Union Law* (Hart Publishing, 2009)

Barnard, Catherine and Steve Peers (eds.), *European Union Law* (OUP, 2014)

Barton, Barry, Catherine Redgwell, Anita Rønne and Donald N. Zillman (eds.), *Energy Security: Managing Risk in a Dynamic Legal and Regulatory Environment* (OUP, 2004)

Basedow, Jürgen and Wolfgang Wurmnest (eds.), *Structure and Effects in EU Competition Law: Studies on Exclusionary Conduct and State Aid* (Kluwer Law International, 2011)

Batlle, Carlos and Pablo Rodilla, 'A critical assessment of the different approaches aimed to secure electricity generation supply', 38(11) *Energy Policy* (2010), pp. 7169-7179

Benedettini, Simona, 'PJM and ISO-NE forward capacity markets: A critical assessment', *IEFE Research Report Series* (2013) ISSN 2036-1785

Bhagwat, Pradyumna, Jörn Richstein, Emile Chappin, Kaveri Iychettira and Laurens De Vries, 'Cross-border effects of capacity mechanisms in interconnected power systems', 46 *Utilities Policy* (2017), pp. 33-47

Bhagwat, Pradyumna, *Security of Supply During the Energy Transition: The Role of Capacity Mechanisms* (Technische Universiteit Delft, PhD thesis 2016)

Bielecki, Janusz and Melaku Geboye Desta (eds.), *Electricity Trade in Europe: Review of the Economic and Regulatory Challenges* (Kluwer Law International, 2004)

Biondi, Andrea, Piet Eeckhout and Stefanie Ripley (eds.), *EU Law After Lisbon* (OUP, 2012)

Bjørnebye, Henrik, 'Electricity generation capacity tenders in the security of supply interest: EU regulation of internal electricity market facilitation and intervention', 4 *OGEL* (2007)

Bjørnebye, Henrik, *Investing in EU Energy Security: Exploring the Regulatory Approach to Tomorrow's Electricity Production* (University of Oslo, PhD thesis 2009)

Boffa, Federico, Viswanath Pingali and Davide Vannoni, 'Increasing market interconnection: An analysis of the Italian electricity spot market', 28(3) *International Journal of Industrial Organization* (2010), pp. 311-322

Boscán, Luis and Rahmat Poudineh, *Flexibility-Enabling Contracts in Electricity Markets* (Oxford Institute for Energy Studies, July 2016)

Broberg, Morten and Nina Holst-Christensen, *Free Movement in the European Union*, 3rd edition (DJØF, 2010)

Burns, Charlotte, Anne Rasmussen and Christine Reh, 'Legislative codecision and its impact on the political system of the European Union', 20(7) *Journal of European Public Policy* (2013), pp. 941-952

Cameron, Peter and Raphael Heffron (eds.), *Legal Aspects of EU Energy Regulation: The Consolidation of Energy Law Across Europe* (OUP, 2016)

Cameron, Peter, *Competition in Energy Markets* (OUP, 2007)

Caro de Sousa, Pedro, *The European Fundamental Freedoms: A Contextual Approach* (OUP, 2015)

Carstairs, Jamie, 'Market design: The energy-only market model', conference presentation at *Capacity Mechanisms in Europe: The fundamental issues behind the ongoing sector inquiry*, 29 September 2015, Brussels, available at http://ec.europa.eu/competition/sectors/energy/state_aid_to_secure_electricity_supply_en.html (last accessed 5.3.2019)

Cepeda, Mauricio and Dominique Finon, 'Generation capacity adequacy in interdependent electricity markets', 39(6) *Energy Policy* (2011), pp. 3128-3143

Cepeda, Mauricio, Marcelo Saguan, Dominique Finon and Virginie Pignon, 'Generation adequacy and transmission interconnection in regional electricity markets', 37(12) *Energy Policy* (2009), pp. 5612-5622

Černoch, Filip and Veronika Zapletalová, 'Hinkley point C: A new chance for nuclear power plant construction in central Europe?' 83 *Energy Policy* (2015), pp. 165-168

Clift, Ben, 'Economic patriotism, the clash of capitalisms, and state aid in the European Union', 13(1) *Journal of Industry, Competition and Trade* (2013), pp. 101-117

Conway, Gerard, *The Limits of Legal Reasoning and the European Court of Justice* (Cambridge University Press, 2012)

Craig, Paul and Gráinne de Búrca, *EU Law: Text, Cases, and Materials*, 6th edition (OUP, 2015)

Craig, Paul and Gráinne de Búrca, *The Evolution of EU Law* (OUP, 2011)

Cramton, Peter and Axel Ockenfels, 'Economics and design of capacity markets for the power sector', 36(2) *Zeitschrift für Energiewirtschaft* (2012), pp. 113-134

Cramton, Peter and Steven Stoft, 'Forward reliability markets: Less risk, less market power, more efficiency', 16(3) *Utilities Policy* (2008), pp. 194-201

Cramton, Peter, 'Electricity market design', 33(4) *Oxford Review of Economic Policy* (2017), pp. 589-612

Cramton, Peter, Axel Ockenfels and Steven Stoft, 'Capacity market fundamentals', 2(2) *Economics of Energy & Environmental Policy* (2013), pp. 27-46

Cremona, Marise (ed.), *Market Integration and Public Services in the European Union* (OUP, 2011)

Cruz, Julio Baquero and Fernando Castillo de la Torre, 'A note on PreussenElektra', 26 *European Law Review* (2001)

Cyndecka, Małgorzata, *The Market Economy Investor Test in EU State Aid Law: Applicability and Application* (Kluwer Law International, 2016)

da Cruz Vilaça and José Luís, *EU Law and Integration: Twenty Years of Judicial Application of EU Law* (Hart Publishing, 2014)

Davies, Gareth, *EU Internal Market Law* (Cavendish Pub. Ltd, 2003)

de Vries, Laurens and Petra Heijnen, 'The impact of electricity market design upon investment under uncertainty: The effectiveness of capacity mechanisms', 16(3) *Utilities Policy* (2008), pp. 215-227

Delvaux, Bram, *EU Law and the Development of a Sustainable, Competitive and Secure Energy Policy: Opportunities and Shortcomings* (Intersentia, 2013)

Dorsman, André, Wim Westerman, Mehmet Baha Karan and Özgür Arslan (eds.), *Financial Aspects in Energy: A European Perspective* (Springer, 2011)

Enchelmaier, Stefan, 'Moped Trailers, Mickelsson and Roos, Gysbrechts: The ECJ's case law on goods keeps on moving', 190(29) *Yearbook of European Law* (2010), pp. 190-223

Fiedziuk, Natalia, 'Putting services of general economic interest up for tender: Reflections on applicable EU rules', 50(1) *Common Market Law Review* (2013), pp. 87-114

Fiedziuk, Natalia, 'Services of general economic interest and the Treaty of Lisbon: Opening doors to a whole new approach or maintaining the "status quo"', 36(2) *European Law Review* (2011), pp. 226-242

Fiedziuk, Natalia, 'Towards a more refined economic approach to services of general economic interest', 16(2) *European Public Law* (2010), pp. 271-288

Fiedziuk, Natalia, 'Towards decentralization of state aid control: The case of services of general economic interest', 36(3) *World Competition Law and Economics Review* (2013), pp. 387-408

Finon, Dominique and Virginie Pignon, 'Electricity and long-term capacity adequacy: The quest for regulatory mechanism compatible with electricity market', 3(16) *Utilities Policy* (2008), pp. 143-158

Foster, Nigel, *Foster on EU Law*, 6th edition (OUP, 2017)

Freris, Leon and David Infield, *Renewable Energy in Power Systems* (John Wiley & Sons, 2008)

Giacomarra, Marcella and Filippa Bono, 'European Union commitment towards RES market penetration: From the first legislative acts to the publication of the recent guidelines on state aid 2014/2020', 47 *Renewable and Sustainable Energy Reviews* (2015)

Gils, Hans Christian, 'Assessment of the theoretical demand response potential in Europe', 67 *Energy* (2014), pp. 1-18

Glachant, Jean-Michel and Sophia Ruester, 'The EU internal electricity market: Done forever?', 30 *Utilities Policy* (2014), pp. 1-7

Gormley, Laurence, *EU Law on Free Movement of Goods and Customs Union* (OUP, 2009)

Gormley, Laurence, 'Reasoning renounced? The remarkable judgment in Keck & Mithouard?', 5(3) *European Business Law Review* (1994), pp. 63-67

Gormley, Laurence, 'Silver threads among the gold ... 50 years of the free movement of goods', 31(6) *Fordham International Law Journal* (2008), pp. 1637-1691

Greening, Lorna, 'Demand response resources: Who is responsible for implementation in a deregulated market?', 35(4) *Energy* (2010), pp. 1518-1525

Gyselen, Luc, 'Services of general economic interest and competition under European Law – A delicate balance', 1(1) *Journal of European Competition Law & Practice* (2010), pp. 491-499

Hancher, Leigh, 'State aid to the nuclear power sector: The General Court's ruling on the UK reactor at Hinkley Point C', *OGEL* (2018)

Hancher, Leigh, Adrien de Hauteclocque and Francesco Maria Salerno (eds.), *State Aid and the Energy Sector* (Hart Publishing, 2018)

Hancher, Leigh, Adrien de Hauteclocque and Malgorzata Sadowska, *Capacity Mechanisms in the EU Energy Market* (OUP, 2015)

Hancher, Leigh, Tom Ottervanger and Piet Jan Slot, *EU State Aids*, 5th edition (Sweet & Maxwell, 2016)

Harbo, Tor-Inge, *The Function of Proportionality Analysis in European Law* (Brill Nijhoff, 2015).

Hary, Nicolas, Vincent Rious and Marcelo Saguan, 'The electricity generation adequacy problem: Assessing dynamic effects of capacity remuneration mechanisms', 91 *Energy Policy* (2016), pp. 113-127

Hatzopoulos, Vassilis, 'The court's approach to services (2006-2012): From case law to case load?' 50(2) *Common Market Law Review* (2013), pp. 459-501

Hatzopoulos, Vassilis, *Regulating Services in the European Union* (OUP, 2012)

Hawker, Graeme, Keith Bell and Simon Gill, 'Electricity security in the European Union – The conflict between national capacity mechanisms and the single market', 24 *Energy Research & Social Science* (2017), pp. 51-58

He, Xian, Nico Keyaerts, Isabel Azevedo, Leonardo Meeus, Leigh Hancher and Jean-Michel Glachant, 'How to engage consumers in demand response: A contract perspective', 27 *Utilities Policy* (2013), pp. 108-122

Heffron, Raphael and Gavin Little (eds.), *Delivering Energy Law and Policy in the EU and the US: A Reader* (Edinburgh University Press, 2016)

Heffron, Raphael and Kim Talus, 'The development of energy law in the 21st century: A paradigm shift?', 9(1) *The Journal of World Energy Law & Business* (2016), pp. 189-202

Heffron, Raphael, Darren McCauley and Benjamin Sovacool, 'Resolving society's energy trilemma through the Energy Justice Metric', 87 *Energy Policy* (2015), pp. 168-176

Heimler, Alberto and Frédéric Jenny, 'The limitations of European Union control of state aid', 28(2) *Oxford Review of Economic Policy* (2012), pp. 347-367

Held, Christian and Jan Ole Voss, 'Legal limits for electricity capacity markets in the EU and Germany', 245 *Renewable Energy Law & Policy Review* (2013)

Helm, Dieter (ed.), *The New Energy Paradigm* (OUP, 2007)

Helstroffer, Jenny and Marie Obidzinski, 'Codecision procedure biais: The European legislation game', 38(1) *European Journal of Law and Economics* (2014), pp. 29-46

Henriot, Arthur and Jean-Michel Glachant, 'Capacity remuneration mechanisms in the European market: Now but how?' Robert Schuman Centre for Advanced Studies Research Paper No. 84 (2014)

Hildmann, Marcus, Andreas Ulbig and Göran Andersson, 'Empirical analysis of the merit-order effect and the missing money problem in power markets with high RES shares', 30(3) *IEEE Transactions on Power Systems* (2015), pp. 1560-1570

Hindelang, Steffen, *The Free Movement of Capital and Foreign Direct Investment: The Scope of Protection in EU Law* (OUP, 2009)

Hirst, Eric and Stan Hadley, 'Generation adequacy: Who decides?', 12(8) *The Electricity Journal* (1999), pp. 11-21

Hofmann, Herwig and Claire Micheau (eds.), *State Aid Law of the European Union* (OUP, 2016)

Hogan, Michael, '"Energy-only markets" or "a given form of capacity mechanism"? Asking the wrong question', conference presentation at *Capacity Mechanisms in Europe: The Fundamental Issues Behind the Ongoing Sector Inquiry*, 29 September 2015, Brussels, available at http://ec.europa.eu/competition/sectors/energy/state_aid_to_secure_electricity_supply_en.html (last accessed 5.3.2019)

Hogan, William W., 'On an "Energy Only" electricity market design for resource adequacy', Harvard University papers, 2005, available at www.hks.harvard.edu/fs/whogan/Hogan_Energy_Only_092305.pdf (last accessed 5.3.2019)

Horsley, Thomas, 'Subsidiarity and the European Court of Justice: Missing pieces in the subsidiarity jigsaw?', 50(2) *Journal of Common Market Studies* (2012), pp. 267-282

Höschle, Hanspeter, Cedric De Jonghe, Hélène Le Cadre and Ronnie Belmans, 'Electricity markets for energy, flexibility and availability – Impact of capacity mechanisms on the remuneration of generation technologies', 66 *Energy Economics* (2017), pp. 372-383

Huhta, Kaisa, 'A new era for capacity mechanisms: Reviewing the commission's clean energy for all Europeans legislative package', 1 *OGEL* (2018)

Huhta, Kaisa, *Capacity Mechanisms in EU Law: A Comment on the Free Movement of Goods* (Oxford Institute for Energy Studies, May 2018)

Huhta, Kaisa, 'Too important to be entrusted to neighbours? The dynamics of security of electricity supply and mutual trust in EU law', 43(6) *European Law Review* (2018), pp. 920-933

Huhta, Kaisa, 'Prioritising energy efficiency and demand side measures over capacity mechanisms under EU energy law', 35(1) *Journal of Energy & Natural Resources Law* (2017), pp. 7-24

231

Huisman, Ronald, Christian Huurman and Ronald Mahieu, 'Hourly electricity prices in day-ahead markets', 29(2) *Energy Economics* (2007), pp. 240-248

Johnston, Angus and Guy Block, *EU Energy Law* (OUP, 2012)

Jones, Christopher (ed.), *EU Energy Law: Volume I: The Internal Energy Market – The Third Liberalisation Package* (Claeys & Casteels, 2010)

Joskow, Paul and Jean Tirole, 'Reliability and competitive electricity markets', 38(1) *RAND Journal of Economics* (2007), pp. 60-84

Joskow, Paul, 'Capacity payments in imperfect electricity markets: Need and design', 16(3) *Utilities Policy* (2008), pp. 159-170

Jürgen, Franz, Säcker, Lydia Scholz and Thea Sveen, *EU Renewable Energy Law: Legal Challenges and New Perspectives* (Oslo Sjørettsfondet, 2014)

Kaczorowska-Ireland, Alina, *European Union Law* (Routledge, 2009)

Kalicki, Jan H. and David L. Goldwyn (eds.), *Energy & Security*, 2nd edition (John Hopkins University Press, 2013)

Kapff, Lionel and Jacques Pelkmans, 'Interconnector investment for a well-functioning internal market: What EU regime of regulatory incentives?', *Bruges European Economic Research Papers* 2010, available at http://aei.pitt.edu/58594/ (last accessed 5.3.2019)

Kaupa, Clemens, *The Pluralist Character of the European Economic Constitution* (Hart Publishing, 2016)

Keppler, Jan Horst, 'Rationales for capacity remuneration mechanisms: Security of supply externalities and asymmetric investment incentives', 105 *Energy Policy* (2017), pp. 562-570

Kiiver, Philipp, *The Practice of Public Procurement: Tendering, Selection and Award* (Intersentia, 2014)

Konstadinides, Theodore, *Division of Powers in European Union Law: The Delimitation of Internal Competence Between the EU and the Member States* (Kluwer Law International, 2009)

Koopmans, Tim, 'Subsidiarity, politics and the judiciary articles EC 5, draft convention I-9; protocol on the application of the principles of subsidiarity and proportionality', 1(1) *European Constitutional Law Review* (2005), pp. 112-116

Koutrakos, Panos and Jukka Snell, *Research Handbook on the Law of the EU's Internal Market* (Edward Elgar Publishing, 2017)

Koutrakos, Panos, Niamh Nic Shuibhne and Phil Syrpis (eds.), *Exceptions from EU Free Movement Law: Derogation, Justification and Proportionality* (Hart Publishing, 2016)

Larouche, Pierre and Péter Cserne (eds.), *National Legal Systems and Globalization: New Role, Continuing Relevance* (T.M.C. Asser Press, 2013)

Lenaerts, Koen, 'Defining the concept of 'Services of General Interest' in light of the 'Checks and Balances' set out in the EU treaties', 19(4) *Jurisprudence* (2012), pp. 1247-1267

Liu, Yingqi, 'Demand response and energy efficiency in the capacity resource procurement: Case studies of forward capacity markets in ISO New England, PJM and Great Britain', 100 *Energy Policy* (2017), pp. 271-282

Lynch, Muireann Á., Richard S.J. Tol and Mark J. O'Malley, 'Optimal interconnection and renewable targets for north-west Europe', 51 *Energy Policy* (2012), pp. 605-617

Makkonen, Mari, *Cross-Border Transmission Capacity Development – Experiences from the Nordic Electricity Markets* (Lappeenranta University of Technology, PhD thesis 2015)

Mantzari, Despoina, 'The quest for reasonable retail energy prices in Europe: Positive and normative dimensions', 36(1) *Yearbook of European Law* (2017), pp. 599-627

Marzooghi, Hesamoddin, Gregor Verbič, and David J. Hill, 'Aggregated demand response modelling for future grid scenarios', 5 *Sustainable Energy, Grids and Networks* (2016), pp. 94-104

Mastropietro, Paolo, Pablo Rodilla, Carlos Batlle, 'National capacity mechanisms in the European internal energy market: Opening the doors to neighbours', 82 *Energy Policy* (2015), pp. 38-47

Matos, Nuno Albuquerque, 'The role of the BUPA judgement in the legal framework for services of general economic interest', 16(1) *Tilburg Law Review* (2011), pp. 83-104

Mayr, Stefan, 'Putting a leash on the Court of Justice? Preconceptions in National Methodology v Effet Utile as a Meta-Rule', 5(2) *European Journal of Legal Studies* (2012), pp. 8-21

Meyer, Roland and Olga Gore, 'Cross-border effects of capacity mechanisms: Do uncoordinated market design changes contradict the goals of the European market integration?', 51 *Energy economics* (2015), pp. 9-20

Mezősi, András, Zsuzsanna Pató and László Szabó, 'Assessment of the EU 10% interconnection target in the context of CO2 mitigation', 16(5) *Climate Policy* (2016), pp. 658-672

Mortensen, Bent Ole Gram, 'The European Court of Justice decision in case C-206/06, Essent Netwerk Noord BV', 17(6) *European Energy and Environmental Law Review* (2008), pp. 389-393

Neuhoff, Karsten et al. 'A coordinated strategic reserve to safeguard the European energy transition', *Utilities Policy* (2016), pp. 1-12

Newbery, David, 'Missing money and missing markets: Reliability, capacity auctions and interconnectors', 94 *Energy Policy* (2016), pp. 401-410

Nicolaides, Phedon and Maria Geilmann, 'What is effective implementation of EU law?', 19(3) *Maastricht Journal of European and Comparative Law* (2012), pp. 383-399

Nicolaides, Phedon and Maria Kleis, 'Critical analysis of environmental tax reductions and generation adequacy provisions in the EEAG 2014-2020', 4 *European State Aid Quarterly* (2014)

Nowag, Julian, *Competition Law, State Aid Law and Free-Movement Law: The Case of the Environmental Integration Obligation* (University of Oxford, PhD thesis 2014)

Oliver, Peter (ed.), *Oliver on Free Movement of Goods in the European Union* (Hart Publishing, 2010)

Oliver, Peter and Stefan Enchelmaier, 'Free movement of goods: Recent developments in the case law', 44(3) *Common Market Law Review* (2007), pp. 649-704

Parvania, Masood, Mahmud Fotuhi-Firuzabad and Mohammad Shahidehpour, 'Optimal demand response aggregation in wholesale electricity markets', 4(4) *IEEE Transactions on Smart Grid* (2013), pp. 1957-1965

Pecho, Peter, 'Good-Bye Keck?: A comment on the remarkable judgment in commission v. Italy, C-110/05', 36(3) *Legal Issues of Economic Integration* (2009), pp. 257-272

Pereira, Rita et al., 'A fuzzy clustering approach to a demand response model', 81 *Electrical Power and Energy Systems* (2016), pp. 184-192

Piernas López, Juan Jorge, *The Concept of State Aid Under EU Law: From Internal Market to Competition and Beyond* (OUP 2015)

Quigley, Conor, *European State Aid Law and Policy* (Hart Publishing, 2015)

Rebours, Yann, Marc Trotignon, Vincent Lavier, Thibault Derbanne and François Meslier, 'How much electric interconnection capacities are needed within Western Europe?', *7th International Conference on the European Energy Market*, 23-25 June 2010

Recchi, Ettore, *Mobile Europe: The Theory and Practice of Free Movement in the EU* (Palgrave Macmillan, 2015)

Reich, Norbert, Annette Nordhausen Scholes and Jeremy Scholes, *Understanding EU Internal Market Law* (Intersentia, 2015)

Riesenhuber, Karl (ed.), *European Legal Methodology* (Intersentia, 2017)

Righini, Elisabetta and Juan Carlos González Fernández, 'Capacity mechanisms and state aid: Between PSOs, market liberalisation, and security of supply', 7(10) *Journal of European Competition Law & Practice* (2016), pp. 661-675

Ringler, Philipp, Dogan Keles and Wolf Fichtner, 'How to benefit from a common European electricity market design', 101 *Energy Policy* (2017), pp. 629-643

Rodilla, Pablo and Carlos Batlle, 'Security of electricity supply at the generation level: Problem analysis', 40 *Energy Policy* (2012), pp. 177-185

Rodilla, Pablo, Álvaro Baíllo, Santiago Cerisola and Carlos Batlle, 'Regulatory intervention to ensure an efficient medium-term generating resource planning in electricity markets', *Working Paper IIT-10-008A* (2010)

Roggenkamp, Martha and François Boisseleau (eds.), *The Regulation of Power Exchanges in Europe* (Intersentia, 2005)

Roggenkamp, Martha, Catherine Redgwell, Anita Ronne, and Inigo del Guayo (eds.), *Energy Law in Europe: National, EU and International Regulation* (OUP, 2016)

Roques, Fabien, 'Market design for generation adequacy: Healing causes rather than symptoms', 16(3) *Utilities Policy* (2008), pp. 171-183

Rosas, Allan and Lorna Armati, *EU Constitutional Law: An Introduction* (Hart Publishing, 2010)

Ruiter, Rik, 'Under the radar? National parliaments and the ordinary legislative procedure in the European Union', 20(8) *Journal of European public policy* (2013), pp. 1196-1212

Rusche, Tim, *EU Renewable Electricity Law and Policy: From National Targets to a Common Market* (Cambridge University Press, 2015)

Sankari, Suvi, *European Court of Justice Legal Reasoning in Context* (Europa Law Publishing, 2013)

Sauter, Wolf and Harm Schepel, *State and Market in European Union Law: The Public and Private Spheres of the Internal Market before the EU Courts* (Cambridge University Press, 2009)

Sauter, Wolf, 'Case T–289/03, British United Provident Association Ltd (BUPA), BUPA Insurance Ltd, BUPA Ireland Ltd v. Commission of the European Communities, Judgment of the Court of First Instance of 12 February 2008, nyr', 46(1) *Common Market Law Review* (2009), pp. 269-286

Sauter, Wolf, 'Proportionality in EU Law: A balancing act?', 15(2) *Cambridge Yearbook of European Legal Studies* (2012), pp. 439-466

Sauter, Wolf, 'Public services and the internal market: Building blocks or persistent irritant?', 21(6) *European Law Journal* (2015), pp. 738-757

Sauter, Wolf, *Public Services in EU Law* (Cambridge University Press, 2015)

Schütze, Robert, 'Subsidiarity after Lisbon: Reinforcing the safeguards of federalism?', 68(3) *The Cambridge Law Journal* (2009), pp. 525-536

Sencar, Marko, Viljem Pozeb and Tina Krope, 'Development of EU (European Union) energy market agenda and security of supply', 77 *Energy* (2014), pp. 117-124

Shuibhne, Niamh Nic, *The Coherence of EU Free Movement Law: Constitutional Responsibility and the Court of Justice* (OUP, 2014)

Siegel, Scott, *The Political Economy of Noncompliance: Adjusting to the Single European Market* (Routledge, 2011)

Sioshansi, Fereidoon (ed.), *Evolution of Global Electricity Markets. New Paradigms, New Challenges, New Approaches* (Elsevier Science & Technology, 2013)

Skouris, Vassilios, 'Effet utile versus legal certainty: The case-law of the Court of Justice on the direct effect of directives', 17(2) *European Business Law Review* (2006), pp. 241-255

Sovacool, Benjamin K. and Michael H. Dworkin, *Global Energy Justice: Problems, Principles, and Practices* (Cambridge University Press, 2014)

Sovacool, Benjamin K. (eds.), *The Routledge Handbook of Energy Security* (Routledge, 2013)

Sovacool, Benjamin K., Roman V. Sidortsov, Benjamin R. Jones, *Energy Security, Equality and Justice* (Routledge, 2014)

Strange, Susan, *The Retreat of the State: The Diffusion of Power in the World Economy* (Cambridge University Press, 1996)

Supponen, Matti, *Influence of National and Company Interests on European Electricity Transmission Investments* (Aalto University, PhD thesis 2011)

Syrpis, Phil (ed.), *The Judiciary, the Legislature and the EU Internal Market* (Cambridge University Press, 2012)

Szydło, Marek, 'Export restrictions within the structure of free movement of goods: Reconsideration of an old paradigm', 47(3) *Common Market Law Review* (2010), pp. 753-789

Szyszczak, Erika (ed.), *Research Handbook on European State Aid Law* (Edward Elgar 2011)

Szyszczak, Erika and Johan Willem van de Gronden (eds.), *Financing Services of General Economic Interest: Reform and Modernisation* (T.M.C. Asser Press, 2013)

Szyszczak, Erika, 'Modernising state aid and the financing of SGEI', 3(4) *Journal of European Competition Law & Practice* (2012), pp. 332-343

Szyszczak, Erika, *The Regulation of the State in Competitive Markets in the EU* (Hart Publishing, 2007)

Talus, Kim (ed.), *Research Handbook on International Energy Law* (Edward Elgar, 2014)

Talus, Kim, 'Decades of EU energy policy: Towards politically driven markets', *Journal of World Energy Law and Business* (2017), pp. 1-9

Talus, Kim, *EU Energy Law and Policy: A Critical Account* (OUP, 2013)

Talus, Kim, *Introduction to EU Energy Law* (OUP, 2016)

Torriti, Jacopo, Mohamed G. Hassan and Matthew Leach, 'Demand response experience in Europe: Policies, programmes and implementation', 35(4) *Energy* (2010), pp. 1575-1583

Verbong, Geert and Derk Loorbach (eds.), *Governing the Energy Transition: Reality, Illusion or Necessity?* (Routledge Studies in Sustainability Transitions, 2012)

VerLoren van Themaat, Weijer and Berend Reuder (eds.), *European Competition Law: A Case Commentary* (Edward Elgar, 2014)

Vesterdorf, Peter and Stephen Harris, *State Aid Law of the European Union* (Sweet & Maxwell, 2008)

von Bogdandy, Armin and Jürge Bast (eds.), *Principles of European Constitutional Law*, revised 2nd edition (Hart Publishing, 2011)

Weatherill, Stephen, 'After Keck: Some thoughts on how to clarify the clarification', 33(5) *Common Market Law Review* (1996), pp. 887-908

Weatherill, Stephen, *The Internal Market as a Legal Concept* (OUP, 2017)

Weiss, Friedl and Clemens Kaupa, *European Union Internal Market Law* (Cambridge University Press, 2014)

Werner, Philipp and Vincent Verouden (eds.), *EU State Aid Control: Law and Economics* (Wolters Kluwer, 2017)

Whish, Richard and David Bailey, *Competition Law*, 8th edition (OUP, 2015)

Documents by EU Institutions

ACER, Annual Report on the Results of Monitoring the Internal Electricity and Gas Markets in 2016. Electricity Wholesale Markets Volume, 6 October 2017

ACER, ACER Market Monitoring Report 2015, available at www.acer.europa.eu/official_documents/acts_of_the_agency/publication/acer_market_monitoring_report_2015.pdf (last accessed 5.3.2019)

ACER, Capacity Remuneration Mechanisms and the Internal Market for Electricity of 30 July 2013, available at www.acer.europa.eu/official_documents/acts_of_the_agency/publication/crms%20and%20the%20iem%20report%20130730.pdf (last accessed 5.3.2019)

Capacity Mechanisms Working Group, Enabling the Participation of Interconnectors and/or Foreign Capacity Providers in Capacity Mechanisms, 30 June 2015, available at http://ec.europa.eu/competition/sectors/energy/capacity_ mechanisms_working_group_6_draft.pdf (last accessed 5.3.2019)

Capacity Mechanisms Working Group, The Participation of Non-Generation Activities, Demand-Side, and Storage in Generation Adequacy Measures, 22 January 2015, available at http://ec.europa.eu/competition/sectors/energy/capacity_mecha nisms_working_group_4.pdf (last accessed 5.3.2019)

Commission Communication on the application of the European Union State aid rules to compensation granted for the provision of services of general economic interest (OJ C 8, 11.1.2012, p. 4-14)

Commission Communication, A Quality Framework for Services of General Interest in Europe, COM(2011) 900 final

Commission Green Paper on services of general interest, COM(2003) 270 final

Commission Green Paper, A European Strategy for Sustainable, Competitive and Secure Energy, COM(2006) 105 final

Commission Green Paper, Towards a European strategy for the security of energy supply, COM(2000) 769 final

Commission Notice on the notion of State aid as referred to in Article 107(1) of the Treaty on the Functioning of the European Union (OJ C 262, 19.7.2016, p. 1-50)

Commission Q&A, Consultation paper on generation adequacy, capacity mechanisms and the internal market in electricity, February 2013, available at https://ec. europa.eu/energy/sites/ener/files/documents/20130207_generation_adequacy _question_answers.pdf (last accessed 5.3.2019)

Commission Staff Working Document accompanying the document Report from the Commission Final Report of the Sector Inquiry on Capacity Mechanisms, SWD(2016) 385 final

Commission Staff Working Document accompanying the document Report from the Commission Interim Report of the Sector Inquiry on Capacity Mechanisms, SWD(2016) 119 final

Commission Staff Working Document Delivering the internal electricity market and making the most of public intervention, SWD(2013) 438 final

Commission Staff Working Document, Best practices on Renewable Energy Self-consumption, accompanying the document Communication from the Commission to the European Parliament, the Council, the European Economic and Social Committee and the Committee of the Regions, Delivering a New Deal for Energy Consumers, SWD(2015) 141 final

Commission Staff Working Document, Energy infrastructure investment needs and financing requirements, SEC(2011) 755

Commission Staff Working Document, Evaluation Report covering the Evaluation of the EU's regulatory framework for electricity market design and consumer protection in the fields of electricity and gas Evaluation of the EU rules on measures to safeguard security of electricity supply and infrastructure investment (Directive 2005/89) accompanying the document Proposal for a Directive of the European Parliament and of the Council on common rules for the internal market in electricity (recast), Proposal for a Regulation of the European Parliament and of the Council on the electricity market (recast), Proposal for a Regulation of the European Parliament and of the Council establishing a European Union Agency for the Cooperation of Energy Regulators (recast), Proposal for a Regulation of the

European Parliament and of the Council on risk-preparedness in the electricity sector, SWD(2016) 412 final

Commission Staff Working Document, Generation Adequacy in the internal electricity market, Guidance on public interventions accompanying the document Communication from the Commission, Delivering the internal electricity market and making the most of public intervention, SWD(2013) 438 final

Commission Staff Working Document, Incorporing demand-side flexibility, in particular demand response, in electricity markets, SWD(2013) 442 final

Commission White Paper on Services of General Interest, COM(2004) 374 final

Communication from the Commission, European Union framework for State aid in the form of public service compensation (2011) (OJ C 8, 11.1.2012, p. 15-22)

Communication from the Commission, Delivering the internal electricity market and making the most of public intervention, C(2013) 7243 final

Communication from the Commission on the application of the European Union State aid rules to compensation granted for the provision of services of general economic interest (OJ C 8, 11.1.2012, p. 4-14)

Communication from the Commission to the European Council and the European Parliament, An Energy Policy for Europe, COM(2007) 1 final

Communication from the Commission to the European Parliament and the Council, Achieving the 10% electricity interconnection target Making Europe's electricity grid fit for 2020, COM(2015) 82 final

Communication from the Commission to the European Parliament and the Council, Energy Infrastructure and Security of Supply, COM(2003) 743 final

Communication from the Commission to the European Parliament and the Council, European Energy Security Strategy, COM(2014) 330 final

Communication from the Commission to the European Parliament and the Council, Energy Efficiency and its contribution to energy security and the 2030 Framework for climate and energy policy, COM (2014) 520

Communication from the Commission to the European Parliament, the Council, the European Economic and Social Committee and the Committee of the Regions, Making the internal energy market work, COM(2012) 663 final

Communication from the Commission to the European Parliament, the Council, the European Economic and Social Committee, the Committee of the Regions and the European Investment Bank, Third Report on the State of the Energy Union, COM(2017) 688 final.

Communication from the Commission to the European Parliament, the Council, the European Economic and Social Committee, the Committee of the Regions and the European Investment Bank, A Framework Strategy for a Resilient Energy Union with a Forward-Looking Climate Change Policy, COM(2015) 80 final

Communication from the Commission to the European Parliament, the Council, the European Economic and Social Committee, the Committee of the Regions and the European Investment Bank, Clean Energy For All Europeans, COM(2016) 860 final

Communication from the Commission to the European Parliament, the Council, the European Economic and Social Committee and the Committee of the Regions, Progress towards completing the Internal Energy Market, COM(2014) 634 final

Communication from the Commission to the European Parliament, the Council, the European Economic and Social Committee and the Committee of the Regions, Launching the public consultation process on a new energy market design, COM(2015) 340 final

Communication from the Commission, Delivering the internal electricity market and making the most of public intervention, C(2013) 7243 final

Communication from the Commission, Guidelines on State aid for environmental protection and energy 2014-2020 (OJ C 200, 28.6.2014, p. 1-55)

Communication from the Commission, Services of general interest in Europe (OJ C 17, 19.1.2001, p. 4-23)

DG Competition, The economic impact of enforcement of competition policies on the functioning of EU energy markets, 2016, available at http://ec.europa.eu/competition/publications/reports/kd0216007enn.pdf (last accessed 5.3.2019)

DG Energy, Permitting procedures for energy infrastructure projects in the EU: evaluation and legal recommendations, July 2011

European Commission, Consultation paper on generation adequacy, capacity mechanisms and the internal market in electricity, November 2012, available at https://ec.europa.eu/energy/sites/ener/files/documents/20130207_generation_adequacy_consultation_document.pdf (last accessed 5.3.2019)

European Commission, Electricity and natural gas price statistics, 4.9.2014, available at http://ec.europa.eu/eurostat/statistics-explained/index.php/Electricity_price_statistics (last accessed 5.3.2019)

European Commission, Investment perspectives in electricity markets, July 2015, available at http://ec.europa.eu/economy_finance/publications/eeip/pdf/ip003_en.pdf (last accessed 5.3.2019)

European Commission, Consultation Paper on generation adequacy, capacity mechanisms and the internal market in electricity, 15.11.2012

European Commission, State aid: Commission opens in-depth investigation into British Capacity Market scheme, 21 February 2019, available at http://europa.eu/rapid/press-release_IP-19-1348_en.htm (last accessed 5.3.2019)

European Commission, State aid modernization, COM(2012) 209 final

European Council, Presidency Conclusions, 15-16 March 2002, available at http://ec.europa.eu/invest-in-research/pdf/download_en/barcelona_european_council.pdf (last accessed 5.3.2019)

European Network of Transmission System Operators for Electricity, Communication Paper on Capacity Remuneration Mechanisms, available at www.entsoe.eu/fileadmin/user_upload/_library/position_papers/120510_MC_TOP_11_CRM_memorandum_external.pdf (last accessed 5.3.2019)

Eurostat, Consumption of energy, June 2017, available at http://ec.europa.eu/eurostat/statistics-explained/index.php/Consumption_of_energy (last accessed 5.3.2019)

Eurostat, Renewable energy statistics, July 2016, available at http://ec.europa.eu/eurostat/statistics-explained/index.php/Renewable_energy_statistics (last accessed 5.3.2019)

Expert Group for Regulatory Recommendations for Smart Grids deployment, Regulatory Recommendations for the Deployment of Flexibility, Report, January 2015, available at http://ec.europa.eu/energy/sites/ener/files/documents/EG3%20Final%20-%20January%202015.pdf (last accessed 5.3.2019)

Keynote speech by European Commissioner for Competition Margrethe Vestager, Securing electricity supply in the EU: How to optimise public support, at *Capacity mechanisms in Europe: The fundamental issues behind the ongoing sector inquiry*, 29 September 2015, Brussels, available at http://ec.europa.eu/competition/sectors/energy/state_aid_to_secure_electricity_supply_en.html (last accessed 5.3.2019)

Note of DG Energy & Transport on Directives 2003/54/EC and 2003/55/EC on the Internal Market in Electricity and Natural Gas: Measures to Secure Electricity Supply, 16.1.2004, available at www.rae.gr/old/europe/sub4/security_of_electricity_supply_DGTREN.pdf (last accessed 5.3.2019)

Opinion of the European Economic and Social Committee on the communication from the Commission on 'Delivering the internal electricity market and making the most of public intervention' C(2013) 7243 final (OJ C 226, 16.7.2014, p. 28-34)

Opinion of the European Economic and Social Committee on the economic effects from electricity systems created by increased and intermittent supply from renewable sources (exploratory opinion) (OJ C 198, 10.7.2013, p. 1-8)

Proposal for a Directive of the European Parliament and of the Council amending Directive 2003/54/EC concerning common rules for the internal market in electricity, COM(2007) 528 final

Proposal for a Directive of the European Parliament and of the Council on common rules for the internal market in electricity, COM(2016) 864 final ('Recast Electricity Directive')

Proposal for a Regulation of the European Parliament and of the Council on the internal market for electricity, COM(2016) 861 final/2 – (2016)379 (COD) ('Recast Electricity Regulation')

Proposal for a Regulation of the European Parliament and of the Council on risk-preparedness in the electricity sector and repealing Directive 2005/89/EC, COM(2016) 862 final ('Security of Supply Regulation')

Proposal for a Regulation of the European Parliament and of the Council, Establishing a European Union Agency for the Cooperation of Energy Regulators, COM(2016) 863 final

Regulatory Commission for Electricity and Gas, Study on capacity remuneration mechanisms, 11 October 2012, available at www.creg.info/pdf/Etudes/F1182EN.pdf (last accessed 5.3.2019)

Report from the Commission, Final Report of the Sector Inquiry on Capacity Mechanisms, COM(2016) 752 final

Documents by Governmental and International Institutions

Consultancy paper for FERC, 'Resource Adequacy Requirements: Reliability and Economic Implications', 2013, available at www.ferc.gov/legal/staff-reports/20 14/02-07-14-consultant-report.pdf (last accessed 5.3.2019)

Department of Energy and Climate Change, 'Overarching National Policy Statement for Energy (EN-1)', 2011, available at www.gov.uk/government/uploads/system/ uploads/attachment_data/file/47854/1938-overarching-nps-for-energy-en1.pdf (last accessed 5.3.2019)

Energy Authority, Decision no 389/451/2015 on the procurement of a strategic reserve (Energiaviraston päätös, Tehoreservikapasiteetin hankinta, 389/451/2015), 23 April 2015

FERC, 'Electric Power Markets: New England (ISO-NE)', August 2017, available at www.ferc.gov/market-oversight/mkt-electric/new-england.asp (last accessed 5. 3.2019)

Government of Western Australia, 'Electricity Market Review', Discussion paper 2014, available at www.treasury.wa.gov.au/uploadedFiles/Site-content/Public_ Utilities_Office/Industry_reform/electricity-market-review-discussion-paper.pdf (last accessed 5.3.2019)

Government of Western Australia, 'Electricity reforms ensure fairer system for all', 7 April 2016, available at www.mediastatements.wa.gov.au/Pages/Barnett/2016/ 04/Electricity-reforms-ensure-fairer-system-for-all.aspx (last accessed 5.3.2019)

NYISO, 'Installed Capacity Market (ICAP)', 2018, available at www.nyiso.com/ installed-capacity-market (last accessed 5.3.2019)

OFGEM, 'Electricity Capacity Assessment Report 2013', available at www.ofgem.gov. uk/sites/default/files/docs/2013/06/electricity-capacity-assessment-report-201 3_0.pdf (last accessed 5.3.2019)

WTO, 'Energy Services', Background Note by the Secretariat, S/C/W/52, 9 September 1998

Table of Cases

General Court

Table of Legislation

Directives

Commission Decisions (Excluding State Aid Cases)

Commission Decision 2012/21/EU of 20 December 2011 on the application of Article 106(2) of the Treaty on the Functioning of the European Union to State aid in the form of public service compensation granted to certain undertakings entrusted with the operation of services of general economic interest (notified under document C(2011) 9380) (OJ L 7, 11.1.2012, pp. 3-10), 102, 111, 112, 114

Commission Decision of 24 April 2007 on the State aid scheme implemented by Slovenia in the framework of its legislation on qualified energy producers (OJ L 219, 24.8.2007, pp. 9-24), 107

Commission Decision of 29.4.2015 initiating an inquiry on capacity mechanisms in the electricity sector pursuant to Article 20a of Council Regulation (EC) No 659/1999 of 22 March 1999, C(2015) 2814 final, 2, 21, 27, 84, 85

National Legislation

Lag (2003:436) om effektreserv (The Swedish Power Reserve Act), 25

Laki sähköntuotannon ja -kulutuksen välistä tasapainoa varmistavasta tehoreservistä (117/2011) (The Finnish Capacity Reserve Act), 25

ENERGY AND ENVIRONMENTAL LAW & POLICY SERIES

1. Stephen J. Turner, *A Substantive Environmental Right: An Examination of the Legal Obligations of Decision-makers towards the Environment*, 2009 (ISBN 978-90-411-2815-7).
2. Helle Tegner Anker, Birgitte Egelund Olsen & Anita Rønne (eds), *Legal Systems and Wind Energy: A Comparative Perspective*, 2009 (ISBN 978-90-411-2831-7).
3. David Langlet, *Prior Informed Consent and Hazardous Trade: Regulating Trade in Hazardous Goods at the Intersection of Sovereignty, Free Trade and Environmental Protection*, 2009 (ISBN 978-90-411-2821-8).
4. Louis J. Kotzé and Alexander R. Paterson (eds), *The Role of the Judiciary in Environmental Governance: Comparative Perspectives*, 2009 (ISBN 978-90-411-2708-2).
5. Tuula Honkonen, *The Common but Differentiated Responsibility Principle in Multilateral Environmental Agreement's: Regulatory and Policy Aspects*, 2009 (ISBN 978-90-411-3153-9).
6. Barbara Pozzo (ed.), *The Implementation of the Seveso Directives in an Enlarged Europe: A Look into the Past and a challenge for the Future*, 2009 (ISBN 978-90-411-2854-6).
7. Henrik M. Inadomi, *Independent Power Projects in Developing Countries: Legal Investment Protection and Consequences for Development*, 2010 (ISBN 978-90-411-3178-2).
8. Nahid Islam, *The Law of Non-Navigational Uses of International Watercourses: Options for Regional Regime-Building in Asia*, 2010 (ISBN 978-90-411-3196-6).
9. Yasuhiro Shigeta, *International Judicial Control of Environmental Protection: Standard Setting, Compliance Control and the Development of International Environmental Law by the International Judiciary*, 2010 (ISBN 978-90-411-3151-5).
10. Katleen Janssen, *The Availability of Spatial and Environmental Data in the European Union: At the Crossroads between Public and Economic Interests*, 2010 (ISBN 978-90-411-3287-1).
11. Henrik Bjørnebye, *Investing in EU Energy Security: Exploring the Regulatory Approach to Tomorrow's Electricity Production*, 2010 (ISBN 978-90-411-3118-8).
12. Véronique Bruggeman, *Compensating catastrophe victims: A Comparative Law and Economics Approach*, 2010 (ISBN 978-90-411-3263-5).
13. Michael G. Faure, Han Lixin & Shan Hongjun, *Maritime Pollution Liability and Policy: China, Europe and the US*, 2010 (ISBN 978-90-411-2869-0).

14. Anton Ming-Zhi Gao, *Regulating Gas Liberalization: A Comparative Study on Unbundling and Open Access Regimes in the US, Europe, Japan, South Korea and Taiwan*, 2010 (ISBN 978-90-411-3347-2).
15. Mustafa Erkan, *International Energy Investment Law: Stability through Contractual Clauses*, 2011 (ISBN 978-90-411-3411-0).
16. Levente Borzsa´k, *The Impact of Environmental Concerns on the Public Enforcement Mechanism under EU law: Environmental protection in the 25th hour*, 2011 (ISBN 978-90-411-3408-0).
17. Tarcísio Hardman Reis, *Compensation for Environmental Damages under International Law: The Role of the International Judge*, 2011 (ISBN 978-90-411-3437-0).
18. Kim Talus, *Vertical Natural Gas Transportation Capacity, Upstream Commodity Contracts and EU Competition Law*, 2011 (ISBN 978-90-411-3407-3).
19. WangHui, *Civil Liability for Marine Oil Pollution Damage: A Comparative and Economic Study of the International, US and Chinese Compensation Regime*, 2011 (ISBN 978-90-411-3672-5).
20. Chowdhury Ishrak Ahmed Siddiky, *Cross-Border Pipeline Arrangements: What Would a Single Regulatory Framework Look Like?*, 2012 (ISBN 978-90-411-3844-6).
21. Rozeta Karova, *Liberalization of Electricity Markets and Public Service Obligations in the Energy Community*, 2012 (ISBN 978-90-411-3849-1).
22. Sandra Cassotta, *Environmental Damage and Liability Problems in a Multilevel Context: The Case of the Environmental Liability Directive*, 2012 (ISBN 978-90-411-3830-9).
23. Mark Wilde, *Civil Liability for Environmental Damage: Comparative Analysis of Law and Policy in Europe and US*, 2013 (ISBN 978-90-411-3233-8).
24. Bernard Taverne, *Petroleum, Industry and Governments: A Study of the Involvement of Industry and Governments in Exploring for and Producing Petroleum*, 2013 (ISBN 978-90-411-4563-5).
25. Anton Ming-Zhi Gao & Chien Te Fan (eds), *Legal Issues of Renewable Energy in the Asia Region: Recent Developments in a Post-Fukushima and Post-Kyoto Protocol Era*, 2014 (ISBN 978-90-411-4856-8).
26. Sabina Manea, *The Instrumentalization of Property: Legal Interests in the EU Emissions Trading System*, 2014 (ISBN 978-90-411-5420-0).
27. Joseph A. Tolorunse, *Protection of Property Rights in Discovered Petroleum Reservoirs*, 2014 (ISBN 978-90-411-5604-4).
28. Katelijn Van Hende, *Offshore Wind in the European Union: Towards Integrated Management of Our Marine Waters*, 2015 (ISBN 978-90-411-5613-6).
29. Ken'ichi Matsumoto & Anton Ming-Zhi Gao (eds), *Economic Instruments to Combat Climate Change in Asian Countries*, 2015 (ISBN 978-90-411-5408-8).

30. Eduardo Pereira (ed.), *Joint Operating Agreements: Challenges and Concerns from Civil Law Jurisdictions*, 2015 (ISBN 978-90-411-5934-2).
31. Ying Shen, *China's Way to Carbon Emissions Reduction: The Choice of Regulatory Instruments and Its Legal Challenges*, 2015 (ISBN 978-90-411-6049-2).
32. Roy Andrew Partain, *Environmental Hazards from Offshore Methane Hydrate Operations: Civil Liability and Regulations for Efficient Governance*, 2017 (ISBN 978-90-411-8730-7).
33. Anton Ming-Zhi Gao & Chien-Te Fan (eds), *The Development of a Comprehensive Legal Framework for the Promotion of Offshore Wind Power: The Lessons from Europe and Pacific Asia*, 2017 (ISBN 978-90-411-8397-2).
34. Tade Oyewunmi, *Regulating Gas Supply to Power Markets: Transnational Approaches to Competitiveness and Security of Supply*, 2018 (ISBN 978-90-411-9869-3).
35. Huseyin Cagri Corlu, *Application of Anti-manipulation Law to EU Wholesale Energy Markets and Its Interplay with EU Competition Law*, 2018 (ISBN 978-90-411-9603-3).
36. Kaisa Huhta, *Capacity Mechanisms in EU Energy Law: Ensuring Security of Supply in the Energy Transition*, 2019 (ISBN 978-94-035-1451-2).